Reinventing Race, Reinventing Racism

Studies in Critical Social Sciences Book Series

Haymarket Books is proud to be working with Brill Academic Publishers (www.brill.nl) to republish the *Studies in Critical Social Sciences* book series in paperback editions. This peer-reviewed book series offers insights into our current reality by exploring the content and consequences of power relationships under capitalism, and by considering the spaces of opposition and resistance to these changes that have been defining our new age. Our full catalog of *SCSS* volumes can be viewed at www.haymarketbooks.org/category/scss-series.

REINVENTING RACE, REINVENTING RACISM

Edited by
JOHN J. BETANCUR
CEDRIC HERRING

Haymarket
Books
Chicago, IL

First published in 2013 by Brill Academic Publishers, The Netherlands.
© 2013 Koninklijke Brill NV, Leiden, The Netherlands

Published in paperback in 2014 by
Haymarket Books
P.O. Box 180165
Chicago, IL 60618
773-583-7884
www.haymarketbooks.org

ISBN: 978-1-60846-346-6

Trade distribution:
In the U.S. through Consortium Book Sales, www.cbsd.com
In the UK, Turnaround Publisher Services, www.turnaround-psl.com
In Australia, Palgrave Macmillan, www.palgravemacmillan.com.au
In all other countries by Publishers Group Worldwide, www.pgw.com

Cover design by Ragina Johnson.

This book was published with the generous support of Lannan Foundation
and the Wallace Global Fund.

10 9 8 7 6 5 4 3 2 1

Library of Congress Cataloging-in-Publication Data is available.

CONTENTS

ACKNOWLEDGEMENTS

This edited volume is the culmination of a journey that began several years ago with the planning of a conference to celebrate the 40th Anniversary of the Kerner Commission. During that conference, we assembled dozens of scholars and policymakers to examine post-1960s developments in race, especially new versions and expressions of racism. Along the way, we benefitted tremendously from the generosity and assistance of several people and organizations. Now, having completed our voyage, we would like to thank Maria Ayala for her capable assistance, both in organizing the conference that featured many of the papers that became chapters in this book, and for her contribution to the early logistics in making this book a reality. We owe a debt of gratitude to Phil Bowman, James Compton, Vernon M. Briggs, Jr., Alice Palmer, Jose Lopez, Robert Rich, Clarence Wood, Eduardo Bonilla-Silva, and the other participants in the original conference. Finally, we would also like to thank the Institute for Research on Race and Public Policy at the University of Illinois at Chicago and the Institute of Government and Public Affairs at the University of Illinois for their support.

John J. Betancur and Cedric Herring

LIST OF TABLES AND FIGURES

TABLES

FIGURES

ABOUT THE CONTRIBUTORS

COEDITORS

JOHN J. BETANCUR is an Associate Professor in the Urban Planning and Policy Program in the College of Urban Planning and Public Affairs of the University of Illinois at Chicago. He has published on urban restructuring, housing and community development, the impact of socioeconomic restructuring on Latinos and Blacks, black-Latino relations, gentrification, economic development and urban impacts of globalization on Latin American cities. He is the coeditor (with Douglas Gills) of *The Collaborative City: Opportunities and Struggles for Blacks and Latinos in U.S. Cities*.

CEDRIC HERRING is Professor in the Department of Sociology at the University of Illinois at Chicago (UIC) and the Institute of Government and Public Affairs at the University of Illinois. Dr. Herring is former President of the Association of Black Sociologists and the Founding Director of the Institute for Research on Race and Public Policy at UIC. He has published widely on topics such as social policy (e.g., social welfare and affirmative action), labor force issues and policy, stratification and inequality and the sociology of African-Americans. He has published seven books and more than 60 scholarly articles. His books include *Skin Deep: How Race and Complexion Matter in the "Color-Blind" Era* (with Verna Keith and Hayward Derrick Horton), and more recently, *Combating Racism and Xenophobia: Transatlantic and International Perspectives*. His forthcoming book is entitled *Critical Diversity: The New Case for Inclusion and Equal Opportunity*. Dr. Herring has received support for his research from the National Science Foundation, the Ford Foundation, the MacArthur Foundation, the Joyce Foundation and others. Dr. Herring has shared his findings in community forums, in newspapers and magazines, on radio and television, before government officials and at the United Nations.

OTHER CONTRIBUTORS

ASMA ALI is a graduate student in the department of Urban Planning and Policy at the University of Illinois at Chicago.

TOMÁS ALMAGUER is Professor of Ethnic Studies at San Francisco State University. He is the author of *Racial Fault Lines: The Historical Origins of White Supremacy in California*.

FABRICIO BALCAZAR, PhD. is Professor in the Department of Disability and Human Development at the University of Illinois at Chicago. His PhD. is in Community Psychology. He is the Director of the Center for Capacity Building for Minorities with Disabilities Research.

LISA MARIE CACHO is an Associate Professor of Latina/Latino Studies, Asian American Studies, Gender and Women's Studies, and the Department of English, University of Illinois at Urbana-Champaign. Lisa Cacho's research interests include Asian and Latina/o gendered immigration, comparative race and ethnic studies, militarism, and racial segregation. Cacho is an interdisciplinary scholar, who is engaged in blurring the boundaries between the humanities and social sciences. Her most recent publication examines Proposition 187 through law, print media, and short fiction.

KAREN J. GIBSON is Associate Professor of Urban Studies and Planning at Portland State University. Her research focuses primarily on racial economic inequality and its spatial manifestations in the urban United States. Currently she is conducting a study of the political economy of neighborhood change in Portland's historic black community, the Albina District. Her publications have appeared in Feminist Economics, Transforming Anthropology, and the Journal of Planning Education and Research. She is board president of Portland Community Reinvestment Initiatives, Inc (PCRI) and a board member of the Urban Affairs Association.

DOUGLAS C. GILLS is an Associate Professor of Urban Planning and Policy and at the Center for Urban Economic Development in the College of Urban Planning and Public Affairs at the University of Illinois at Chicago. A Political Science PhD from Northwestern University, he has written extensively on African American mayoral politic, community development and coalition politics.

EDWARD G. GOETZ, professor, specializes in housing and local community development planning and policy. His research focuses on issues of race and poverty and how they affect housing policy planning and development. Before coming to the University of Minnesota in 1988, Goetz worked at the mayor's Office of Housing and Economic Development in San Francisco and for several nonprofit community developers in Los Angeles and San Francisco. He has served on the board of directors of nonprofit housing agencies in the Twin Cities, and on several regional commissions related to affordable housing and development. Goetz is the author of *Clearing the Way: Deconcentrating the Poor in Urban America* (2003, Urban Institute Press), *Shelter Burden: Local Politics and Progressive Housing Policy* (1993, Temple University Press), and co-editor of *The New Localism: Comparative Urban Politics in a Global Era* (1993, Sage Publications).

ISABEL MOLINA-GUZMÁN is an associate Professor of Latina/Latino Studies and Media & Cinema Studies and Chair of the Department of Latina/Latino Studies at the University of Illinois Urbana-Champaign. She is author of *Dangerous Curves: Latina Bodies in the Media* (New York Press, 2010). Her work has been published in numerous edited collections and academic journals such as *Latina/o Studies* and *Journalism*.

ROOSHEY HASNAIN, PhD. is a visiting Research Assistant Professor in Asian American Studies at the University of Illinois at Chicago.

DEVORAH HEITNER is a Chicago based media scholar. She earned a PhD in Media, Technology and Society at Northwestern University and has taught at DePaul University, Lake Forest College and various community sites. She studies media in relation to social justice, activism and identity. She is grateful to the many individuals who spoke with her about their experiences at the Black Journal Workshop and other tuition-free training programs for African American media makers in the Black Power era.

LOREN HENDERSON is a PhD Student in the Department of Sociology at the University of Illinois at Urbana-Champaign and an Adjunct Faculty Member in the Department of Social Science at Wright College. Her research has focused on race, class, gender, sexuality, and the changing meanings and controversies surrounding diversity. Her work has been published in the *Journal of African American Studies, Families as They Really Are,* and *The Illinois Report.*

HAYWARD DERRICK HORTON is a Professor of Sociology and the School of Public Health at the State University of New York at Albany. A native of Norfolk, VA, he holds a BA in Sociology from Norfolk State University, and an MA and Ph.D. from the Pennsylvania State University. He has also held professorships at the University of Central Arkansas and Iowa State University. Professor Horton specializes in demography, race/ethnicity, public sociology, and sociology of place. He has published over 30 articles on topics such as: the demography of rural black families; differences in black-white levels of homeownership; population change and the employment status of college-educated blacks; race, ethnicity and levels of employment; the demography of black entrepreneurship; and the feminization of poverty.

N. MICHELLE HUGHES is a doctoral student in the Department of Sociology at the University of Michigan, Ann Arbor. Her interests include racialized gender, the semiotic analysis of race, and feminist theory. Hughes's current research involves the exploration of meanings of black womanhood at the intersections of race, class and gender. She is currently serving on the editorial board for the journal Michigan Feminist Studies.

JACQUELINE JOHNSON is an Assistant Professor in the Department of Anthropology and Sociology at Adelphi University.

KECIA JOHNSON is assistant professor of sociology at the University at Albany, SUNY. She completed the National Science Foundation postdoctoral research fellowship at the Criminal Justice Research Center of Ohio State University. Her current research interests include the impact of racial/ethnic inequality on labor market outcomes, the consequences of incarceration on individuals and communities, and the influence of racial segregation within schools and educational resources on adolescent delinquency.

ANGELA MASCARENAS is the Executive Director and one of the original founders of CIRCA-Pintig, a not-for-profit community arts organization dedicated to the development and popularization of community arts that speak of the immigrant experience within the changing multicultural landscape of America. Mascarenas holds a PhD in Sociology from the University of Illinois at Chicago. Her scholarly work is focused on social movements and cultural identity.

JUNAID RANA is an associate professor of Asian American Studies with appointments in the Department of Anthropology, the Center for South Asian and Middle Eastern Studies, and the Unit for Criticism and Interpretive Theory. His interests include transnational cultural studies, diaspora studies; community organizing and social movements; critical and comparative race studies, political economy, the postcolonial state; South Asia/Pakistan/US.

YOLANDA SUAREZ-BALCAZAR, PhD. is Professor and Head of the Department of Occupational Therapy at the University of Illinois at Chicago. Her PhD is in Community Psychology. She is also the Co-Director of the Center for Capacity Building for Minorities with Disabilities Research.

ELIZABETH L. SWEET is a visiting assistant professor in the Department of Geography and Urban Studies at Temple University. She has published on issues related to the role of planning and policy in the production and reproduction of social, economic, and spatial inequalities, particularly examining issues of race, gender, and migration.

TINA TAYLOR-RITZLER, PhD. is an Assistant Professor in the Department of Psychology at Dominican University. She received her PhD. in Community Psychology.

MELVIN THOMAS is an Associate Professor of Sociology at North Carolina State University. His areas of specialization include racial inequality, social stratification, religion, and social psychology. He is currently involved in research on the impact of race, class, and local labor market characteristics on career earnings disparities.

CHAPTER ONE

REINVENTING RACE, REINVENTING RACISM:
AN INTRODUCTION

John J. Betancur and Cedric Herring

In 1964, the Civil Rights Act prohibited discrimination by reason of race, religious belief, and gender. In 1965, the Voting Rights Act extended full voting rights to African Americans. In 1968, the Fair Housing Act prohibited race-based discrimination in housing. Altogether, these acts formally corrected centuries of exclusion and discrimination on the basis of race. Yet, in 1968 the Kerner Commission issued its now-famous quote about the United States' "moving toward two societies, one black, one white— separate and unequal." More inclusion of black people was seen as the answer to the "What can be done" question. The Commission wrote, "We believe that the only possible choice for America is...a policy which combines ghetto enrichment with programs designed to encourage integration of substantial numbers of Negroes into the society...." In essence, the Commission called for desegregation and diversity.

Over the past forty-plus years, the rhetoric about inclusion has changed substantially in the United States, but has the reality? Today, the discussion is as polarized as the reality. Authors like Omi and Winant (1994) have argued that race relations between majorities and minorities have gone from domination to hegemony. Many others have claimed that structures and signifiers established when discrimination was legal remained untouched. Although *de jure* federal legislation prohibited discrimination, *de facto* structures and mechanisms of distribution of resources and opportunity, along with vast accumulated advantages acquired in centuries of race-based discrimination and rule, remain in place.

Race continues to be a critical issue with significant effects in many areas of national policy, especially as the U.S. population has become increasingly diverse. Hispanics, blacks, Asian and Pacific Islanders, American Indians and Alaska Natives currently constitute nearly a third of the U.S. population (U.S. Bureau of the Census 2011). These same groups are expected to become the majority of the U.S. population by 2042 (U.S. Bureau of the Census 2008). The Hispanic population increased by 43 percent between 2000 and 2010. This increase of 15.2 million, from

35.3 million to 50.5 million residents, accounted for more than half of the total U.S. population increase. Similarly, the Asian and Asian American population increased by 43 percent between 2000 and 2010. This was an increase of 4.4 million, from 10.3 million in 2000 to 14.7 million in 2010. The black population had the third-largest numeric increase in population size over the decade (4.3 million). It grew by 12 percent between 2000 and 2010, from 34.7 million in 2000 to 39 million in 2010. These changes will present this nation with a variety of social and economic opportunities and challenges.

The historic rise in international migration over the past forty years has brought a tide of new immigrants to the United States from Asia, Latin America, and other parts of the globe. The American dream of opportunity and upward mobility is still appealing to the more than one million immigrants who arrive in the United States each year, especially from the Third World. But the competition for jobs and other resources has made America an unwelcoming place for many new immigrants. Rising anti-immigrant sentiments have served the cause of those who favor deportation and harsh immigration limits against people from Third World countries. These forces have also been at play in producing mass incarceration of the minority poor; criminalization of people with non-Christian religions (most explicitly Islam but also others); zero tolerance toward behaviors that do not conform to white middle-class notions; increased and intense racialization of minority and low-income spaces; ghettoization of education; stigmatization of minority mothers (e.g., classification of Latino mothers as producers of "anchor babies"); further racialization of jobs and neighborhoods, and so forth.

Despite the notion that America is a country of immigrants, this dramatic growth in the number of foreign-born residents concerns many U.S.-born white Americans. A growing number believe immigrants are a burden to this country. Moreover, a majority of U.S.-born white Americans believe that immigrants take jobs and housing and put strains on schools and the health-care system. Some are also concerned about the ethnic and cultural impact of the expanding number of newcomers. Interestingly, these are many of the same concerns that U.S.-born white Americans had about African Americans traditionally.

But what are the realities of race and immigration in the second decade of the twenty-first century? What are the impacts of race and immigration on the social, political, and economic well-being of residents of this nation? Below, we review some of these issues in the context of the Great Recession, which has made access to resources and opportunities for people of color even scarcer.

ECONOMIC WELL-BEING AND THE GREAT RECESSION

In December 2007, the United States officially entered into the Great Recession. . For many people of color, the economic downturn was more severe than a recession. Indeed, it has been argued that Americans of color experienced "a silent economic depression that, in terms of unemployment, equals or exceeds the Great Depression of 1929" (Rivera, Huezo, Kasica, and Muhammad 2009). Considered a rare and extreme form of recession, a depression is characterized by its length and abnormal increases in unemployment, bare-bones availability of credit, shrinking output and investment, high bankruptcy rates, and reduced amounts of trade and commerce. By all these criteria, it could be argued that African Americans and Latinos have experienced an economic depression.

The Great Recession increased unemployment rates for all racial and ethnic groups. An estimated 8.1 million jobs were lost. But because higher unemployment rates for people of color relative to those for whites are an enduring part of the U.S. economy, people of color normally face catastrophic "recession levels" of unemployment. In October of 2009, the nationwide unemployment rate was 9.5 percent for whites, 15.7 percent for blacks, and 13.1 percent for Latinos.

The Great Recession also had a human toll that went beyond unemployment. Jobless people cannot contribute to the economy as taxpayers or as consumers. Indeed, among those without jobs, it is often difficult to meet basic economic needs. In 2007, 13 million U.S. households experienced "food insecurity," or difficulty providing enough food for all family members. More than 4 million families faced a severe disruption in the normal diet for some members (Nord, Andrews, and Carlson 2009). Again, there are some substantial racial differences in the relationship between employment status and various economic hardships. For example, jobless African Americans were more likely than their white counterparts to report that they could not afford to pay for needed food and medicine. According to data from the General Social Survey, 56 percent of jobless African Americans reported bankruptcies or property losses compared with 13 percent of jobless whites. Among whites, 28 percent of the jobless experienced housing problems. In comparison, 44 percent of jobless African Americans reported housing difficulties. Similarly, the results also show that 52 percent of unemployed whites said that they are worse off financially. This compares with 81 percent of unemployed African Americans who report that they are worse off financially.

According to a 2010 U.S. Foreclosure Market Report, more than 2.3 million families have had their homes repossessed since the Great

Recession began (RealtyTrac 2010). Nearly one million additional foreclosure filings—default notices, scheduled auctions, and bank repossessions—were reported in the third quarter of 2010 alone. This represented about one in every 130 housing units and more than a 20 percent increase over the same period in 2008. It was the third highest number of foreclosures in a quarter since such data have been collected. Bank repossessions increased by more than 20 percent from the second quarter to the third quarter. The foreclosure crisis has brought black and Latino homeownership rates down to the levels that preceded the homeownership boom of the past decade. According to a study by the Applied Research Center, "high-cost loans were marketed in aggressive, sometimes predatory ways to poor communities of color. They were frequently sold through direct broker solicitation and were characterized by higher interest rates" (Applied Research Center 2009: 18). Often, these were adjustable rate loans that started off with lower "teaser" rates and then ballooned when they included high fees, prepayment penalties, and climbing interest rates.

Not surprisingly, during the Great Recession, poverty levels increased for all racial and ethnic groups. Nationwide the poverty rates for whites increased from 12 percent to 16 percent. For blacks, there was an increase from 33 percent to 36 percent. And for Latinos, the poverty rate increased from 21 percent to 22 percent.

HEALTH DISPARITIES AND LOSS OF HEALTH INSURANCE

Many apparent racial and ethnic differences in health outcomes are closely linked to socioeconomic inequalities (Hummer 1996; Smith and Kington 1997). Generally, groups with lower socioeconomic status do worse on most indicators of healthiness (LaVeist 2005; Jackson 2005; and Williams 2005). But there is a notable exception. Despite facing economic barriers to health care, on most indicators Latinos have better health outcomes than do groups with higher average incomes, such as non-Hispanic whites (Abraido-Lanza et al. 1999; and Zsembik and Fennel 2005). Given their generally lower socioeconomic status and more limited access to quality health care in the United States, these patterns are surprising. African Americans, in contrast, fare worse on health indicators than do whites (LaVeist 2005). And African Americans die at a rate that is 1.5 times higher than that of whites (LaVeist 2005).

The Great Recession also affected the health insurance coverage of groups differentially (Holahan and Cook 2009). According to the U.S.

Census Bureau, the number of uninsured adults grew by more than 1.5 million between 2007 and 2008. As the unemployment rate grew, all racial and ethnic groups experienced a decline in employer-sponsored insurance. This drop was partially offset by increases in Medicaid and Medicare. However, the uninsured rates increased from 13.9 percent to 14.7 percent for whites and from 25.3 percent to 25.4 percent for blacks. More Latinos turned to public coverage in 2008. So, despite a decrease in employer-sponsored insurance, their uninsured rate declined slightly. However, because of growth in the Latino population, the number of uninsured Latino adults increased by 100,000. It should also be noted that because of the increase in the size of the low-income population, the number of uninsured, low-income Americans increased by 1.4 million. As the Great Recession continued through 2009, the percentage of uninsured adults also increased. A 1 percentage point rise in the unemployment rate reduces the share of adults with employer-sponsored insurance by 0.9 percentage points (Holahan and Cook 2009). Such reductions are not being offset by increases in public coverage such as Medicaid and Medicare.

EDUCATION

Education, a form of "human capital," plays an important role in producing economic growth. Factors that lead to less education can have major consequences for years to come. Recessions can affect educational achievement in several ways. Because early education is driven primarily by parental options and funding, factors that reduce families' resources affect the quality and level of education available to their children. Studies suggest that family income has a direct effect on math and reading test scores. Furthermore, there is evidence that nutrition affects cognitive development. In recessions, when many families face financial troubles and hardships, childhood nutrition can suffer. After-school and summer educational activities also affect in-school achievement and learning. Forced housing dislocations—and in the extreme, homelessness—affect educational outcomes as well. All of these influences on educational success are clearly shaped by economic downturns.

In 2010, the United States Census showed that 84 percent of African Americans over age 25 had completed high school. This compares with 87 percent of whites. This suggests that the high school completion rate of African Americans is only slightly lower than that of whites. In contrast, high school graduation rates for Latinos are much lower, as 62 percent of Hispanics over age 25 had completed high school. Asians had the highest high school completion rate at 88 percent.

In recent decades, college enrollment rates increased for all races. Similarly, the college graduation rate also increased. In 2010, 19 percent of African Americans had completed college. This compares with 29 percent of whites, 13 percent of Hispanics, and 52 percent of Asians.

There is an irony with respect to higher education and economic recession: the Great Recession initially led to a surge in college enrollments, but when revenue shortfalls were allocated among state services, higher education absorbed larger cuts than other sectors. Public higher education had to compete with K–12 schools, welfare, Medicaid, corrections, and other services for state funding. Relative to these other services, colleges and universities were often perceived by state policy makers as having more fiscal and programmatic flexibility. Thus, when higher education faced cuts in state funding, the state and higher education institutions often shifted the burden of such shortfalls to students and their families by raising tuition and fees. According to a 2009 College Board study, four-year public colleges in the United States raised annual tuition and fees by an average of 6.5 percent because of reduced state spending on higher education and diminished campus endowments. Moreover, during the Great Recession, states became less likely to make new or additional investments in student financial aid to offset increases in tuition. Indeed, student aid was reduced. The report also showed that 65 percent of 2007–08 bachelor's degree recipients graduated with student loan debt, and the median burden was $20,000.

Families struggling to get by were often forced to delay or abandon plans for continuing education. A recent survey of young adults found that 20 percent of people aged 18–29 left or delayed college (Greenberg and Keating 2009). This delay or reduction in college attendance was costly. Not only does college attendance yield higher earnings, lower unemployment, and other benefits to the individual, but it conveys many social benefits as well, including better health outcomes, lower incarceration rates, greater volunteerism rates, etc.

CRIME, RACIAL PROFILING, AND INCARCERATION

According to a U.S. Department of Justice report published in 2006, over 7.2 million people were in prison, on probation, or on parole (Glaze and Bonczar 2006). That means that with roughly one in every thirty-two

Americans being held by the justice system, the U.S. has the highest incarceration rate in the world. According to a 2009 report by the Pew Hispanic Center, Latinos "accounted for 40 of all sentenced federal offenders-more than triple their share (13) of the total U.S. adult population" (Lopez 2009: 14). Similarly, blacks accounted for 30.4 of the prison and jail population in 2009 (Bureau of Justice Statistics 2010). For men in their early thirties, African Americans were about seven times more likely to have a prison record than whites. African Americans are disproportionately represented in both the arrest and victimization reports which are used to compile crime rate statistics in the United States. The data reveal that although white Americans constitute the vast majority of total arrests made, African Americans and Latinos are disproportionately represented among those incarcerated, with average rates of representation that are two to three times higher than their representation in the general population (Gabbidon and Greene 2005).

One explanation for racial minorities' being arrested and incarcerated disproportionately is discrimination by the police and the criminal justice system more generally. For example, racial profiling—the discriminatory practice by police of treating racial or ethnic minority status, per se, as an indication of possible criminality—has become commonplace (Herring 2001). More than four out of ten African Americans and Latinos report such experiences. This compares with less than one out of fifteen whites (6 percent) (Newport 1999). Racial profiling is not just another form of discrimination against racial minorities. It often carries the force of the state behind it and therefore is even more repugnant. It is not just the haphazard lawlessness of a few individual police officers who act on their prejudices; rather, it is so systematic that many critics point to it as an example of institutionalized discrimination. But perhaps most disturbing about such practices is the fear that they may be symptomatic of persisting racial inequities in the criminal justice system (Harris 1999).

The use of racial profiling by the police has been justified with the idea that most drug offenses are committed by racial and ethnic minorities. But a study on U.S. drug policy issued by Physician Leadership on National Drug Policy (PLNDP) concluded, contrary to popular perceptions, that drug users are not primarily members of minority racial and ethnic groups. They found that illicit drug use reaches across all strata of society, with affluent, educated whites being the most likely drug users, and the most likely to be addicted. In other words, even though drug use and possession by minorities is supposedly the basis for racial profiling, that premise is factually untrue. Nevertheless, it becomes a self-fulfilling prophecy: because police look for illegal drugs mostly among blacks and Hispanics, they find a higher number of them with illicit substances. Therefore, more minorities are arrested, prosecuted, convicted, and imprisoned. In particular, blacks constitute 13 percent of the country's drug users; 37 percent of those arrested on drug charges; 55 percent of those convicted; and 74 percent of all drug offenders sentenced to prison (Hawkins and Herring 2001). These patterns reinforce the perception that drug offenses are primarily committed by racial and ethnic minorities.

In addition to the issue of racial profiling as a reason for elevated rates of minority arrest and incarceration, the troubled state of the U.S. economy revived the long-standing debate concerning whether economic factors can be linked to increases in the nation's crime rates. Several studies have found that unemployment rates (which are substantially higher in minority communities) are correlated with property crime rates. There is also a correlation between abandoned houses and the property crime. And there is also evidence that foreclosures have an impact on the violent crime rate.

A 2009 Congressional Research Service study found that racial and ethnic minorities experience substantially higher rates of violent victimization than non-Latino whites in the United States. The study shows that the higher rates of poverty, urban residence, and differential age distributions of blacks and Latinos help to explain these groups' higher victimization rates. Moreover, the study uses data from the early 1970s to the present to document an association between economic downturn and increases in victimization rates among minorities over this period (Finklea 2009).

INCOME AND WEALTH

According to Economic Policy Institute calculations, a basic budget required for a family with two adults and two children was $48,778 in 2008. This is well above the median income of black families ($38,269) and Latino families ($40,000). The median income of white families was $61,280. More than 50 percent of black and Latino families fall below the basic family budget, as compared with 20 percent of white families.

Between 2007 and 2009, the real median household income in the United States fell from $52,163 to $50,313. All racial and ethnic groups saw large declines in income in 2008. The median white income declined by 2.6 percent from 2007 to 2008, while African American households experienced a decline of 2.8 percent. The median Latino household income declined 5.6 percent from 2007 to 2008. In 2000, the median black family earned 63.5 percent of what the median white family did. By 2009, that ratio had dropped to 62.4 percent.

As great as the racial and ethnic differences in income are, they pale in comparison to the racial and ethnic differences in wealth. Several studies have documented racial and ethnic differences in wealth ownership (Parcel 1982; Horton 1992; Oliver and Shapiro 1995; Lewin-Epstein, Elmelech, and Semyonov 1997; Conley 1999; Keister 2000; Avery and Rendall 2002; Oliver and Shapiro 2006; and Semyonov and Lewin-Epstein forthcoming). In 1984, the black-white wealth gap, for example, was roughly $20,000. By 1994, it had increased to more than $60,000. By 2007, the black-white wealth gap increased to $95,000. In other words, in a generation (i.e., less than twenty-five years), the black-white wealth gap increased by more than 350 percent. In 2007, for every dollar of wealth owned by a white family, a Latino family owned twelve cents of wealth, and an African American family owned less than a dime (Lui 2010). The typical white family had more than $170,400 in wealth. In contrast, the typical Latino family had a net worth of $21,000, and the typical African American family owned $17,100 of wealth.

As Lui (2009: 2) points out:

> The financial security that wealth brings correlates to success in many areas, including educational attainment, good health, and intergenerational well-being. It increases civic participation and encourages social responsibility. A neighborhood of homeowners has a deeper level of engagement in their community than a neighborhood of renters; their personal stake propels them to take greater action for communitywide success. Ownership promotes engagement, prompting interest in policy from the neighborhood to the national level. Wealth builds "citizenship" in the broad sense.

In short, it is difficult to overestimate the impact of wealth. And it is clear that the racial wealth gap is not only staggering but growing.

POLITICAL INVOLVEMENT AND INCLUSION

Forty years after the National Advisory Committee's report declaring that the United States was moving toward two separate and unequal nations, the first person of African ancestry was elected to the office of the presidency of the United States of America. Barack Obama's election has been hailed as marking a fundamental change in race relations in America. How else can one explain this event, which was believed by most people of all races as inconceivable in the United States? Many people have concluded that the election of Obama is proof that the United States has reached the postracial, colorblind society that so many have struggled to attain for over four hundred years.

In the 2008 presidential election, 64 percent of voting-age citizens voted, and a record 131.3 million votes were cast (U.S. Census Bureau 2010). Among registered voters, while less than half of Latinos (49 percent) and Asian Americans (49 percent) voted, nearly two-thirds of whites (66 percent) and blacks (65 percent) participated in the historic election of Barack Obama. The vote for Obama was racially polarized, as substantially less than half (43 percent) of white voters voted for him, and more than 95 percent of African Americans did so (Herring 2008). Latinos (67 percent) and Asian Americans (62 percent) also overwhelmingly cast their votes for Barack Obama. Such results suggest neither a postracial nor colorblind society.

Indeed, despite the election of Obama, there were still reports of massive efforts to disenfranchise people of color during the election (Herring 2008). Voter suppression was carried out through activities such as providing obstacles to voter registration; improper purges of voter lists; impediments to voting, such as excessively long lines in heavily minority areas; inaccurate and unreliable voting machines; problems with absentee and provisional ballots; voter intimidation; and legal disenfranchisement due to arrest records.

In addition to voter suppression is the fact that voting is not an avenue of participation available to many people of color living in the United States. Noncitizens, in particular, are barred from voting. They are, however, eligible to participate in other modes of political involvement, from volunteering for political campaigns to petition signing to participating in political rallies and political protest marches. Leal (2002: 367) reports that "contrary to stereotype, a number of non-citizens are civic-minded and do invest their time in communities in which some are not even legally allowed to live...Non-citizens do participate in community and political activities...." Indeed, as several chapters in this volume discuss, hundreds of thousands of non-citizens participated in mass mobilizations prior to the 2008 presidential elections in order to influence policy and give voice to those without the franchise.

Overview of Remaining Chapters

The remainder of *Reinventing Race, Reinventing Racism* discusses new developments in the conceptualization of race, racial inequality, and the practice of racism in the last four decades. It explores how issues of race have been reflected in laws, legislation, and the media. Specifically, it examines the social construction of race and citizenship; misapplied public policy, disasters, and displacement; labor markets and racial inequality; racialization in the global era; criminalization of youth and families; political empowerment and immigrant mobilizations; and race and health disparities.

This volume also addresses racial developments and policies with particular implications for families and communities. Here, we ask, has racism moved from a direct frontal attack on racial communities to more nuanced institutional and structural expressions? Has socioeconomic restructuring affected in new ways the living environments and advancement of communities of color? Has the socioeconomic gap between majority and minority communities narrowed or widened? Lastly, *Reinventing Race, Reinventing Racism* asks, "How much progress has been made in the last forty years in the struggle against racism, and what are the priorities of today?"

The chapters in *Reinventing Race, Reinventing Racism* not only address the theoretical implications of the new forms of race and racism, but also provide empirical evidence and look at the policy implications of race, new forms of racism, and racial disparities. The chapters present new policy-relevant developments in the conceptualization of race and the practice of racism in the last four decades. These issues are tackled by some of the nation's most prominent race and public policy scholars. In addition, the volume has contributions by some of the most innovative up-and-coming voices that are often neglected in such volumes. Below, we provide a brief sketch of the various chapters and authors included in *Reinventing Race, Reinventing Racism*.

In the next chapter, John J. Betancur asks, "How much control do Latinos and African Americans have of their mutual relations?" He critically examines the dynamics between Latinos and African Americans in the United States. Although the Kerner Commission focused on the black-white bipolarity, race in the United States may be best explained in terms of a hierarchy in which white hegemony gets exercised in part through the competition of racialized communities for opportunities, power, and wealth but principally through the ongoing reproduction of the structures of race-based domination. Largely invisible to the general public through the years, Latinos became a major focus of attention after they surpassed the African American population. Unfortunately, this attention has taken highly negative directions. The community has become a favorite target of anti-immigrant forces and has been often blamed for taking the pie sliced for African Americans. These sentiments and structures have produced tension between blacks and Latinos that the media often brings to a boiling point. This chapter argues that much of the black-Latino tension actually comes from forces external to the community and from structures they have limited control of. As such, black-Latino relations are largely shaped and manipulated from outside.

In "*Juntos pero no Revueltos*: Race, Citizenship, and the Conundrums of Latinidad," Tomas Almaguer (San Francisco State University) argues that we need to give more serious attention to racializing practices that are fundamentally fused upon a previously existing set of colonial constructions of race in order to make sense of the increasing ethnic antagonisms that scholars have been ethnographically documenting in powerful ways. He suggests that this foundational racialization process provides a far more fruitful way of understanding racial conflict than notions of the "traditional" and the "modern" that have been largely relied upon in ethnographic studies. It allows us to better appreciate the profound role that race and citizenship have played in the contemporary conundrums of Latinidad that are so palpably and painfully articulated in urban areas in the United States.

Edward Goetz (University of Minnesota) is the author of "Public Housing Redevelopment and the Displacement of African Americans." This chapter addresses the degree of displacement and disparate impact of public housing redevelopment. It does so by examining two databases that allow for the examination of the racial impact of the direct displacement due to HOPE VI program activity and estimate the degree and the nature of indirect displacement caused by public housing redevelopment. The evidence presented in this chapter, however, indicates that the HOPE VI program has had a greater displacement impact on African Americans than would be expected. African American residents of public housing are 19 percent more likely to be directly displaced by HOPE VI projects than other public housing residents. This is a pattern that occurs across all of the projects for which data are available and across the life of the program. On the other hand, there is little evidence of systematic indirect displacement in HOPE VI neighborhoods (the area surrounding the project site). The scale of the public housing displacement accounts for virtually all of the neighborhood change seen between the 1990 and 2000 census dates. While there are examples of significant secondary displacement in some project areas, on the whole this is not a pattern of all HOPE VI neighborhoods. Many neighborhoods see little or no change in the African American population, while others see increases.

In "Problems of Racial Justice in Portland, 1968–2010: Revisiting the City's 'Kerner Report,'" Karen Gibson (Portland State University) analyzes how institutional discrimination, especially within the real estate industry (bankers, real estate agents and city redevelopment agencies) has become more subtle since 1968. Using examples from institutions in Portland, Oregon, she demonstrates how relations with the community have changed. In the summer of 1967, for example, black youth across our nation violently expressed their anger and frustration at being "locked in" urban reservations that were devoid of legitimate economic opportunity. There was a "common denominator" across all areas which aggravated the situation of racial injustice: governmental neglect of citizen involvement. Disinvestment in the Albina District from this period through the 1980s drove property values down to 58 percent of the city's median by 1989. Reinvestment then resulted in rapid gentrification and significant population turnover from black to white. Despite the efforts of residents (both black and white) to improve their community over the preceding decades, public and private investments in the 1990s were biased toward white newcomers. One longtime neighborhood activist called it "revitalized racism." Economic measures reveal that black Albina residents have fared poorly since 1968.

The next chapter, "After the Storm: Race and Victims' Reactions to the Hurricane Katrina Aftermath" by Hayward Horton (State University of New York at Albany), Melvin Thomas (North Carolina State University), and Cedric Herring uses a Du Boisian framework to analyze racial differences in Hurricane Katrina victims' perceptions about rescue and relief efforts after the storm. The data collected from survivors show that blacks and whites drew very different lessons from the tragedy. There was widespread agreement among black survivors that the government's response to the crisis would have been faster if most of the storm's victims had been white. Whites, in contrast, were more likely to feel that the race of the victims did not make a difference in the government's response. Less than half of white victims, but more than three-quarters of black victims, held the view that Hurricane Katrina pointed out persisting problems of racial inequality. There were, however, few racial differences in perceptions about the role of income in the aftermath of Katrina. Most blacks and whites agreed that low-income and middle-income victims of the hurricane received similar treatment. But when asked a similar question about the role of race, racial differences reemerged. Also, despite the idea that it was mostly a difference of opinion between poor blacks and middle-class whites, these results suggest that there were also differences between lowest-income blacks and middle-income blacks, and perhaps an even larger difference between middle-income blacks and middle-income whites in terms of how they viewed the government's response. Income and other sociodemographic differences did not explain racial differences in perceptions about the role of race in the aftermath of the hurricane. The chapter concludes that the aftermath of Hurricane Katrina exposed the wide gulf between the nation's haves and have-nots as well as the nation's persisting racial divide.

The next chapter is entitled "Race, Class, and the Political Economy of Urban Uneven Development: The Restructuring of Community Development." In it, Douglas Gills (University of Illinois at Chicago) examines the structuring and restructuring of the field of community development. To show how such restructuring occurs, he examines interventions of the local state. He also asks how community development, as a field, can understand this restructuring and overcome it successfully. His general working thesis is that the local development policy process, like the politics that informs it, has two aspects: (1) a mainstream of insiders and (2) a fringe of outsider agents and actors who are marginalized where these two forces both complement and contest with each other. Moreover, Gills suggests that racism and class dynamics are both causes and effects of community development. Further, community development, as a field of collective practices, emerged in response to effects of adverse local development policies which spilled over into urban communities. Finally, he argues that once community development efforts have significant energy and creativity, they are often restructured into irrelevant vehicles of social change in the social conditions of their communities.

N. Michelle Hughes (University of Michigan) and Cedric Herring examine the effects of skin tone and beauty on the treatment of African American women, especially in the work setting. "Fairness on the Job: Skin Tone, the Beauty Myth, and the Treatment of African American Women at Work" shows that skin tone and beauty are related to how African American women are treated at work: the more attractive an African American woman is, the more likely she is to report that she is hassled at work. Similarly, when taking the interaction between skin tone and perceived beauty into consideration, the more attractive an African American woman is considered to be, the more likely she is to report that she has been unfairly fired or denied a promotion. The results also suggest that when interacting with whites, African American women with lighter complexions generally receive better treatment, but those who are considered more attractive receive worse treatment. When interacting with blacks, the lighter an African American woman's complexion and the more attractive she is, the better is the treatment she receives. Hughes and Herring show that although skin tone and beauty are important to African American women's treatment on the job, it is not always the "fairest" women who receive the most favorable treatment.

In "Training Black Media Makers after Kerner: *The Black Journal Workshop*," Deborah Heitner (Lake Forest College) examines a national movement for black media access and representation in the Black Power era and beyond (1968–1980.) The urban uprisings in this era, she argues, combined with a concerted demand for access to the airwaves, brought about black public affairs programs such as Brooklyn's *Inside Bedford-Stuyvesant*, Boston's *Say Brother,* Chicago's *Our People*, and national shows such as *Black Journal* and *Soul!*. These black television shows documented African American artistic and political achievements and gave African America spectators a chance to see themselves and their communities represented positively on television; indeed, they served as a training ground for a new generation of African American producers, journalists, and technicians. She suggests that, while increased broadcast regulations and enforcement by the FCC during the Black Power era supported the wave of new black public affairs television, both the programs and the increased regulatory enforcement were products of the same social, cultural, and political forces. This chapter focuses on the history black media training programs created in the wake of the Kerner Report.

In "Rupturing U.S. Racial Formations: The *New York Times* Coverage of Latina/o Immigration and Immigration Rights (1997–2007)," Isabel Molina-Guzmán (University of Illinois at Urbana-Champaign) examines the role of the news media in shaping public discourses about race, citizenship, and immigration over a ten-year period. Specifically, she examines a selective sample of the *New York Times* coverage of immigration from 2005 to 2007 to document how the U.S. general-market media framed Latina/o immigration and immigration legislation. During this historically significant period, the Republican-controlled Senate attempted to pass the politically moderate Comprehensive Immigration Reform Act of 2006, while the House of Representatives attempted to pass the restrictive immigration legislation HR 4437. Immigration rights activists responded to both pieces of legislation by launching the largest set of protests and marches in U.S. history. Both bills failed to get out of Congress and ultimately died in 2007, handing President George W. Bush a legislative defeat. By engaging in a framing analysis of news coverage of Latina/o immigration, she asks the following research questions: What were the news frames surrounding Latina/o immigrants during this period?

What were the news frames surrounding the Latina/o immigrants' rights marches? How do the frames about the march compare and contrast to discussions of Latina/o immigration? Finally, how are these news frames informative of social conflict and tensions resulting from shifts in U.S. ethnic and racial demographics? Understanding the journalistic news framing of important social issues, such as immigration, contributes to understanding ethnic and racial relationships in the United States more generally and for the Latina/o community more specifically.

Junaid Rana (University of Illinois at Urbana-Champaign) is the author of "Muslims in the Global City: Racism, Islamophobia, and Multiracial Organizing in Chicago." In this chapter, he refers to the challenges of racism and combating anti-immigrant rhetoric through the emergent social movements based in Chicago's history of radical organizing, the consequence of which is an important model of multiracial organizing that is forging a new path to contest racism and other forms of systematic oppression through the platform of faith-based organizing and the recognition of immigrant rights. Central to this congruence is the complex migration history of domestic and immigrant people of color. And herein lie many of the contradictions, conflicts, and potential of organizing paralysis that are brought forth in contesting racism, particularly in its anti-immigrant form, while also dealing with an internalized racism that pits anti-black against anti-immigrant forms of racism. That is to say, that competing forms of racism and anti-racism have called for multiple organizing strategies and tactics in the effort to find common cause. Specifically, the chapter refers to the formation of the Muslim American community that has often pitted African American Muslims against Arab and South Asian American Muslims. Through various efforts and historical circumstances, a new paradigm of Muslim American organizing with the imperative of overcoming these divides has gained prominence.

In the next chapter, "New Configurations of Racism after 9/11: Gender and Race in the Context of the Anti-Immigrant City," Elizabeth Sweet (Temple University) begins to explore the nature and dimensions of the contemporary intersection of race, gender, and perceived immigrant status, especially in the anti-immigrant city. She suggests that the anti-immigrant city is predicated on gender stereotypes/images and the increased criminalization of brown people. Gender and criminalization have become important points of intersection that add density to the racism inherent in the anti-immigrant context. Brown women, particularly Mexican American women, are experiencing increased challenges strongly correlated to their race and gender as well as their perceived "illegal" immigrant status. She explores the implications of child-care emergencies, sudden changes or elimination of income streams, displacement, challenges to reproduction processes, increased vulnerability to state and intimate partner violence, and health deterioration for brown women.

"Gang Members, Juvenile Delinquency, and Direct Democracy," by Lisa Marie Cacho (University of Illinois at Urbana-Champaign), examines how one of the legal challenges to Proposition 21 was presented to the public in print media, paying particular attention to how race, criminality, and whiteness have been "reinvented," or rather resignified, for the twenty-first century. Youth of color were unable to be representative victims of Proposition 21 legally or in media, so this chapter analyzes representations of white ethnic gang members' legal challenges to the initiative. It reads race as an analytic and as a political strategy to demonstrate 1) how race does not need to be invoked when people and places are already marked as criminal and illegal and 2) how criminality is racialized and spatialized even when the bodies referenced do not neatly correspond. In other words, most racial analyses see race as an arbitrary marker of human difference that perpetuates or exacerbates class exploitation; through this framework, race excludes people of color not only from economic opportunities and social resources, but also from the democratic principles of freedom and equality. Cacho's analysis of how young Armenian gangsters were represented by print media illustrates how race and culture operate to render "other" people and places of color irrevocably illegal while enabling legal escape mechanisms for nontargeted whites.

In "Racial Disadvantage and Incarceration: Sources of Wage Inequality among African American, Latino, and White Men," Kecia R. Johnson (University at Albany-SUNY) and Jacqueline Johnson (Adelphi University) investigate the depreciative impact of incarceration on earnings. They also assess racial differences in wage penalties to incarceration among African American, Latino, and white men. Conceptualizing prior incarceration as a supply-side factor that individuals bring to labor markets along with human capital attributes, they employ fixed-effects models and data from the National Longitudinal Survey of Youth (1979–2002) for their analysis of wage trajectories which compare men who were formerly incarcerated with those who were never incarcerated. They find that while incarceration depresses wages for all men, there are significant racial differences in the impact of incarceration on wage trajectories. They find that the earnings trajectories of Latino ex- and non-offenders are similar to whites, and that both groups manage to maintain a higher rate of earnings growth across their careers than African Americans, regardless of their former incarceration status. Their results demonstrate that incarceration is not the only factor that structures the wage trajectories of ex-offenders. They conclude with a theoretical argument that considers racial disadvantage as a key determinant of wage disparities among ex- and non-offenders across their careers.

In "Casualties of War: The War on Drugs, Prisoner Re-entry and the Spread of HIV/AIDS and Hepatitis C in Chicago's Communities," Cedric Herring focuses on the connection between incarceration for illegal drugs, prisoner re-entry into Chicago's communities, and the spread of infectious diseases such as HIV/AIDs and Hepatitis C. pointings out even more insidious effects of elevated rates of incarceration, especially among people of color and their communities. He uses data from the Illinois Department of Public Health to demonstrate that when most offenders enter the prison system they are not infected with HIV/AIDS nor Hepatitis C. Upon exiting the system, however, 30–40 percent are infected with HIV and/or Hepatitis C. Of those infected, more than 60 percent say that they contracted the diseases while in prison. Yet, most were unaware of their condition upon release. These patterns of incarceration and low rates of appropriate treatment are not only endangering inmates but also individuals in the communities to which they return. He shows the link between the disastrous "War on Drugs," elevated incarceration, increased rates of infectious disease, and increased need for access to health care and other social support programs for ex-offenders as they return to their communities upon release.

Angela Mascarenas (CIRCA-Pintig) and Cedric Herring are the authors of "Marching in March: Early Participation in Chicago's Immigrant Mobilizations." In their chapter, they write about the March 10, 2006, mass demonstration of more than one hundred thousand participants protesting in Chicago in favor of immigrant rights. That demonstration for immigrant rights was the first of its kind, and it greatly exceeded the expectations of immigrant rights organizers. As events unfolded, however, it became evident that the March 10 Chicago demonstration was part of a growing tidal wave of immigrant protests across the country that were linked to the debate on immigration reform. In their chapter, Mascarenas and Herring use survey data from the May 1 immigrant mobilization in Chicago to assess competing formulations about why activists participate in social movement activities. They test propositions derived from competing social movement theories about the nature and characteristics of activists involved in the March 10 and May 1 immigrant rights demonstrations in

Chicago. They compare the characteristics and behaviors of activists who participated in both the March 10 mobilization and the May 1 mobilization to those who were involved only in May. In doing so, they shed light on what distinguishes early adopters from others, and possibly what makes such early adopters unique.

In "From Political Novice to Veteran: Youth Participation in the Immigrant Mobilization," Loren Henderson (University of Illinois at Urbana-Champaign) uses data from the 2006 Immigrant Mobilization Project Surveys to examine political activism among young participants (ages twelve to twenty-eight) in the May 2006 Chicago Immigrant Rights Marches. In particular, she shows how youth of various races differ in their levels of experience in unconventional political participation and how factors such as race/ethnicity, immigrant status, having immigrant family members, income, and work status affect their levels of experience in participation. Her analysis shows three distinct groups of youth: political novices, political repeaters, and political activists. For the "political novices" the immigrant rights marches were the first time they became involved in protest politics. The "repeaters" had attended at least one previous rally or march, while the "political activists" had participated in more than three rallies or marches. This chapter also shows that Latinos were more likely than other racial and ethnic groups to be political novices and repeaters but less likely to be political veterans. Similarly, those who were immigrants were more likely to be repeaters but less likely to be political veterans. Having relatives who are immigrants and coming from mixed immigrant-citizen families were not systematically related to levels of political experience. Work status was not related to political experience, but those who were college students were less likely than others to be political novices and more likely to be political veterans. She discusses the implications of these results.

The next chapter is "Race, Poverty, and Disability: A Social Justice Dilemma," by Yolanda Suarez-Balcazar (University of Illinois at Chicago), Fabricio Balcazar (University of Illinois at Chicago), Tina Ritzler-Taylor (Dominican University), Asma Ali (University of Illinois at Chicago), and Rooshey Hasnain (University of Illinois at Chicago). In the chapter, they discuss the relationship between poverty, race, and disability from a social justice perspective. They argue that people of color with disabilities confront several marginalizations due to the interaction of racial and class factors that add to their oppression, discrimination, and segregation. They first examine the relationship between poverty and disability and between poverty, disability and race. Then, they examine how the social justice literature has influenced the debate about disability, race, and poverty. Finally, they propose a social justice agenda to address the marginalization of low-income people with disabilities from multiethnic backgrounds. They also discuss the implications of this discourse in light of the 1968 Kerner Commission Report.

The final chapter by John J. Betancur offers an overview of themes and approaches in the book. In particular, he examines the question of neoracism and associated implications, both for theory and practice. He points out that researchers in this collection demonstrate continuing inequality of outcomes by race, especially in the most vulnerable sectors of minority communities. Most of the chapters focus on how public policies and practices disadvantage racial minorities and increase social polarization by race. He adds that beneficiaries of racism do not want to give up their advantages. Summarizing the book, he suggests that

> this book examines the timely issues of racialization of new groups and causes; the differential effects of public policies and actions by race; the effects of racial perceptions; sources of contention and collaboration among racial minorities; the differential effects of racism at the overlapping of race, gender, class, sexuality and disability; processes of production and reproduction of race and racism today; the relationship between structures of racial power and ideology; the ubiquity of racism and the ways in which racial minority struggles are neutralized; developments and structures of racial minority relations with each other; effects at the intersection of race and other sources of minoritization; and differences between and within the races.

In short, we believe that *Reinventing Race, Reinventing Racism* is an important work on a timely subject. We believe that we have assembled the works of leading scholars, new voices with new perspectives, and experts in the area who have written an accessible book about how new forms of race and racism continue to affect the lives of Americans of all shades and ethnicities.

REFERENCES

Applied Research Center, 2009. *Race and Recession: How Inequity Rigged the Economy and How to Change the Rules*. Oakland, CA: Applied Research Center.

Finklea, Kristin M. 2009. *Economic Downturns and Crime*. Washington: Congressional Research Service.

Gabbidon, Shaun L. and Helen T. Greene. 2005. *Race and Crime*. Thousand Oaks: Sage Publications.

Glaze, Lauren E. and Thomas P. Bonczar. 2006. *Probation and Parole in the United States*. Washington: U.S. Bureau of Justice Statistics, U.S. Department of Justice.

Greenberg, Anna and Jessica Keating. 2009. *Young Adults: Trying to Weather a Recession: National Survey Results*. Washington, DC: Greenberg, Quinlan, Rosner Research.

Harris, David. 1999. *Driving While Black: Racial Profiling on our Nation's Highways*. New York: American Civil Liberties Union.

Hawkins, Darnell and Cedric Herring. 2001. "Race, Crime, and Punishment: Old Controversies and New Challenges." Pp. 240–275 in *New Directions: African Americans in a Diversifying Nation*. J. Jackson (ed.). Washington, DC: National Policy Association.

Herring, Cedric. 2001. "Racial Profiling and Illinois Policy." *Policy Forum* 14: 1–5.

Holahan, Jonathan and Allison Cook. 2009. *Changes in Health Insurance Coverage, 2007–2008: Early Impact of the Recession*. Washington: Kaiser Family Foundation.

Knopp, Lawrence. 1998. "Sexuality and Urban Space." Pp. 149–176 in *Cities of Difference* edited by Ruth Fincher and Jane M. Jacobs. New York: Guilford Press.

Lopez, Mark Hugo. 2009. *A Rising Share: Hispanics and Federal Crime*. Washington: Pew Hispanic Center.

Newport, Frank. 1999. "Racial Profiling is Seen as Widespread, Particularly Among Young Black Men." *December 9, 1999 Poll Release*. Princeton, NJ: Gallup News Service.

Nord, Mark, Margaret Andrews, and Steven Carlson. 2009. *Household Food Security in the United States, 2008*. Darby, PA: Diane Publishing Co.

Omi, Michael and Howard Winant. 1994. *Racial Formations in the United States*. New York: Routledge.

RealtyTrac Staff. 2010. "Foreclosure Activity Increases 4 Percent in Third Quarter." *U.S. Foreclosure Market Report*. Irvine, CA.

Rivera, Amaad, Jeannette Huezo, Christina Kasica, and Dedrick Muhammad. 2009. *State of the Dream 2009: The Silent Depression*. Boston: United for a Fair Economy.

U.S. Bureau of the Census. 2011. "Overview of Race and Hispanic Origin: 2010." *2010 Census Briefs*. Washington: U.S. Bureau of the Census.

U.S. Bureau of the Census, 2008. *An Older and More Diverse Nation by Midcentury*. Washington: U.S. Bureau of the Census.

U.S. Bureau of Justice Statistics. 2010. *Prison Inmates at Midyear 2009, Statistical Tables*. Washington: U.S. Bureau of Justice Statistics.

CHAPTER TWO

CRITICAL CONSIDERATIONS AND NEW CHALLENGES IN BLACK-LATINO RELATIONS

John J. Betancur

For the most part, the literature has discussed black-Latino relations in a rather essentialized way that fails to explore what these relations truly stand for while treating blackness and Latinoness as natural and mono-lithic formations and relations. This chapter intends to present some critical questions based on the insights and experiences of the author in black-Latino coalitions and relations as well as through decades of strug-gling with this and related matters theoretically and practically. I start with what I consider necessary qualifications of the parties involved and the relationship itself, and then go into a qualified discussion of black-Latino relations. Lastly, I examine new challenges and developments with an impact on definitions and relations.

BLACKNESS AND LATINONESS

Race and ethnicity, I agree with constructionist and critical authors, are not *natural* conditions or genes or traits found in people; they are socially constructed categories that frame people in certain ways and establish particular historical formations/relationships. Race emerged in the actions of colonizers to set themselves apart from the colonized within a relationship of domination that they justified on the rationale of Manifest Destiny. Based on color/phenotype or place of origin, such separation and relationship truly stood for European versus non-European origin and resulted from the exercise of power that colonization represents. In the resulting order, blackness and whiteness belonged together within a social relation of submission and othering. Thus, at root, racialization places whites in opposition to blacks/others through "the identity and [social] property that produce privilege for itself" (Martinot 2003: 205).

Established in the process of colonization of the Americas, and continued after independence, the relationship of blackness-whiteness assumed the form of slavery; meanwhile, the relationship between

European colonizers and nonblack colonial subjects assumed other forms of submission and racialization ranging from protectorate to peonage to extermination. Most specifically, in the United States of America, racial domination included extermination of Native Americans and containment of survivors in reservations, peonage of Mexicans (and Indians) in the Southwest, slavery of blacks, and indentured servitude of Asians and others (including some Europeans before independence). Early relationships had a major effect on future ones, shaping the white-black matrix and the relationships between whites and each of the nonwhite groups included in the process of colonization/domination. These relationships continued after U.S. independence from Britain, eventually assuming forms that caused Barrera (1979) to speak of internal colonialism. With the legal abolition of these forms, the condition and relationships they produced remained in structural, representational, and multiple other forms and created social formations ranging from jobs/market segments through residential segregation, to layers of unequal distribution of opportunities.

The struggles of dominated groups, however, managed to poke holes in the system of race-based domination, eventually securing civil rights legislation and achieving major gains in education, wealth, and class formation. These gains have been limited, however, and unequally distributed among groups, as some nonwhite groups obtained or were granted more opportunities and standing than others and as the differential conditions resulting from such relations, generated layers of opportunities, accumulated advantages and disadvantages, and differentiated representations and self-perceptions among nonwhites. As a result, the racial order in the United States of America has been shaped into a hierarchy dominated by the majority white in power, with the rest ordered into somewhat fluid layers struggling to achieve the white condition. This hierarchy pits racialized groups and subgroups within them against each other.

Particularly interesting is the racialization of groups by continent of origin, each shaped into this or that version of the white-black divide. As much as the Bureau of the Census explicitly states that groups such as Latinos are ethnics rather than races, the historical process of construction of groups fully reflects the white-black divide and relationship. In fact, this relationship turned different origins and phenotypes into different races; ideologies, representations, and stereotypes consecrated these divisions, assigning contending and differential identities to the parties involved. Eventually, as Omi and Winant (1986) claim, with the changes of the civil rights movement, white-nonwhite relationships went from dominant to hegemonic; although the terms got softened somewhat, differences survived and continue reproducing in new versions. Although *de jure* groups are no longer inferior, structure, legacy, and practice continue producing and reproducing the hierarchy. As much as the law prohibited race-based discrimination, structures continue producing very much the same divisions, separations, and conditions as in the past—at least for a majority of them. Ultimately, spaces of opportunity are, in theory, open to all racialized persons, but they are already occupied for the most part by the traditionally dominant race and, thus, are barely available to them.

Built on this division and relationships, U.S. capitalism is deeply rooted in genocide, slavery, and colonization – now transformed into more subtle and sophisticated mechanisms of race-based difference, social categorization, and subsequent mechanisms of value extraction and monopoly of wealth and opportunity. Subsequently, race has been a major determinant of position in the class structure, dictating the primordial class structure. Different from Europe, in the United States of America, race is a major mechanism of class ascription and reproduction; it creates white advantage together with disadvantage for the others. The role of race in class ascription and reproduction is such that the class position of middle- and upper-class minorities largely maintains the segregation of this group through black-on-black or Latino-on-Latino class relations (e.g., class exploitation within the race/ethnic enclave). In fact, the class position of many blacks and Latinos is a function of relations to their own (as reflected in the clienteles of black and Latino physicians and many other professionals). Furthermore, many Latinos and blacks become fronts for white power and class control, somewhat sharing in this power and position as a function of their position/role.

Racial relationships, meanwhile, are not generic or cast in stone and, hence, need qualification. Racialized groups are certainly not monolithic and, in fact, have diversified further over time to the point that practically any generality we may make will have exceptions. The major tenet of racialization (production and bestowing of race on people by institutional social action) (Martinot 2003: 13) remains today.

Although race and racism have been considered primarily black and white, racialization of nonwhite others is the result of the same foundational act of colonization and submission. In this way, it has its own different forms and connotations. Altogether, however, racialization exists within a common matrix of white submission of the nonwhite other.

In this way, blackness and Latinoness are variations of the same theme of racialization.

The fact that racialization assumed differentiated forms has led to claims as to which group's condition has been harsher or which group should get priority when it comes to reparations or distribution of the minority pie. Thus, at the root of racialization is always the possibility of competitive racialization. By the same token, there are many segments of class, phenotype, and other factors of diversification (field and house slave, lighter or darker skin, mixed, white, or Asian heritage for the case of Latinos, and so forth) or gradations within each of the groups. As much as the overall hierarchy ranks groups by race, individual Latinos or blacks or even segments of them occupy different layers within the racial hierarchy. Similarly, overall, national groups within the so-called Latino community have different ascriptions within the racial hierarchy, with Cubans and South Americans enjoying higher statuses and opportunities than Puerto Ricans and Mexicans. Such differentiations have made struggles against racism more complex by the day, building wedges and competitive races between and within groups while often neglecting the larger and common relationship of race hegemony and advantage.

RACIAL IDENTITY

Thus, primordially, racial identity is an imposed identity, a statement of white superiority and hegemony. Under the circumstances, minorities may reject it and declare alternative identities (e.g., African American, Mexican, Panamanian, or otherwise). Or they may choose the racial identity in direct opposition to the founding action (a la queer identity) of domination. To a large extent, groups have responded to ascribed statuses with chosen identity. Yet, the foundational element looms on the horizon as a statement of inferior condition within the hegemony ratified each and every day by racial structures, institutions, and representations of social practice, and by inferior economic and social standing, thus opportunity and position in U.S. society. In this way, racial identity for minorities moves between a chosen and an imposed identity. This situation results in differences between self-perception and perception by others and between aspirations and declarations of self-determination and subordination. Such ambiguity has a significant impact on racial minorities as they move from identities of culture and self-determination to the realities of social practice and dominant structures. They may seek to compensate by trying to look white or conform to white expectations; alternatively, they may counter with identities of opposition, confrontation, or resistance that still keep them within the tension between reality and aspirations.

Foundational Premises of Black-Latino Relations

Thus, underlying black-Latino relations is a shared foundation of oppression. As such, they are relationships between two subgroups within an imposed hierarchy in which they rank at or near the bottom. Their primary agency is determined by the hierarchy itself (level one). Then, it is not a relationship between two communities with the full power to determine their position in society and the relationship with each other, but between two groups whose constitution is itself an act of oppression. It is a relationship between two groups at the bottom of the racial hierarchy, bearing an identity they did not choose and over which they have limited control. At the same time, as indicated earlier, although constituted by the same act of racialization, they are affected differently as individuals or as segments of class or else (level two). Here, the relationships have two primary dimensions: the relationship of two distinct racial groups and the relationships of individuals or segments from each of the groups with those of the other.

By definition, when we talk about black-Latino relationships, we are primarily referring to relationships around their racial condition, that is, around race. A relationship of racism between them would imply the ability to influence or overpower each other on the basis of race power. Relationships of racism, thus, are not much of a possibility between them. At the same time, the existence of different classes and social categories and their close overlapping with race opens the doors for relationships of class or other categories or for relationships at their convergence. We need to determine in each case which type of relationship is involved. We should be aware of the differences between relationships of race, relationships of class, and relationships of any other type or intersection. This is not to say that they can be separated. It means that in certain relationships, class may prevail, with race being a secondary connotation, and vice versa. Certainly, they are always intertwined as race mediates class and other impacts. The study of black-Latino relations should make these differentiations if it is to reflect properly the actual nature of these two groups. By the same token, a wave does not lift all boats, and addressing one problem does not necessarily resolve the other.

Framing Black-Latino Relations

Within these qualifications, the following considerations are in place:

1. Starting with the group as a whole, I pose that, as the powerhouse of racialization and the main force in support of the racial hierarchy, whites hold primary control of the relationships between blacks and Latinos. Not only did they define the primordial terms and create the original structures, but they control most of the resources blacks and Latinos struggle for. They also own and manage the instruments that define groups and shape racial representation. Since many of the issues and conflicts the media and researchers pay attention to in black-Latino relations relate to these struggles and those resources and representations, whites *tienen la sarten por el mango* (have the upper hand), opening or closing access to the resources they control. Thus, for instance, by determining the size of "the minority pie," they can produce conflict/competition among nonwhites over limited resources, entice them to coalesce in their common opposition to an inadequately sized pie, or make things smooth when the pie is large enough for all. One case in point is the media and their role in black-Latino relations. For the most part, the media are rather sensationalist in their coverage of interracial conflicts that do not involve whites or that demean minorities. They can stir up conflicts among them by portraying one or the other in certain ways or in the way they cut issues (e.g., the current depiction of Latino immigration as a "brown threat" invites blacks to think of Latinos as causing their employment problems or as crowding social services to the point of depriving them of access)—along the way absolving whites of any possible fault.

   For the most part, blacks learn from the (white-controlled) media their prejudices about Latinos and Latinos their prejudices and stereotypes about blacks. This is also true of the portrayals the media make of them in the practice of daily life (or the ways in which people self-define in the United States of America by taking distance in negative ways from other races). At the end of the day, group members may end up repeating or acting out the socially dictated script. Most black-Latino relations are tainted by such powers and practices. The context underlying and determining black-Latino relations is one of prejudice and the assumption that the other causes their plight. In short, black-Latino relations are primordially determined/shaped by white power and structurally conditioned by this factor.

2. Most matters researchers and the media focus on or blacks and Latinos clash over refer to resources and opportunities they have to compete for (the minority pie), to institutions that serve them both, or to the issue of who is more or less worthy and deserving. They often involve resources or power they do not control for the most part. In this sense, relationships depend on an outside party that, knowingly or not, has the ability to determine who gets what, that can pit one against the other or dictate the terms of their relationships. In this way, the root nature of their conflict gets obscured and the status quo reinforced. Conflicts over or around institutions they depend on are perhaps the most common sources of tension in the daily life of poor and working-class Latinos and blacks. By focusing on control of these institutions or clashing over what may appear to benefit one or the other, they fall into the trappings of racial subordination and blaming that the situations call for when they don't know better. In this way, they play the script that domination uses to divide people by race in the first place. This includes the stereotypes used to define each group and the ways in which the other is racially constructed. This is a manifestation of the internalization of oppression under logics of underrepresentation, competition, and advantage.

3. The grassroots movement that brought Harold Washington (HW) to power in Chicago constitutes a great illustration of the dynamics of black-Latino relations when it comes to the confluences of class and race, race and power, and the representations surrounding race relations. Latino support for HW in the primary elections was very low, as one of the candidates, Mayor Jane Byrne, had formed alliances with sectors of the Latino community and appeared as the candidate they would benefit most from. Yet, once she was out of the way, Latinos voted overwhelmingly for HW, in part enticed by a different set of also-well-known Latino leaders, in part due to overall Latino support of the Democratic Party in the city, and in part enticed by an agenda that gave priority to redistribution of public resources and opportunities. United to elect him, Latinos and blacks broke off, however, when it came to governing. Although Harold Washington managed to keep the coalition together, internally, sectors of both communities fought bitterly over high-level positions, control of contracts and jobs, and many other middle- or upper-class- divisible goods. In this case, the communities broke off by class and around the contention for positions of power and visibility. Differently, the majority working-class and low-income black

and Latino communities reaffirmed their support for the administration's prioritizing of redistribution embedded in the allocation of collective benefits by voting overwhelmingly for him in his reelection bid.

The media and other vehicles of the public discourse, meanwhile, worked hard to build wedges between the two communities, for instance by making news of and pointing to the race of each appointment or by emphasizing the deficits and stereotypes whites associate with blackness or Latinoness. Thus, while converging around a social movement of redistributive priorities and collective benefits, segments of class or other social categories in the black and Latino communities clashed over distribution of divisible class goods. For this, they invoked slogans such as the claim that the distribution of positions and opportunities should be done according to the vote (a majority of the votes that elected Harold Washington came from the black community), that Latinos were seeking a free ride, or that it was the turn of blacks and Latinos had to wait for theirs. These types of representations certainly copy mainstream priorities and games, especially the practice of blaming the underrepresented on the basis of their deficits and claiming entitlements.

4. A fourth critical factor has to do with the mutual prejudices and stereotypes Latinos and blacks throw at each other. Although it is true that members of each of these groups often engage in such accusations or exchanges, I argue that for the most part, such representations have a common source in ideologies of racial domination or the competition forced on minorities by practices pitting them against each other. Notice, however, that not all Latinos and blacks do this, that stereotypes do not necessarily or usually come from within the communities, that they often repeat each other's self-descriptions or self-prejudices or what whites in power have to say about either group, and that prejudices and stereotypes they do not necessarily amount to racism.

Two Alternative Practices

After these qualifications and nuances, I propose to qualify overall black-Latino relations as reproducing and operating under the premises of racialization they inherited and live under. Short of an explicit effort to engage in transformative efforts, they are driven to regurgitate the structures of domination they have been socialized under. This is best exemplified in apparently retaliatory/compensatory, certainly racist-sounding talk some engage in about each other, often unaware of the structures that produce and reproduce racism all around. It leads to targeting the other, somewhat repeating the experience of oppression and alienation they suffer. By the same token, they often play by default the game of competition against each other that the script predetermines. This is not necessarily mechanical, as users can be aware of what they are doing and play the expected race role, even if for fun or imaginary compensation. What they may not know is that by doing so they are accepting the game that causes their own oppression. Coming from different backgrounds, exposed to different experiences and encounters, holding different values, or making different choices, however, different people and groups have different options, may play the game differently (for instance, getting into racial practices they themselves reject of others), or can stay away altogether.

However, we can also refer to relations that challenge the status quo, especially as they claim agency by taking themselves out of this game of iterations and plays. This can happen at many levels and in many ways, ranging from spontaneous resistance and distance to conscious efforts at change. This has been perhaps the most fruitful form of intervention in black-Latino relations, especially when it translated into actions and movements to end race-based advantage and oppression and struggle for equal rights and opportunities. However, by definition, racial agency often involves high levels of conflict, turning race relations into confrontation. Was/is there an alternative? Perhaps not to the extent that the gains of the underrepresented may affect the interests and privileges of racial power. At the same time, however, the enactment of civil rights legislation and the ensuing advance of many minorities/formation of a minority middle class increasingly detract from this approach as black and Latino communities get fragmented between a majority that still needs such actions for advancement and a minority leadership/elite that has been accommodated. Then, the disadvantaged stay behind, less hopeful by the day as the leadership focuses on further individual mobility or on maintaining its place among the majority. The advancement of the latter, meanwhile, gets used as an argument to dismiss race as a cause of their conditions. Asked to pull themselves up by the bootstraps they lack, Latino and black majorities often turn to each other to vent their frustrations and compete for what each has. But even this type of agency runs into the structural issues discussed later. Internally segmented by class, education, occupation, upbringing, and others, Latinos and blacks break into subgroups of interest and are less likely to converge around the general cause of race disadvantage that now affects or interests different segments differently.

Black-Latino relations become more segmented by the day as they involve different issues or break into different segments and sub-interests. They certainly can become tenser as the majority poor among them get more frustrated and disenfranchised. Agency is a major factor, as the above considerations suggest. For the most part, discussions of their relations ignore such differentiations. Hence, surveys on their relations can miss the major questions or measure the obvious. For instance, a well-publicized rift between members of the two communities can polarize the answers. Studies may capture what people have been predetermined to believe and regurgitate mechanically. Along the way, they may miss the differences mentioned here. They certainly do not necessarily predetermine their actual relations or behaviors on the ground.

Altogether, all-encompassing analyses may be misleading or partial and may need disaggregating and qualifying to properly represent these nuances. We may focus too much on "public opinion" and too little on structural factors producing it. We may have more to learn from positive relations or from the external forces mediating black-Latino relations than from the regurgitation of scripts.

Blaming?

The point here is not so much about blaming whites or exonerating Latinos and blacks, but about looking at relations beyond those "public opinions" that usually repeat a script or at expected outcomes while missing the structural dynamics that determine and shape such relations and roles. Members of all communities have fought bravely for centuries against race-based oppression and suppression. Many gave their lives for the cause of equality. In this sense, they dared to assume counterinsurgent agency, constructing their dignity in different ways and transforming a demeaning into a constructive relation—thus turning the manifest destiny, the founding rationale of racial advantage and disadvantage, on its head.[1] In contrast, people within the black and Latino communities also

---

[1] Born into a structure of race advantage and disadvantage, all groups are trapped in relations that they act out and, a priori, benefit or suffer from. In this order, the underrepresented obviously perceive and blame the racially advantaged, but the latter discard or deny any race-based privileges. At the end of the day, echoing Hegel's dialectics of master and slave, the racially advantaged may be as alienated as the disadvantaged to the extent that they did not produce but inherited their position. However, they cannot accept that their advantage does not come from themselves, but from the structure—unless they resort

play the race card to gain advantage—or to put the other down. Similarly, they manipulate the representations and actions of race to seek favor against the other or as tools in their competition for position or advantage. Notice that blacks and Latinos are socialized into a world defined mostly by racial power, and that the production and reproduction of meaning are only marginally in their hands. As such, they can become racial surrogates against their own or against each other.

For the most part, the white community believes that race and racism can be only blamed on the past and that most racial tension today is caused by blacks (Knowledge Networks 2008). A recent poll by this group shows that blacks and whites hold almost opposite positions, with a majority of the former believing that there is discrimination against blacks and the latter that there isn't. A majority of whites (51 percent) indeed disagree that generations of slavery created conditions that make it difficult for blacks to work their way out of the lower classes. In other words, a majority of them have come to believe in a leveled playing field and to deny any racial advantage or any responsibility for past or present race outcomes. Meanwhile, blacks and Latinos are far below whites in practically every category of capital (human, social, cultural, class) in the United States of America. How can we explain this contradiction? How can we address a problem that nobody accepts responsibility or agency for?

White Mediation?

Based on these considerations, I wish to postulate that black-Latino relations are largely controlled and mediated by white power. I posed earlier that the fields, issues, and often the terms are part of the U.S. hierarchical system of race. In this sense, black-Latino relations operate within a structure of rules they have little control of. I posed earlier two major overall possible forms of agency: that of users and that of insurgency or resistance. For the most part, the ruling structures have the upper hand. As major power holders and as controllers of most of the resources and issues involved in black-Latino interactions, they have the ability to mediate these relations. For instance, they can choose between black and Latino

---

to an analysis of a higher order. Although both can intervene to change this order, it is only natural for the oppressed to try to shake it off. Or who is going to accept that his/her advantage occurs at the expense of somebody else's disadvantage without feeling shame of his/her condition or justifying it on some superior standing or destiny, such as Manifest Destiny?

beneficiaries when both aspire to a good or benefit they control (e.g., a job, a contract, a position). Examples abound of white-controlled appointments to important offices or positions in both the public and the private sector that they allocate to one or the other, often provoking the losing party along the way. In Chicago, appointment of a black or a Latino to high positions in the police, the Department of Human Relations, or Streets and Sanitations always raises eyebrows in these communities.

Moreover, power holders have a controlling role in the media and the institutions that play a major role in the shaping of images, stereotypes, and representations of groups. In conversations with ordinary Latino and black folks, they often confirm that they have not had much direct exposure to each other and have formed their opinions on the basis of what they hear or what they see in the media. Their positions and perceptions are often reactive. Sensationalist news exposing black or Latino incidents of crime, editorials and analyses of immigration, the choice of images and people to portray good and bad are all factors with a deep incidence on the conversation, the information the public gets, and the images they form of each other. In this way, it is often the case that blacks learn about Latinos through white-controlled outlets and that Latinos learn about blacks in the same way.

Using universities as an example, the presence or absence of Latinos and blacks, the distribution of opportunities among them, and the amount of resources invested in each of the groups are decisions made for the most part by whites, often creating the impression that they only have a responsibility towards blacks. Certainly, many of these decisions result from the challenges of sectors from these communities. Employment in public-sector jobs often translates into chains of patronage or concessions to particular demands or a system of payments for political support. At the same time, however, it is whites who decide between them, often causing a pingpong of reactions, sometimes pitting them against each other, oftentimes controlling who gets in and who does not. For the most part, whites controlled affirmative action positions. For the most part, they make hiring decisions. For the most part, they control the institutions operating in black and Latino areas and ineluctably end up producing mixes that one or the other group disputes and hence mediating between them or setting the terms for their contentions.

These matters are certainly not cast in stone. Race and racism have been ever-evolving social relations. They are continuously reshaped in response to the challenges of those negatively affected or those in the majority committed to social change; they are also reshaped by ever-changing and adjusting political economies. U.S. society has come a long way from slavery, peonage, and extermination. Yet, the effects of race and racism are still rather dramatic, as reflected in differential institutional treatment by race (e.g., racial profiling), perceptions,[2] and structures of distribution of opportunity. Whereas the most blatant and clear forms of racism may have been abolished, race and racism have proven resilient to the point of reproducing many of the old patterns and at times conditions that remind society of the old forms associated with the practices of Manifest Destiny.

New Challenges

I could not possibly include all the challenges impacting black-Latino relations that have emerged since the 1960s. Practically any challenges affecting race have an impact on black-Latino relations. I will select a few associated with postrace/postracism or neorace/neoracism, depending on the nomenclature or the appreciation of changes.

I start with the challenge posed by the claim that no decisions/allocations can or should be made on the basis of race. This formulation has been applied literally against race-based solutions to race-caused problems or to the accumulated and new effects of race and racism particularly on the racially disadvantaged. This interpretation opposes any reparations, quotas, or even affirmative action programs opening the doors to reverse discrimination. It has been posed by the Right as a clean slate, wiping out all responsibility for past discrimination, for accumulated disadvantage, and denying the existence of any racism today. By doing this, they end up sanctioning and perpetuating existing race-based advantages or disadvantages. Its most recent applications actually define race-based gains or losses as self-inflicted or even related to alleged racial traits.

Proclamation of the end (denial?) of race and racism has effectively wiped out redress, shrinking the pie for racially underrepresented groups in the United States of America. Calls for bootstrapping have replaced affirmative action. Ultimately, racially underrepresented groups have been

---

[2] In the survey of the Associated Press conducted by Knowledge Networks, 77 percent of white respondents found blacks to be violent, 81 percent to be boastful, 77 percent to be complaining, 65 percent to be lazy, and 70 percent to be irresponsible. At the same time, however, they also found them to be friendly (91 percent) and determined.

blamed for their disadvantage, criminalized, and asked to accept their condition as self-inflicted. Pushed against the wall, they have often responded with predation on each other or have blamed the most proximate other. A shrinking "minority pie" and a growing population in need do not help black-Latino relations in a structural context of racism and economic polarization that drives these groups to blame each other or to compete bitterly for what is left.

The second set of challenges comes from transformations attributed to globalization. Some authors and activists talk about globalization of racism or of white hegemony. This is not necessarily new, as colonialism and its legacy divided the world long ago between Europeans and non-Europeans under European or European-origin supremacy and Manifest Destiny. In reality, hence, they are referring to so-called postcolonial rule that has driven millions off the land and off their countries of origin. Although race is by no means new to Europe, the masses of new immigrants from the Third World, have stirred the waters and caused Europeans to worry about the integrity of their countries and cultures. In the United States of America, most attention has been placed on new mass immigration from Latin America. As massive uprooting in the region has brought and continues to bring millions of low-income, often undocumented immigrants, racial representations speak of a "brown invasion" threatening the U.S. way of living and civilization (e.g., Huntington). Such developments and perception have further exacerbated black-Latino relations as U.S. society blames Latino immigrants for "taking the jobs of blacks," snatching their social services, and competing for their pie. These claims have caused many in the black community to concede that Latinos are causing their demise and impoverishment.

Many others, however, have put this in perspective and have spoken positively of the formation of networked diasporas and interventions of solidarity and resistance across nations. As a result, discourses of racism compete with those of cultural diversity in a world in which economic and social polarization and intolerance are the order of the day.

Most influential here are the practices and doctrines of free market known today as neoliberalism. Under claims such as a hidden hand maximizing utility for all, provided that the market is left to its own devices and inertias, this doctrine also renders social policy, and hence redistribution and redress, unjustified while declaring inequalities as racially neutral outcomes of the marketplace. Whereas in the past racism was based on the belief and practice of Manifest Destiny, it is now dismissed in the name of the market, stupid! Thus, income and opportunity distribution are just market outcomes. People get back according to what they input. We need not look for explanations beyond what it is all about, namely, market outcomes. In other words, you deserve what you get; it is that simple.

Claiming or assuming a leveled plain field, market advocates and practitioners direct attention away from race and into factors of capital (human, social, cultural or class). Race is no longer a factor, many claim. Class is, poor play is, personal deficits are. Hence, results/outcomes are self-caused. This is the dominant form of structural racism today. Under it, race and racism do not need to be blatant or intentional. They are so built up in the institutions of society that even members of racial minority groups are part of their implementation. Such are the cases of the law and its application, of housing and financial institutions, of education, the job market, and so forth. Unless we recognize that there are certain traits associated with race, and hence essentialize race, we probably cannot explain the disproportionate rates of incarceration of racial minorities, or residential segregation, or market segmentation, or educational outcomes; then we would need to turn to the law and its implementation (who engages in illegal activities and who actually gets punished and why), to housing institutions and the ways they structure markets, to the allocation of jobs (e.g., word of mouth), or to the institutions delivering education. Structural racism makes matters mechanical and racism more subtle and undetectable, indeed more pervasive and permanent.

These factors affect black-Latino relations in new ways. To the extent that racism gets denied, race-based solutions attacked as reverse racism, claims of racism individualized, and solutions left to the courts, the removal of racism is a function of individual claims or blatant action. Cases get resolved one by one (if at all), processes are stuck in court endlessly, and remediation outlawed. If it is the case, as I argue with most authors that racism has become primarily structural, this treatment actually perpetuates race and makes racism impossible to address. At the end of the day, the disadvantages of Latinos and blacks have been naturalized. under claims that they are the result of deficits or cultural traits. Such diagnosis then justifies criminalization. The resulting dead end adds to the mutual blaming between the two communities, increased disenfranchisements of both, and a race to the bottom in the competition for the crumbs.

Thus, today, allegedly, the condition of blacks and Latinos can no longer be attributed to race and racism but to their alleged cultures of poverty and capital deficits. Disenfranchisement or racial disadvantage is being vanished from the conversation, forcing Latinos and blacks to compete within a culture and game of blaming in which surviving subsidies or public services are deemed a black entitlement. Under the circumstances, immigration or any other changes in the Latino community become a challenge to these "entitlements." In other words, a sense has been created that U.S. society is only indebted to (if anyone) blacks, and that anything Latinos get comes at the expense of blacks. Where does this come from? Who does it serve? It certainly pits Latinos and blacks in sad ways against each other.

The same rationale is present among middle classes for the limited opportunities open to minorities and women in jobs and contracts and procurement associated with the public budget. It supports claims on elected positions, appointed positions in government, proportional employment, and even the private sector. Particular niches or job categories get somehow allocated to blacks or Latinos, attracting the attention of the other group, which then comes to claim its piece of the pie. At that point, the group with the jobs assumes a territorial attitude and those controlling the jobs, rather than opening the field or expanding the pie to include the other, end up taking sides and further polarizing the situation. A culture has developed as a result in which, rather than fighting against these structures, blacks and Latinos are driven to fight against each other; instead of challenging the entire game (or the entitlements of whites), they have to compete for a fixed "minority pie." This is very much the new game, one in which everybody loses because the issue of racism becomes highly defensive and counterproductive, losing the forest for the tree as it becomes a matter of this or that job, this or that position. In short, the Civil Rights movement or the struggle against race-based injustice has been turned into a competition for the limited opportunities available—rather than a struggle for opportunities for all and measures to make up for accumulated disadvantage (to ignore the common issue of class or of a system of uneven development for all).

Lastly, we wish to call attention to two additional "new" aspects of the struggle, namely, renaming and multiplication of minorities within a shrinking pie and "identity reduction." Renaming refers both to the redefinition of disadvantage and the associated assumption of a "clean slate" or new beginning at a time of postracism and to the confusions caused by languages such as diversity lumping all issues into a generic pot. Postracism operates on the assumption that race-based inequalities are behind us and that the real issue is a legitimate one of class or one of different identities. Not only does this reduce the discussion to the assumption that there is a single root for all alienations and that they all amount to class, but it assumes that all it takes to resolve the issue of race and racism is to leave it behind and describe it as "a different identity" among many equal others. Race inequalities do not count anymore, as they are not the result of race but something else. All the inequities inherited from the past, all the accumulated disadvantages of centuries of race-based white advantage get wiped out in a single stroke. No reparations or redress are in place. The fact that different groups start the race at a different point and thus have a longer or shorter way to go does not count. Structural racism is just a name for inequities caused elsewhere. Interestingly enough, ignoring race and racism perpetuates its effects and the racial condition. Languages such as diversity and identity get introduced in such a way that all groups become equal and equally deserving of recognition without the need to change the status quo—and white advantage. Actually, the recognition of other groups occurs largely at the expense of underrepresented racial and ethnic groups, as feminist movements benefit primarily white women, gay-lesbian-bisexual-transgender (GLBT) movements benefit white males for the most part, the advances of people of disabilities are basically those of whites with disabilities, and so forth. At the end, many of these movements easily become surrogates for movements of disadvantaged segments of the white community at the same time that black and Latino women, black and Latino GLBTs, or black and Latino people with disabilities sink further along with the disadvantaged among the black and Latino majorities.

Similarly, the new struggle prioritizing identity over any other source or form of difference has multiplied the number of causes, making them often compete against each other for attention and redress. Not only does this struggle fall in the fallacy that a wave lifts all boats equally, but it trivializes the cause of race or reduces it to one of identity comparable to all other minority claims. Is it all truly about identity? Is it about forms of oppression that create all kinds of questionable identities? Should we accept the identity of race and its ensuing "culturization"? This struggle has certainly made race second or third or, at any rate, subservient to white sexual identity, white gender identity, white disability, and so forth. Is this how we should define the struggle? Once again, in the same way in which identity is founded by an act of alienation, the struggle gets primarily defined by exclusions and ascribed difference and in this sense is primarily a negative identity.

CONCLUDING REMARKS

The cause of race came a long way from direct domination to hegemony and from legal discrimination to its outlawing in the 1960s. After that, the struggle got undermined by class diversification within racially or ethnically underrepresented groups, confused by the trappings mentioned earlier, perpetuated by structural racism, and certainly delegitimized or undermined by new discourses of diversity, identity, poverty culture, and capital deficits. Similarly, black-Latino relations variably took forms ranging from solidarity around the struggle against race-based discrimination and inequality to adversarial competition for a fixed "minority pie" within a racially controlled environment of white mediation and advantage.

Different from positivist accounts that describe black-Latino relations as willingly perpetrated by these groups, this analysis qualifies such agency, arguing that most of the agency of these relations lies with white advantage and racial manipulation. Not only are these relations largely predetermined by a racial structure of white advantage, but they are at the mercy of white control of the resources blacks and Latinos compete for. On a daily basis, practically every encounter between the two groups implies opportunities and resources under control of whites.

Most recently, an environment of race denial and the subsequent unwillingness on the part of those in power to guarantee effective equal opportunity and access have pit Latinos and blacks in very unique and adversarial ways. Thus, black-Latino relations have been pushed to a realm of bitterness that displaces the problem from one of white racial hegemony to one of intergroup conflict. This context, however, needs qualification, as different segments within each of these communities are affected differently by race and racism and as many of them actually have secured position at the expense of their own, as white surrogates or in representation of white interests vis-à-vis their own. Similarly, globalization has made redistribution and redress more complicated as labor markets become global, disadvantages structural, and race and racism a marketplace casualty. Some hope, meanwhile, comes from the networked struggles of a black and Latino diaspora and the possibilities of an internationalized racial or ethnic struggle pushing changes in the United States and elsewhere.

References

Barrera, Mario. 1979. *Race and Class in the Southwest, A Theory of Racial Inequality.* South Bend, IN: University of Notre Dame Press.

Martinot, Steve. 2003. *The Rules of Racialization, Class Identity, Governance.* Philadelphia: Temple University Press.

Omi, Michael and Willen Winant. 1986. *Racial Formation in the United States from the 1960s to the 1990s.* New York: Routledge.

CHAPTER THREE

JUNTOS PERO NO REVUELTOS: RACE, CITIZENSHIP, AND THE CONUNDRUMS OF LATINIDAD[1]

Tomas Almaguer

The title of this chapter is drawn from a phrase used by Latinos in New York City to describe the spatial geography of the Mexican and Puerto Rican communities in that city. In *Barrio Dreams: Puerto Ricans, Latinos, and the Neoliberal City* (Berkeley: University of California Press, 2004), Arlene Davila reports the Mexican community in New York as being "consistently described by Puerto Rican residents as a self-contained group, with whom they lived 'juntos pero no revueltos' (together but not mixed). Mexicans and Puerto Ricans live side by side in El Barrio, yet Mexicans are nowhere to be found in Julia's Jam, or La Palma Night club, or in the pages of *Siempre*, whereas Puerto Ricans were entirely absent from Salon Cinco Dancing Lounge, or the pages of *La Voz de Mexico*" (p. 155).

The construction of these ethnic boundaries, Davila writes, "has been accompanied by tensions between Mexican and Puerto Rican populations, traced to their different histories, citizenship status, and/or self-conception as residents, racialized minorities, or temporary immigrants" (pp. 20–21). However, the 'Puerto Ricans' colonial status and history of racialization in the city also renders them a racialized minority closer to African Americans than to other Latino groupings in the city's racial and ethnic hierarchy, a position increasingly shared by Dominicans" (p. 18).

In contrast, the ever-growing Mexican immigrant population in New York has been accompanied by an image of them "as a relatively homogenous community of vulnerable workers, striving to maintain their identity as 'good immigrants' by working hard, keeping their cultural traditions, and maintaining their transnational connections back home.

---

[1] This essay reflects an initial attempt at exploring the contested meaning of race and racialization among the Latino population. For a more recent discussion of these issues see: Tomas Almaguer, "Race, Racialization, and Latino Populations" in Daniel HoSang, Oneka Bennett, and Laura Pulido, Eds. *Racial Formation in the Twenty-First* Century (Berkeley: University of California Press, forthcoming).

This dominant picture echoes the discourses through which Mexican leaders have maneuvered anti-immigrant sentiments by presenting themselves as worthy and hard-working immigrants" (p. 156).

This positioning by the Mexican community, Davila maintains, helps "to establish the relative value, achievement, and hard work of Mexicans and other recent immigrants when compared to the 'privileges' of citizenship afforded to Puerto Ricans... In New York City's hierarchy of Latinidad, for instance, to distance oneself from the lowest ranked racial/ethnic groups in the city is to estrange oneself from Puerto Ricans and, increasingly, Dominicans. These two groups are considered to be lazy, uneducated, loud, less 'cultured' as compared to the more cultured, hard working, and ethical Mexicans, a discourse positioning them as the premier 'good immigrant' and prospective model citizen" (p. 171).

Evidence of this self-positioning can be found in the Mexican newspaper *El Dario*, which proclaimed: "We Mexicans are hard workers and don't depend on welfare as do Dominicans...many Mexicans are deported because they are illegal. Each month, Dominicans are deported because they've been jailed for selling drugs, committing robberies, crimes and fraud. We are humble and respectful of our neighbors, Dominicans play radio out loud without caring about their neighbors" (pp. 171–72).

Dominicans and Puerto Ricans, on the other hand, are not often lost for words in characterizing the Mexican community in that city. For instance, Davila observes that Herman Badillo, the Puerto Rican chairman of the board of trustees at the City University of New York and unsuccessful candidate for mayor in 2001, conveyed the not-too-uncommon view that Mexicans " 'came from the hills,' from countries with little tradition of education, and were mostly short and straight haired Indians. These racist comments," Davila notes, "exposed stereotypes of Mexicans as less educated or unsophisticated 'newcomers,' as opposed to the 'urban savviness' of Puerto Ricans. In this case, it is the 'seniority' of one Latino group over the other that is deployed to maintain the 'traditional/modern binary,' although this binary is also maintained by the politics of citizenship that permeates relations between Mexicans and Puerto Ricans" (p. 173).

Davila's invocation of the "traditional/modern binary" to characterize key aspects of these ethnic differences draws directly from the collaborative comparative study by ethnographers Nicolas De Genova and Ana Ramos-Zayas. In their fascinating book *Latino Crossing: Mexicans, Puerto Ricans, and the Politics of Race and Citizenship* (New York: Routledge, 2003), De Genova and Ramos-Zayas invoke the notions of a discreet "civility" to characterize the Mexican community in Chicago and an assertive "modernity" to capture the Puerto Rican community's ideological self-construction.

According to De Genova and Ramos-Zayas: "What emerge are competing visions of each group's 'civilized' or 'modern' qualities in juxtaposition to the other's purported 'rudeness' or 'backwardness'...Mexican immigrants often generalized from the allegation that Puerto Ricans were 'lazy' to posit variously they were likewise untrustworthy, deceptive, willing to cheat, disagreeable, nervous, rude, aggressive, violent, dangerous, and criminal. In constructing these racialized images of the character of Puerto Ricans as a group, Mexicans were implicitly celebrating themselves as educated, well-mannered, and civilized. In contrast, Puerto Ricans frequently elaborated further upon their perceptions of Mexicans as uninitiated into the workings of the sociopolitical system in the United States and inclined to sacrifice their dignity in a desperate quest for work. Puerto Ricans commonly coupled these judgments with allegations that Mexicans, as a group, were submissive, obliging, gullible, naïve, rustic, outmoded, folksy, backward, and predominantly 'cultural,' in contrast to a vision of themselves as political, principled, sophisticated, stylish, dynamic, urban, and modern. Remarkably, these parallel discourses on the part of both groups served to sustain their own divergent claims of civility or modernity, in ways that implied their differential worthiness for the entitlements of citizenship" (p. 83).

This particular framing of the ethnic tensions between Mexicans and Puerto Ricans in Chicago is largely a product of the "charged and conflicting meaning associated with the palpably racialized notions of 'civilization' and 'modernity'" that "came to inflect the interrelationships of Mexicans and Puerto Ricans" in that city.

While there is considerable merit to De Genova and Ramos-Zayas's characterization of these conundrums in Latinidad, I am troubled by their framing of this ethnic antagonism by invoking the "civilization/modernity" binary. I suspect that there is something far more fundamental taking place here that has far deeper roots than this binary formulation suggests.

It seems to me that what is at the core of these tensions are the different ways in which each group constructs the meaning of race in Mexico and Puerto Rico as well and how these views are re-racialized in the United States. Briefly stated, I want to propose that it is the distinct constructions of race in both of these colonial contexts that lead to each group viewing one another through the eyes of the colonial regimes that have structured their historical experiences. In other words, Mexicans principally view

Puerto Ricans through the lens of how blackness is constructed in both Mexico and in the United States. Puerto Ricans, on the other hand, essentially view Mexicans through the lens of how Indianness is given meaning in Puerto Rico and in the United States. While notions of "civilization" and "modernity" undeniably play a role in these racialized constructions, they do so through the way that blackness and Indianness have been infused with racialized cultural meaning in their distinct historical experiences.

At its most fundamental level, Puerto Rican political luminary Herman Badillo has perhaps best captured one side of this racial construction in suggesting that Caribbean Latinos generally view undocumented Mexican immigrants as "short and straight-haired Indians" that "come from the hills." In contrast, Mexican immigrants tend to quickly view Puerto Rican and Dominican immigrants in the same way that they perceive African Americans. They are all seen as fundamentally "black" and part of the African diasporic experience that did not play as significant a role in the colonial experience in Mexico. That Puerto Ricans also share a common status as U.S. citizens with privileged access to the state-sanctioned rights and entitlements like African Americans is at the heart of the way that Mexicans racialize both Puerto Ricans and Dominicans. The line of difference that refracts around both racial signification and citizenship status in this context is central to the particular construction of race on the part of each Latino group.

But there is some irony here, because these recent Mexican immigrants also view earlier generational cohorts of their compatriots (i.e., Mexican Americans or Chicanos) in exactly the same way: as privileged U.S. citizens with a qualitatively different relationship to the state, a different racialized status (as "mestizo" rather than primarily as "Indian"), and a different cultural worldview and English language facility that has been undeniably recast in the United States. Consequently, Chicanos are also subjected to the same troubling characterizations that recent Mexican immigrants often deploy against the Caribbean Latino population.

CONTRASTING VIEW OF MEXICANS AND PUERTO RICANS ABOUT ONE ANOTHER

Before outlining this alternative interpretation of these conundrums of Latinidad, I want to draw upon the perceptive ethnographic data written recently about the ethnic tensions between Mexicans and Puerto Ricans in both the Midwest and East Coast. In so doing, I rely upon the exciting studies that have been written about Latinos in both Chicago and New York City by Nicolas De Genova, Anna Ramos-Zayas, Gina Perez, and Jorge Duany. I draw from their work because of the powerful way in which Mexican and Puerto Rican voices are so starkly juxtaposed in their qualitative studies. In what follows I want to further contrast the Mexican and Puerto Rican voices in order to more concretely problematize the line of analysis that I am attempting to develop here.

Let me begin with Gina M. Perez's perceptive ethnographic study of the Puerto Rican community in Chicago, *The Near Northwest Side Story: Migration, Displacement, and Puerto Rican Families* (Berkeley: University of California Press, 2004). In one particular passage Perez discusses the way in which the Puerto Rican community has been increasingly encroached upon by Mexicans immigrants in a previously Puerto Rican section of that city. In so doing, she draws upon the voice of one respondent named Aida, who poses the antagonisms between Mexicans and Puerto Ricans in Chicago in this way:

> [Y]ou know, *los puertorriqueños* [are] disappearing here in Chicago. It's becoming more of a *Mexican* place. Everywhere that you go now, it's like, Mexican restaurants, Mexican owners and stores, you know. I don't see the Puerto Ricans that much anymore. The only Puerto Ricans that you see…are the ones in Humboldt Park. And I love going to Humboldt Park because my kids, I like to take them there so they know that at least there's a piece of us here in Chicago—even though it's a little piece. Everywhere you go it's 'La Villita.' I'm not being a racist, but I feel, you know, if they got theirs, why can't we have ours? You know, we're not as bad as people think we are (p. 174).

Aida adds to this portrait the following thoughts about Mexican immigrants purportedly stealing Puerto Rican jobs, taking over their schools, and then turning around and depicting Puertorriqueños as lazy, dangerous, and on drugs. According to Aida:

> I'm just mad because a lot of people here…they think that's what we're about. Taking welfare, being in gangs. That's not right. Selling drugs. No. It's not. I don't think we've had our chance to progress, because everybody else has taken it. Everybody else has taken it. That's the way I see it…You can't get a good job here. Why? Why? Because they [the Mexicans] come here, other people come here and get our jobs and then when we go to work, what is it? We got to earn what they are? When you know you're supposed to be earning more for the job?! I know…where my husband works, that's all you see there is Mexicans. You know…where he's working now, he's the only Puerto Rican working there…And my husband comes home and says, 'These Mexicans, you know.' He's not being a racist because like now, they changed his hours… he'll work from five o'clock in the morning to five o'clock in the afternoon….

I tell him, 'Hey, you don't have to be killing yourself for them.' 'No, but if the other guys do it, I have to do it. Otherwise, I won't get my hours and they'll get more hours and they'll work for anything, you know' (pp. 174–75).

The issue of competition for jobs among Puerto Rican and Mexican workers in one particular Chicago tool and die factory is also captured in Nicolas De Genova's *Working the Boundaries: Race, Space, and "Illegality" in Mexican Chicago* (Durham: Duke University Press, 2005). Therein he discusses the tensions that existed between Puerto Rican and Mexican workers in this factory as captured in an incident involving the graduation of Mexican workers in the English-as-a-second-language course he taught on the site. De Genova explains this particular scenario in the following way:

> The occasion of the graduation ceremony at Die-Hard [tool and die] provided other revealing moments that helped to trace the broader outlines of the racialized condition of the Latino workers in the factory. Afterwards, for instance, when Raul (a Puerto Rican worker who was fluent in English) was talking to me, a white co-worker teased that the next time Raul also would need to go to class to learn English. Raul turned abruptly, and pointing demonstratively at the flesh of his forearm, replied forcefully, 'I don't go to the classes—I'm white!' Reconfirmed was the way that the stigma of having to attend ESL classes, itself, operated within the larger process of racialization for Latino migrant workers whose Spanish language was rendered as a 'lack' of English, a 'need' for remediation, and a general failure to have learned English by their own devices of ingenuity and intelligence. In this instance, a Latino who did indeed speak English replied upon his language proficiency as a resource with which to produce his own surrealist claim to a whiteness that could (as if magically) be conferred upon his skin through the tenacious insistence of his index finger, as well as the fluency of his mouth (p. 185).

Gina Perez also makes mention of the way the Puerto Ricans often draw upon their claims to whiteness, English fluency, and citizenship status to distance themselves from the "short and straight-haired" undocumented Mexican immigrants with whom they compete for jobs in the city. According to Perez, "Many Puerto Ricans recognize that undocumented *mejicanos* are vulnerable both as employees and as residents living in an increasingly hostile society characterized by the nativist backlash of the 1990s. Yet by possessively investing in their own citizenship—in a way similar to white Americans' investment in the 'resources, power, and opportunities' whiteness offers them—Puerto Ricans contribute to the discourse of illegality that further marginalizes Mexican immigrants and erects barriers of exclusion that prevent Puerto Ricans from seeing their shared social location with *mejicanos* and Mexican Americans in Chicago's racialized political economy. In an effort to create an economic, social, political, and cultural space, many Puerto Ricans use citizenship to victimize, demonize, and marginalize Mexican immigrants who have been, and continue to be, allies in civil rights struggles" (p. 175).

Whether or not Mexican undocumented immigrants and U.S.-born Puerto Rican citizens occupy a "shared social location" and are equally invested in a common "civil rights struggles" as Perez suggests remains an open question. Nonetheless, the magnitude of the ethnic antagonism between Mexicans and Puerto Ricans in Chicago is also vividly captured in another passage from De Genova's book in which he discusses how Mexicans perceive Puerto Ricans in the same way they do African Americans. Both are viewed as U.S. citizens with privileged access to the state, public assistance entitlements, and having access to life chances and social opportunities not granted the Mexican undocumented population in that city. According to De Genova:

> While attending a baptism party in the spring of 1997, a recent [Mexican] immigrant in his early twenties told me a joke that was circulating in Mexican Chicago. Pared down to its basic elements, the joke can be summarized as follows. It is the time of the Mexican Revolution, and Pancho Villa's army has just captured the invading U.S. regiment. Addressing his lieutenants, Pancho Villa gives the order: 'Take all of the Americans [*americanos*]— shoot them, kill them; the Blacks [*morenos*] and Puerto Ricans—just let them go.' The lieutenants are confused and dismayed: 'What? What are you saying? But why?' Coolly, Pancho Villa replies: 'Don't waste the bullets— they'll all just die of hunger—because *here,* [in Mexico] there's no welfare' (p. 199).

De Genova interprets this joke as reflecting a "fundamental opposition between 'Mexicans' (as migrants) and an array of variously racialized U.S. citizens. Three of the four operative categories might be mistaken for nationality, but the key to the puzzle is precisely the remaining term— *Blacks.* Although the lines of conflict are drawn around the critical axis of citizenship, the antagonism becomes overtly apprehensible only when it is fractured in racialized terms. However, both African Americans and Puerto Ricans, like Mexicans, are perceived to be separate, distinct, and indeed excluded from the category 'Americans'.... As such, neither for African Americans nor for Puerto Ricans does birthright U.S. citizenship secures the status of 'American'-ness. From the Mexican/migrant standpoint of the joke, then, 'American'-ness is unavailable to both Blacks and Latinos, because it is understood, in itself, to be a national identity that is intrinsically racialized—as white" (p. 199–200). Despite their shared exclusion from 'American'-ness, the Mexican protagonists of the Pancho Villa joke, as 'aliens,' are nonetheless pitted against both African Americans and Puerto Ricans whose specific association with 'welfare' signals a substantive entitlement of their U.S. citizenship" (p. 200).

De Genova seems to be saying that Puerto Ricans and blacks are both racialized as nonwhite, on the one hand, while also vividly capturing in his first vignette that Puerto Ricans occasionally make specific claims to being both "white" and U.S. citizens, in which case Raul's earlier claims to whiteness underscores that they may not be so "surreal" after all. Rather, as Gina Perez perceptively maintains, it reflects a possessive investment in whiteness that cannot be claimed by the largely indigenous undocumented Mexican population in Chicago. While both Mexicans and Puerto Ricans have a long and convoluted historical claim to being white, it has primarily been the second- and third-generation Mexican American or Chicano population that have made specific their claims to "Caucasian rights."[2]

---

[2] Like Mexicans, Puerto Ricans have also had a long and complex history of making claims to whiteness and, in the process, distancing themselves from the more devalued racial categories of being either Indian or black in these two cultural contexts. Both groups, for example, would often racially describe themselves as "white" when asked to define their race through use of the five racial categories utilized on the decennial census (which were, in Census 2000, defined as being white, black or African American, American Indian or Alaska Native, Asian, or Native Hawaiian and other Pacific Islander).

In this regard, Duany's interesting analysis of the Bureau of the Census's 2000 survey in Puerto Rico has documented that, when given only these options, over 80 percent of Puerto Ricans on the island racially self-defined as "white," while only 8 percent claimed a black identity. Another 11.5 percent chose to simply define themselves as being of some "other race." (Which could signify being of one of the number of intermediate racial categories used on the island or of some mixed-racial group).

Statistics drawn from the Bureau of the Census's Current Population Survey conducted in 1999 among Puerto Ricans in the United States reflected a similar racial mapping when given only these racial options. In that year over 90 percent of the Puerto Ricans surveyed self-identified as "white," while only 8 percent defined themselves as "black" and a mere .03 percent claimed to be Indian.

However, when not forced to make use of only the five racial categories (and given the option of self-designating themselves as some "other race"), the percentage of those who claimed being white dropped dramatically. In some of my earlier work on this issue, I was able to show that in 1990, the percentage of Puerto Ricans in the United States who defined themselves as "white" dropped to 45.8 percent, while an even larger number chose to define themselves as simply being of some "other" race. In that year only 5.9 percent of Puerto Ricans surveyed in the 1990s claimed to racially define themselves as being "black."

Mexicans had similar claims to whiteness when asked to racially self-define in the 1990 Census. Like Puerto Ricans, 47.2 percent opted to racially self-define as being of some "other" race. I recall self-defining in that way and then writing in that I was "mestizo." However, over half (50.4 percent) of the Mexican population claimed to be "white" while less than 1 percent (0.9 percent) racially defined themselves as being "black" and a similar percentage (0.8 percent) as being "Indian."

The more recent undocumented Mexican population, who are generally viewed as more distinctly Indian than mestizo, are unable to similarly claim to being white or the entitlements that come with that legal status.

Perhaps another voice, that of a Mexican woman in Chicago, helps capture and throw into broad relief the associations made by Mexicans of both Puerto Ricans and blacks that are at the heart of the Pancho Villa joke. In this case, a Mexicana named Juana offers the following widespread view held by her compatriots that "the poor Mexicans (*los pobres mexicanos*) want to work and are ready to work very hard (*duro*), for very little." Juana points to various examples of how Mexican/migrant workers (and especially the undocumented) are taken advantage of, but increasingly punctuates her troubling narrative with the singular refrain: "All the Mexicans who work in factories tell you how very lazy the blacks are (*que son muy flojos los morenos*)."

As Juana explains the situation, it is recent Mexican immigrants who do the blacks' work and, by extension, that of Puerto Ricans in the workplace as well. According to Juana:

> They are so lazy—they just stand around watching while the Mexican does everything...and then if they hear anything about it, they'd sooner go on welfare because they're able to collect from the government...and they don't live in luxury, true, but they can pay for their needs because the government won't let them die of hunger. The government in Mexico *will* leave to die of hunger, which is why we Mexicans are all over here! But then the Mexicans do all the work because they have to be in fear all the time about getting sent back...And you see it in the stores, too—the Blacks have their carts stacked with meat and all kinds of food, and the bottom is a pile of food stamps. Meanwhile, the Mexicans are eating beans and tortillas! And the Blacks all have nice cars—although many don't even go to work!—while the Mexicans may not even have a car. The post office in Ashland [in Pilsen] is full of Blacks—all Blacks [*puros morenos*]! I don't think there are any whites [*gueros*] there—no whites, no Mexican...And on the buses, too (as drivers), the Blacks have all the jobs (p. 193).

On the basis of this part of his ethnographic work in Chicago, De Genova painfully acknowledges that "such articulations of the hegemonic racism against Black people in the United States were nevertheless quite ubiquitous in Mexican Chicago...Juana's account of the "laziness" of Black people was largely informed and mediated by what other Mexican migrants recounted, and although it was supplemented by her own observations, its authority relied upon the collective common sense" (p. 194).

How are we to make sense of these vignettes? Where does the visceral antipathy captured in Juana's diatribe against blacks, and by extension

Puerto Ricans as well, come from? Why are both blacks and Puerto Ricans viewed by Mexicans as lazy, violence-prone, welfare-dependent, shiftless, and essentially unworthy citizens? Where does the Puerto Rican perception of Mexicans as a largely docile, highly exploitable, naïve, unsophisticated country bumpkin come from?

As we have seen, the most common explanation for these conundrums in Latinidad, proposed by scholars, has centered on the contradictions of groups caught up in the antinomies between a "discreet civility" and "assertive modernity." In other words, it reflects the recent Mexican immigrants' roots in the more traditional (dare I say "pre-modern") world of Mexico and the Puerto Rican being anchored in the more modern, fast-paced world of the United States and Commonwealth of Puerto Rico. But are these ethnic antagonisms simply the straightforward product of the contradictions between what Davila has un-problematically termed the "traditional" and the "modern"?

Part of the answer to these questions can be found in the very different ways that Mexicans and Puerto Ricans have undergone their respective colonization at the hands of Spain and then by the United States. Each of these white supremacist regimes imposed its own particular meaning of race and different racial hierarchies that unambiguously privileged those socially defined as white. Both of these colonial systems also summarily relegated the "non-white" Indian and black populations into a subordinate colonial status. While I do not minimize the powerful structural or material underpinnings of these ethnic antagonisms, I want to argue that it is the ideological or discursive dimensions of this conflict that have not been fully appreciated. While globalization, transnational labor migration, state-sponsored recruitment initiatives, etc., all play a foundational role, it is the way in which racial signification is given cultural meaning among both Mexicans and Puerto Ricans that is central to the alternative analysis being proposed here.

THE CONTESTED MEANING OF RACE IN DIFFERENT
COLONIAL SITUATIONS

What seems to me to be most important in both of these racial systems is the different ways in which Africans and indigenous peoples have been differentially racialized and how those racialist attitudes have been internalized. Spanish colonization conferred different constructions of what it meant to be black or Indian in Mexico and Puerto Rico. The longstanding history of racial mixing in these colonial contexts involved two different colonial populations ensnared as colonial workforces by the Spanish in these settings. It is clear that it was the African diaspora that provided the colonial labor in what became the Spanish Caribbean, while it was the Indian population that was relegated to a similar status in the case of Mexico.

While the racial mixing in these colonial contexts lead to a more fluid, gradational racial hierarchy in Puerto Rico and Mexico, the intermediate racial categories were defined differently in each case. The principally Spanish and African racial project in Puerto Rico led to various inter-mediate racial categories between these two groups, such as *trigueño* or a number of other racially inflected terms. In the case of Mexico, the most prominent racial category was *mestizo* or reference to skin color such as *moreno*.

I want to suggest that the way these racial categories were constructed in the Spanish colonial era lies at the heart of the racial tensions and cultural dissonance that have been captured in the ethnographic studies I have been discussing.

Mexicans have come to racialize Puerto Ricans as a fundamentally debased black population. Alternatively, Puerto Ricans have essentially come to view Mexicans as a fundamentally backward Indian population. These racialized constructions are the product of how each group has internalized their Spanish colonial fathers' view of the Africans and Indians they subjugated in Mexico and Puerto Rico. Added to that foundation, these groups then re-racialize one another under the logic of the black-white binary that largely structures the meaning of race in the United States. Mexicans take what they learned from their Spanish colonizers and fuse that with what they quickly learn about the meaning of race in the United States. These constructions of blackness that Mexican immigrants bring with them from Mexico are exacerbated by the way in which African Americans and black Latinos are racially constructed by the white population in the United States, while Puerto Ricans, and I would suggest also African Americans, tend to immediately position Mexicans as a largely backward population that they fundamentally view as Indian.

MEXICAN VIEWS OF RACE IN MEXICO AND THE UNITED STATES

It is interesting to see the way that blackness has been defined in Mexico and then re-racialized onto Puerto Rican and African American bodies in the United States. One of the most insightful discussions of this racialization is captured in De Genova's *Working the Boundaries*. His chapter titled "Re-racialization: Between 'Americans' and Blacks" offers a perceptive analysis of how Mexican immigrants give racial significance to blackness in both Mexico and then in the United States. There are some very curious and even profoundly ironic differences that are central to these mappings that I want to now turn to.

Mexicans do very often see themselves primarily in relation to Indianness and often discuss their increasing presence in Chicago with reference to that racial designation. Take the case of Leobardo, a Mexican immigrant interviewed by De Genova in his ethnographic work in that city. According to Leobardo:

> [J]ust like Aztecs who were a very good people and knew how to dominate other people and places, the Mexicans are going to take over....I bought this building and fixed it up when I was still illegal. And nobody gave me any problems; I was never discriminated against. But it's because I work—not like the Puerto Ricans or the Blacks who just go on welfare and don't do anything for themselves. They're very conformist, very resigned, but Mexicans are not. Mexicans work two jobs, sometimes three. I would work for $400 a month if I had to, just to make something of myself. I would sleep only two or three hours a night, if I had to. And that's why we're going to take over everything (p. 70).

Yet this type of racial invocation belies the way that being Indian is most often used in less-than-flattering terms by Mexicans themselves. While De Genova notes that Mexicanos often refer to one another as Indios, this does always carry an unambiguously positive connotation. To the contrary, in common usage throughout Mexico (and much of Latin America) *Indio* is not just a neutral term for being "Indian" or "Indigena." Instead, it is most often used as a derogatory epithet that is synonymous with being "rude," "uncouth," and generally "backward." Other anthropologists suggest that the term *indio* went hand in hand with the notion of Indians being lazy, idle, or shiftless, as in laboring "como indio."

There is, in other words, a long and sordid history in the way in which Spanish-Indian relations in Mexico clearly elevated the white Spanish population and summarily subordinated the indigenous population to the bottom of that racial regime. In the Southern California world in which I was born and raised, for example, to call another Mexican an *indio* was to invoke a derisive racial epithet that connoted being ugly, dumb, and primitive. Consequently, it comes as no surprise to me that other Latino groups (such as Puerto Ricans) would also describe the Mexican population

as simply Indians. This is about the most offensive things one could possible say. It captures and reflects the negative status of the Indian population under Spanish colonial dominion of Mexico and in the American
Southwest.

Blackness was also marked in a similar way by recent Mexican immigrants, as well as among the second- or third-generation Mexican
Americans or Chicanos. While it may be true that the term *negrito* is often
used as a diminutive term of endearment (I was always referred to in this
way, as *negrito*, while growing up as a child in Southern California), it is a
problematic construction. Another racialized term that was also used in
this era was the term *chinito*, which generally referred to someone that
had Asian features. But it was also used to refer to young Mexican children
with curly hair and a dark complexion that signaled some African ancestry. But these diminutive terms of endearment carried far more negative
connotations when used to describe an adult person.

In the case of Chicago, De Genova has insightfully discussed the way
that being black carried racial significance for the Mexican immigrant
population's description of African Americans in that city. The most common and benign constructions were made with reference to their being
dark complexioned; such as references to them as *Negroes*, (blacks) morenos, (dark brown or dark-skinned) or prietos (dark or swarthy). The most
common of these terms used by Mexicans to refer to African Americans
was *morenos*, which De Genova maintains was often used as a way of
avoiding the use of the term *Negros*, which could be easily taken as just
another way of saying "niggers." According to him:

> What is remarkable in the ubiquitous usage of the *moreno* in place of *Negro*,
> however, is that many Mexicans (perhaps the majority) would have been
> most commonly inclined to describe *themselves* in Mexico (before migrat-
> ing) as *morenos*, and—excluding diminutive uses that are always relative
> and highly contextual—would have tended to reserve the category *negro* for
> Mexicans considered to be of recognizable African ancestry. In the course of
> re-racialization in the United States, however, the two were conflated as
> markers of Blackness, and the term *moreno* was displaced onto African
> Americans as a generic and collective (racial) category....Thus, the fairly
> ambiguous, highly contextual, sweeping middle term *moreno*—the color
> category that brushes the broad mass of 'brown' Mexicans within Mexico's
> distinct and relatively fluid racial order—is deflected altogether from
> Mexicans *as a group* in the United States and tends to be fixed unequivocally
> upon African Americans as a rigid generic racial category (pp. 196–97).

On the other hand, among the most derogatory and derisive terms used by
Mexicans to describe African Americans in Chicago were as *changos*

(monkeys) or else as *xicotes* or *mayates* (a large black dung beetle). These terms were also the ways in which African Americans were depicted in the southern California world in which I was raised. *Mayates* was the most common of these racial epithets and was used in a very derogatory way.

Puerto Rican Views of Race in Puerto Rico and the United States

In his interesting analysis of racial identity among Puerto Ricans, anthropologist Jorge Duany has documented that there exist at least nineteen different ways in which Puerto Ricans have racially defined themselves on the Island. Among these are *blanco* (white), *trigueno* (wheat colored or brunette; usually light mulatto), *moreno* (dark skinned; usually dark mulato), *mulato* (mixed race; rarely used in public); *indio* (literally Indian; brown skin with straight hair); *prieto* (dark skinned; usually derogatory); *negro* (black; rarely used as a direct term of reference); and *negrito* (literally, little black).

What is so interesting about this racial classification is the way in which Indianness is marked among Puerto Ricans. It is here where the role of the indigenous Taino population has taken on importance in the way Puerto Ricans come to infuse that racial category with cultural meaning. In this regard, there are certain social associations made to being of Taino ancestry among Puerto Ricans that capture the way in which Indianness is infused with meaning. The dominant characterizations of the Tainos, according to Duany, are as the prototype of Rousseau's "noble savage" (in which these indigenous people are seen as "docile, sedentary, indolent, tranquil, and chaste") (p. 268).

In terms of skin color or race, the most relied upon descriptions of the Taino as "neither white or black but brown or 'copper like' and that their intermediate phenotype placed them between Europeans and Africans in moral and ascetic terms" (p. 270). Duany contends that few "standard descriptions of the Taino Indians fail to mention their skin color, physical stature, bodily constitution, hair texture, and facial features....For example, one third-grade textbook widely used in Puerto Rico today lists the following 'characteristics of the Taino race': medium build, copper-tone skin, black and straight hair, prominent cheekbones, slightly slanted eyes, long nose, and relatively thick lips. These features are sharply contrasted with the phenotypes of both Spaniards and Africans" (p. 270).

While Duany maintains that "[r]acialized images of Indians and Africans have dominated how Puerto Ricans imagined their ethnic background" (p. 276), he states that "Puerto Rican identity reveals the systematic overvaluation of the Hispanic element, the romanticization of Taino Indians, and the underestimation of the African-derived ingredients" (p. 280).

These racial categories and system of cultural meanings, I want to suggest, have shaped how Latino groups similarly ensnared in racial projects elsewhere in the Spanish colonial empire have come to view one another. This brings us back to Mexico and how Puerto Ricans view the Mexican immigrant population in Chicago as essentially Indians. It is their construction of the Taino that lays at the heart of how they have come to construct recent Mexican immigrants. This is, in one respect, just the other side of the way Puerto Ricans have been constructed as black by the Mexican population in Chicago.

While I would not deny the powerful role of the media in the re-racialization that both groups undergo upon arriving in the United States, these racializing practices are fundamentally fused upon a previously existing set of Spanish colonial constructions of race. It is here that we need to give more serious attention in order to make sense of the increasing ethnic antagonisms that scholars have been ethnographically documenting in such powerful ways. This foundational racialization process provides a far more fruitful way of understanding this conflict than notions of the "traditional" and the "modern" that have been largely relied upon in the ethnographic studies I have discussed in this chapter. It allows us, in conclusion, to better appreciate the profound role that race and citizenship have played in the contemporary conundrums of Latinidad that are so palpably and painfully articulated in the troubling first-person narratives that I have drawn upon here.

CHAPTER FOUR

PUBLIC HOUSING REDEVELOPMENT AND THE DISPLACEMENT OF AFRICAN AMERICANS

Edward G. Goetz

Since the early 1990s the U.S. Department of Housing and Urban Development (HUD) and local public housing authorities (PHAs) have pursued an aggressive strategy of public housing demolition and redevelopment. The initiative has been accomplished through a mix of demolition, redevelopment, and sale of public housing units. The major—though not exclusive—tool in this effort has been the HOPE VI program. Hackworth (2007) argues that HOPE VI embodies neoliberal policy principles applied to the American urban setting. The program simultaneously retrenches the central New Deal housing policy aimed at providing safety-net housing for very low income families, while activating an urban regeneration effort characterized by the displacement of poor households on the one hand and by inducements to the entry of private sector investors and the urban gentry on the other.

Thousands of units of low-cost public housing, most of which was occupied by people of color, have thus been taken down in cities large and small all across the country. The displaced families have been for the most part relocated to other low-cost housing, usually in other low-income and/or racially segregated neighborhoods (Comey 2007; Buron et al. 2002). Where this redevelopment has succeeded in leveraging significant private sector real estate investments, the communities surrounding the former public housing sites have also undergone tremendous change. The dismantling of public housing in the U.S., thus, has both *directly displaced* thousands of low-income families through demolition and *indirectly displaced* thousands more through subsequent neighborhood change induced by redevelopment.

The direct and indirect displacement that is the central legacy of public housing redevelopment has had a disparate impact on people of color. The projects chosen for demolition disproportionately house people of color even given the very high minority residence rates throughout the public housing program, and the neighborhoods in which these projects are located are also typically high-minority neighborhoods.

This chapter addresses the degree of displacement and disparate impact of public housing redevelopment. Specifically, I find that the dismantling of public housing has had a disparate impact on African Americans. Projects that have been eliminated are, in general, disproportionately occupied by African Americans compared to other projects in the same cities that are left standing. The indirect displacement effects of public housing redevelopment are mixed. In some communities it is leading to gentrification and racial change, while in other cases one or neither of these phenomena result.

Public Housing Redevelopment in the United States

Public housing in the United States has been heavily concentrated in central cities, and within central cities it is concentrated in poorer communities and communities of color. This is due in part to the fact that public housing was historically tied to slum clearance activities (Hirsch 1996). But, local authority over site selection also led to the concentration of public housing in high minority and high poverty areas (Goetz 2003). At the outset of the program in the 1930s and 1940s, public housing residents were low-income families, but typically the heads of households were employed. Initially, families on welfare were generally excluded from public housing in favor of working class families (see Vale 2000, Bloom 2008, Hunt 2009, and Williams 2004). By the 1960s, larger numbers of welfare families were entering public housing as pressures increased to reserve public housing for the neediest (Hunt 2009). Over time Congress mandated resident preference rules that gave priority consideration to needy families (Spence 1993). Over the same period African Americans became the largest racial group in public housing in many of the country's largest cities. In the post-war decades African American families, both the working class and the welfare-dependent, faced an absolute shortage of housing due to the strict maintenance of residential segregation in most U.S. cities, discrimination in the market, and the destruction of housing caused by the Urban Renewal program. Lower-income whites by comparison had greater choice in the housing market as the private sector began to meet the pent up demand caused by the Second World War. As more public housing was built, it was typically placed in racially-mixed or predominantly black neighborhoods (Newman and Schnare 1997), and was therefore more attractive to African American families than to whites (Vale 2000; Bloom 2008; Hunt 2009). In older projects, as whites moved out of public housing, blacks moved in.

As the profile of residents changed, the political support for the program, always tenuous and fragile, waned even further. The program became politically marginalized and chronically underfunded. Budgetary constraints led to the abandonment of New Deal designs and ushered in an era of high-rise development and Spartan modernist architecture that produced the greatest number of units for the least cost. The design and construction shortcuts that were taken to cut costs soon manifested themselves in a rapid decline in the physical state of the buildings.

The corollary (some might argue the consequence) of this concentration of public housing in disadvantaged or declining central city neighborhoods is the subsequent and negative impact that such housing has had on its immediate surrounding environment. Some studies argue that public housing has contributed to neighborhood decline and disinvestment (e.g., Schill 1991, Schill and Wachter 1995, and Turner 1998). Others demonstrate that public housing has led to high neighborhood-level concentrations of poverty (Holloway et al. 1998; Massey and Kanaiaupuni 1993; Schill and Wachter 1995). Massey and Kanaiaupuni argue that public housing contributed to concentrations of poverty both directly and indirectly. The direct contribution was related to the tenant selection rules that Congress imposed on local housing authorities (see Spence 1993) and the steadily declining incomes of public housing residents relative to the general population (by 1995, the median family income for public housing residents was $6,500 compared to the national median of $35,000, Zielenbach 2002). Indirectly, public housing projects depressed local housing markets, according to Massey and Kanaiaupuni (1993). This led to a downward spiral of disinvestment that left many neighborhoods with declining housing values and a deteriorating housing stock, few commercial outlets, a lack of jobs, and an increasingly poor population.

In 1989, Congress created the National Commission on Severely Distressed Public Housing (NCSDPH) to consider strategies for dealing with the nation's worst public housing. The commission visited public housing in twenty-five cities and held public hearings on the conditions faced by residents and neighbors. The commission found that the worst public housing shared a set of physical characteristics that contributed to the poor conditions found there. These characteristics included poor site design, the use of "superblock" developments that cut off the projects from their surrounding communities, the lack of defensible public space, inappropriately high densities for families and children, and the use of inferior materials and construction techniques (NCSDPH 1993; Epp 1996). Equally disturbing to life in distressed public housing projects were the widespread and debilitating effects of drug-related crime and crack cocaine (HUD 2002a).

Congress took up the commission's report and enacted the Urban Revitalization Demonstration Program (the program that came to be known as HOPE VI) in 1992. The deconcentration of poverty was one of the central objectives of HOPE VI (Kingsley, Johnson and Pettit 2003). Several dimensions of the program have evolved over time, including the relative importance of rehabilitation and demolition in redevelopment strategies, the relative emphasis on leveraging of private sector invest- ment, and the allowable scope of the projects (see Zhang and Weismann 2006). The program as originally established was limited to the forty largest public housing authorities and an additional twelve that were on HUD's list of "troubled" housing authorities (Fosburg, Popkin and Locke 1996). Subsequent changes opened up the program to all PHAs, though projects still had to meet the threshold of distress.

The most important part of the evolution of the HOPE VI program relates to how it moved from an orientation toward rehabilitation to a program that relies on demolition. HUD acknowledges that when the program was created, it was "an embellished modernization program" for public housing (GAO 2002), little different than the existing MROP pro- gram (Major Reconstruction of Obsolete Public Housing). Indeed, the NCSDPH did not emphasize demolition as the preferred policy response to distressed public housing (Center for Community Change 2003). In a relatively short period of time, however, the program became more oriented toward demolition of existing public housing projects. Demolition efforts were constrained in the early years of the program by the require- ment that public housing be replaced on a one-for-one basis. This made demolition financially challenging and diluted the de-concentration objectives of the program. In 1995, however, Congress repealed the one- for-one replacement requirements, allowing demolition to become the centerpiece of the HOPE VI program.

In the same year, HUD began to emphasize the leveraging of private sector capital in HOPE VI projects. One year later, in 1996, the program began to allow mixed financing, allowing public housing authorities to use other public and private financing to build public housing, or to channel public housing funds to third parties to develop public housing units. HUD additionally encouraged local housing authorities during this time to be entrepreneurial and innovative (to "incorporate boldness and creativity," according to Fosburg, Popkin and Locke 1996) in their HOPE VI applications, fundamentally rethinking the public housing model that had prevailed for close to sixty years. These changes and the reorientation of the program away from a relatively staid concept of public housing improvement was part of the political response of HUD to the 1994 mid-term elections and the efforts on the part of a new conservative majority in Congress to question HUD's legitimacy. The overall scope of the HOPE VI program has expanded over time as well. The 1992 NCSDPH report identified eighty-six thousand units of public housing as severely distressed. It was this set of units that drove the creation of the HOPE VI program. Yet, from the beginning there was an effort to expand the reach of the program. The program quickly moved beyond eighty-six thousand units and now affects well over one hundred thousand public housing units. While the level of distress of the early projects may have seemed obvious, that has not been the case in subsequent years.

In a similar fashion, the HOPE VI program has grown into one that is meant to generate significant spillover effects in the neighborhoods in which it operates (Zielenbach 2002). The emphasis on leveraging private capital is, in practice, an incentive for projects located in neighborhoods ripe for private investment. By Fiscal Year 2002, local housing authorities were required to demonstrate how their proposed HOPE VI redevelopment would "result in outside investment in the surrounding community" (GAO 2003a). Part of the emphasis on the neighborhood impacts of HOPE VI is driven by the belief among HUD officials that the program *must* generate spillover effects to succeed: "If the HOPE VI process does not help to solidify and revitalize the neighborhoods that surround each development, then the sustainability of these developments is thrown into question" (HUD 2002, p. 36).

Beyond HOPE VI, public housing units are being lost through demolition that is not accompanied by redevelopment. Congress initiated a policy of "viability tests" for public housing projects in the mid-1990s that has led to the demolition of thousands of units. Finally, some local housing authorities have sold off part of their public housing stock to non-residents in order to address budgetary problems. In St. Petersburg, Florida, for example, the housing authority sold its largest development in 2008, a 486 unit project to a private developer for conversion to condominiums (Silva 2008). In September 2008 the Oakland, California Housing Authority sold more than 1,000 units of public housing, converting the subsidy in the units to Section 8 Housing Choice Vouchers in order to bring greater subsidies to the agency (Burt 2008).

The effort to dismantle public housing has not been an even one across the nation's largest cities. Some cities such as Atlanta, Chicago, and

Memphis, have been very aggressive in downsizing public housing while in other cities very little demolition or conversion has taken place. The reasons for this variation have changed over time. During the 1990s, cities with higher crime rates and greater gentrification pressures were the most aggressive in dismantling their public housing systems (Goetz 2011). After 2000 the importance of gentrification declines and in its place we see that the cities that are taking down the most public housing are those cities in which Blacks are disproportionately represented among public housing residents. That is, the greater the disparity in racial profile between public housing and the city's population at large (i.e., the more racially-identified public housing is in a given city), the greater is the effort to dismantle it (Goetz 2011). Thus, at the city scale, race has become an important factor in public housing demolition and redevelopment. The analysis to follow will examine whether race is also important at the scale of individual projects.

Methods

The research questions of interest are whether the families directly and indirectly displaced by public housing demolition are disproportionately African American. Of course, we know that public housing generally is already disproportionately occupied by people of color, so the research question attempts to get at whether, given the overall racial distribution in public housing units, the dismantling of public housing is focusing on projects with disproportionately high minority occupancy. Similarly, we know that public housing across the board is disproportionately located in minority neighborhoods. The research question more precisely investigates whether HOPE VI has triggered racial change in those neighborhoods by displacing residents of color.

Measuring Direct Displacement

The analysis of direct displacement is based on a database of public housing projects demolished, sold, or converted to other uses between 1995 and 2007. The data are restricted to the largest 150 cities in the United States.[1] No consistent data are available in any form on the racial

---

[1] Eleven of these cities are suburbs with no public housing. Thus, the analysis focuses on the 139 largest central cities in the country.

breakdown of those directly displaced by HOPE VI projects. As a result, we are forced to make estimates based on other HUD data on the occupants of subsidized housing. HUD's "Picture of Subsidized Households" databases provide racial and other details about the residents of public housing projects across the country. We attempt to estimate the racial impact of displacement by looking at the racial breakdown of public housing units prior to their demolition. HUD's database is available for the years 1996, 1997, 1998, and 2000. In general, I use the dataset that corresponds to the year prior to the demolition of a given project. Thus, for projects demolished in 1997, the 1996 database provides information on the resident mix. No resident information is available for projects demolished prior to 1997. For all projects demolished after 2000 I use the most recently available database, the 2000 version.

For example, the Bernal Heights Dwellings in San Francisco were demolished in 1997. HUD's "1996 Picture of Subsidized Households" database indicates that in 1996, the 208 units in the Bernal Heights Dwellings were 93 percent occupied (193 units). Sixty-nine percent, or 133, of the households were African American. We conclude, then, that the Bernal Heights demolition displaced 133 African American households. In cases of partial demolition (e.g., a project with three high-rise towers in which only one is demolished), we assume that the racial breakdown of tenants in the demolished building is identical to that of the overall public housing development.

To determine whether such a distribution is disproportionate, we need a reference. In this analysis we use the overall racial distribution of a city's public housing stock as the reference. That is to say, if the overall public housing stock in San Francisco was 69 percent black, then the Bernal Heights demolition did not have a disproportionate impact. HUD's 1996 database tells us, however, that citywide, public housing in San Francisco was only 49 percent black in 1996. Thus, we conclude that the Bernal Heights Dwellings demolition had a disproportionate impact on African Americans. This analysis is repeated and aggregated for all of the projects for which data are available.[2]

Measuring Indirect Displacement

The analysis of indirect displacement is based on a subset of the projects analyzed above, focusing specifically on HOPE VI projects. A HOPE VI

---

[2] The HUD database is dependent on the reporting by local housing authorities. For some cities in some years, no racial occupancy data are reported for any units.

project is the full set of redevelopment-related activities that take place at spatially separate public housing developments. One implication of this definition is that a single HOPE VI project may receive multiple HOPE VI grants. The most common pairing of grants is one grant for demolition and a second, later grant for redevelopment. A second implication of this definition is that different public housing developments that share physical space are deemed to be a single project for the purposes of this analysis. So, for example, the ABLA projects in Chicago are four separate public housing developments: the Jane Addams Homes, built in 1938; the Robert Brooks Homes, completed in 1943; Loomis Courts, constructed in 1951; and the Grace Abbot Homes, built in 1955. In all, the four developments had thirty-six hundred apartments, all in a single contiguous location on the city's near south side. For the purposes of this study, ABLA, which received eight separate HOPE VI grants, is considered a single HOPE VI project.

A matter of some difficulty in estimating indirect displacement is the operational definition of neighborhood. The most frequently used method of identifying neighborhoods is by using census tract boundaries. This is certainly a convenient means of defining neighborhoods when decennial census data are used in the research. Jargowsky's (1996) national study of concentrated poverty, for example, uses the census tract as the basic unit of analysis. He argues that census tracts are "the only realistic choice" for national studies, because they approximate the appropriate size and homogeneity of neighborhoods and are available and comparable across time and space.

Zielenbach (2002) examined the census tracts in which HOPE VI projects were located in his study of the neighborhood effects of the program. His definition of neighborhood included the tracts that contained the HOPE VI project and all other tracts that abutted but did not include the site. Each tract with public housing units was weighted by the percentage of the project's units in each tract. The abutting tracts were counted as 5 percent of the weighted average. Zielenbach compared the HOPE VI neighborhoods to citywide averages instead of identifying control neighborhoods. Zielenbach's study of HOPE VI impacts also uses the census tract as the unit of analysis. Of course, when investigating the spatial impact of a community development effort like a HOPE VI redevelopment, it is as likely that the project site is on the very edge of a tract, or indeed saddling two tracts, as it is that the project lies in the very middle of the tract. Zielenbach's study attempts to account for that by computing a weighted average of census tracts that encompass or abut the HOPE VI site. Tracts are weighted by the percentage of the HOPE VI site in each.

Tracts that abut but do not contain any of the HOPE VI site constitute 5 percent of the weighted average.

GAO defines the neighborhood as the set of census block groups that are adjacent to the block group containing the HOPE VI site. For its analysis of lending patterns (for which data are only available at the census tract level), they adjust their definition of neighborhood to be the census tract that contains the HOPE VI site.

Fosburg, Popkin, and Locke (1996) allow local research associates to define neighborhood according to local usage. This has the advantage of conforming to local understandings of what neighborhoods are, but it runs the risk of complicating comparability across cities.

Our definition of "neighborhood" is determined in the following manner. The address of each HOPE VI project was geocoded. The neighborhood of the HOPE VI project was defined as all of the census block groups whose centroid is within a half-mile radius of the HOPE VI project address. These trapezoidal areas were truncated wherever significant man-made or natural boundaries occurred, such as rivers or major highways. Once the relevant block groups were identified, we used the Geolytics Neighborhood Census database to collect social, physical, and economic characteristics for the neighborhoods in 1990 and 2000. The Geolytics database standardizes census boundaries across the two census years, allowing for comparison of identical spatial areas.

Because we wish to detect the degree of neighborhood change that is induced by the HOPE VI project, we need to control for changes taking place more broadly within the city. Thus, we will look at the degree of neighborhood change relative to changes taking place at the city level.

In the analysis to follow we examine the degree to which HOPE VI projects have triggered the displacement of African Americans in the surrounding neighborhoods. We measure African American displacement as a decline in the neighborhood African American population at a rate greater than occurring in the city at large. A simple measure of the relative change in the African American population is computed as follows: $(CB2k - CB90) - (NB2k - NB90)$, where:

CB2k = percentage of citywide population that is black in 2000;
CB90 = percentage of citywide population that is black in 1990;
NB2k = percentage of neighborhood population that is black in 2000;
NB90 = percentage of neighborhood population that is black in 1990.

This produces a difference in score in which a positive value indicates greater decline in the black population at the neighborhood level than was experienced at the citywide scale (i.e., a disproportionate impact).

Timing the HOPE VI Intervention

One challenge in this analysis is determining how much redevelopment activity is necessary to trigger neighborhood change. Some of these projects are located in neighborhoods poised to gentrify, and thus change will take place quickly. Other neighborhoods with different conditions may need more dramatic efforts before change occurs. Because of this, we test for three different intervention points.

A HOPE VI project is typically announced to much fanfare as the local housing authority and local public officials herald a multimillion-dollar reinvestment effort. Thus, it is possible that private investors waiting for a signal to trigger neighborhood change will take the grant announcement as the time to act. In the analysis to follow, we will examine the neighborhood change for projects funded before 2000.

Alternatively, the first stage in a HOPE VI redevelopment is the relocation of the project residents. This event may also potentially serve as the critical "intervention" point in the redevelopment process. Thus, we will also examine HOPE VI projects in which relocation occurred before 2000. Finally, the most visible sign of redevelopment may be the demolition of the old public housing structures. Thus, we also look at those projects which moved to the demolition stage before 2000.

ANALYSIS

Direct Displacement

There were 394 public housing projects demolished in the 139 largest U.S. central cities between 1995 and 2007. These projects accounted for 163,393 units of public housing (an average of 415 units per project). Of these units 110,227 (67 percent) were occupied during the year for which we have occupancy data. The HUD data contains resident demographic information for 313 cases, or 87,251 households. The average size of the projects in the database is 397 units, though the median is 293. The mean is skewed upward by a relatively few large projects; one quarter of the projects had more than 515 units prior to demolition. The number of people displaced in the 313 projects for which resident information is available is

estimated at 239,844 people.[3] This is an underestimate of the total number
of people displaced because it excludes 83 projects for which HUD reports
no resident information despite the fact that they were at least partially
occupied the year before demolition.

The overwhelming majority of households directly displaced by public
housing demolitions across the country are African American. Of the
87,251 displaced households for whom demographic information is
known, 71,373 (82 percent) households (or more than 192,000 residents
given average household size in these projects) were African American.
The average demolition displaced 229 African American households (or
641 African American residents). In half of the demolished projects,
African Americans were 95 percent or more of the households. Are these
figures higher than one would expect to find in these cities during these
years? Table 4.1 compares demolished projects with the rest of the public
housing stock in the same cities.

The data suggest a disparate racial impact of public housing demolition
across more than 300 demolitions in these large American cities. The average project demolished was 79.5 percent African American while other
projects in the same cities were on average 73.2 percent African American.
For Hispanic residents, however, there was no disparate impact; the average demolished project was 11.5 percent Hispanic compared to 11.2 percent
citywide.

Table 4.1: Demographic characteristics of demolished public housing,
1996–2007.

	Pct Black	Pct Hisp	Pct Minority	Pct LT $5k	Pct with Wages	Pct with Welfare	Pct FHH	Pct Senior	Pct Disabled
Demolished projects	79.5	11.5	94.2	32.2	24.9	28.6	82.8	15.4	16.9
Other public housing projects	73.2	11.2	87.5	25.2	22.2	21.5	78.5	25.9	20.2
sig.	***	–	***	***	***	***	***	***	***
N	305	306	306	296	296	296	305	304	304

*** p < .001

---

[3] The number of residents displaced is estimated by multiplying the average household
size in each project by the number of occupied units.

The data in Table 4.1 also provide evidence of other statistically significant differences between projects that have been demolished and other public housing. In the average demolished project, 32.2 percent of residents had incomes less than $5,000, compared to only 25.2 of residents in comparison projects. Conversely, demolished projects had higher relative populations of wage earners and residents with welfare income. This is likely due to the fact that demolished projects also had significantly fewer seniors and disabled households than public housing that was not demolished.

These averages mask a wide range of outcomes across projects. Disparity ratios were derived by dividing percent black in a given project by percent black in the rest of the city's public housing. For example, the Christopher Columbus Homes in Paterson, New Jersey, demolished in 2000, were 97 percent black-occupied in 1999. The rest of the public housing stock in Paterson in 1999 was 70 percent black. This produces a disparity ratio of 1.39 (97/70). The ratios range from 0 (in projects that displaced no African American households) to 5.08. A disparity ratio of 1.0 signals a demolished project that exactly matched the racial profile of the rest of the public housing stock in the same city for the same year. Table 4.2 shows projects with the highest disparity ratios.

Table 4.2: Ten projects with highest disparity ratios.

Rank	Project, City	Disparity ratio	Project Pct Black	Other PH Pct Black
1	Springview Apts, San Antonio	5.08	61	12
2	Iris Court, Portland, OR	2.76	58	21
3	DN Leathers II, Corpus Christi	2.67	32	12
4	320 – 23rd St, Denver	2.63	71	27
5	Arapahoe Cts, Denver	2.60	65	25
6	Curtis Park Homes, Denver	2.44	61	25
7	Arrowhead Apts, Denver	2.41	65	27
8	Mulford Gardens, Yonkers	1.92	96	50
9	College Hill Homes, Knoxville	1.91	90	47
10	Lonsdale Homes, Knoxville	1.88	90	48

The highest ratios occurred in cities in which African Americans made up half or fewer of all public housing households. Demolitions in those cities, nevertheless, affected some projects with very large proportions of African American residents. The unweighted average disparity ratio for the 305 projects for which all data are available is 1.096, indicating that the average public housing project demolished had 9.6 percent more African American households as a percentage of all households than other public housing in the same cities in the same year. Twenty-two percent of the demolished projects had ratios of less than 1.0, meaning that there were fewer African American households in those projects compared to other public housing in the cities studied. Thirty-seven percent of the projects had disparity ratios between 1.0 and 1.10, one-quarter (24.6 percent) had disparities from 1.10 to 1.25, and the rest (16.7 percent) had disparity ratios of 1.25 or more.

The *overall disparity ratio* is determined by dividing the total number of black households displaced in all 305 projects by the expected number displaced, where the expected number is simply the citywide percent black applied to each project. In the Christopher Columbus Homes example, in Paterson, New Jersey, if there had been no disparate impact on blacks, one would expect that 70 percent of the 314 households in that project would have been Black (matching the rest of the city's public housing stock 1999). This means 220 African American households would have been displaced. In fact, 97 percent of the project was African American, or 305 households. Thus, this project displaced 85 more African American households (or 39 percent more) than would have been expected given a non-disparate outcome. Summing this calculation across all 305 projects produces a weighted disparity ratio of 1.077; in the aggregate, projects that have been demolished in these cities have displaced 7.7 percent more African Americans than would have been the case had there been no disparate impact. The weighted ratio is less than the unweighted average because of large projects in cities such as Chicago, Detroit, and Baltimore where virtually all public housing residents are black and therefore the individual-project disparity ratios are close to 1.0.

Disparity ratios are bounded on the upper end by the initial over-representation of blacks in public housing in most of the large cities in this sample. In cities like Washington, DC, Memphis, and Detroit where 98 percent or more of public housing residents are African American, there is essentially no possibility of a disparate racial outcome as defined here. Since both the numerator and the denominator in the disparity ratio have maximum values of 100, as the denominator approaches 100, the possibility of a ratio above 1.0 diminishes. Thirteen percent of the demolitions in the sample (or 40 projects) took place in cities in which blacks make up 99 percent of all public housing households. In one-third of the demolitions (more than 100 projects), blacks make up more than 90 percent of all public housing households citywide. This has the effect of deflating the overall disparity ratio and therefore understating the degree of disparate impact in the demolition of public housing.

Several cities have sizable disparities in the racial makeup of demolished public housing projects compared to their overall public housing profiles. In Portland, Oregon, for example, the public housing that was demolished had 2.03 times as many African American households (as a percentage of all households) than did the rest of the city's public housing stock. Denver has torn down public housing that had 51 percent more African American households as a percentage of all households than the rest of its public housing stock. Other cities have fewer African American households in their HOPE VI projects than would be expected given the overall racial makeup of public housing in the city. Two examples of this are El Paso, Texas and Los Angeles, CA where public housing demolition has affected projects with higher Hispanic populations. Cities in the west and southwest account for seven of the 10 cities with the lowest disparity ratios for African Americans. This suggests that disparity ratios might be an artifact of region and perhaps dependent on whether blacks make up a small percentage of citywide units.

There are two possible alternative explanations for the racial disparities found in this analysis. First, the disparate racial impact of demolition may be an artifact of the fact that "family" public housing is demolished at a greater rate than projects that house seniors, and that senior public housing is less racially segregated. The second counter-explanation for disparate racial impact is that demolition has targeted the most dysfunctional public housing developments and that these are disproportionately occupied by African Americans. The assumptions behind these alternative explanations are only moderately supported by the data. The proportion of a project's population that is black is moderately correlated with the percentage that is below the age of 62 and with vacancy rate (a measure of building quality) $r = .28$ and $.23$, respectively. A logistic regression analysis of *all* public housing projects in the 139 cities of this sample demonstrates that even when controlling for building quality and for the presence of seniors, developments that were predominantly (more than two-thirds) black were 71 percent more likely to be demolished than projects that were not mostly black (see Table 4.3).

The analysis shows that building quality (as measured by percentage of units occupied) is an important predictor of whether or not a public housing project was demolished. Additionally, senior buildings (defined here

Table 4.3: Importance of race controlling for building quality and senior occupancy: Binary logistic regression. Dependent variable: Demolition.

Characteristics of public housing development	B	Exp (β)	Sig.
Number of Units	.000	1.000	***
Pct Units Occupied	–.036	.964	***
Median Rent	–.017	.983	***
Pct Incomes LT5K	.000	.999	–
Pct With Wages	–.003	.994	–
Pct Under 25 yrs old	.001	1.001	–
Senior Building@	–1.693	.184	***
Predominantly Black#	.539	1.714	**
Pct Units with 3+ bedrooms	.002	1.002	–
n = 1926			
Log likelihood = 1102.15. Pct. predicted correctly: 88.6.			

@ = 50 percent or more of the occupants are 62 years of age or more.
# = 66 percent or more of the occupants are African American.

as projects in which more than half of the residents were older than 62) were significantly less likely to be demolished than other projects. But, even accounting for those factors, public housing developments that were predominantly occupied by African Americans were significantly more likely to come down than projects with a more segregated profile. The data in Table 4.3 show that all three of these explanations are accurate in distinguishing demolished public housing from the projects left standing.

Indirect Displacement

The analysis of indirect displacement caused by HOPE VI is based on the expectation that neighborhoods surrounding HOPE VI projects will change due to the redevelopment that occurs on the public housing site. The focus here is on the degree of racial change and poverty reduction in HOPE VI neighborhoods. In order to control for racial and poverty changes taking place more broadly in the local housing market, neighborhood change is calculated relative to citywide change.

The average population in these HOPE VI neighborhoods was 5701 for the 176 that received their funding prior to 2000, 6246 for neighborhoods that began relocation during the 90s, and 6857 for the neighborhoods of projects that had been demolished (see Table 4.4). These neighborhoods were 60 percent African American on average, and 12 to 14 percent

Table 4.4: HOPE VI project characteristics.

Neighborhood characteristics	First grant in 1990s	Relocation in 1990s	Demolition in 1990s
Mean population, 1990	5701	6246	6857
Mean Pct. Black 1990	59.7	61.1	60.3
Mean Pct. Hispanic 1990	11.9	12.3	14.1
Mean pct. Poverty 1990	45.0	45.0	45.6
Mean pct. Owner-occupied housing	28.4	25.6	24.3
Mean pct vacant housing	14.9	14.9	14.7
N	176	100	64

Hispanic. The HOPE VI neighborhoods were characterized by a high poverty rate (45 percent), low-levels of owner-occupancy (24 to 28 percent) and vacancy rates of close to 15 percent. Because the basic patterns of neighborhood change are the same across these three nested sub-samples, the focus is on projects that relocated residents prior to the 2000 census (n=100).

Poverty Reduction in HOPE VI Neighborhoods

The commonly accepted threshold for "concentrated poverty" is an area in which more than 40 percent of the population is below the poverty line (Jargowsky 1996). Thus, on average, HOPE VI neighborhoods were above that threshold when the 1990s began. By 2000, the 100 neighborhoods that had already experienced HOPE VI relocation averaged 36.1 percent poverty, a reduction of more than eight percentage points. The average decline in poverty relative to changes taking place at the city level was 7.6 percentage points. That is, the average HOPE VI neighborhood saw a decline in poverty that was 7.6 percentage points greater than their respective citywide changes during the 1990s.

Most neighborhoods saw a decline in poverty rate that was significantly greater than the secular trends taking place citywide (see Table 4.5). Looking at the projects that moved to relocation during the 1990s (the middle column in the data table), one sees that poverty declined faster citywide than in the HOPE VI neighborhood in 25 projects (25 percent). In 15 cases the neighborhood reduction in poverty was slightly greater (less than five percentage points) than what was experienced citywide. In close to one-half of the cases (46 percent), however, the neighborhoods saw

Table 4.5: Changes in poverty and in African American population in HOPE VI neighborhoods relative to changes taking place citywide, 1990–2000.

	Projects that received grant in 1990s		Projects that relocated families in 1990s		Projects that were demolished in 1990s	
	Poverty	Af-Am	Poverty	Af-Am	Poverty	Af-Am
Neighborhood reduction that trailed the citywide rate of reduction	44 (25)	51 (29)	25 (25)	25 (25)	12 (19)	15 (23)
Decline that exceeded the citywide rate by less than 5 percentage points	29 (17)	49 (28)	15 (15)	25 (25)	12 (19)	19 (30)
Decline from 5 to 10 percentage points greater than citywide decline	28 (16)	43 (25)	13 (13)	27 (27)	7 (10)	15 (23)
Decline of more than 10 percentage points greater than citywide	74 (42)	32 (18)	46 (46)	23 (23)	33 (52)	15 (23)
N	175		100		64	

a reduction in poverty that was at least ten percentage points greater than what was happening citywide. Table 4.5 indicates that projects that were farther along (i.e., had moved to demolition by 2000) were even more likely to show significant poverty reduction (52 percent declined in poverty at a rate at least 10 percentage points more than the city).

Racial Turnover in Predominantly Black Neighborhoods

By limiting the analysis to HOPE VI redevelopments taking place in predominantly (50 percent+) black neighborhoods, it is possible to focus more directly on the issue of black displacement. Sixty two percent of the neighborhoods in the HOPE VI sample can be classified as predominantly black in 1990. Table 4.6 summarizes the displacement information for projects in these neighborhoods.

The data indicate that in HOPE VI neighborhoods in which blacks were the largest racial group, they constituted on average 84 percent of the population in 1990. For all projects that began in the 1990s, the black population declined four percentage points (84.0 to 79.9). For projects that went as far as demolition, the decline was six percentage points (84.7 to 78.8). In absolute numbers, the average reduction in black population over the decade was 1005 persons for projects begun in the 1990s. For projects that completed relocation, the reduction was 1175, and for projects that moved to demolition, the average reduction in black population was 1372.

Table 4.6: Indirect displacement of African Americans in predominantly Black HOPE VI neighborhoods.

Neighborhood characteristics	First grant in 1990s	Relocation in 1990s	Demolition in 1990s
Mean Black pop 1990	4824	4927	5232
Mean Pct. Black 1990	84.0	84.2	84.7
Mean Black pop 2000	3643	3486	3539
Mean Pct. Black 2000	79.9	78.7	78.8
Mean Expected Reduction in Black population[#]	1005	1175	1372
Mean Reduction in Black population	1180	1441	1694
Per-project displacement effect[@]	175	256	322
Excessive Reduction in Black population[*]	19,974	11,155	12,524
N	108	62	39

[#] The reduction in the neighborhood Black population if the neighborhood change had matched the overall city change.
[@] Actual reduction in neighborhood Black population minus the expected reduction.
[*] Sum of per-project displacement effects.

The per-project displacement impact isolates the reduction in black population above (or below) what is expected given citywide trends. Predominantly black neighborhoods with HOPE VI projects initiated in the 1990s saw a reduction in the black population of 175 more than expected given citywide trends. For projects that went to relocation the displacement effect was 256, and 322 for projects that saw demolition during the 1990s.

These national averages, however, obscure significant variation across cities and across projects. Figure 4.1 arrays HOPE VI projects along two dimensions: change in poverty and change in African American population, relative to changes taking place in the city as a whole.[4] The most populated quadrant is the lower left which contains neighborhoods experiencing white gentrification. These twenty-seven HOPE VI neighborhoods (44 percent of this sample) saw a relative and sizable reduction in poverty and a relative and sizable reduction in African American population.

A smaller number of neighborhoods saw a reduction in poverty with little to no change in race, or even an increase in the black population. These neighborhoods (18 percent of the HOPE VI neighborhoods that began the 1990s with a predominantly Black population) could be said to be undergoing black gentrification. These neighborhoods are highlighted in the rectangle within Figure 4.1. While Chicago's Bronzeville neighborhood surrounding the Robert Taylor Homes is included in this group, the data reveal that black gentrification is also occurring in HOPE VI neighborhoods in Pittsburgh, Charlotte, Columbus (Ohio), Louisville, and Wilmington (North Carolina), among other places.

Neighborhoods that are near the intersection of the two axes have not experienced significant change in either poverty or racial profile. In these neighborhoods the HOPE VI project has seemingly not triggered any larger neighborhood change. Finally, the smallest number of neighborhoods see a sizable decline in African American residents but no change in poverty (desegregating neighborhoods) or see an increase in poverty with little racial change. Taken together, the data presented in this section suggests that while significant secondary displacement of African Americans occurs in some cases, there are offsetting examples where no such indirect

---

[4] The data are shown only for those projects that moved to relocation during the 1990s. The distribution of projects along these two dimensions is similar for projects that only received their funding in the 1990s and for those projects that moved to demolition in 1990s.

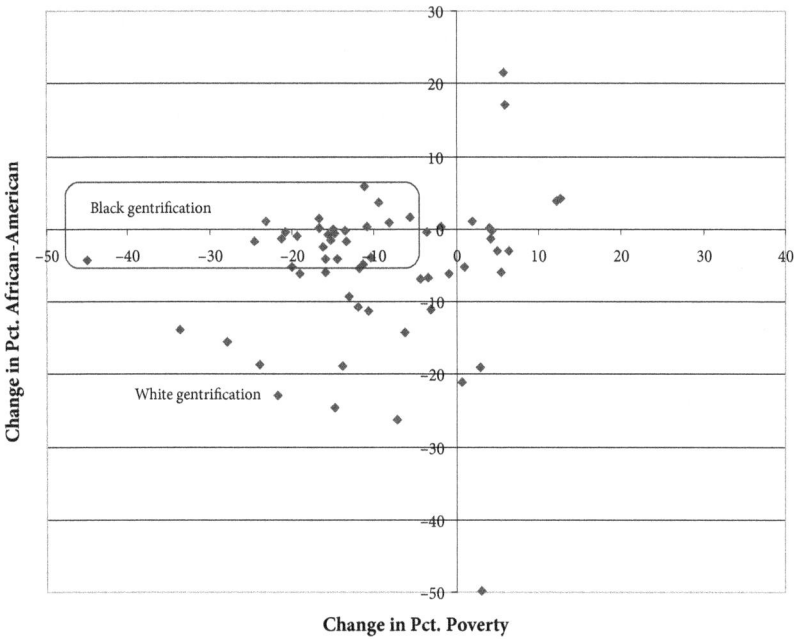

Figure 1: Relative changes in race and poverty in predominantly Black HOPE VI neighborhoods (for projects that were demolished prior to 2000) n = 62.

displacement has occurred or where African American populations have actually increased in the neighborhood. HOPE VI projects seem to generate a range of racial outcomes not easily summarized.

CONCLUSION

Local and federal officials across the United States have energetically pursued demolition of older public housing projects in many cities that have displaced hundreds of thousands of very low income families since the 1990s and disproportionately affected African Americans. The disparate impact, furthermore, is not merely the result of the fact that blacks are over-represented in public housing. Faced with a range of public housing projects to sweep away, local housing authorities have systematically chosen projects that, even by the standards of their own city, are disproportionately inhabited by black families.

The data presented here indicates that public housing demolition and redevelopment is generating a wide range of neighborhood outcomes, the most common of which are patterns of black or white gentrification.

In the aggregate, redevelopment projects that began in the 1990s were not associated with a significant amount of neighborhood racial turnover. Public housing transformation has in some cities led to gentrification that entails significant racial turnover as well as changes in the income profile of the neighborhood. This pattern was found in close to half of the HOPE VI projects in predominantly black neighborhoods. The data also show that one in five predominantly African American communities with a HOPE VI project experience black gentrification, i.e., a significant reduction in poverty without racial change. HOPE VI triggered significant poverty reduction in most neighborhoods, but was associated with racial turnover in a smaller number of places.

The neighborhood change analysis presented in these pages must be regarded as preliminary given three important considerations. First, though the data reveal examples of black gentrification as well as other paths of neighborhood change triggered by public housing transformation, the analysis cannot shed light on why neighborhoods move down one of these paths or another. Second, the amount of indirect displacement is probably under-estimated because very few of the HOPE VI projects that form the basis of this analysis had completed the redevelopment process. As a result, the analysis more closely reflects the initial population changes associated with demolition and displacement. It is possible, indeed probable, that some if not most neighborhood change dynamics would begin or accelerate after redevelopment is complete, producing subsequent settlement patterns that could reflect changes greater than those discovered by this analysis.

Finally, the neighborhood data measures change over a 10-year period. The public housing redevelopment is only one event, albeit a major one, in that 10-year period. Though the analysis controls for broader market changes within the local economy, it is difficult to say, for any given neighborhood, whether public housing redevelopment produced the neighborhood change seen, or was simply a part of a trend that began before demolition. The analysis confirms, however, the observations of previous studies that identify the central importance of public housing transformation to patterns of gentrification in U.S. cities.

References

Buron, Larry, Susan Popkin, Diane Levy, Laura Harris, and Jill Khadduri. 2002. "The HOPE VI Resident Tracking Study." Washington, DC: The Urban Institute.

Burt, Cecily. 2008. "Oakland housing agency reassures tenants who fear Section 8 voucher plans." *Oakland Tribune*, http://www.insidebayarea.com/localnews/ci_10551818, September 24.

Comey, Jennifer. 2007. HOPE VI'd and On the Move. Brief No. 1, Washington, D. Metropolitan Housing and Communities Center, The Urban Institute.

Epp, Gayle. 1998. "Emerging strategies for revitalizing public housing communities." In David P. Varady, Wolfgang F.E. Preiser, and Francis P. Russell (Eds.) *New Directions in Urban Public Housing.* New Brunswick, NJ: Center for Urban Policy Research.

Fosburg, L.B., S.J. Popkin, and G. Locke. 1996. *An Historical and Baseline Assessment of HOPE VI. Volume I: Cross-Site Report.* Washington, DC: U.S. Department of Housing and Urban Development.

Goetz, Edward G. 2011. "Where have all the towers gone? The dismantling of public in U.S. cities." *Journal of Urban Affairs,* 33 (3): 267–288.

Hackworth, Jason. 2007. *The Neoliberal City: Governance, Ideology, and Development in American Urbanism.* Ithaca, NY: Cornell University Press.

Hirsch, Arnold R. 1998. *Making the Second Ghetto: Race & Housing in Chicago, 1940 – 1960.* Chicago: University of Chicago Press.

Holloway, Steven R., Deborah Bryan, Robert Chabot, Donna M. Robers, and James Rulli. 1998. "Exploring the effects of public housing on the concentration of poverty in columbus, Ohio." Urban Affairs Review 33 (6): 767–789.

Jargowsky, Paul A. 1996. *Poverty and place: Ghettos, barrios, and the American City.* New York: Russell Sage Foundation.

Kingsley, G. Thomas, Jennifer Johnson, and Kathryn L.S. Pettit. 2003. "Patterns of Section 8 relocation in the HOPE VI program." *Journal of Urban Affairs* 25 (4): 427–447.

Kingsley, G. Thomas, Martin D. Abravanel, Mary Cunningham, Jeremy Gustafson, Arthur J. Naparstek, and Margery Austin Turner. 2003. "Lessons from HOPE VI for the future of public housing." Washington, D.C.: The Urban Institute.

Massey, Douglas, and Shawn M. Kanaiaupuni. 1993. "Public housing and the concentration of poverty." *Social Science Quarterly* 74 (1): 109–122.

Schill, Michael H., and Susan M. Wachter. 1995. "The spatial bias of federal housing law and policy: Concentrated poverty in urban America." *University of Pennsylvania Law Review* 143: 1284–1349.

Silva, Cristina. 2008. "St. Pete: Housing authority will pay $850,000 to relocate Graham-Rogall residents." *St. Petersburg Times* http://blogs.tampabay.com/breakingnews/2008/04/st-pete-housing.html, April 24.

Turbov, Mindy and Val Piper. 2005. *HOPE VI as a catalyst for neighborhood change.* Washington, D.C.: The Brookings Institution.

US Department of Housing and Urban Development. 2002. *HOPE VI: Best practices and lessons learned 1992–2002.* Submitted to the Committee on Appropriations, United States House of Representatives, Committee on Appropriations, United States Senate.

US Department of Housing and Urban Development. 2003. "HOPE VI report on need for revitalization, lessons learned and reauthorization." Washington, D.C.: Office of Public and Indian Housing, Fiscal Year 2003 Appropriations Required Report.

US GAO. 2003. *Public housing: HOPE VI resident issues and changes in neighborhoods surrounding grant sites. Report to the Ranking Minority Member, Subcommittee on Housing and Transportation, Committee on Banking, Housing, and Urban Affairs, U.S. Senate.* Washington, D.C.: US General Accounting Office. (GAO-04-109).

Zhang, Yan, and Gretchen Weismann. 2006. "Public Housing's Cinderella: Policy Dynamics of HOPE VI in the Mid-1990s," pages 41–67 in Larry Bennett, Janet L. Smith, and Patricia Wright (Eds.) *Where are the poor people to live? Transforming public housing communities.* Armonk, NY: M.E. Sharpe.

Zielenbach, Sean. 2002. *The economic impact of HOPE VI on neighborhoods.* Washington, D.C.: Housing Research Foundation.

CHAPTER FIVE

PROBLEMS OF RACIAL JUSTICE IN PORTLAND, 1968–2010: REVISITING THE CITY'S "KERNER REPORT"

Karen J. Gibson

INTRODUCTION

The City Club of Portland, a group of civic-minded citizens, commissioned its own study about the causes of civil unrest during the summer of 1967 in the Albina District, where black people had been segregated following World War II. Modeled after the Kerner Report, the "Report on Problems of Racial Justice in Portland" documented pervasive racial discrimination.

> The range of deficiencies and grievances in Portland is similar to that found by the Kerner Commission to exist in large cities in general. It includes discrimination or inadequacies in many areas—police attitudes and practices, unemployment, consumer treatment, education, recreation, welfare, health, housing, municipal services—and the underlying behavior and attitudes of the white community. To the extent that its problems differ from those of Watts, Newark, or Detroit, the differences are of *degree*, not of cause and effect, or of urgency." (City Club of Portland, June 14, 1968)

The report concluded that there was a "common denominator" across all areas which aggravated the situation of racial injustice: governmental neglect of citizen involvement. The main complaints of the rebellious youth concerned education, employment, housing, and police. This chapter analyzes how the relations between the black community and institutions such as city redevelopment agencies, the school district, and the police have changed over the past forty years.

THE SOCIOECONOMIC GAP BETWEEN BLACKS AND WHITES HAS WIDENED

Socioeconomic indicators from the city of Portland, Oregon, reveal that not only has the racial gap widened, but that black Portlanders are worse off than they were in the late 1960s. In this section I discuss the following indicators of socioeconomic status of blacks and whites as groups: per capita income, unemployment, educational attainment, and homeownership.

Per capita income is a measure of aggregate income for a population group. It includes earnings as well as other forms of income, such as Social Security or pensions. Figure 5.1 shows that the income gap widened over the past thirty years as black per capita income grew by just 8 percent to $16,258, while white per capita income increased by 32 percent to $33,192 (in 2009 dollars). Thus, the black-white ratio decreased from 60 to 49 percent.

Figures 5.2 and 5.3 compare black and white unemployment rates by gender. Black workers were more marginalized from the labor market in the 2005–09 time period than they were in 1970. Since 1980, the official black male unemployment rate has been above 15 percent and the black female unemployment rate above 10.5 percent. The black male rate has been more than double the white male rate since that time. The same was true for females, until the recent period, when the Great Recession caused the gap to decrease as white female unemployment rates rose.

Figure 5.4 displays the trend in adult educational attainment from 1960 to 2005–09. The ratio of black-white college degree attainment (bachelor's or higher) went from .60 in 1960 to .38 in 2005–09. In 2005–09, less than one in five black adults has a bachelor's degree or higher, compared to

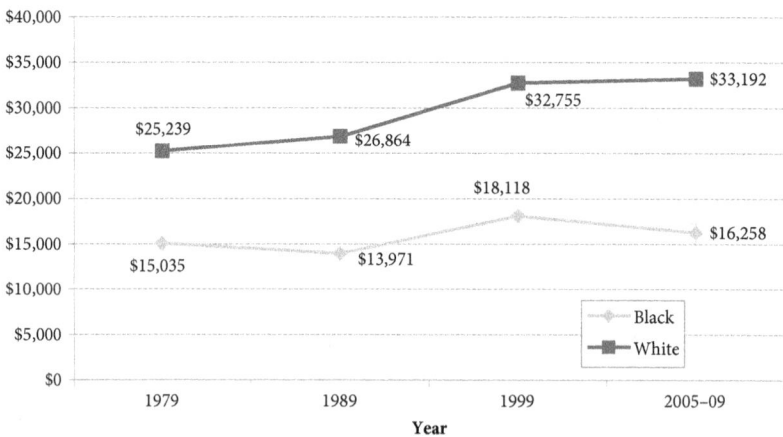

Figure 5.1: Per Capita Income by race in Portland, 1979 to 2005–09.

Note: I-beam lines indicate margin of error of 2005–09 ACS estimate at 90% confidence

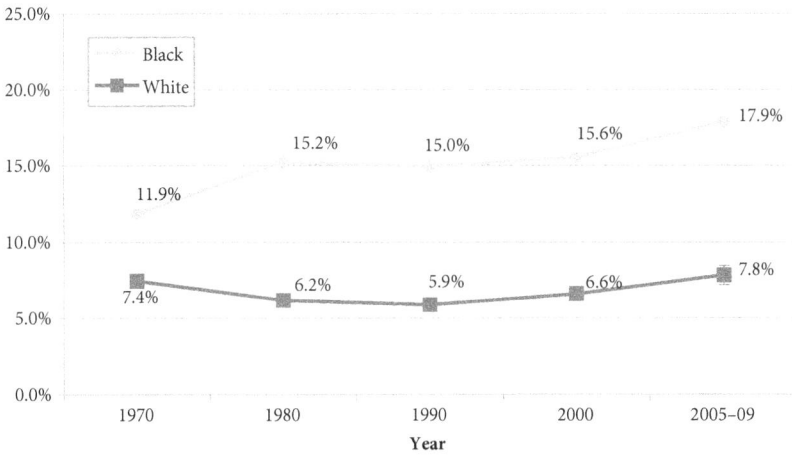

Figure 5.2: Male unemployment trends in Portland, 1970 to 2005–09.

Note: I-beam lines indicate margin of error of 2005–09 ACS estimate at 90% condence level.

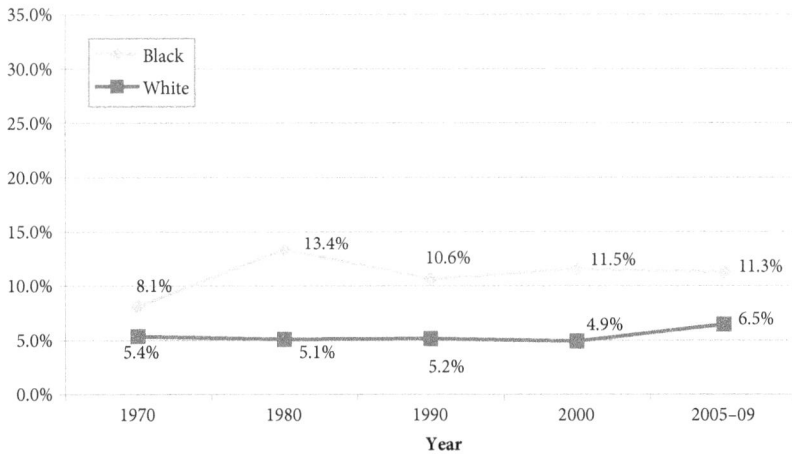

Figure 5.3: Female unemployment trends in Portland, 1970 to 2005–09.

Note: I-beam lines indicate margin of error of 2005–09 ACS estimate at 90% condence level.

nearly one in two white adults. Part of the increase in attainment among whites is due to the immigration of educated white adults to the city of Portland in the twenty years. This gap in higher education means that black adults in the city of Portland are less competitive in the labor market for jobs requiring a college education.

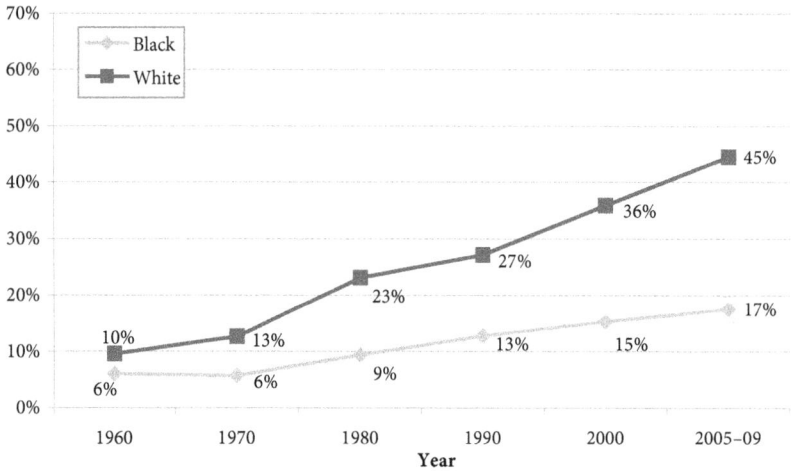

Figure 5.4: Adults 25 and older with bachelor's degree or higher, 1960 to 2005–09.

Note: I-beam lines indicate margin of error of 2005–09 ACS estimate at 90% condence level.

Homeownership is a common path utilized to accumulate wealth. Figure 5.5 shows that Black Portlanders experienced a 15 percentage point decrease in the homeownership rate during the past 50 years. By 2010, just one of three black households owned their homes. While whites also experienced a decrease in the homeownership rate, it was a much smaller loss (4 percentage points), and nearly six in ten white households owned their homes. These trends meant that the racial homeownership gap widened: the ratio of black-white homeownership went from .79 in 1960 to .58 in 2005–09.

It is clear from this empirical portrait that blacks in Portland have not yet achieved the racial justice that was envisioned by the City Club when it wrote its version of the Kerner Report. Nor would the youth involved in the revolts be satisfied with the lack of progress both absolutely and relative to whites. The next section deals with the reasons why we see these outcomes.

Has racism moved from a direct frontal attack to more nuanced institutional and structural expressions?

This chapter analyzes how institutional discrimination, especially within the real estate industry (Portland Development Commission (PDC), Bureau of Housing and Community Development (BHCD), bankers, real

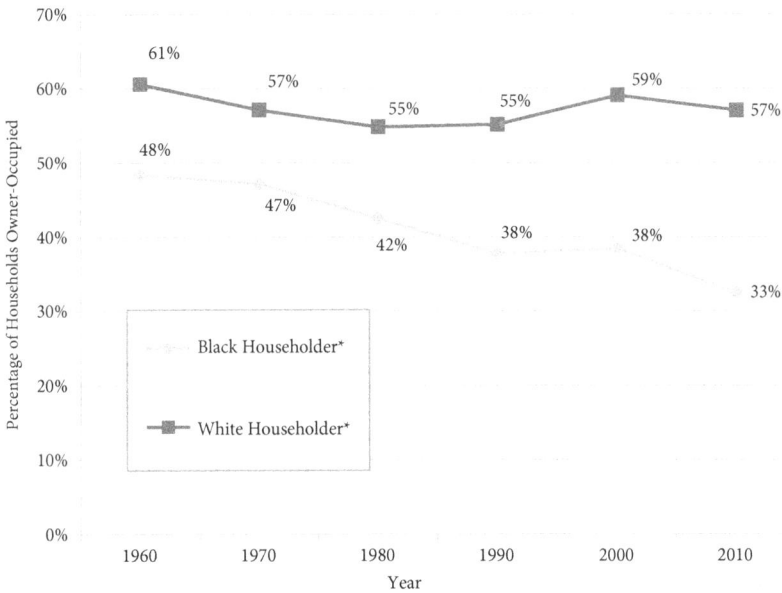

Figure 5.5: Homeownership rates by race in Portland, 1960–2010.

*Non-Latino whites and blacks in 1990, 2000, and 2010

estate agents, etc.) has become more subtle since 1968. Institutions such as the Portland Public School District and the Police Bureau are also analyzed to see how relations with the community have changed. An analysis of institutionalized employment barriers is beyond the scope of this chapter. The chapter also explores the implications of the widening racial economic inequality in the Albina District.

Housing and Urban Redevelopment Institutions

In the 1960s, black residents were excluded from most of the planning that decided the fate of their Albina District neighborhoods. In standard fashion, Portland's planners and business elites had declared the predominantly black area blighted. The future of this district was for institutional and commercial use. Sitting on the east side of the Willamette River, the Albina was once its own town, located very close to downtown in an area called Inner Northeast. This area was designated as a black enclave by real estate agents and bankers after the defense-era City of Vanport was flooded in 1948. Prior to the war, blacks numbered less than two thousand. Although roughly twenty-two thousand blacks migrated here to work in the shipyards during the war, about twelve thousand stayed after it was over. Many left because there were few jobs and the city was unwelcoming, to put it mildly. Others stayed because they were broke and had few other options. So as blacks crowded into the Albina District neighborhoods[1] to which they were "assigned" during the 1950s, the white population declined by twenty-three thousand (54 percent) by 1960.

From the late 1950s through the early 1970s, the Portland Development Commission's urban renewal bulldozer chased black residents from their homes several times in preparation for constructing the Memorial Coliseum, Emanuel Hospital, the Interstate 5 freeway, and various city government buildings such as the school and water district headquarters. The Portland Development Commission has been doing urban renewal since the early 1960s, when Oregon was the second state in the nation to adopt tax increment financing to support urban redevelopment. The first director of the PDC, Ira Keller, was a businessman from Chicago who ran the agency in an autocratic manner. Single-minded and confident, his leadership style set the tone and culture of the agency. Decisions were made in closed-door deals and public commission meetings were scripted. The PDC ignored other planning agencies, including the Housing Authority of Portland and the Planning Bureau (Gibson 2004).

The City Club's Racial Justice Report discussed two key elements associated with a systematic disinvestment process in Albina: mortgage redlining and absentee landlordism. These two operate in concert, as redlining prevents households from owning rather than renting property. Drawing on a Model Cities survey, the report noted that substandard housing and negative environmental health conditions were pervasive in Albina, and that these conditions and their alleviation were made more difficult by absentee ownership. Black homeowners with equity who wanted to move out of Albina faced discrimination in their attempts to buy in other neighborhoods, and those who stayed in the area had "more than normal difficulty in obtaining improvement or building loans" (City Club of Portland 1968: 33).

Although Albina residents had requested housing assistance in the mid-1960s, the PDC barely involved them in planning its application for Model Cities in 1967. The Department of Housing and Urban Development (HUD) criticized the citizen participation provisions of the application because they were designed to "inform" rather than "involve" residents.

---

[1] The neighborhoods that comprised a black majority are Boise, Eliot, Humboldt, Lloyd, Irvington, King, Sabin, and Woodlawn.

Yet the PDC could not prevent resident involvement in Model Cities planning. When the final plan arrived at the city council, it included opinions from the Citizens' Planning Board, which "shocked" the PDC and other agencies because of citizens' complaints about the discrimination they faced, the worst from the county welfare office, the school district, and Portland Development Commission. The PDC feared that it would lose control of urban renewal plans in Albina to citizens. Despite opposition, the agency kept its plans for Emanuel Hospital separate from the Model Cities process. Clearance of seventy-six acres, or twenty-two blocks, for the redevelopment of Emanuel Hospital destroyed the heart of the black community in the early 1970s. The commercial heart of the community at Russell and Williams avenues was torn down. To make matters worse, promised jobs and amenities did not materialize in a meaningful way, and that corner is still vacant today. After this debacle, the PDC did not engage in large redevelopment projects in Albina for two decades. This history explains the intense distrust that members of the black community feel toward various agencies of local government, particularly the PDC, because of top-down projects planned *for them*, rather than *with them*.

In general, city agencies neglected the Albina District until the late 1980s, when the neighborhoods were totally at rock bottom with abandoned housing, drugs, gang warfare, and prostitution, and residents demanded attention. It was the "forgotten stepchild" of urban planning efforts (Gibson 2007). During hard economic times the city had its hands full just trying to keep the downtown from going to ruin. Discrimination of various forms meant that black residents had limited choices of where to live, whether they could buy property, or whether they could fix up property they did manage to buy. Bankers refused to lend in the area; studies during the 1970s and 1980s showed that black neighborhoods received about 10 percent to 20 percent of the loans received in other areas. At one point the excuse was based upon housing characteristics (no off-street parking, too few bathrooms) and in the 1980s it was because they did not make mortgage loans of less than $30,000. Residents could get money to buy a $25,000 car but not a $16,000 home. Often owners refused to maintain rental property. The city and county did not enforce the building codes or enforce property tax collection through foreclosure. Disinvestment drove property values down to 58 percent of the city's median by 1989 (Gibson 2007). In 1990, the *Oregonian* published a series of articles titled "Blueprint for a Slum," which documented that four Albina neighborhoods had received just 10 percent of the loans of an average city neighborhood.

When the city finally turned its attention to the problem, it promoted reinvestment that then resulted in rapid gentrification and significant population turnover from black to white. Sadly, many black homeowners either moved or lost their homes through foreclosure during the 1980s. When greenlining occurred during the 1990s, many black renters were involuntarily displaced by rising property values and rampant housing speculation.

Although longtime residents in the majority black neighborhoods labored to keep their neighborhoods safe during years of neglect, public and private investments in the 1990s were biased toward white newcomers. In 2005, one long-time Boise neighborhood activist, Charles Ford, claimed that both city policies and new resident attitudes were racist and reminiscent of problems he thought were solved forty years before:

> We fought like mad people to keep crime out of here. Had we not fought, I don't know what this area would've eventually been. But the newcomers haven't given us credit for it. I envisioned cleaning up the neighborhood, making the neighborhood livable for all of us. ...We never envisioned that the government would move in and mainly assist whites. They came in to the area, younger whites. (The Portland Development Commission) gave them business and home loans and grants, and made it comfortable and easy for them to come. I didn't envision that those young people would come in with what I perceive as an attitude. They didn't come in 'We want to be a part of you.' They came in with the idea, 'We're here and we're in charge.' ... In the past, blacks and whites worked very strongly together. We were one. This thing that happened in the last 10 years has been most disappointing, most uncomfortable. It's like the revitalization of racism. (Barnett 2005).

Another housing agency involved in neighborhood revitalization is the Bureau of Housing and Community Development (BHCD), which sponsored a small, five-year economic development program bringing technical assistance and a $40,000 annual investment of community development block grant funds to the Boise neighborhood. Howard Cutler, a BHCD program manager, says that in the late 1990s and early 2000 the agency was still in the "anti-blight mind-set" (Cutler, March 20, 2008). The Mississippi Target Area Designation program (TAD) engaged in community planning, encouraged homeownership and issued loans to revitalize a ten-block area along Mississippi Avenue, a street with charming historic buildings and homes and great access to downtown. BHCD connected new small-business owners to the programs available at the PDC. In effect, TAD aided the gentrification and racial transition of Boise as white businesses and homeowners were the major beneficiaries, while many low-income and older residents were forced out by rising housing prices. Efforts to involve black businesses in the revitalization were limited to the few existing businesses. Gary Brown, a black small-business consultant, stated that his efforts to steer resources toward the cultivation of young, black entrepreneurs were discouraged, and that barriers for black business people were poorly understood by BHCD (Brown, March 21, 2008).

Once property values began to rise, low income residents were displaced. It is clear that the city had not anticipated the impact of their effort on residents. Janet Bauer, a program coordinator, said that they were successful at catalyzing commercial revitalization and making the area safer, and she wishes that they had more money to invest in preventing displacement (Bauer, March 20, 2008). The private sector was eager to invest in what they knew to be a desirable area. Low-cost community development efforts stimulated initial investment when the area was very dilapidated and unsafe. But bankers and speculators were lined up to buy foreclosed properties in eager anticipation that the neighborhood would cycle up again. They just needed the match that the BHCD provided to begin the property speculation process that would catch like wildfire.

When I asked Howard Cutler how he would explain the success of the revitalization program on Mississippi Avenue, he responded in this way:

> Community-powered and community-driven revitalization efforts can be in the vanguard of attracting new investment. When you have a community decide "here are what our needs are" and "here is what we would like to focus on," and people come out and clean their own litter and do things on behalf of children who live in those neighborhoods; and who aren't motivated by the traditional capitalistic profit mind. These are oftentimes, you know, white young people from middle-class backgrounds who are willing to have poverty income—but they have a coffee shop, or a bookstore, or a record store. And they are following their passions—and the creative economy, or whatever Portland's lure for those types of people is— [they] came and they saw affordable locations, they saw a mind-set of neighborhood that was thrilling to them and they gave their all to investing in areas that hadn't been invested in for twenty years.(Howard Cutler, BHCD, March 20, 2008)

Cutler's statement substantiates Ford's claim that the city "mainly assisted whites." Does this mean that the BHCD is racist? Certainly the failure to understand the economic situation of neighborhood residents *before* it engaged in the revitalization process is extremely problematic. Displacement occurred too easily. The community was terribly fragile because of the cumulative effect of disinvestment. Should city agencies be accountable for understanding this? The BHCD was surprised at the depth of poverty among existing Boise residents, and surprised that private sector investment took off so rapidly.

> I think the displacement took us by surprise—because for twenty years or so the city flailed away at inner-city problems. So who would have thought that it would come—that it would come in the 1990s and it would be as successful? All this new investment and the market would come in, and then we wouldn't have any control over it, and it would spiral out of...so I think we were surprised. I am mostly okay (with the revitalization and gentrification). I mean I supported it–but it could have been improved so that we protected more people. (Howard Cutler, BHCD, March 20,2008)

I was surprised to hear Cutler point to "white young people from middle-class backgrounds" as the "vanguard" of revitalization efforts. He is very proud that a small amount of Community Development Block Grant money leveraged by "creative class" types seeded investment that revitalized Mississippi Avenue, while other streets (Martin Luther King) with the power of TIF money weren't doing as well.

The result of city efforts was racially skewed; although perhaps contemporary policies are not directly racist because they are built on the scaffolding of prior racist policies, the outcomes are racist. That scaffolding included predatory and exploitative lending practices by speculators, slumlords, bankers, and real estate agents who watched the city's early redevelopment efforts, eagerly waiting to benefit from them. Many long-time black homeowners undersold their properties, as speculators went door to door offering rapid cash ($80,000 for a house bought for $20,000, but with a market value of $160,000) to homeowners around Mississippi Avenue. The BHCD did not protect homeowners from these predators. They did not have an initiative in place early enough or funded well enough to prevent renter displacement. During a door-to-door campaign to survey resident needs, they were surprised to discover a segment of residents who were living in deep poverty. It was very difficult to help them find new housing at a level they could afford when investors and new homeowners forced them out. Why should this have been a surprise? Wouldn't it have been discovered during the community planning phase of the TAD program?

The PDC was a major player in the revitalization of Mississippi Avenue and the Boise neighborhood. But they were not the public face of revitalization policy; the kinder, gentler BHCD was the visual presence, attempting to preserve established black businesses and prevent renter displacement while, in the background, market forces operated at a much larger scale. BHCD was also "surprised" by how market forces propelled out of control. They were naïve about the real estate market and their naiveté caused many longtime residents much trouble. In fact while BHCD was supporting community-level efforts, the private sector was making big plans for the area. The Portland Realty Board was working with a newly established nonprofit called Housing One Street at a Time (HOST) that was started by two real estate agents to help rehabilitate "vacant or abandoned housing in north and northeast Portland." Ostensibly the goal was to make "homeownership opportunities available to low and moderate income individuals," but as Ted Gilbert, president of Gilbert Brothers Real Estate and an originator of HOST, said, "Hopefully the project will change the perception of North/Northeast Portland by impacting the property values and making the area a 'terrific' place to live" (Ethnic Minorities Study, November 8, 1989: 1). Doris Kiel, executive vice president of the Portland Board of Realtors, said that a coalition of twenty-two other associations was involved in the project, which was "needed because the City of Portland has not been active in pursuing vacant and abandoned properties" (Ethnic Minorities Committee, September 25, 1989). So forty years after the Portland Realty Board had insisted that blacks be confined to Albina neighborhoods and, along with the banks, denied them access to the lifeblood of housing (mortgage and rehab loans), they were now working to rehabilitate the neighborhoods! Ironically, the main tool for beginning the revitalization, the "Trojan horse," if you will, was a community development corporation that benefited by getting free tax-foreclosed properties and vacant lands from state and county government (the county had over five hundred properties in the late 1980s). Many of these properties came from black families that could not pay property taxes and whose homes had negative values precisely because of the racism in lending and real estate appraisals. It is an

ingenious form of racism in real estate markets, naively ignored or sometimes perpetuated by community developers and planners at the city.
Next I turn to the school district.

"Broken Promises and Unfulfilled Commitments": The Portland Public
Schools (PPS)

The Racial Justice Report observed that racial residential patterns had
resulted in racially isolated schools. In 1968, four elementary schools
were more than 90 percent black (Boise, Eliot, Humboldt, and Highland—
now named King). Nearly half of the black children in Portland attended
these schools. This was the result of deliberate housing segregation.
Figure 5.6 shows that the black-white dissimilarity index was roughly
77 percent during the 1960s. This means that 77 percent of black persons
would have to move in order to have a spatial distribution proportion-
ate with their representation in the population. Blacks comprised just
6 percent of the city's population at this time, but roughly 75 percent lived
within the Albina District in 1967. In 1964–65, to reduce racial isolation in
the schools, the Portland Public Schools (PPS) began to transfer black children out of their neighborhood schools. That year, 424 Black children were
bused to forty-one schools "where room exists" (City Club 1968: 16).
No white children were bused into black neighborhoods.

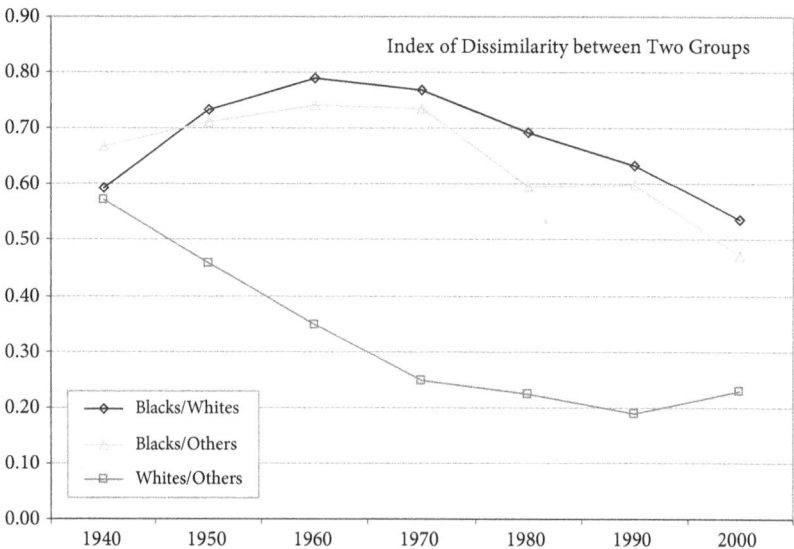

Figure 5.6: Dissimilarity indices in Portland: 1940–2000.

In the spring of 1980 members of the Black United Front protested to the school board about the unequal treatment of black children. Ron Herndon, an activist for racial equality in schooling, stood on desks and kicked board members' "name plates to the floor" to get attention to the issue (Slovic, November 14, 2007). Black parents and community members wanted to stop busing children out of their neighborhoods—the district's desegregation policy burdened black families, whose children were scattered all over the city. Children from one black elementary school were "bused to twenty different schools in the white community, and during the 1970s, no schools in the black community were allowed to serve children in grades five through eight" (Herndon, August 31, 2001: 2). This practice helped to break down social bonds in the black community. PPS responded with a voluntary desegregation plan that ended forced busing, put more money in black neighborhood schools, and allowed all children to transfer out of their neighborhood schools if they wished. This remedy was supposed to improve schools in majority black neighborhoods. But voluntary measures have increased segregation by race and class and the unequal quality of schooling persists. The PPS transfer policy is designed to keep the white middle class in city schools. But there is a cost to the policy that burdens black families, other families of color, and low-income families. When students leave their neighborhood schools, the dollars go with them. In 1990, before gentrification hit inner Northeast neighborhoods, Jefferson High School was 33 percent white and 56 percent black. But after the displacement of poor whites and blacks and the influx of white middle-class families, fewer whites are sending their children to Jefferson. Table 5.1 displays the racial composition and neighborhood capture rate for four schools, two located in (what used to be) majority black areas and two located in majority white areas. (Actually, Alameda Elementary is a six minute drive from King Elementary, but it is situated within an upper-middle-class white enclave). Jefferson High has a population of just 707 students, compared to 1,404 at Lincoln High. Since the dollars go with the students, so do the level of staffing and variety of courses offered at each school. Advanced placement courses are unavailable at Jefferson but abundant at Lincoln. Today, many black education activists are more concerned about school quality than the racial composition of schools. This is part driven by their experience with being bused into white schools as youngsters. It was a negative experience that broke down community, isolated children from others in their neighborhoods, and did not necessarily provide a better quality education. In fact, many have painful memories from attending all-white schools in neighborhoods far from home. So they fight to control educational quality in their neighborhood schools.

Table 5.1: Portland Public Schools: Characteristics by Race and Neighbohood, 2007.

Schools	Black	White	Latino	Neighborhood Capture Rate	Free Lunch
Majority Black Area					
King Elementary	65%	9%	20%	49%	92%
Jefferson High	63%	17%	12%	25%	73%
Majority White Area					
Alameda Elementary	5%	82%	2%	81%	9%
Lincoln High	5%	79%	5%	87%	8%

While the Black United Fund had some success at improving elementary school programs during the 1980s, Jefferson High did not see the same improvement. Gentrification has helped shrink school populations and make them poorer than surrounding neighborhoods. Also, black middle class families have left neighborhoods, or they send their children to other schools. Yet some argue that Jefferson High School faces more problems than it should because the PPS administration does not listen to community members, it patronizes them. *Parents* and community members have had to use confrontational tactics just to get heard. In 2001, frustrated with the school board inaction on a plan to improve school quality, even after engaging in formal mediation sessions, Ron Herndon editorialized in the *Portland Tribune* that the PPS school board was engaging in a "decades-long devotion to protect Portland Public Schools' bureaucratic status quo" (Herndon, August 31, 2001). Herndon has been a thorn in the side of local public agencies for many years as an agitator for racial and social justice. His statement below evokes a feeling that not much has changed for relations between the black community and the public sector since 1968, especially as it pertains to the report's finding that the "common denominator" in all areas was "governmental neglect of citizen involvement" (City Club, 1968: 46).

> The Portland school board's history is littered with broken promises and unfulfilled commitments. There are common themes: the district's institutional racism and its resulting academic carnage for low-income children and changes that come only after boycotts, demonstrations, and relentless community pressure. We've come to expect little if any help from governors, mayors, city commissioners, county commissioners, civic organizations, or others of purported goodwill. (Ron Herndon, August 31, 2001)

If promises and commitments made are not kept, then that means that even with citizen involvement, justice is elusive. Is this how racism has changed? Do we have the illusion of inclusion? In 1968 the City Club said neglect of public involvement aggravated deficiencies in services. What does involvement that is ignored do to community trust in governmental institutions? The next section turns to police relations.

Portland Police: A Long Racist Tradition

The Racial Justice Report began its section entitled "Police Policies, Attitudes, and Practices" with the following statement:

> The Mayor and the Chief of Police have indicated that in their opinions the Kerner Report is not applicable to Portland. Satisfactory police-citizen relations are not likely to be achieved as a reality in Portland in the absence of a fundamental change in the philosophy of the officials who formulate policy for the police bureau.(City Club 1968: 39)

It went on to discuss the findings of the Kerner Report, which "cited deep hostility between police and communities as a primary cause of the disorders" in the many cities which had such disorders since 1964. But it argued that in a "fundamental sense" it would be wrong to characterize the problem "solely as hostility to police" because the policeman represented not just law enforcement, but the larger society: "the policeman in the ghetto is a symbol, finally, of a society from which many ghetto Negroes are increasingly alienated" (City Club 1968: 37). This alienation is aggravated by experience with discrimination from the police, however. The Racial Justice Report said that although it didn't have "firm evidence," there were numbers of reports of "police discrimination against minorities," including slow responses to calls from black neighborhoods, police harassment, rudeness, and abusive behavior (p. 38). Five "problem areas" were identified where public officials should help police in order to minimize the "risks of further disorders" in Portland:

1. Need for change in police operations to ensure proper individual conduct and elimination of abrasive practices
2. Need for more adequate police protection of ghetto residents to eliminate high sense of insecurity to persons and property
3. Need for more effective citizen grievance process
4. Need for policy guidelines to assist police where police conduct can create tension
5. Need to develop community support for law enforcement

Although the City Club didn't have evidence to substantiate the charges of discrimination, the black community had long recognized that public safety was a low priority in their neighborhoods. Richard White's study of faith-based community organizing in Portland documents the grassroots perspective on police-community relations.[2] In an interview, the Reverend Boyd, a black minister who was part of the Albina Ministerial Alliance, discussed the difficulty of gaining police services within Albina neighborhoods: "We knew that our part of the city had been designated as where all this stuff [crime, drugs, prostitution] should go on" (p. 156). In the early 1960s, he and "a small contingency of pastors and neighbors met with a deputy police chief who referred to Albina as 'the Tombstone territory,' indicating the 'law of the streets' would have to prevail because the police would offer no additional help." When the same group met with Mayor Terry Schrunk, he "calmly asserted that illicit drug use was 'relatively confined to black neighborhoods' and was 'not really a large enough concern to warrant an additional police presence' " (p. 156). According to James Mason, a resident of the King neighborhood, in the 1980s, "the crack houses were known" but they "didn't do anything about it" (Gibson 2007). Reverend Boyd was present at a meeting with Mayor Bud Clark when he told African American pastors and residents of inner northeast Portland, "The gangs will go back to California as soon as it rains, don't worry about it" (p.156). Mayor Clark's reliance on the weather to combat drug dealing was, at least in part, due to his weak authority over the police bureau. When another faith based group, the Portland Organizing Project, which was largely white, was trying to get a drug house ordinance, he confided to them that he had "little power to control Chief Walker" (p. 157). Later, when Chief Walker publicly announced his opposition to a drug house ordinance, Mayor Clark responded to community pressure and fired him. Yet, according to Reverend Boyd, city actions helped to marginalize and alienate black citizens on the basis of race. "A couple of times they could have helped the black community, but they missed the opportunity… We did not envision a lot of things [that are now taking place], we were just trying to survive. There are always new road blocks, a new wrinkle, with the same objective—keep blacks from being accepted by the whole community" (p. 156).

Have the police-community relations improved in the five areas identified by the Racial Justice Report? It appears that these same areas are quite

---

[2] *Faith, Hope, and Leverage: Attributes of Effective Faith-Based Community Organizations.*

problematic today and tensions remain high because of racial profiling and even unwarranted shooting deaths in black neighborhoods. Citizens complain of discriminatory police conduct and lack of effective grievance procedures or responsiveness from elected officials. One community organizing group, Oregon Action, insisted that the city's racial profiling plan address the following: the collection and analysis of traffic stop data, procedures that result in racial profiling, residency requirements for new officers, making police personnel more representative of local community, accountability for police behavior, and training. These issues were identified in a series of listening sessions between community members and police in 2006. That October, Portland's city commissioners accepted the report that came out of these sessions, and created a commission called the Mayor's Racial Profiling Committee, which has been meeting since early 2007.

The committee discussed the traffic stop data which showed that in 2006, black stops comprised 13 percent of all stops (although they are 6 percent of the city's population), while white stops comprised 68 percent of all stops (79 percent of population). Yet one activist argued that the statistics on use of force are "far more significant" (Loving 2008: 3). From late September 2004 to December 2006, black citizens "comprised 29 percent of all uses of force," which included takedowns, control holds, pepper spray, Taser strikes, and "point weapon" use of firearms. In the Northeast precinct, where black residents are 23 percent of the population, they comprised 48 percent of all arrests and 53 percent of all use of force. Citizens are frustrated that action has yet to be taken, since the listening sessions revealed their grievances about racial profiling.

Racial discrimination in the application of exclusions from "drug-free" zones in the city had resulted in black citizens being more likely to be banned from areas by police than whites or Latinos. Since 1992, based upon suspicion of drug possession or sales, police had been able to ban people from an area for ninety days. Conviction was not necessary—suspects were guilty until proven innocent. The law meant that citizens can't wander through drug-free (and prostitution-free) zones in the central city, North and Northeast Portland, and East Eighty-Second Avenue. The practice was terminated in September 2007 because a report showed a racial disparity in enforcement of the exclusion zone law (Dworkin, *Oregonian*, September 27, 2007). Since 2003, 63 percent of the prosecuted violations were against black persons. Often the same people were excluded and jailed dozens of times.

Mayor Potter, a former police chief who commissioned the report, wanted to know why methamphetamine dealers/users were the least likely to be excluded. The report found that from September 2006 to July 2007, nearly 70 percent of the people arrested for qualifying cocaine crimes were excluded, compared with 30 percent of methamphetamine arrests (Dworkin, September 27, 2007). Potter said he hasn't "heard anybody give me a good answer of why" meth was treated differently even though he has asked Chief Sizer and others (Dworkin, September 27, 2007: 2). Race plays an important role because blacks overwhelmingly deal in cocaine rather than meth: 91 percent of 1,015 exclusion-eligible black arrests were for cocaine (compared to 40 percent of 756 white arrests). Of those arrested for meth, 82 percent were white and 7 percent were black. Even a lawyer for the public defender's office thought that the racial disparity was "worse than I thought" (Dworkin, September 27, 2007: 2). The mayor has proposed a citywide increase in jail beds and drug treatment beds in lieu of the exclusion zones, which had been challenged by opponents over many years. Critics argued that the zones do not end crime or fix the drug addiction and they make people afraid to connect with their communities.

DISCUSSION

Has racism become more subtle? Using the definition of subtle that means "clever, cunning, sly, devious, crafty, or shrewd," I would say yes. It is clear in the case of housing and redevelopment, schools, and police that these institutions have learned how to devise policies that enable them to pursue goals that perpetuate severe racial inequality. Because of civil rights law, they can no longer directly declare that they will discriminate on the basis of race, but they continue to do so through indirect means. Table 5.2 displays examples of policies that are racist in sly ways. They are not racist on the surface, but the racism is more nuanced (defined as a "finer distinction").

Policies in the area of housing and urban redevelopment have directly contributed to the decline in black homeownership since 1970, which is now 37 percent below the national average for black homeownership of 46 percent.

The policies of disinvestment, which were allowed to continue through the late 1980s, meant that black homes were valued less than white homes. The black community in Albina was not supported in their efforts to create a viable settlement in Portland after World War II. The ghettoization

Table 5.2: Subtle Institutional Policies with Racist Outcomes.

Institutions	Subtle or Sly Policies	Racist Outcomes
Housing and Redevelopment	Target Area Designation program	White home and business ownership privileged over black home/business ownership
	HOST CDC	Gentrification with racial transition; white ownership and displacement of black and low income residents
Schools	Neighborhood transfer policy	Schools are segregated by race and class; less money available for schools in majority black areas despite influx of white gentrifiers
	Paternalistic Planning Processes	Paternalistic attitude toward Jefferson High School community results in disparate educational quality for students of color and low-income students
Police	Exclusion Zones	Racial profiling and racially discriminatory law enforcement; white meth users/dealers less likely than black crack users/ dealers to be excluded or prosecuted. Hence blacks are more likely to be "guilty until proven innocent"

which made black youth feel trapped meant that they had fewer housing choices and often had no recourse to substandard housing conditions, which absentee landlords allowed to persist as they milked properties. City neglect and private sector predation meant that conditions got bad enough that middle-class residents left during the 1980s. The cycle had come full circle and now the time was ripe to sweep blacks out and reinvest in a new white settlement.

The subtle racism of school district policy is embodied in the school transfer policy, which lets students leave their neighborhood schools. Middle-class black and white parents tend to send their children away from schools when they live in majority black neighborhoods. As the dollars follow students to their new schools, low income students of color (and poor whites) remain isolated in neighborhood schools with fewer resources. The decision-making processes which govern the schools' curricula and overall educational policy do not allow for participation beyond token levels. Parents and school advocates from low-income or majority black neighborhoods are frustrated by what they see as a paternalistic mode of interaction: the school district knows best what to do for their children.

Buchanan defines paternalism as the "usurpation of decision making power, by preventing people from doing what they have decided, interfering in how they arrive at their decisions, or attempting to substitute one's judgment for theirs, expressly for the purpose of promoting their welfare..." (Buchanan, 2008: 15). The Jefferson parent quoted above lamented the longstanding PPS stance of not seriously utilizing parental input. Middle-class whites do not have to listen to black voices especially since they comprise such a small fraction of the overall population.

The paternalistic mode of interaction with the black community also applies to neighborhood revitalization and public safety. Jennie Portis, who worked for the Northeast Coalition of Neighbors and counted the nine hundred or so vacant and abandoned buildings in the late 1980s, said that when black community members told city officials that there was a serious and growing problem with gangs, they turned their heads in denial (Portis, May 23, 2008). Thus city officials, by remaining in denial about the severity of the problem, refused to allow community members to control the fate of their neighborhoods. This is racism by refusing to make decisions, by refusing to make appropriate choices in terms of public safety.

Paternalism explains the attitudes of government and private citizens toward black citizens of Portland. White Portlanders were unaccustomed to black people, as they had no exposure to black culture except through racial stereotypes. Figure 5.7 shows the isolation indices for whites, blacks, and others in Portland from 1940 to 2000. In 1960, the average neighborhood of whites in Portland was about 96 percent white while the average neighborhood for blacks was 46 percent black. Thus the ghettoization of black Portlanders into a four-square-mile area of Albina meant that the issues facing blacks were confined to a small, concentrated area, and average white citizens did not have to address these issues. The majority had

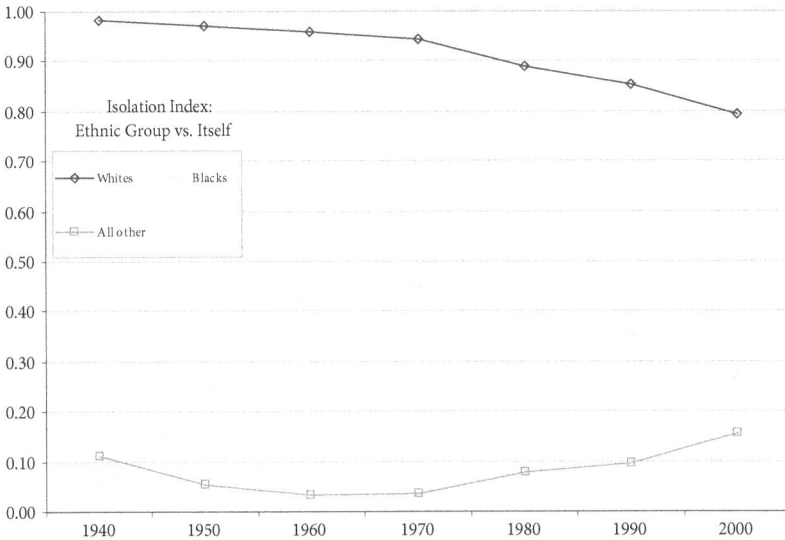

Figure 5.7: Isolation indices, City of Portland, 1940–2000.

no idea of how the ghettoization of blacks created the conditions for economic and social decline. Ora Hart, a black real estate agent who moved to Portland in 1965, said that "White folks did not understand black folks. They tolerated them, but it was as if black folks did not see what was really going on" (personal interview, September 11, 2007).

Black Portlanders are worse off today than they were in 1970, and they have fallen further behind whites, and even their national counterparts. This is a result of racist attitudes and policies of whites in Portland. While there has always been a courageous set of white folks who championed the cause of racial equality in Portland, they have been outnumbered by the general population, who embraced white superiority. Edwin C. Berry, the Urban League leader brought to Portland just after the war, warned city officials that they were "blueprinting a slum" by confining black residents to an "overcrowded ghetto" (Berry 1945: 161). Elites, primarily real estate brokers and bankers, concerned with the maintenance of property values, followed the recipe utilized in black urban settings across the nation: confine blight so that it does not infect property values or the white way of life.

In addition, the race relations were not just a matter of avoidance and paternalism, but they have always been characterized by exploitation. Profiles of the postwar conditions facing blacks in West Coast cities were published in the *Journal of Educational Sociology*. Edwin C. "Bill" Berry discussed the model of exploitation developed by the boilermakers' union:

> No reference to race relations on the West Coast would be complete without some comment on the boilermakers' union (International Brotherhood of Boilermakers, Iron Shipbuilders, and Helpers of America), which has had a stranglehold on the shipbuilding industry. In Portland, as elsewhere, auxiliary unions were formed for Negro workers. The auxiliaries were nothing more than a method of exacting tribute from Negroes for the right to work. Negroes paid union dues, but had no union status, could not vote, were required to voice complaints through a white and unfriendly steward, and received only partial benefits at death. The influence of the Boilermakers is widespread and its methods of adjustment racially have been adopted or attempted by civic and social groups. Indeed, one Portland Parent Teachers Association recommended a nonvoting auxiliary for Negro parents. This was not permitted, but indicates the extent to which "boilermakers' thinking" has permeated the community.(Bill Berry 1945: 162–163)

It appears that while institutional racism has become more subtle and nuanced, it still stands on the same foundation of "boilermaker thinking": blacks are part of a "nonvoting auxiliary" in the city of Portland. And this is how and why decisions are made for and not with them. This is why things have not changed much since the city declared in the 1968 Racial Justice Report that the common thread among all problem areas was governmental neglect of citizen involvement. Thus despite the mythology surrounding Portland as one of the most civically engaged cities, the truth is that this applies only to those who are considered worthy of full citizenship.

But it is the police who are the most obstinate about maintaining a racist posture. In 1968, the mayor and the police chief declared that the Kerner Report had no application in Portland. In 2006, the Portland Police Association challenged the Racial Profiling report by commissioning an independent study which found no evidence of racial profiling. Little has changed among the rank and file police who supervise black neighborhoods—the most intrusive symbols of a social system from which black people are economically marginalized and alienated.

It is another example of the extreme paternalism that characterizes police-community relations that even after an airing of public grievances (as was recommended by the Racial Justice Report), the police remain the ones *who know better*. An activist with Oregon Action said, "As we come up on the two-year anniversary of the listening process, in which story after story of racial profiling were heard, it is ridiculous that the PPA commissions a study to falsely refute the reality of police racial profiling"

(Loving, 2008: 1). Portland remains in denial: a denial that not only keeps the city from facing reality, but that denies the humanity of black citizens and other citizens of color.

References

Buchanan, David R. 2008. *Autonomy, Paternalism, and Justice: Ethical Priorities in Public Health*. American Journal of Public Health, Vol. 98, Issue 1.

City Club of Portland. *Problems of Racial Justice in Portland*. 1968. City Club of Portland Bulletin, 49: 2.

Gibson, Karen J. 2007. *Bleeding Albina: A History of Community Disinvestment, 1940–2000*. Transforming Anthropology, 15: 1.

Loving, Lisa. 2008. "Citizens Demand Anti-Profiling Plan" *The Skanner*. May 14, p. 1.

Dworkin, Oregonian, drug exclusion zone articles, 9/27/07 and 9/29/07.

CHAPTER SIX

AFTER THE STORM: RACE AND VICTIM'S REACTIONS TO THE HURRICANE KATRINA AFTERMATH

Hayward Derrick Horton, Melvin Thomas, and Cedric Herring

This chapter provides an analysis of data from victims of Hurricane Katrina to determine whether there were racial differences in their perceptions about rescue and relief efforts after the storm. The data collected from survivors show that blacks and whites drew very different lessons from the tragedy. There was widespread agreement among black survivors that the government's response to the crisis would have been faster if most of the storm's victims had been white. Whites, in contrast, were more likely to feel that the race of the victims did not make a difference in government's response. Less than half of white victims, but more than three-quarters of black victims, held the view that Hurricane Katrina pointed out persisting problems of racial inequality. There were, however, few racial differences in perceptions about the role of income in the aftermath of Katrina. Most blacks and whites agreed with the idea that low-income and middle-income victims of the hurricane received similar treatment. Despite the idea that it was mostly a difference of opinion between poor blacks and middle-class whites in their views, these results suggest that there were also differences between the lowest-income blacks and middle- and high-income blacks, and perhaps an even larger difference between middle-income blacks and middle-income whites in terms of how they viewed the government's response. Income and other sociodemographic differences did not explain racial differences in perceptions about the role of race in the aftermath of the hurricane. The chapter concludes that the aftermath of Hurricane Katrina exposed the wide gulf between the nation's haves and have-nots as well as the nation's persisting racial divide.

AFTER THE STORM: RACE AND VICTIMS' REACTIONS
TO THE HURRICANE KATRINA AFTERMATH

When disaster strikes, Americans like to believe that no matter the race, color, creed, or socioeconomic level of the victims, "we are all in it together."

Unfortunately, this is seldom the case. Hurricane Katrina did not affect all people of the Gulf Coast equally. The aftermath of the storm had racial and class dimensions. Any analysis of the tragedy that fails to acknowledge this basic truth misses the opportunity to understand the underlying power structures and patterns of inequality that have made recovery from the storm more difficult for some.

Questions of race and class came into focus as news coverage of the disaster showed primarily black residents stranded in New Orleans. The U.S. Census Bureau estimated the New Orleans population to be 20 percent white and 68 percent black. According to a Population Reference Bureau Report, of the fifteen U.S. metropolitan areas with the most African Americans, New Orleans had the highest black poverty rate, at 33 percent (Saenz 2005). Within the city itself, the poorest tended to live in the lowest parts that are most vulnerable to flooding. Moreover, only half of African American males were employed (Saenz 2005). African Americans were also much more likely than whites to lack basic amenities, such as an automobile or a telephone (Saenz 2005). Given their limited social and economic resources along with their geographic isolation, poor urban African Americans were disproportionately vulnerable to being left behind during crisis situations.

Surveys of the American general public indicated that African Americans and whites held very different perceptions about the aftermath of Hurricane Katrina (CBS News/*New York Times* 2005; and Pew Research Center 2005). But it is not as clear what effects the storm and its aftermath had on black and white victims. Did black and white victims of Hurricane Katrina differ in how they viewed the disaster? And if so, did socioeconomic differences account for apparent racial disparities in perceptions about the aftermath of the hurricane? This chapter uses data from survivors of the hurricane to examine racial differences in their experiences during the hurricane and their perceptions about the aftermath of the hurricane.

RACE AND DU BOISIAN ANALYSIS

What is a Du Boisian analysis? W.E.B. Du Bois was a noted African American scholar, activist, and co-founder of the NAACP. His analysis self-consciously incorporated race and was "committed to empirical research as a source of knowledge to replace ignorance about race, and firmly believing that such knowledge was the basis for movement toward social equality" (McKee, 1993: 31). As Morris (2009) puts it, for "Du Bois, the goal of science was the search for truth using the best scientific methods available. In particular, he argued that sociological generalizations and interpretations needed to be based on carefully collected empirical data and measurement. Moreover, Du Bois' "conceptual framework was driven in a novel direction because of its insistence from the beginning that sociological interpretations should rest on empirical data rather than grand theorizing" (Morris 2009).

Throughout his illustrious career, Du Bois addressed the burning questions of his day: the relationship between race and class (Smith and Green, 1993; and Hattery and Smith, 2005). Du Bois agreed with Marx that poverty and oppression are caused by an unjust economic system (Zuckerman, 2004). Both Du Bois and Marx argued that in a capitalistic structure, the wealth created by labor out of natural resources is surplus. Du Bois (1933: 102) was also in accord with Marx in the belief that "a true just society could be realized only if democracy is extended to the realm of industry." The most important factor for Du Bois, however, was race. He knew the shortcomings of the Marxian theory of economic determinism that did not include race as a major consideration. Indeed, Du Bois was the first social theorist who attempted to link class to race. One of his most distinctive theoretical convictions was that race never stands apart from economic realities.

As Zuckerman (2004) suggests, Du Bois recognized that racial distinctions and racial constructs are central to how people experience the world, from health to wealth, from literacy to religion, from crime to politics, and from city governance to international relations. Du Bois also linked racial analysis with class analysis.

Given Du Bois' theoretical innovation of linking race and class, it is apparent that although he appreciated the heart of Marxian analysis, he saw its shortcomings in that it ignored the color line. Du Bois corrected this omission by adding racial dynamics to class dynamics (Du Bois, 1933). As DeMarco (1983: 192) notes, "Du Bois' ... objections to [Marxian] theory and practice involved racial considerations: Blacks formed a special group without a significant class opposition, essentially a proletariat group. Yet, blacks were separated from the proletariat movement by racism; the proletariat as an economic class was split along racial lines." This was an occurrence Du Bois viewed Marxism as being incapable of explaining (Zuckerman, 2004).

The insights of Du Bois can take a long way toward understanding differences in perceptions of African American and white victims of

Hurricane Katrina. They may also be useful in accounting for income-based differences. Before examining the role of race and income, this chapter provides a brief overview of the events that constituted Hurricane Katrina and her aftermath.

A BRIEF TIMELINE OF HURRICANE KATRINA

A central issue surrounding the aftermath of Hurricane Katrina was whether rescue and relief efforts were slow in coming, and, if so, whether they were slower than they would have been if the race and/or class of the victims had been different. Because this issue of timing is central to understanding perceptions of the disaster (especially in New Orleans), this section of the chapter provides a brief timeline of the central events surrounding Hurricane Katrina.

On Thursday, August 25, the National Hurricane Center upgraded Tropical Storm Katrina to Hurricane Katrina. That evening, Katrina made landfall in Florida as a category 1 hurricane. The next morning, the Hurricane Center upgraded Katrina to a category 2 hurricane and issued an advisory forecasting that she would soon be a category 3 hurricane. Louisiana Governor Kathleen Blanco declared a state of emergency for Louisiana, and Mississippi Governor Haley Barbour declared a state of emergency for Mississippi (Roig-Franzia and Hsu 2005).

President George W. Bush—still on vacation at his ranch in Crawford, Texas—gave his weekly radio address on Saturday of that week. His radio appearance made no mention of the events unfolding around Hurricane Katrina. Nevertheless, later on that day, he officially acknowledged that a state of emergency existed in Louisiana. He ordered federal aid to the affected areas to complement state and local relief efforts. On the same day, New Orleans Mayor C. Ray Nagin declared a state of emergency for New Orleans and issued evacuation orders. That night, the Hurricane Center issued a warning suggesting that Katrina was moving in a western direction to an area that included New Orleans. By early Sunday morning, Katrina was declared a category 4 storm, and before noon it reached the status of a category 5 hurricane, the highest possible rating.

On Sunday afternoon, National Hurricane Center Director Max Mayfield personally briefed President Bush as part of his regular FEMA briefing. That same day, Governor Blanco sent a letter to President Bush requesting federal aid. President Bush declared a state of emergency for both Mississippi and Alabama, and declared Florida a federal disaster area in light of damage done by Hurricane Katrina. He did not, however, offer federal government assistance to Louisiana at that time (Phillips 2005).

Although the federal government did not offer assistance to Louisiana, New Mexico's Governor Bill Richardson offered Louisiana Governor Kathleen Blanco help from his state's National Guard. Blanco accepted the offer, but paperwork needed to get the troops en route did not come from Washington until late Thursday, September 2 (Theimer 2005).

Katrina made landfall in Louisiana as a category 4 hurricane with 145 mph winds on Monday, August 29. Storm surges sent water over the Industrial Canal near New Orleans, and a barge crashed through the flood-wall and opened a breach that accelerated flooding into the Lower Ninth Ward in New Orleans and St. Bernard Parish. At approximately 9:00 a.m., the eye of Hurricane Katrina passed over the city of New Orleans. By that time, six to eight feet of water covered New Orleans Lower Ninth Ward. By 10:00 a.m., Hurricane Katrina was ripping holes in the Superdome's roof. More than ten thousand storm evacuees were inside. More than three thousand other evacuees were also stranded at the convention center (where officials had encouraged them to go for aid and comfort). By 10:30, President Bush made emergency disaster declarations for Louisiana, Mississippi, and Alabama. This freed up federal funds for the situation. Nevertheless, FEMA Director Michael Brown urged emergency service personnel not to respond to hurricane-impacted areas unless dispatched by state or local authorities. He waited five hours after Katrina had hit to ask his boss, Director of Homeland Security Michael Chertoff, for a thousand Homeland Security employees to be sent to the region. It took them more than two additional days to arrive (CNN.com 2005).

On Tuesday morning, August 30, President Bush delivered a speech in San Diego on the sixtieth anniversary of Victory over Japan (V-J) Day. He began the speech with brief remarks on hurricane relief efforts, and he told the audience, "The federal, state and local governments are working side by side to do all we can to help people get back on their feet." The remainder of the speech was dedicated to the need to "stay the course" in Iraq (Phillips 2005). The next day, Governor Blanco ordered that all of New Orleans, including the Superdome, be evacuated. An exodus from the Superdome began, with the first buses leaving for Houston's Astrodome, more than 350 miles away. The New Orleans police force was ordered to abandon search and rescue missions and to turn their attention toward controlling looting. A curfew was placed in effect, and Mayor Nagin called for increased federal assistance.

On Thursday, September 1, evacuees from the New Orleans area and the Louisiana Superdome began arriving at the Astrodome in Houston. In Washington, FEMA announced guidelines to contractors interested in "doing business with FEMA during the Hurricane Katrina recovery." In New Orleans, Mayor Nagin called the situation critical and issued "a desperate SOS." Reportedly, looting, carjacking, and other violence spread, and the military decided to increase National Guard deployment to thirty thousand.

As the city descended into chaos and squalor in the days following the hurricane, about two hundred people from New Orleans—mostly African Americans—were told by police to cross the Greater New Orleans Bridge over the Mississippi River on foot. There, police told them, buses would meet them to take them to shelter and aid. Instead, policemen from the neighboring suburb of Gretna met them. The police formed a line across the foot of the bridge. Before the evacuees were close enough to speak, the police began firing gun shots over their heads. This sent the crowd fleeing in various directions. After the evacuees retreated down the bridge and set up camp, the Gretna authorities pursued them. The police forced the evacuees off the freeway at gunpoint.The police said that their city was in lockdown and their job was to protect property and lives in Gretna (Charnas 2005).

Members of the Congressional Black Caucus, Black Leadership Forum, National Conference of State Legislators, National Urban League, and the National Association for the Advancement of Colored People (NAACP) held a news conference expressing anger and charging that the government's response was slow because those most affected are poor. Critics say city, state, and federal officials did not bother to consider citizens who cannot afford private transportation when planning for a natural disaster in New Orleans (Associated Press 2005). Mayor Nagin was criticized for failing to formulate an evacuation plan that provided transportation out of the city for those without private means. However, the greatest amount of criticism was directed at the slow reaction of the Bush administration to the crisis. No meaningful help for thousands of people stranded at the city's Convention Center occurred until the fifth day of the flood. They went without food, water, electricity, and toilet facilities. People stranded in the Superdome and on highway overpasses fared only slightly better (Phillips 2005).

On the fifth day of the state of emergency, Chertoff claimed, "I have not heard a report of thousands of people in the convention center who don't have food and water." That night, on ABC's *Nightline*, Michael Brown told

Ted Koppel "We just learned of the convention center—we being the federal government—today."

On Friday, September 2, President Bush toured Alabama, Mississippi, and Louisiana to survey Katrina's damage. He described the result of relief efforts up to that point as "not acceptable." Afterward, however, while visiting Mobile, President Bush said about the efforts of FEMA and its director, Michael Brown: "Again, I want to thank you all for—and, Brownie, you're doing a heck of a job. The FEMA director is working twenty-four— (applause)—they're working twenty-four hours a day." FEMA released a statement asking for "patience in the wake of Hurricane Katrina" (Phillips 2005).

After having met with Federal Reserve Chairman Greenspan to discuss the economic impact of Hurricane Katrina, President Bush requested and Congress approved an initial $10.5 billion aid package for immediate rescue and relief efforts. President Bush returned for a second visit to the Gulf Coast region on Monday, September 5. The Associated Press reported that Kellogg Brown and Root—a subsidiary of Halliburton that has been criticized for its reconstruction work in Iraq—had begun work on a $500 million U.S. Navy contract for emergency repairs at Gulf Coast naval and marine facilities that were damaged by Hurricane Katrina. On Wednesday, September 7, the White House announced it would send a $51.8 billion supplemental budget request to Congress for expenses in excess of the $10.5 billion Congress approved earlier in the week (Carson 2005).

On Monday, September 19, Mayor Nagin urged residents to return to New Orleans. As residents began coming back into the city, Hurricane Rita gathered strength off the coast of Florida, and Mayor Nagin called off his plan to allow residents to return to their homes in New Orleans, urging those who had come back to evacuate.

As of December 2005, the confirmed death toll from Hurricane Katrina stood at 1,383, mainly from Louisiana (1,075) and Mississippi (230). Moreover, most experts anticipate that Katrina will be recorded as the most expensive natural disaster in U.S. history. Some estimates put the damages in excess of $100 billion (Carson 2005).

In the time since that tragedy, the debate has continued about why the federal government made so few resources available to victims of Hurricane Katrina for so long, especially in New Orleans. Moreover, there have been questions about why, when help finally arrived, selected groups of people were evacuated sooner than those who were poor African Americans. It is now fairly well documented that the black and white public saw these issues differently (CBS News/*New York Times* 2005; and Pew Research Center 2005). But did black and white victims of Hurricane Katrina differ in how they viewed the disaster? And if so, did socioeconomic differences account for apparent racial disparities in perceptions about the aftermath of the hurricane? The remainder of this chapter examines these questions from the vantage point of survivors of Hurricane Katrina themselves.

DATA AND METHODS

Data Sources

The data used in the analysis come from a September 21 through October 5, 2005 Web-based survey of victims of Hurricanes Katrina and Rita. This survey collected information about the experiences and long-term needs of a sample of Gulf Coast residents and others affected by Hurricanes Katrina and Rita who registered with the International/American Red Cross Family Links. This American Red Cross Family Links Web site (http://www.familylinks.icrc.org/-katrina/people) included more than 250,000 records with contact information of victims of Hurricanes Katrina and Rita and their family members. International/American Red Cross Family Links is the largest consolidated Web site with the most current contact database and accurate information available about those who survived Hurricanes Katrina and Rita (American Red Cross 2005). From the contact database, 66,342 records contained e-mail addresses. It should be noted that the American Red Cross and Microsoft Corporation provided e-mail access to tens of thousands of people who may not have had e-mail access otherwise. From the list, more than six thousand e-mail addresses were randomly selected, and messages were sent to potential study participants. The data collection was anonymous and voluntary. Because it was not possible to verify which messages reached their destinations (nor who responded), it is not possible to calculate a final response rate. Nevertheless, this strategy did yield 1,642 valid surveys. Thus, approximately 25 percent of those contacted participated in the study. For the purposes of this chapter, the 465 survivors of Hurricane Rita were excluded from the analysis. Therefore, the base sample size for this (Hurricane Katrina survivors) analysis is 1,177.

The survey asked about evacuees' lives before, during, and shortly after the disasters. It also sought their opinions about the efforts of public officials and private agencies to meet their needs.

Operationalizations

The analysis included three dependent variables, race, income, and several control variables to gauge net differences in perceptions about responsiveness to the hurricane situation. Variable names are indicated in all capital letters.

Dependent Variables

FASTER IF WHITE: Respondents were asked, "Most of the people stranded in New Orleans following the hurricane were African American. Do you think the government's response to the situation would have been faster if most of the victims had been White, or don't you think this would have made any difference?" Responses were coded (1) "Yes, would have been faster," and (0) "No, wouldn't have made any difference."

RACIAL INEQUALITY A PROBLEM: Respondents were asked "In your view, did this disaster show that racial inequality remains a major problem in this country, or don't you think this was a particularly important lesson of the disaster?" Responses were coded (1) "Showed that racial inequality remains a major problem," and (0) "Not a particularly important lesson of the disaster."

INCOME TREATED SAME: Respondents were asked to agree or disagree with the following statement: "Low-income and middle-income victims of the hurricane have received similar treatment." Responses were coded (1) "Agree" and (0) "Disagree."

Independent Variables

The central independent variables for the analysis are race and income. Respondents were asked, "What is your race or ethnicity?" Responses were dummy variable coded to indicate whether the respondent was "White," "Black/African American," or from some "Other racial/ethnic group." In addition, respondents were asked to indicate their family income for 2004. Responses included: under $10,000; $10,000–$19,999; $20,000–$34,999; $35,000–$49,999; $50,000–$74,999; $75,000–$99,999; $100,000–$149,999; and $150,000 or more. Values were coded as the midpoint of the category range, with the open-ended category coded as $175,000. These categories were collapsed into five income levels: under $20,000; $20,000–$34,999; $35,000–$49,999; $50,000–$74,999; and $75,000 or more, and respondents were dummy variable coded.

In addition, the multivariate analysis includes several sociodemographic control variables. Respondents were asked to indicate whether they were male (coded 0) or female (coded 1). They were asked about the last grade or class that they completed in school, and responses were coded to indicate their level of educational attainment (i.e., less than high school, high school graduate or equivalent, some college, or college graduate or more). Age was recorded in years, and ranged from eighteen through seventy-three. Respondents were also asked about their religious preference, and the were dummy variable coded to indicate whether they were Catholic, Protestant Christian, or some other religion (or had no religious preference). Finally, respondents were asked whether they considered themselves to be Republican, Democratic, independent, or something else, and they were dummy variable coded to reflect their responses.

ANALYSIS AND RESULTS

Did black and white victims of Hurricane Katrina differ in how they viewed the disaster? And if so, did socioeconomic differences account for apparent racial disparities in perceptions about the aftermath of the hurricane? In other words, can racial differences be explained by other sociodemographic factors? This section attempts to address these questions.

Figure 6.1 illustrates substantial racial differences on questions about race in the aftermath of Hurricane Katrina. This diagram shows, for example, that while fewer than one in four white victims (24 percent) thought the government's response to the situation would have been faster if most of the victims had been white, three in four black survivors (75 percent) held such views. Figure 6.1 also shows that the racial groups differed a great deal on their views about whether the disaster showed that racial inequality remains a major problem in this country. Less than half of whites (48 percent), but more than three-quarters of blacks (79 percent) held the view that Hurricane Katrina pointed out persisting problems of racial inequality.

In contrast to the racial differences in perceptions about the role of race in the aftermath of Hurricane Katrina, there were few racial differences in perceptions about the role of income. In particular, 55 percent of whites and 57 percent of blacks agreed with the proposition that low-income and middle-income victims of the hurricane received similar treatment.

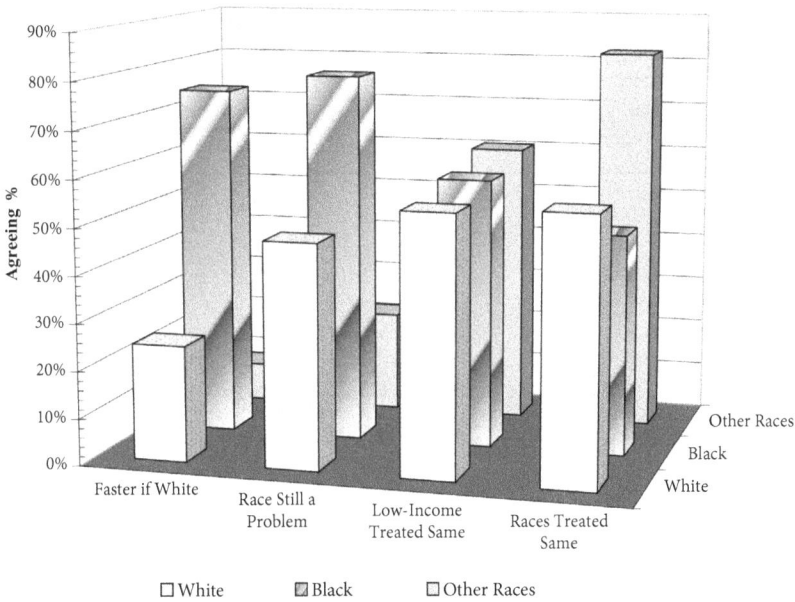

Figure 6.1: Racial differences in victims' beliefs about responses to Hurricane Katrina.

It is possible that apparent racial differences in views about the aftermath of Hurricane Katrina could be explained by racial differences in income, education, and so forth. Table 6.1 and Figure 6.2 present means and percentage distributions of selected characteristics of survivors of Hurricane Katrina by race. The table shows, for example, that racial groups differed by a great deal in their average incomes. Blacks had incomes of just over $36,000 on average. This compares with an average exceeding $64,000 for whites. Roughly three in ten blacks have incomes that were less than $20,000 per year. About two in ten whites (22 percent) have incomes below $20,000, but more than half (52 percent) report incomes of $50,000 or more. This contrasts with the fewer than two in ten blacks (18 percent) who do.

Educationally, black victims and white victims appear to be much more similar. For example, 70 percent of whites report that they graduated from high school and/or attended some college, and 62 percent of black survivors say they have this level of educational attainment. Black and white hurricane victims also report roughly the same one-in-four rate of college graduation. So, education does not appear to be a particularly strong candidate for accounting for racial differences of opinion about the aftermath of Katrina.

Table 6.1: Means and Percentage Distributions for Selected Characteristics of Victims of Hurricane Katrina by Race/Ethnicity.

Characteristics	Race/Ethnicity	
	Whites	Blacks
Mean Income	$64,345	$36,160
% < $20,000	22.2	31.3
% w/ $20,000 - $49,999	25.7	50.4
% w/ >$50,000	52.1	18.3
% Male	30.4	37.6
% Female	69.6	62.4
% < High School	6.5	12.1
% w/High School/Some College	69.7	62.9
% College Graduate+	23.8	25.0
Mean Age	30.2	37.1
% Protestant	35.9	66.3
% Catholic	26.4	25.4
% Other Religion	37.7	8.3
% Democrat	33.3	67.2
% Independent	45.3	28.0
% Republican	21.4	4.8

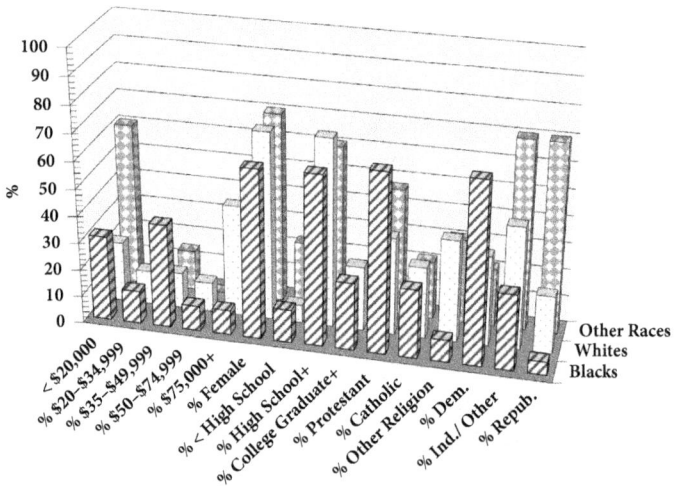

	< $20,000	% $20-$34,999	% $35-$49,999	% $50-$74,999	% $75,000+	% Female	% < High School	% High School+	% College Graduate+	% Protestant	% Catholic	% Other Religion	% Dem.	% Ind./Other	% Repub.
Blacks	31.3	12.1	38.3	9.2	9.1	62.4	12.1	62.9	25	66.3	25.4	8.3	67.2	28	4.8
Whites	22.2	12.5	13.2	10.9	41.2	69.6	6.5	69.7	23.8	35.9	26.4	37.7	33.3	45.3	21.4
Other Races	60.7	8.2	14.8	0	16.3	70.4	23	60.7	16.3	47.4	21.5	31.1	21.5	70.3	70.3

Figure 6.2: Selected Characteristics of Respondents by Race.

On average, black victims (thirty-seven years old) tend to be slightly older than white victims (thirty years old). And while roughly the same proportions of black and white victims are Catholics (25 percent and 26 percent, respectively), black victims (66 percent) are substantially more likely than are white victims (36 percent) to report that they are Protestant Christians. Finally, another rather large sociodemographic difference between black victims and white victims is political party identification. Blacks (67 percent) are more than twice as likely as whites (33 percent) to say that they are Democrats. Conversely, whites (21 percent) are more than four times more likely than blacks (5 percent) to say that they are Republicans.

Although informative, the descriptive statistics do not provide much information about the net impact of race on perceptions of the aftermath of Hurricane Katrina. In order to address this issue more rigorously, Table 6.2 presents the results from multivariate analysis. These results are presented as predicted probabilities (i.e., estimated proportions) in order to make presentation of the results more accessible. Still, it should be kept in mind that these results compare racial groups and income categories, but are net of other factors such as gender, education, age, religion, and political party affiliation.

Table 6.2 confirms that black survivors (75 percent) were significantly more likely than whites (25 percent) to believe that the government's response to Hurricane Katrina would have been faster if most of the victims had been white. In this case, however, the differences are net of the effects of income, gender, education, age, religion, and party affiliation. Still, race alone explains nearly a fifth of the variance in perceptions about these perceptions.

Table 6.2 also shows that, net of other factors, black victims with low incomes were significantly less likely than blacks with higher incomes to believe that the government's response would have been faster if most of the victims had been white. This table also shows that whites with high incomes were more likely than those with low incomes and those with middle incomes to believe that the government's response would have been faster if most of the victims had been white. There is, however, a significant interaction between race and income such that black victims with middle and high incomes are more likely than low-income blacks to believe that the response would have been faster if most of the victims of Hurricane Katrina aftermath had been white. In other words, not only was there a distinct difference of opinion between poor blacks and middle class whites in their views, but these results suggest that there was also a

Table 6.2: Predicted Probabilities of Perceptions about the Response to Hurricane Katrina by Race and Income Category, Net of Gender, Education, Age, Religion, and Political Party Affiliation.

Characteristics	Income Category							
	Lowest < $20,000		Middle $20,000 − $49,999		High > $50,000		Overall	
	Black	Whites	Blacks	Whites	Blacks	Whites	Blacks	Whites
% Believing Rescue Faster If White	58.7	24.0	82.3	5.9	89.9	34.7	75.0	24.6
% Believing Racial Inequality a Problem	70.7	56.9	85.2	39.4	75.0	47.9	78.8	47.7
% Believing Income Groups Treated Same	44.0	56.8	59.5	69.2	75.0	47.3	57.5	55.0
N	75	130	121	150	44	305	240	585

difference between the lowest-income blacks and middle- and high-income blacks. There was an even bigger difference between middle-income blacks and middle-income whites. Middle- and high-income blacks were the most likely to say that the government's response to the situation would have been faster if most of the victims had been white; middle-income whites were the least likely to say this.

This table also confirms that black victims (79 percent) were significantly more likely than were white victims (48 percent) to believe that Katrina showed that racial inequality is still a problem in this country. Middle-income blacks were the most likely to hold such beliefs, and middle-income whites were the least likely to agree with such statements. Again, this suggests a race-class interaction.

Table 6.2 presents some very different patterns with respect to perceptions about the treatment of people from different income levels. Here, there are no systematic differences in perceptions by race. Black victims in the lowest income group are the least likely to believe that low-income and middle-income victims received similar treatment after Hurricane Katrina. However, high-income blacks are more inclined than their white counterparts to believe that low-income and middle-income victims received similar treatment. These patterns also suggest that there is a race-class interaction.

Table 6.3 offers various logistic regression models predicting the log-odds of believing that black and white survivors of Hurricane Katrina received similar treatment. In Models I-III, blacks are significantly less likely and victims of other races are significantly more likely than are white victims to believe that blacks and whites received similar treatment. In Model IV, however, the statistically significant difference between blacks and whites becomes nonsignificant, net of the other factors. Still, this model suggests that victims who are black and middle income or black and high income are less likely than their counterparts to believe that black and white victims received similar treatment. So again, contrary to the idea that poor blacks and middle class whites viewed the hurricane's aftermath differently, these results suggest that there was also a difference between the lowest income blacks and blacks with higher incomes and an even bigger difference in perceptions between middle and high income blacks and middle and high income whites and others. In other words, not only do income differences not explain apparent racial differences, but also in this case, they appear to amplify racial differences in perceptions.

Conclusions

This chapter began with the observation that Americans like to believe that "we are all in it together" when disaster strikes. It then pointed to surveys of the American general public that indicated that African Americans and whites held very different perceptions about the aftermath of Hurricane Katrina, and that blacks and whites drew very different lessons from the tragedy. The chapter then asked whether black and white survivors of Hurricane Katrina differed in how they viewed the disaster. And, if so, did socioeconomic differences account for apparent racial disparities in perceptions about the aftermath of the hurricane?

The chapter linked issues of race and class (income) to examine victims' experiences during the hurricane and their perceptions about the aftermath of the hurricane. The results provided evidence of large racial differences on questions about race in the aftermath of Hurricane Katrina. Much like national surveys of the general public, the findings indicated that fewer than one in four white victims thought the government's response to the situation would have been faster if most of the victims had

Table 6.3: Logistic Regression Models Predicting the Log-Odds of Believing Black and White Victims of Hurricane Received Similar Treatment, with Race, Income, and Other Characteristics.[a]

Independent Variables	Model I	Model II	Model III	Model IV
	Race Only	Race and Income	Race and Income, Net of Other Factors	Race by Income Interaction, Net of Other Factors
Constant	$-.759^{***}$	-2.698^{***}	-2.468^{***}	$-.355$
Race				
Black/African American	$-.903^{***}$		$-.726^{***}$	$-.956^{***}$
Other Race/Ethnicity	-1.019^{***}		-1.184^{***}	-1.02565^{***}
Income Category				
$20,000-$34,999				
$35,000-$49,999		1.295^{***}	1.380^{***}	$.959^{***}$
$50,000-$74,999		$.621^{***}$	$.466^{*}$	$.166$
$75,000 +		$.046$	$.133$	$.145$
Other Characteristics				
Female				$-.005$
High School Graduate				$.678^{*}$
Some College				$.0002^{*}$
College Graduate+				$.800^{**}$
Age				$-.810^{***}$
Married				$.157$
Catholic				$-.009^{*}$
Born-Again Christian				$.054^{**}$
Democrat				$-.810^{***}$
Independent				$.157$
Race by Income Interaction				
Black*$20,000-$34,999				
Black*$35,000-$49,999				$.0002^{*}$
Black*$50,000-$74,999				$.800^{**}$
Black*$75,000 +				$-.810^{***}$
R2 Analog	$.043^{***}$	$.197^{***}$	$.225^{***}$	$.317^{***}$
N	474	421	409	353

* p < .1 ** p < .05 *** p < .01

[a] Coefficients are unstandardized. For the dummy (binary) variable coefficients, significance levels refer to the difference between the omitted dummy variable category and the coefficient for the given category.

been white, but three in four black survivors held such views. Similarly, less than half of whites but more than three-quarters of blacks held the view that Hurricane Katrina pointed out persisting problems of racial inequality. There were, however, few racial differences in perceptions about the role of income in the aftermath of Hurricane Katrina. Most whites agreed with the idea that low-income and middle-income victims of the hurricane received similar treatment. The results did, however, suggest that there were differences between the lowest-income blacks and middle- and high-income blacks. There were even bigger differences between middle-income blacks and middle-income whites in terms of how they viewed the government's response to Hurricane Katrina. Not only did income differences not explain racial differences in perceptions about the role of race in the aftermath of the hurricane in the cases examined, but they actually appeared to increase racial differences in such perceptions between people with similar income levels.

Using a Du Boisian analytical frame, this chapter linked issues of race and class (income) to examine victims' experiences during the hurricane and their perceptions about the aftermath of the hurricane. The results provided evidence of large racial differences on questions about race in the aftermath of Hurricane Katrina. Much like national surveys of the general public, the findings indicated that fewer than 1 in 4 white victims thought the government's response to the situation would have been faster if most of the victims had been white, but 3 in 4 black survivors held such views. Similarly, less than half of whites, but more than three-quarters of blacks held the view that Hurricane Katrina pointed out persisting problems of racial inequality. There were, however, few racial differences in perceptions about the role of income in the aftermath of Hurricane Katrina. Most whites agreed with the idea that low-income and middle-income victims of the hurricane received similar treatment. But when asked a similar question about the role of race, racial differences re-emerged. Also, despite the idea that there was a difference of opinion between poor blacks and middle class whites in their views, these results suggested that there was also a difference between the lowest income blacks and middle income blacks and perhaps an even bigger difference between middle income blacks and middle income whites in terms of how they viewed the government's response to Hurricane Katrina. Not only did income differences not explain racial differences in perceptions about the role of race in the aftermath of the hurricane in the cases examined, they actually appeared to increase racial differences in such perceptions between people with similar income levels.

African Americans across the country had stronger reactions to the disaster in New Orleans and the Gulf Coast than did whites. Blacks made harsher judgments of the federal government's response to the crisis, perceived the plight of disaster victims in a different light, and felt more emotionally connected to what happened.

Hurricane Katrina put issues of poverty, class, and race in America back on the front burner when the world saw the plight of poor, mostly black storm victims all but abandoned in New Orleans. But the results of this survey also tell another story: there were substantial differences in how black and white victims viewed the aftermath of the storm. The aftermath of Hurricane Katrina exposed the wide gulf between the nation's haves and have-nots. As a society, America needs to address the gross disparities that Hurricane Katrina exposed. Failure to take such actions will have enormous economic and social costs—not just for African Americans, but also for a society living with a disconnect between its ideals and the reality of continued inequality along the color line. Unfortunately, many whites in the United States are so unwilling to see or even discuss issues of race and class that it is possible that these issues will soon be casualties of the storm, too.

REFERENCES

American Red Cross Family Links Website, Available at: http://www.familylinks.icrc.org/-katrina/people

Associated Press. 2005. "Black U.S. Lawmakers Angry about Federal Response to Katrina." Wire Service Story, September 2, 2005.

Carson, Emmett D. 2005. "Beyond Relief and Recovery: Philanthropy's biggest challenge in the wake of Hurricanes Katrina and Rita is to move past just doing the familiar." *Mona Reeder*/Dallas Morning News/*Corbis*

CBS News/New York Times. 2005. "The Economy, Gas Prices, and Hurricane Katrina." CBS News/New York Times Poll, September 9–13, 2005.

Charnas, Dan. 2005. "The Bridge To Gretna." *The Blog of Dan Charnas*. Tuesday, September 13. Available at http://www.Dancharnas.Com/2005/-09/Bridge-To-Gretna.Html

DeMarco, Joseph P. 1983. *The Social Thought of W. E. B. Du Bois*. Lanham, MD: University Press of America, Inc.

Du Bois, W.E.B. 1933. "Marxism and the Negro Problem." *The Crisis* 40(3): 101–116.

Hattery, Angela J. and Earl Smith. 2005. "William Edward Burghardt Du Bois and the Concepts of Race, Class and Gender." *Sociation Today* 3.

McKee, James B. 1993. *Sociology and the Race Problem: The Failure of a Perspective*. Urbana and Chicago: University of Illinois Press.

Morris, Aldon D. 2009. "Sociology of Race and W. E. B. Du Bois: The Path Not Taken." *In Sociology in America: The American Sociological Association Centennial History*. C. Calhoun (ed.).

Pew Research Center. 2005. "Huge Racial Divide Over Katrina and its Consequences: Two-in-Three Critical of Bush's Relief Efforts." Pew Research Center for the People & the Press.

Phillips, Stone. 2005. "What went wrong in hurricane crisis?: Why did it take so long for help to arrive? Were warnings ignored?" Dateline NBC, September 9, 2005.

Roig-Franzia, Manuel and Spencer Hsu. 2005 "Many Evacuated, but Thousands Still Waiting: White House Shifts Blame to State and Local Officials." *Washington Post.* September 4, Page A01.

Saenz, Rogelio. 2005. *Beyond New Orleans: The Social and Economic Isolation of Urban African Americans.* Population Reference Bureau Report. Washington, DC.

Smith, Earl and Dan Green. 1983. "W.E.B. Du Bois and the Concepts of Race and Class." *Phylon: The Atlanta University Review of Race and Culture* 44(4).

Theimer, Sharon. 2005. "Congress Likely to Probe Guard Response." Associated Press Wire Story, September 03, 2005, Available at: http://www.kansascity.com/mld/kansascity/ -news/world/12551986.htm

Zuckerman, Phil, (Editor). 2004. *The Social Theory of W. E. B. Du Bois.* Thousand Oaks, CA, Pine Forge Press.

CHAPTER SEVEN

RACE, CLASS, AND THE RESTRUCTURING OF URBAN COMMUNITY DEVELOPMENT

Douglas C. Gills

Overview

The purpose of this chapter is to examine the structuring and restructuring of the field of community development (CD). To show how this occurs, I examine interventions of the local state and how CD, as a field, can understand this restructuring and overcome it successfully. The general, working thesis is that: a) the local development policy process, like the politics that informs it, has two aspects—a mainstream of insiders and a fringe of outsider, marginalized agents and actors; these two forces both complement and contest with each other; b) racism and class dynamics are both causes and effects of community development; c) CD, as a field of collective practices, emerged in response to effects of adverse local development policies, which spilled over into urban communities; and d) once having significant energy and creativity, CD has now been restructured into irrelevance as a vehicle of social change in the social conditions of these communities.

Premises

Community development was used as an instrument of disadvantaged urban communities to gain equity and power in struggles over economic and political life and to gain access to decision making about the distribution of resources and benefits on behalf of disadvantaged and marginalized community constituents. From the mainstream perspective, if it is to be accommodated, community development has to be continually restructured in order to meet the requirements of political-economic reproduction of relations of exploitation. To do this, capitalists must have hegemony and, ultimately, control of urban communities. This includes maintaining relations of dominance/subordinance between a majority, mainstream (U.S.) society and its marginalized, urban communities.

Both exploitation and other oppressive relations (such as racism) must be made a part of the normal process of the working out of these contradictory social relations. Only liberals and academics seem not to understand the realities of this type of politics.

I revisit Giloth (1996), Mier (1993), and Betancur and Gills (1993). None of these works anticipated the changes in the CD environment that were taking place at the time. While aware of restructuring on the global and international comparative level, none of these writings prepared us for the crisis that has befallen CD during the past two decades. At the time of their writings, I describe the leading roles of Chicago communities in the Harold Washington's regime in formation, which included the Eugene Sawyer administration. I show that Washington kept his promises. I will give some examples of where even this reform administration fell short of a standard of contributing to the improvement of community life for the poorest sections of the City. I will show how that role of a local reform administration under Washington has shifted to one of neoliberalism, resulting in cooptation under the leadership of the Richard M. Daley regime. Furthermore, I offer some reflections on the lessons gained over both periods, specifically as related to redevelopment and to CD. Finally, I make some recommendations on what we must do in the current period.

Some Definitions

By reference to *structure,* I mean the frame for the incorporation, formalization, and institutionalization of organizational forms and mechanisms setting limits on CD as a set of practices. Structure is the set of rules by which the CD game is to be played. When house elites note that the skill and adroitness in which players use the given mechanisms of the game cuts too deeply into the amount of profits or the rate of profits, they call for a change in the rules: a restructuring of the field of play or the hoops that must be negotiated by the players. It is an admission of a problem or a crisis.

By *restructuring,* I mean the rearranging of the terms of discourse and the matters open for negotiating who is winning and who is losing by the agreed-upon set of rules. From the standpoint of the mainstream policy makers, this restructuring must be done in conformity to local development interests, such that their agents profit from it. From the standpoint of constituents of urban communities, they have an interest in producing and maintaining counterstructures, which would be designed to capture as much value as possible for retention and for further redistribution to community members or to the community as a whole.

By urban *development*, I mean those activities that build up values and amenities in the locality, in terms of people and material that generate or facilitate the production of value.

For the city, investments in building up residential, commercial, and industrial property result in a higher volume of tax revenues and, perhaps, lowering the tax rates on these types of properties. For property owners, building up of private and institutional properties tends to raise the values of owner-occupied properties in the area. For communities, investments in area housing stock and in workforce skills enhancement are likely to make prospective workers more employable and reduce the number of persons on the welfare rolls.

Community development (CD) is a process by which collectivities collaborate to pursue and secure the well-being of their members. CD is a process of social action in which the people of a community organize for planning and action; further, it is a special set of collective activities of groups and aggregated individuals, or it is collectively pursued by agents of communities to build up the economic, political (power), and social values of a community and/or its constituents. The aim is not purely the pursuit of individual benefits or divisible private goods, but CD activities have some expressed social mission that cannot be realized by individual initiative alone. It is related to the build-up or mobilization of resources associated with enhanced capability to solve collective problems and to seize opportunities for the well-being of the collective. It leads to the capacity to, collectively, get things done, productively and effectively.

Social scientists, typically, base definitions of community on turf or territory; shared ideas and expectations; adherence to networks or ties of associations and affiliations; or a collective framework conveying constructions of legitimacy in governance, authority, and leadership in times of crisis (Keller 2003:. 6–7). Urban planners, who study CD from a political-economic and/or a social action framework, emphasize social relations as both units of social analysis and action. They concentrate on urban communities of bounded space (place), interest-based (class) communities, and communities of (racial or nationality) disadvantaged condition. Urban communities are of central concern to us because of their relations to the production and reproduction of both social order and social change in society, through collective initiatives. In these contradictory relations to wealth, property, and power, people are likely to have split perceptions of legitimacy, authority, power, and leadership.

Planners, operating from political, economic, and social action frameworks, focus on what is the structure of real, actually existing relations and how change is to be brought about in unjust relations leading to unjust outcomes. The focus is upon the motion of urban communities that are significantly connected to the political economy that they possess sufficient *social agency* through collective actions (Harris 1992: 33–54). That is, the capacity to lift whole sections of the society, improving their conditions and quality of life progressively, even going beyond the affected community itself. Social agency is that initiative that, in improving the lot of the initiating community, brings about even broader changes of benefit to persons and groups with less contradiction to the political economy system.

These collective initiatives are generally responses due to: a) failure of the market to adequately serve a community in certain places, or to respond to its members' special needs or conditions, or due to withdrawal of capital investment from specific places; b) the historical and persistent existence of racial segregation and economic and political discrimination; or, otherwise, c) public sector indifference or neglect, related to policy and bureaucratic failure to administer services or social goods to certain populations, which may be assigned or relegated to certain places and social spaces in urban settings (Gills 1991).[1]

Urban communities are distinguished by being juxtaposed to the urban mainstream, whose members are, routinely, absorbed, integrated, and accepted into the main flow of societal practices, benefits, and values. On the other hand, communities connote aggregates of persons who are otherwise marginalized and pressed to the fringe. They are much like being put in a boat without oars and paddles and expected to navigate a winding river. Pretty soon they find themselves drifting outside the main current or drifting toward backwaters.

Community, in the urban context, consists of collectivities whose members share affinity with each other based on: 1) a common *place*, where they are settled; 2) a common *condition* or *identity* due to a historical persistence of a social condition of disadvantage or oppression or, into relations of dominance/subordinance; and/or 3) whose members share a set of common, objective, *social interest* conditions which they have stakes in promoting or resisting (Harvey 2001). These are prerequisite conditions; there are also subjective conditions, where people come to

---

[1] Collective efforts taking place in a community, such as entrepreneurialism and business enterprise development are often pursued by CD practitioners, inclusive of self-employment and capital enhancement. But unless these strategies are undertaken with some specifically community or collective aim or benefit as its aim, I am inclined to exclude them (save for strategies such as worker-owned businesses and cooperatives or community-owned ventures, etc.).

accept or to reject their imposed identity, conditions, and social place in the extant order. Typically, it is the awareness of some flashpoint issue or crisis that jolts them into a liberative consciousness or awareness (McAdam 1982).

The state: the state is the authorized agent for the owning class. The state is the managing organ of the league. It consists of the owners and league officials and some retired players. It manages the affairs for the sports league; it sponsors amateur and little leagues. It does these things to create a *sports culture*. Some fans become caught up in the culture, they become overly indulgent; and though it is symbolic, they live out the lives of the team and some of the players; they even mimic some owners.

The league officials are representative of the state. They are hired by the owners to moderate the rules between teams during the games and, even after the games, to manage events and regulate competition on the field. Some are called referees; their roles are to be judges. They are to judge when fouls are registered. Fouls occur all the time; they are not called all the time. League officials have their favorites, on and off the field. There are three key levels of competition in the CD game. They are: a) fans to fans; they buy tickets and consume the games; b) players to players; they rally the fans; and c) owners to owners; they own the equipment and balls, players, the stadiums, even the league officials.

Theory of Urban Community Convergence-Divergence

There is a theory of local social movement formation, wherein, during periods of urban crisis, diverse urban communities tend to converge and unite; however, after the threat or opportunity subsides, or the immediate objective is attained, these agents diverge, and the movement ebbs and recedes. This theory has been used to explain the Harold Washington mayoral campaign, the widespread unity around the 1992 Chicago World's Fair opposition; and the politics underpinning the Chicago Empowerment Zone process (Alkalimat and Gills 1989; Gills 1991; Betancur and Gills, 2000, chapters 1 and 2). I argue that this theory can be usefully deployed to explain the rise to prominence, the decline, and the resurgence of CD practice in Chicago. I will use the political process model of resource mobilization to augment this theory (McAdam 1982, chapters 1–3).

The methods used in this essay will be from current social and urban studies literature focusing on movement processes in big cities like Chicago and my previous work in the area of urban social movements and the community development experience (Alkalimat and Gills 1989; Gills 1991; Betancur and Gills 1993; Betancur and Gills 2000b).

A subthesis is that: 1) a viable community movement that is democratic and a radicalized movement presence are necessary to advance community development gains in the city; and 2) a progressive regime presence is crucial to counteract the development growth industry.

Post-Industrialization Today

This is the age of global, *service capitalism*. Globalization is buttressed by neoliberalism and a type of revanchist city politics, which aimed its main blows at the most vulnerable and defenseless populations of color still highly concentrated in the big cities of the United States. New electronic technologies make possible time-sequence production in decentralized sites on a global scale; near-instantaneous communications; the separation of production and administrative functions on a global scale, etc. This is a period of redundant labor due to cybernation and roboticization of the workplace. Many workers, especially from among blacks and Latinos, are increasingly being marginalized through means of disqualification and criminalization (Body-Gendrot 2000).

Earlier in the period, factory closings and factory relocations to suburban campuses and to national and global points southward were associated with layoffs of thousands of workers of all nationalities, although blacks and Latinos were hit hardest. There is a downward leveling of wages and earnings of U.S. workers in the service sector that is currently being felt by a large and growing sector of the middle class.

This period also has witnessed the dismantling of the welfare state and a vicious attack on the most vulnerable sectors of the working class, poor families, young adults, and children. Civil rights gains made in an earlier phase were withdrawn within the next two decades, as the broad, intense movement of the 1960s turned to the local level of policy. The trend toward devolution meant that the federal government was absolving itself of any social responsibility to address *group* claims of impoverishment and racial discrimination based on a structural analysis. There has been wholesale dismantling of affirmative action programs. The assumption of neoliberalists is that there are no racists and racism is a phenomenon of the past: that racism persists but without racists (Bonilla-Silva 2003). This is one aspect of the new racism. It is structured; it does not depend upon the volition of persons, only their assent to it.

The workers' social contract with monopoly capital as consolidated by state regulation was essentially rescinded; it was replaced by a more informal understanding of the existence of a reinvented racial contract: the assurances that the broad, disproportionately white but expanding middle class would share in reduced taxes and indirect subsidies as the economy is strengthened. The working poor and displaced workers were hit hardest. As transfer payments, targeting the poorest of families, were reduced, they were traded for policies raising ceilings on eligibility requirements, which benefited the middle class and wealthy, affluent class, presumably. The assumption was that this segment would invest in industries where jobs would be created. The workers' contract seems to have been replaced by a racial contract (Mills 1997).[2]

There has been a shift in national and local politics toward conservatism. The state became even more "revanchist": insensitive and indifferent to any group claims of economic and social injustice. It was based on new, neoconservative policies that if the state were going to invest in programs to assist the poor and racially oppressed, this could best be done by the private sector (Smith 1996). This policy is popularly called *privatization*. It was based on the misapplied assumption that the corporate business model and principles should be applied to all public sector and social institutions. The thought driving these developments is called "neoliberalism."

The Daley Regime and Local Development Policy: The Main Danger

Mayor Daley, a Democrat, has "out-Republican-ed" Republicans like President Bush. In 1991, he represented the cutting edge of *republicanism* in the Democratic Party. He was the first big-city mayor to endorse privatization—the use of private contractors to do public services and displace public service workers. That is because he was a neoliberal. He was a frontrunner in privatizing public schools—establishing corporate schools and charter schools in Chicago. Moreover, he paved the way in the use of money earmarked for low-income people—mainly blacks—to attract and subsidize middle-class homebuyer programs.

More than any mayor, Daley has used development finance tools designed to grow and build in areas of the city where developers would probably go on their own by using tax increment financing (TiFs) schemes

---

[2] Mills suggests that whites' life standards and life quality will remain higher than blacks and other peoples of color; that this is still whites' country and they are still in charge; this was most apparent with the emergence of the Republican "Contract for America" and the reform and collapse of the social welfare system.

that may, ultimately, bankrupt the city's schools and parks. How? By rob-
bing these entities of their shares of property tax revenues as the City
expands the number of TiFs and reduces the value of properties not
included in TiF-designated areas. What, then, is neoliberalism?

Neoliberalism is is the ideology that justifies the current policy thrust
that government should not support the social *demand* side but invest in
the *supply* side of the economy. If the economy has to be stimulated by
the public sector, then stimulate the supply side through private sector
investments. It was launched in the 1980s with Reagan and continued to
be promoted through Bush I and Bush II and the Clinton federal administrations. The thinking behind neoliberalism is: "markets, good; state, bad."[3]
Moreover, it privileges the private sector through public sector contracts
for goods and services.

Growth Ideology: The Foundations of Neoliberalism in Localities

First, neoliberalism means a process of community fragmentation, of
disintegration of the structures, of the networks of support, of solidarity
and of mobilization of the people in pursuit of collective well-being and
a personal sense of worth. Second, neoliberalism consolidated itself
by privatizing public resources. It seeks to impose itself on the entire
society on a worldwide scale through privatization, through the private

---

[3] Neoliberals argue that when markets are "free" from interference by the state, it is
good for business, which is good for the economy and good for citizens. So, neoliberal policies aim to liberate markets by removing controls on trade, corporate investment, and
international finance. At the same time, neoliberals want to roll back the state, producing
weaker environmental or worker safety regulations, privatization of schools and water services, and cutbacks in social welfare programs. Neoliberalism supports restructuring, globally and domestically.

It is responsible for the continual retrenchment of the welfare state, and it now has its
sights set on the public goods aspect, while holding sway over U.S. civil society—its public
institutions, the ecology, even the sense of social and collective responsibilities to each
other. Market talk dominates ordinary thought; and, more, markets rule increasing aspects
of our lives. Everything now is valued in terms of the dollar. Everything "public" can only be
bad—schools, housing, welfare assistance, transportation, health care—but public subsidies might be good. Neoliberalism connects many pressing issues, today—increased
inequality; deepening poverty, particularly along racial lines; exploitation of immigrant
communities; environmental debasement; deregulation and wanton corporate behaviors;
privatization of schools, social services, even water; the trampling over small, local businesses by large chains ("big box" development); the military-prison-industrial complexes;
and the "theme park" model of culture.

Neoliberalism is the flag of global and domestic imperialism—the exploitation and
oppression of nations, peoples, communities, at home and abroad, by wealthier and more
powerful interests.

appropriation of the collective wealth, even the collective public savings of the people.

Third, neoliberalism enters the state, twisting and contorting it; it belittles the state. It trivializes what is the best idea of the state. This is in the sense that the state has the potential to represent that which is held in common, the collective wealth and will of the people. It exposes the state as a friend, only to capitalism—big developers and bankers. Further, neoliberalism has to destroy the idea that the state is a collective repository of all people. It must "gang-bang" the state (a corporatist view of government). It does this by capturing its more advanced, if more romantic conception, and making it an instrument of profit-seeking at every opportunity.[4]

Fourth, neoliberalism implanted itself by expropriating the participation of the public, reducing democracy to a ritual—vote every four years— but one in which substantial decisions are held out of civic discussion. These decisions were no longer based on the citizen, the voter, but on little cabals, negotiating in secret how to steal shares of the public wealth. They are political elites, who arrogated to themselves the representation of the people. In the context of Chicago, this could be called "growth ideology" or "growth machine" politics (Squires, Bennett, Nyden and McCourt 1987; Ferman 1996).

Local political regimes have been penetrated by local growth coalitions. In the restructured "local state;" its policies have become corporatist, where private sector interests are articulated into formal roles in the design of urban development policies; the government facilitates economic growth based on optimal revenue generation and steers its public investments strategy toward enhancing property values. This is development growth based on a land interest with bank financing. The good of the people is viewed as that which is good for profit making.

Paradigm Shifts

From the end of World War I through the Reagan-Bush presidential years nationally, and the Washington-Sawyer mayoral terms (1983–89) locally, in Chicago, the dominant way of thinking in urban politics and public

---

4 One of the lessons of Katrina is that some businesses took advantage of suffering people by appropriating collective wealth even as they called upon charities and ordinary people to give. Similarly privatization fails us in times of war, no matter how we claim it is just war, because some companies claim exorbitant profits for services that just men would do for free.

policy was the white/black racial paradigm. However, today, there is a new urban sociopolitical reality that forcibly impresses on our thinking about urban politics, policy, and the sociopolitical movements in light of a new demographic: the presence of Latinos as a maturing, vibrant political force. Be it a mainstream view or social movement view politics, this political reality compels students of politics, policy, and planning to recognize the need for a paradigmatic shift. We no longer define political realities in racial terms, but in demographic terms of nationalities.

Early in this period, the concentration of black people in a compressed area of the city led to seriously overcrowded conditions. This taxed the normal maintenance requirements on rental buildings and the normal incidences of wear and tear. White property owners were reluctant to invest in maintenance of these properties. Banks would not lend in these areas, and insurance companies would not insure these properties except at high premiums. Banks charged the highest rates when they did make loans. These areas were "redlined," being targeted for disinvestment as "slum and blighted." There was typical public sector neglect of enforcement of housing and building codes. Many whites either sold these buildings or walked away from them.

Absentee ownership was chronic. Some property owners depended on realty companies to manage their properties and to collect rents. They frequently "milked" the properties: collecting rents and deferring maintenance on them. Since the 1980s, racial segregation is no longer de facto. If you have the resources, blacks and browns and whites as well, can move very much wherever they can afford to. However, significant numbers of them cannot afford to move. This is structured economic segregation. This is a new paradigm.

Now, there has been a restructuring of community development in the most recent period. Essentially, CD has been co-opted, politically and economically. Many CD technical applications to property development worked; perhaps, too well. There were creative uses of publicly conceived but conservatively aimed finance instruments, especially housing rehab and new construction. But developers loathed partnering with Community Development Organizations (CDOs); they were too democratic. Therefore, they wanted to circumvent these democratic aspects of CD and supplant CDOs in the use of these finance development tools. The growth coalition has been able to supplant them and create their own version of low-income market mechanisms (Squires 1989, 1991). CDOs were, hereafter, incorporated into a public–private partnership as junior partners; and, under the current regime, they have been marginalized. Thus, this has become another aspect of the paradigmatic shift in local politics and policy: that developers are using tools demanded or created by constituent driven-CDOs to fashion their profits, while squeezing out CDOs as significant players in the market.

Reclaiming the Central City: Displacement of the Poor

A recent trend has been the movement of middle-class whites back to the city. This movement has been a near-two-decade-long process. The local government has used first-time home buyer seductions and affordable housing marketing tools, coupled with selling good, safe neighborhood schools and community safety, as key features of attraction to young families. This effort has been done to broaden the tax base while keeping the tax rate low. Moreover, this tactic has resulted in |aggressive enforcement of parking regulations, vehicle registrations, and increases on consumer sales taxes. All these forms of taxation are regressive on the incomes of poor working people (Varady and Raffel 1995).

URBAN CRISIS IN COMMUNITIES: THE CONVERGENCE OF CLASS, RACE, AND PLACE

Investment Determinants

Given an urban real estate property market, there would be some uneven valuation of property due to uneven supply and demand and uneven concentration of desirable property by location. Thus, uneven development is an expected outcome of the build-up or concentration of property. There is also unevenness in the rate of wear and tear on existing property. The more persons per unit, the more frequent the repair schedule must be on these units.

Reinvestment in property follows a cyclical pattern. Some areas would tend to be built up and deteriorate at faster rates than other places (Logan and Molotch 1987). Class and race differentials exacerbate these cycles of development and underdevelopment of property by location (Squires 1994). Historically, social consumption investments in capital mirror the pattern of private development in locations. Areas and subareas with the greatest private and public build-up of capital tend to attract greater levels of reinvestment in property. Most blacks and Latinos cannot afford the higher cost of occupancy in these areas. They are forced to find places outside these high-build-up areas.

Areas with the proportionately high concentrations of poor, propertyless settlers, relative to more affluent areas occupied by property owners and settlers tend to attract less private and public investment. People of color, highly concentrated in areas where there are proportionately fewer affluent property owners in settlement, are likely to receive lower, more irregular private and public investments, over time, than majority areas, especially areas with high concentrations of affluent property owners (Suttles 1990; Logan and Molotch 1987; Smith 1996; Squires 1987; Squires 1992).

The political structure favors white, affluent, property-owning areas because a greater proportion of these areas' occupants pay taxes; and because they pay taxes, they are more likely to be concerned where their taxes go. Mainstream property-owning areas can maintain their advantage and preferred status in the political process by establishing and sustaining an institutional presence in the process. Allocation decisions, then, tend to be racist in effect or outcome. But tenant-based areas are no match in the political process unless they organize for collective action. And communities of color can only neutralize their racial disadvantage by persistent collective action efforts (Squires 1992).

The development design plan for Chicago features build-up of property development in the central business district (CBD) and O'Hare Airport; north and south of the CBD; the Lakefront westward to Ashland; and mega-institutional build-up including educational medical and sports complexes and parks and boulevards moving north to south and east to west. As these areas are redeveloped, then adjacent communities can expect to be subject to redevelopment forces and pressures as new investment nears from these prime development zones.

The redevelopment process goes through several stages. First, by disinvestment in adjacent residential and commercial residential areas, forcing many residents to move; second, by divesting: this leads to slum and blighted designation and a first wave of gentrifiers move in; then, third, by wresting control over community planning initiatives, gentrifiers support developer interests over and against tenant and senior homeowner interests in affordable housing, and the redevelopment process goes forward.

Disinvestment

Generally, beginning in the 1960s, capital disinvestment from low-income community markets was a prime accelerant of earlier CD efforts. Note that disinvestment does occur in working-class and poor neighborhoods with majority (white) populations and where the residents of these communities are relatively marginalized politically. However, more often, the norm is that some types of communities are unfairly locked out of certain markets. This is due to discrimination; or, they suffer paying higher-than-normal interests or premiums than white, communities. These communities suffered neglect from the public sector as rental properties deteriorated. Housing code enforcement officers were found to be corrupt, making deals between landlords and machine cronies that sometimes included housing court judges, who were contriving to ignore the code violations for a price. The 1950s through the '70s was a period of banking, finance, and insurance institutional "redlining," especially targeting blacks, then, later, Latinos (Squires, 1992).

The national civil rights movement (CRM) and the Chicago grassroots response to increasing poverty and blight provided an opportunity for local community empowerment. By 1965, a radical network of poor and welfare recipients union emerged. They were also active within a broader coalition united against poverty and joblessness. Their struggles were subsumed by civil rights activism across the nation and in Chicago. Yet, these initiatives set the tone for subsequent community-based organizations. Civil rights work in Chicago was led by the *Congress of Racial Equality* (CORE) and an umbrella coalition called the *Coordinating Council of Community Organizations* (CCC-O). It was pivotal in targeting the national state as a vehicle against the local state in gaining and enforcing anti-discriminatory laws and regulations.

Poor people's organizations served as an underbelly to the more prominent civil rights actions that captured more newspaper clippings. However, the struggle around jobs for blacks to get into unions and public works construction sites sparked a broader grassroots protest related to other economic issues of importance to the broader black community (Anderson and Pickering 1986).

The constituencies of welfare rights and anti-poverty groups were displaced workers (Piven and Cloward 1977). The poor peoples' movement in Chicago was undermined because of several factors: 1) the CRM was essentially led by middle-class blacks and supported by liberal whites who shunned partnering with poor blacks; moreover, it was not in their class interest to build unity; 2) most CRM leadership did not want to be identified with Leftist organizations, which were influencing the direction of poor peoples' groups like the *Chicago Welfare Rights Organization* and the *Illinois Welfare Rights Coalition* (ibid.); and, 3) local civil rights activists could not identify a basis of unity with groups focused on social consumption struggles while its first priority was legal and access questions of enforcement of equal rights. These were insurgents wanting inside the system more than its transformation. This was a failed opportunity to open up the political and urban social policy process.

Saul Alinsky-styled organizations were subsequently charged with being racist. This was due to the practice of allowing black activists to initiate work around the issue; then, they would join the action, as a public ally, only to kill the motion by secretly negotiating a settlement of the conflict with City Hall and resolving their differences.[5]

CD MOVEMENT FORMS: STAGE I: RADICAL, GRASS OUTSIDERS; DEMOCRATIZATION AND INNOVATION

By the time that the Kerner Commission Report released its findings, the cities were the key battle ground for anti-poverty, anti-racist struggles for justice and nationality liberation. While the framers of the report could not reveal the full extent of the class divide, by implying that the United States was dividing into two nations, one black and one white, it revealed far more about the emergence of nationality content of struggles than most analysts wanted to admit. The struggle for social transformation had shifted from the factory floor to the streets and to differentiated neighborhoods of America's cities. Between 1968 and 1984, the *nationality* content of the urban movement pushed the institutional elite (white power) to the brink. The slogan was: "cut us in or cut it out!" This was a period of the largest, most rapid expansion of what we now call the black middle class, but, more appropriately, the incorporation of a middle-class-aspirant black insurgency, which was followed, within the decade, by Latinos.

This movement appeared to be race based; however, it was, in essence, a movement of a class in transition (on a trajectory from workers to middle-class supervisors and managers) within the framework of national democratic liberation. This class-based incorporation came as a result of leaving behind the poorest majority of these nationality communities. But what they had was a significant capacity to organize, to protest, and to

---

[5] This practice served the purposes of their self-interested brand of neighborhood politics. It gave coalition building a bad name and set back biracial community collaboration on economic and social consumption issues for decades in Chicago. See Alkalimat and Gills 1989; also, Coleman and Akins 1989 for their discussions of early community coalition building.

disrupt. By the mid-1980s, the grassroots communities of color would lose many of their middle-class allies, aligned in anti-racist struggle. They were united in anti-racist struggles. They separated based on class differences between poor, working class, and middle class blacks. The black poor were left, presumably, with their own organizations and agenda.

The community based organizations (CBO)/CDO movement has undergone three periods of development since the 1960s. The first was a stage of radical experimentation, innovation, and democratization of the local political and development policy process. The second stage was one of empowerment and institutionalization during the 1980s. The third stage, beginning in the 1990s, was one of cooptation and hegemony.

In the 1960s, a new generation of community grew out of neighborhood struggles: some of them pressed for equality; for public services and against public sector neglect; antipoverty actions; and fights against redlining. Some of them focused on basic social services. They also had a peculiar character of being popular and democratic, perhaps a reflection of their longings to govern themselves; most of them adhered to democratic principles. In this period, grassroots players were considered bush leaguers and amateurs. They were little noticed by the big leagues. Their prizes were marbles, bragging rights, and big dreams.

Unlike most ethnic-based organizations, which were organized around block clubs, reflecting a homeowner bias, these, essentially black community organizations were composed of tenants and welfare recipients, who had equal standing with homeowners, who were frequently seniors on fixed income. This "community participation" influenced their early diversity: their advocacy agendas; their service missions; and their development orientations. For when the government was unresponsive, they collectively practiced self-reliant development. They did vacant lot clean-ups and post fenced them in to deter "fly-dumping" of trash and refuse; they did cosmetic rehab of rented buildings, when neither government nor the owners acted.

This led to tenant forms of governance; to tenant self-management; and, ultimately, to tenant-based organizing for housing code enforcement, court appointed receiverships, and CBO-tenant co-management. Paralleling these developments, some CBOs setup ancillary CDOs (CDCs, CHDOs, etc.) for the purposes of producing substantial housing rehab and property management toward the end of the 1970s. However, the country was embracing neoliberalism.

Generalized Disinvestment and the Early CD

Disinvestment in predominately black communities came from several sources. First, banks would not loan in high-risk areas for fear of arson-related fires or fires due to squatters occupying vacant and abandoned buildings. Second, property owners of buildings stopped investing in the maintenance of their own properties occupied by or rented to black tenants. Insurance companies would not insure properties in areas which had a high incidence of arson. Third, the public sector failed to enforce tenant housing codes. More specifically, capital disinvestment is likely to occur in low-income areas with high concentrations of residents of color, e.g., blacks and browns. These communities are more likely to be doubly, even trebly, affected by dislocations in the economy.

These communities had a history of racial discrimination in the labor market (blacks were typically "last hired, first fired," and less well paid, while Latinos, typically, took over jobs and service work that few blacks wanted). Thus, their communities' common *condition* of oppression, their common, collective *interests* (opposed to poverty and relative powerlessness), and their concentration in devalued *places* of settlement tended to overlap and to converge. CD approaches would identify factors most likely to mobilize human, material, and spiritual resources to seek collective, long-term solutions to problems affecting them. One possible alternative is a cooperative, or worker-owner buyouts to keep the firm in place, but under local ownership.

CD is likely to be a strategy deployed where significant industrial or commercial employment centers have closed or relocated, resulting in widespread unemployment and the closing of related industries and secondary businesses. This occurred in white working-class neighborhoods. Local businesses were dependent upon local workers and their families with discretionary incomes. CD activity took an historical form of industrial, business, and commercial retention and attraction strategies and pursued jobs, development, worker retraining, and vocational-technical education. To the extent a significant proportion of community residents were likely to be homeowners, they were most likely interested in mortgage refinancing strategies to preserve whatever they valued about their community.

If they come together to consider a strategy of collective borrowing to reduce the mortgage rates, or collective ownership ventures to replace individual ownership, these approaches would be considered a form of CD. Whites tended to call it "neighborhood development." On the other hand, blacks were likely to call their approach "community development."

It was more all-encompassing. This CD strategy would be more likely to consider the conditions of retired workers or seniors and of neighboring tenants.

Contested Local Development Policy:
The Growth and Anti-Growth Coalitions

For most of the twentieth century, Chicago had a pro-growth, pro-development coalition, network, or consortium. Its resurgence can be documented from the 1960s;[6] it has become more prominent in the past two decades (Suttles 1990; Squires, et al., 1987; Ferman 1996). It is traceable back to the policy interventions on behalf of land development interests by the "Boss" Daley regime of the mid-1950s. Other followers of Chicago politics admit there is a loose network of actors shaping local development politics, but they may differ with each other over any given issue of development policy; it was not monolithic. But what I mean by a "development growth consortium" is that the local state has been captured by this network of interests in real estate, sports/entertainment facilities, construction, and, finance institutions, who collaborate to shape or to influence the main contours of local development policy in Chicago.

Edwards found evidence that the industrial factory and corporate service workplaces were "contested terrains" (Edwards 1979); Davis found similar evidence in the arena of social consumption struggles that neighborhoods were equally "contested grounds" between polar class forces. Both contested zones require collective action (Davis 1991). Perry views the modern (urban) state as being a contested zone between competing class interests, who battle over control and the direction of local and social spaces, including mega-institutions and local development policies, especially at the local level of politics and public policy (Harvey 2001.; Wiewel and Perry 2008). These development policies have become quite salient to determining the conditions of urban communities. In the most current period, developer interest has seized the initiative and is contesting community agencies for growing shares of urban community development resources and CD finance tools under public control. They have been able to redefine CD in the global urban and neoliberal contexts.

---

6 The political machine subsumed a development politics and policy from the 1930s to the 1970s. As the machine weakened, the development growth consortium became more prominent.

Some are so salient to require realignments of political forces as regime change. Their relevance to a policy issue could mean shifts of billions of dollars. So, the development growth consortium has members that not only are privileged by the taxes they pay but by campaign contributions they make to assure access to policy formation tables. Therefore, the chief policy maker invites members of this interest to sit on important development policy boards and commissions, or to be his policy advisors, even cabinet members, up to and including the oversight of purchases and contracts.[7]

The growth machine has been shown to date back to the Progressive Era, and it has changed in correspondence to the economic requirements of the city by the dominant interest (Squires, et al. 1987, chapters 1 and 2). Of course, through the end of World War II, the leading sector was factory-based capital. But in the post-industrial period, it has been commercial and residential property development using federal funds to subsidize private investment. Today, the key actors in the development growth consortium are the following: real estate development interests with the capacity to acquire and transfer consolidated pieces of property; developers with the capacity to raise moneyed capital; large construction companies with a monopoly of specialized building equipment and machines; banks and finance houses interests with cash reserves for the largest development projects; sports/entertainment facilities developers; and property managers.

Representatives of this consortium have been incorporated into government, particularly, its policy-making boards, commissions, and various development departments, and even as advisors in the executive offices. Their agenda is implicit: to support the mayor's agenda in such a way that it facilitates a climate favorable to the conduct of business. They bring this orientation into government (Squires et al, 1987, chapter 6; Ferman 1996; Mier and Moe 1991: 64–99).

Mayor Washington's reform regime may have dismantled patronage, but he did not displace machine-based regimes. Washington died before he could consolidate them on a new institutional basis. That basis was most likely community-based organizations, whose representatives were

---

[7] I depart from Ferman and from Squires, et al., in the use of the term *growth machines* and use the term *development growth* at the local level, because at the center of their concern is that of development and the city facilitating development engines which lead to real estate development. The faster property can become underdeveloped, the faster that this elite can make money. See Shlay and Giloth 1987.

incorporated into governance at all levels, between 1983 and 1989 (Clavel & Wiewel 1991).

In the recent period, a straightforward analysis of growth-directed development in Chicago's city government is complicated by the emergence of a regime that is infused with what some observers call "pinstripe patronage." This is where campaign contributions are made to the mayor's election coffers by affluent persons in return for appointments and no-bid contracts.[8] Since 1991, pinstripe patronage has been routinized, consolidated, and reinforced by privatization in the several terms of office of the current mayor. The lines of this political fusion into governance are blurred today. However, it is thought to have centralized much of policy making in the mayor's office.

Just as there is a development growth consortium, there are networks aligned on the opposing side. Initially, these groups were organized outside the mainstream development process. As much as fifteen years before 1975, this opposition centered on urban communities of poor welfare recipients, displaced workers, and tenants, led by racially marginalized black and (then) brown activists. They practiced raw democracy; everyone had a say. These collectivities were truly grassroots. They had volunteer board members and part-time staff. They were organized out of church basements and homes of members.

By the mid '70s, many of these CBOs had launched their own specialty development organizations (CDO) and community development corporations (CDCs). Then, more specialty housing development organizations were organized by communities and their allies (CHDOs). These groups and their leadership were diligent, "quick students." They learned the legalities of being CDOs. They struggled through remaining democracy, accountable to their constituents. Since the mid-1970s, there has been a network of community housing and development groups. They fought hard to be incorporated. They won. They were frequently opposed by the city officials and the development growth consortium (referred to as the "DGC"). Their numbers were sufficient enough to shape the direction of local development policy formation from the bottom up.

About the same time, the first mass action coalition against development growth networks occurred. This was about the same time that black-led CDCs came to prominence in the neighborhood context.

---

[8] As opposed to party members having direct jobs on the public payroll, these pinstripers, typically, want access and contracts from local government; second, they only work in precincts on Election Day.

Around the mid 1970s, a multiracial, multinational coalition surfaced against the "Chicago 21 Plan." This was the grand plan to redevelop areas adjacent to the central business district north to Division Street, south to 39 th Street from the Lakefront, westward to Ashland Avenue (Coleman and Atkins 1989). In this broad area, whole communities and several neighborhoods would be destroyed and then rebuilt on the basis of a new demographic. The activist communities forestalled the plan and forced the growth consortium to accomplish its mission piecemeal.

By 2005, this entire area has been redeveloped. Someone revisiting Chicago thirty years after 1975, who was familiar with the neighborhoods, would not know either the people or the place landmarks were he blind-folded. The demographic (racial and class) profile of these areas has been transformed.

Key lessons were learned from this early period of CDO-driven coalitions. First, these experiences put community activists on the urban politics and policy map as viable social forces. Second, communities were successful in demonstrating that they could come together around a common, sustainable program of resistance and that they would be per-sistent in pressing their demands for change. Moreover, unlike early cross-community coalition efforts, not one group broke ranks, making their own deal, sacrificing the other agents in the process. Third, many of the CBO-type groups were broadly based on local area constituencies, yet they attempted to build alliances, successfully.

Stage II: Community Empowerment and CD Institutionalization

The 1980s were the golden age of CDOs. This form gained increasing capacity and organizational and technical sophistication. They practiced parliamentary democracy and used every encounter as teachable moments about how aspects of the local system operated. The leadership, typically, remained organically connected to the members and constitu-ents. They still knew everybody in local places. There was respect for local opinion and voices. After the mid-1980s, the CDO staffs had become pro-fessionalized. Most had degrees from planning schools. So, they were smart, but were their orientations toward constituents, who placed them there? Or, were the voices of the grassroots being filtered or censored by these representatives? The agendas of the community-directed networks and coalitions have been fuzzier and less sharply focused on low-income residents. The distance between these leaders and their grassroots, legitimating bodies has become wider. The business of the organization is given as a series of written reports.

Radicalized community voices would appear to have become delegitimated. The old neighborhood-based organizations were parochial and place-insulated. They mainly mounted campaigns around single issues. The newer forms of CBOs had reluctantly reached outward, across boundaries to form alliances. This explains the proclivity to coalesce and build coalitions even where most of the outreach was initially black-led activists doing the outreach. They were insistent on finding ways to organize groups around issues into a progressive program, leading to sustainable networks and coalitions.

The Chicago Rehab Network (CRN) was the first successful CD-based attempt to build a sustained network across boundaries of neighborhoods. It was followed by the Community Workshop on Economic Development (CWED) and several more during the early 1980s. These coalitions were led by radical activists and progressives. But in another decade, pragmatic professionals were assuming leadership roles at the community and cross-community level. Most would not have organic connections to community constituents whom they represented.

The greater significance of these two developments (opposition to the Chicago 21 Plan and the formation of CRN and CWED) is that many of these community and neighborhood activists were in the leadership of the movement to elect Harold Washington mayor of Chicago. And many of this leadership joined the government thereafter. CBO leadership had further distanced itself from the constituents. They were the government, at least for a moment.

In 1983 came the reform government of Harold Washington; his stated goal was to destroy the "machine as we now know it." Washington had come to power at the helm of a black-led, multinational, all-community coalition of blacks, a majority of Latinos, and significant numbers of liberal whites. He rode the crest of a massive mobilization of his electoral base, featuring an enlarged electorate composed of segments of the population that had been politically disaffected or that had rarely, or never before, voted. This history and its political analysis have been done elsewhere (Alkalimat and Gills 1989; Gills 1991).

Washington's governance coalition mirrored and approximated his electoral coalition and the policy agenda reflected the issues that these communities were most concerned about: jobs, vocational training for jobs; affordable housing for tenants in multifamily units; adequate education; saving and changing public housing; an end to the high number of incidences of police brutality and misconduct; community safety and alternative, constructive activities for youth and children. Transparency, openness, and accountability were hallmarks of his governance as reflected in public policy (see *Chicago Works Together* 1984, City of Chicago). This planning document became the development policy framework of the Washington administration; it was continued under Eugene Sawyer as mayor. It incorporated the central demands of activist-led, community-directed coalitions.

A hallmark of Washington's policy was balanced or ("linked") development between the downtown central business district and the neighborhoods. A key feature of his development policy was that if there were developers interested in receiving public support, they must build partnerships or collaborative support of the affected local area and citywide communities. If a community demanded a policy change, it should build unity before coming for his endorsement of the new policy direction. A salient theme in his style of governance was effective citizen participation in policy formation, and also participation in the benefits of public goods on the bases of equality and proportional equity.

In 1982, under Mayor Jane Byrne, there were about forty CBOs receiving federally funded and locally administered *Community Development Block Grant* (CDBG) funding. During 1984, 120 CBOs were designated delegate agencies. There were nearly forty CDOs and CDCs alone receiving CDBG contracts. By 1987, there were over three hundred contracts extended to CBOs in Chicago. There was a steadily increasing number and variety of CDOs being incorporated into the mainstream local development policy processes. Moreover, the whole field proliferated with community-based groups, CD technical assistance and support organizations, and research institutes. Local, regional, and state intermediaries were growing, and by the late 80s, there were at least seven community-directed networks and coalitions in Chicago (Gills 1991; Alexander 2000).

This was the stage of institutionalization of CD as a field within mainstream local policy. This was the second phase of incorporation of CDOs. It set the tone for CDO cooptation and the hegemony of the DGC. Now, this was an announcement that CD was a big-time game. CD practitioners and activists had arrived. They were playing in high-stakes competition with the big boys.

End of the Myth of Race Paradigm in Chicago Politics and Policy

The movement underpinning the successful election of Harold Washington exploded the myth of the *race* paradigm in Chicago politics and ushered in the salience of multinational, community politics in Chicago. It is also promising for other big cities attracting immigrants of color. Because Chicago, as a global city, values international tourism and trade, it can no longer ignore being tagged a racist city. Racism is bad for business.

In 1989, Richard M. Daley (son of the first Richard) defeated Eugene Sawyer in a special mayoral election, held to complete the unexpired term of Harold Washington. Washington had died earlier, in November 1987. In his first two years, Daley did little to alter the policies of Harold Washington and his successor, Eugene Sawyer, save for the Tax Reactivation Program (TRP), where he permitted for-profits to be included in the partnership between the City, the County, and nonprofit CDOs.

Started by Mayor Byrne but enlarged under Mayor Washington, TRP was a novel program that grew out of the demand for low-income, affordable family housing in minority neighborhoods across the city. It saved many small, multifamily dwellings from being met by the wrecking ball as either unsafe or unproductive buildings that attracted molesters, squatters, and building scavengers. In each case, something bad was the likely outcome if these buildings were allowed to stand vacant and unattended.

A successful struggle for pro-community development forces against the DGC was the fight against the proposed Chicago World's Fair and the front work of the Chicago 1992 World Fair Commission (Shlay and Giloth 1987). This was a blue-ribbon commission that spearhead the growth consortium's public and civic work, and was intent on using the fair as a development engine to spearhead and accelerate housing development between Thirty-Fifth Street south, north to about Fifth Street, from the Lakefront westward to Halsted Street. (Sounds familiar?) Its objective was to get the State (Illinois) and City to fund its losses and the City would supply infrastructure so that when the party was over, the land could be reassembled for development at cost significantly lower than the developers would have to pay for it unassembled. Mayor Washington supported the idea of a fair but wanted a "fair fair"; he was opposed to the City having to fund the debt of the fair. The fair developers would have to fund their own debt without the City funding its infrastructure (Shlay and Giloth 1987; Giloth 1996).

The last success of the community development coalition was the policy advocacy around the campaign for a "tenants Bill of Rights," which was essentially codified as the *Chicago Landlord Tenants Relations Ordinance*. This ordinance culminated a three-year struggle against major propertied interests and for tenant protections. It gained rights and protections for nearly a million tenants in private and public rental housing units across Chicago. This reform, although respecting property rights, put some weapons in the hands of the individual tenant and his/her group.

Stage III: CD Co-optation and Mainstream Incorporation

The first loss of the CD coalition was the Tax Reactivation Program—an initiative designed to restore dilapidated but salvageable abandoned properties back to the tax rolls while temporarily providing seriously needed units of multifamily housing for low income households. Daley did little to alter the policies of Harold Washington and his successor, Sawyer, save for the Tax Reactivation Program, where he permitted for-profit developers to be included in the partnership between the City, the county and nonprofit, community-based development organizations.

Started in 1983–84, under Mayor Jane Byrne and expanded under Mayors Washington and Sawyer, TRP was a novel program that grew out of the demand for low-income affordable housing in neighborhoods across the city. Under Mayor Daley, the private developers displaced non-profit developers, producing on scale and something worse happened. The housing units were subsidized for fifteen years using CDBG funds. Many of the units went for market rate afterward, thereby displacing poorer families.

Big Loss: The Empowerment Zone

Chicago had one of the broadest, most effective Empowerment Zone planning processes in the United States between (late) 1993 and 1995. It was celebrated as having broad, extensive, and intensive participation. In all respects, it had signaled a significant CD and human development victory for the affected communities. The cluster-driven action plans offered the promise of significant goods for the nominated, poor community areas: the mid-South; Pilsen–Little Village; and the heart of West Side Chicago. After an elaborate planning process and deferred decisions about governance and fund control, the three core plans had the potential to significantly impact on blighted but development-capable areas included in the general plan. However, big troubles were soon to come.

After the announcement that Chicago had been a winner of $100 million, all kinds of development and power politics were set into play. Many groups who had sat on the fence during planning now jockeyed for a piece of the action. The west wing of the Joint Governance Council of the six clusters split. The West Cluster joined with ambitious interests in Pilsen/ Little Village to sell out the more radical Southside Cluster leadership. Meanwhile, the power play of the day was played by an alderman in the affected EZ area. The councilman staked prerogatives to name a majority of the EZ Coordinating Council members to this policy board that would oversee award of grants and contracts throughout the EZ. The monies represented windfall resources into a few of the fifty wards in Chicago. It touched off intense conflict in City Council and between the nominated communities and their respective leadership.

Moreover, some Aldermen insisted that proportionality drive the appointment of board nominees, since most of the EZ area lay within their respective wards, and they insisted that their respective wards be awarded a greater share of the dollars. There would be no respect given to the planned expenditures called for in the Chicago EZ plan. The cluster plans were discounted altogether. This corrupted the entire EZ plan process, rendering it redundant.

Furthermore, the plan had called for a trust structure that would last over the life of the EZ. This would provide accrued interest to fund initiatives beyond the two-year funding period well into the obligatory ten-year period that state and local governments were to sustain the EZ through their resources. This was the most salient provision in the EZ planned provision. Finally, the plan called for a majority, community-driven governance process. This element, too, was corrupted. Also, a certain City Council member argued that ordinary citizens could not be entrusted to govern the funds. Ironically, the alderman who argued the most for CDO exclusion was one who was most proud of his CRM and community affiliations.

So what was learned in these or through these experiences? All of these successes were attended by the following factors. First, these broad, progressive community forces acted in ways which were democratic and egalitarian. Second, community leadership was supported by professionals and radicalized activists associated with applied research centers and institutes. Third, CDOs facilitated a broad extension of diverse development practices based upon new translation language between development organizations and human service groups that had been lost or never previously existed. Fourth, we learned that multinational alliances could be built even if the circumstances were to protect the narrow interest of middle-class leaders against the interests of the masses at the community level.

But the dominant experience was that of popular collaboration and cross-nationality cooperation. This experience is likely to be transferable in future efforts of coalition building, but with a more accountable leadership.

SETBACKS AND COOPTATION

The setbacks occurred when the generalized crisis of urban centers subsided. For example, the greatest gains were registered during the Reagan administration and the social cutbacks accompanying his policies. Blacks and Latinos perceived Reagan's assault on the poor as a threat to them as whole communities. On the other hand, setbacks of the movement have occurred during the periods of relative prosperity (Clinton and Bush eras) of politics and development policy. Now, cutting across the Clinton and Bush era at the local level has been the local administration of Mayor Richard M. Daley (Daley II).

Few community level leaders assume "neoliberalism" as a danger. From a local perspective, Daley's regime has been associated with neoconservative policy: the growth development, growth ideology, and privatization, all these developments have occurred along with the demise of CD as progressive, community-driven praxis. Of course, if we place these developments in a global, economic, and political context of neoliberalism, it is easier to see the connections between the market crisis in Asia, the Iraqi war, the collapse of the Bear Stearns investment house, and the national and local home mortgage crisis. It is less of a leap to see their connection to low-income, affordable, rental, multifamily housing.

All these are manifestations of neoliberalism visited locally as the playing out of local development policy. The crisis in housing markets is occurring at the same time as the crisis in CDC. Moreover, the vertical and horizontal mechanisms that held CD leadership accountable have become titular or nonextant. This means that grassroots, community organization forms of meeting have become less substantially democratic. In the past period, neighborhood constituencies held leadership accountable. Also, the coalition form, which, earlier, had some semblance of peer review and self-policing of CDO practitioner actions, was no longer available to hold them accountable. Many of these organizations, so prominent a feature of CD in Chicago, were now closing their doors; and they were no longer viable as networks or coalitions. They had ceased to be representative of bottom-up political democracy. The CD movement has to be rebuilt.

Once more, CDOs (CDCs and CHDCs) were fast becoming ineffective vehicles for the democratic expression of grassroots voices and conveyers of their respective demands for development and change. Stoecker (1995, 1996) noted this as a weakness a decade or so ago. But the more significant aspect of democracy that has been lacking is the accountability of leadership to constituents.

Moreover, Stoecker (1995) noted the other failure of the CDC mode of organization as being its lack of production of scale. CD was never viewed as a competition to the private market production. It was viewed as a transitional alternative to the market production of housing. Rather than being perceived as a failure or deficit, this observed tendency is most likely consistent with CDC's mission, which was to model the future of a society in transition and to show its constituents what is possible through collective efforts.

The CDC model was not conceived as "competitors" with market production organizations. It was envisioned as an alternative to capital-laden production of social consumption goods, services, or community values. Housing for low-income residents should be socially produced for social consumption. It was a political challenge to market processes, not an economic one. In fact, when development capital sees that collective models of development can be done profitably, it will attempt to capture or subsume them. Under neoliberalism, CDC and CHDCs had to be removed from the contest over (low-income) affordable housing, targeting low-income families. The market for affordable housing had to be expanded to include middle-income families as consumers. This would provide the necessary production of scale that the market requires.

And this is exactly what happened to CDCs after the mid-1990s. By that date, private developers had displaced most CDCs in the low-income affordable-housing field. This was because most public and donor subsidies had been removed from it prior to this date. Prior to 1990, private developers did not have access to public finance and regulatory mechanisms, at sufficient scale, to make affordable housing production marketable. In Chicago, by this date, they had gained such access. To do this, developers have to have control over this aspect of local development public policy.

CRISIS OF CD AND THE GROWTH CONSORTIUM

There is a crisis in community development practices. It parallels the crisis of mortgage housing. This crisis is a reflection of a deeper crisis of global capitalism and of the U.S. political economy, in particular. It is not merely a crisis of competing networks of capitalists and capitals (M. Hart-Landsberg and Burkett 1999), nor of overproduction (Chesnais 1998). Neither is it merely of underconsumption (Walsh 1998); nor is it one of working-class high unemployment rates and of declining real wages (Kotz 1992). It is none of these things, alone, but all of these working in tandem to produce a general, pandemic, multidimensional crisis. This crisis is more deeply visited upon disconnected urban communities of interest, place, and condition.

It is a crisis where the state is shifting an increased burden upon working wage and salary earners to bear the cost of federal spending on war preparations and conduct and for social and public services (Petras 2006). They are concealing this debt loading through externalizing the conflict. This is reflected in growing rates of home foreclosures, growing indebtedness of working families, and a growing problem of meeting family health insurance costs. Even retired workers are finding it more difficult to live despite Social Security, health care, and their own retirement plans (Petras 2006).

At the level of the *local state* (Mokonnen 1995), the general crisis is one that manifests in multiple dimensions. They are:

1. Economic: Production increases lead to under consumption; high-end wage and salary workers are soothed with games where the government partners with developers in the building of unproductive sports/entertainment mega-projects while unemployment and under-employment are high, and highest within communities of color. More middle-income persons are falling into the ranks of the poor. The wealthy are getting wealthier and the country is deeply in debt to foreign capitals.
2. Political: Politicians want to govern in the same way but cannot; the people find it difficult to live under the same arrangements; people's democracy is opposed by a hierarchy of elite power and privilege.
3. Fiscal and managerial: Increasing legitimate demands for services while the growth consortium benefits privately from public resources; revenues to meet these demands are shrinking; new forms of taxation fall disproportionately on the poorer section of workers. The state can no longer manage, with or without regulation.
4. Sociocultural: New forms of racism attack and divide the poor and young with increasing rates of disqualification and criminalization (see Alkalimat and Gills 1989).

CD had been an approach and a strategy of the urban dispossessed and the powerless to be used collectively to address poverty and inequality in the city. The current version has no vision of a future that includes the transformation of current generations of the poor and powerless. Most families who resided in high-rise public housing units have been relocated to fringe settlements adjacent to the central city (Wilson 2006). There has not been, nor was there intended to be, adequate supplies of replacement, affordable housing targeting low- and very-low-income residents (Newman 1999; Patillo 2007).

Moreover, the working poor are still here. CD is practically too tied to political and economic mechanisms that wed it to the mainstream development policy process and its finance mechanisms to be of service to them.

The mainstream of urban development is deeply ensconced in values of individualism, private property, and pursuit of success through private accumulation of things. Currently, there is little connection of development practices to indigenous community leaders and to a broader movement for social justice ends in the economy, the extension of democracy, and the affirmation of diversity as a social value. Here are the conditions that prevail:

· Communities of color, principally composed of blacks and browns, have had populations which are, disproportionately, laborers: they comprise working class, displaced workers who are relatively poor or propertyless persons and families. Their members who share these conditions of lack and powerlessness are more readily mobilizable. They are more amenable to strategies of collectivization because they have few monetary resources at their discretion and, therefore, it represents a lower entry level of social investment. The returns are perceived as greater than the investment or, otherwise, they had little to lose.
· Typically, these communities are, collectively, subjected to racial or national oppression, which threatened all those identified for exclusion from mainstream social, economic, and political processes based on their current status as marginals. Thus, they are more readily mobilizable in resistance to these forms of oppression. Unity is their best option because of skin color and language distinctions from the U.S. mainstream population (Body-Gendrot 2000).
· As a part of a nationality community, sharing a common historical experience of oppression, a common legacy of struggle, and structurally concentrated in shared spatial proximity, their members are

more amenable to and more readily mobilizable to support collective action.

· Class becomes increasingly significant within communities of color or among nationalities, shaping a divided interest in politics and policy matters along class lines (Landry 1987; Patillo 1999, 2007). This represents a marked growth in the significance and mass of the middle class over the past forty years.

During times of urban crisis, common features of *place, condition, and interest* tend to serve as confluent factors, motivating collective efforts, which also tend to reproduce and to sustain a will to act collectively. Thus, we can speak of these factors being prominent in internal coalition building processes (see McAdam 1982). During the 1960s and '70s, all the contradictions of a racist, exploitative, political economy were dramatically manifest among them and in their communities. Many of those factors are still extant, though not so intensively. But since 1995, there has been a class-specific split in black politics and public policy. Pretty much, it has been over what to do with and for the poorest of the poor among blacks and Latinos (Patillo 2007, 1999; Wilson 2006; Lawson 1992; Bonilla-Silva 2003).

At this point, our modeling of CD as a game breaks down. It has too many serious consequences. The owners have taken their balls and equipment back to invest in some other big-league sport. For them, it was never about people, except to the extent that people bought (tickets) into the game. The CD game was never serious; it was a temporary means to make money. There was never any serious competition. CD activists, advocates, and practitioners took the game too seriously. Why? For them, they saw too many lives shattered, too many babies dying, and young kids shot by other young kids. For the owners and even league officials, they know too little about homelessness, joblessness, broken families, dead babies, and gang-infested neighborhoods. For them, these are all collateral damages in the undeclared war for profits.

The Structuring of Race and Class Differentiations into Urban Policy

The sociopolitical process comprises two aspects: a) formalized, institutionalized relations; and b) informalized, noninstitutionalized relations. The former, we call "mainstream," representing orderly, structured relations and normal, patterned, expected activity. The latter consists of nonroutine patterns of irregular, unexpected activities and informal patterns of relations. Thus, we have *insiders* and *outsiders* in the same political-policy process (Mc Adam 1982; also, Wilson 1995)

Within the political economy of society, exploitative and oppressive relations are part of the mainstream, routine patterns of relations and expected interactions between those who work and do not own and those who own and control and manage the production process and those who are ordered to produce and to serve. Workers as laborers and servants are excluded from participation in the proceeds. This exploitation is hidden and concealed by agreement, for which a formal wage is paid for the workers' ability to labor. Owners, reluctantly, agree to adhere to a policy of paying workers a *minimum wage* by which they are able to survive, sustain their families, and return to work the next day after pay day. Property, which is a legal relation, is presented as a "thing in itself."

These same workers are oppressed *outside* the production process, as consumers, where they are treated differentially in terms of access to quality and amount of goods, services, access to power, privilege and influence, owing to their position in the primary political-economic structure. This same structure of relations is reproduced in noneconomic institutions (e.g., schools and higher education, religious houses, politics and government, financial houses, other specialized institutions, etc.).

The *state* (at the local and national levels) is called upon to regulate, to bring order, and, by its authority, legitimates these structured relations. The state does this in several ways. First, the state appears to be impartial to the conflict between owners and workers, appearing to stand above class conflict. The system is first a system of laws and rules, not of men. Thus, it is assured to all its citizens as members that justice through the system works and every man can "have his day in court." Yet, these rules are rationalized in the interests of protecting class rule.

Second, the state plays a key role in redistribution, providing transfer payments and subsidies to compensate for market failures to pay sufficient wages, and in the provision of social consumption of public goods and services.

Third, the state is essentially partial to the privileged place (or social space) of the propertied class. Agents of the state are duty bound to respect and protect property: the interests of the rich and wealthy *in property* are placed over and above the interest of the propertyless class. This is done through the connection of propertied class to government authorities in the following mechanisms:

1. Property owners pay local property taxes; they tend to pay more attention to how these taxes are spent; nonproperty owners as tenants pay indirect taxes. On the other hand, poor, local consumers pay a disproportionate portion of their incomes on sales taxes and user fees.

2. Most occupants of the highest offices tend to come from the affluent and privileged classes. They have the resources, including access, to recruit and attract persons to their campaigns who tend to reflect the same background and interest of policy makers.

3. Property owners and the wealthy tend to contribute more money, time, and talent to the campaigns of candidates for public offices, and therefore they are likely to recruit these persons into governance when they win. Policies of government officeholders tend to reflect the interests of this class.

4. Government administrators, appointed to the highest levels of policy making, tend to be recruited from the affluent and privileged class. So, their policy preferences tend to reflect the interest of the dominant class.

5. There is a "back office" to the public face of government. We see and know the mayor, city council members, and other elected officials. They are public figures. Most often, we do not know boards and commissions members. Boards and commissions tend to be highly specialized, requiring specialized expertise about matters of limited concern to ordinary, generally disinterested citizens (e.g., planning commission, capital development commission, real estate board, tax board, and board of tax appeals all confront intricate, specifically interested questions). Much urban development policy thought begins in these specialized regulatory boards and commissions.

Even, though a given city government may have adopted rules governing openness and transparency in government, each one of these parameters of interface between public authority and private interests might only surface to the light of public scrutiny months, and even years, whole election cycles, after their relevancy to a current policy debate. The wheels of government turn slowly; and of justice, even more slowly.

RACISM IN THE URBAN DEVELOPMENT PROCESS

Race, as a social construct, is institutionally reproduced and ingrained into social relations, culture, including language, and becomes operationalized as racist effects and outcomes. It results in disparities and differential distributions of wealth, power, incomes, and privileges, where a power majority (whites) believe that they are superior and, further, acts on or condones the belief that they are entitled to an advantaged position in their patterned relations with "racialized" minorities, i.e., blacks, browns, et. al. Furthermore, it justifies this assumed racial inferiority as a rationale for unequal outcomes or the disadvantaged position that minorities retain in these racialized social relations and conditions. In this structured context, it is possible to subjectively have racism without racism (Bonilla-Silva 2003). This is where all put the leaders, in an institutional context, merely following orders or going "strictly by the book."

In the interest of brevity, I will address the matter of racialized language briefly. Language has a descriptive construct that is more or less denotative and a connotative component that is more or less implicit and symbolic. Within development policy, when researchers and policy analysts see certain terms, such as, "urban," "inner city," "immigrant workers," "community development," "underprivileged," "under class," "welfare," "public housing," etc., and assume that the referents are metaphors for "blacks" (or "Latinos"), they impute race to these constructs; then, most likely, the term itself has become racialized (although poor whites and workers are likely eligible to be included in these constructions). The attitude or predisposition of the listener is projected on to construction of the speaker and his/her subjectivity about the construct drives his/her actions when he/she operates in the social context.

By 1980, or shortly thereafter, to say "affordable housing, public housing, public transit, public schools, public health," etc., in the policy context was to think "poor black and brown service recipients," since, these groups are likely to be the primary consumers of these services. However, many whites who are poor, working class, and even middle income would take a subsidy if it or the main product is made "privatized." In the popular lingua of the period, to refer to any service as "public" is bad, a derisive referent to be distant from, subjectively.

From this brief discussion, in the era of neoconservatism or neoliberalism, we can more readily understand and appreciate how language has been used to prejudice the discussion of most socially progressive public policy in the post-Reagan period.

Today, even in the academy, discussions of "community development" practices and its subjects are racialized, if not derided by social class referents to the poor and disadvantaged. Mainstream biases suggest that an enterprising planner should have a certain level of cognitive dissonance with respect to it.

But the most important structuring of racism flows from a similar place that class relations are structured and reproduced. In the United States today, we admit to a structured unemployment rate of about 5 percent. Ninety-five out of one hundred workers can find employment.

Five percent will not. For blacks the rate is 8.2, and for white workers it is 4.2 percent. Blacks are about twice as unfortunate as whites to not have a job. Thus, the structuring of unemployment and race are joined at the hip. Of one hundred black workers who show up looking for a job, only ninety-two will get a job; sometimes fewer.

Given differentials of class disparities, economically, if we did the same thing in accounting for median income differentials, occupational wages and salary differentials, and wealth or net worth differentials, these measures are the extent that racism affects the operation of class relations. Imagine aggregating these differentials by demographic concentrations and, if location patterns follow property valuations, then we could map the zones occupied by blacks and we could generate an economic model with the effects of race differentials operating on class as a predictor of property valuations by census tracts.

STRUCTURAL LIMITATIONS ON CD FREEDOMS OF ACTION

Legal and Political Constraints

Community-based organizations, to be legitimate in the policy process, had to give up certain freedoms of their field of acceptable actions. This is problematic for CBOs with protest and direct action traditions. However, they do have rights to protest and assert their grievances before the public. There are certain legal and political constraints set upon them if they decided to enter into and operate within the mainstream process.

Now, to be incorporated as a not-for-profit collective, an organization set upon raising funds in the public arena must declare its purposes, its mission, and certify a fiscal agent having an address in the state. Moreover, it must also declare its chartering members and list its officers. This is a trap door that says that you are a legitimate organization, carrying an ongoing concern in the public interest. To remain in the public interest, you must meet several other conditions:

- You must have a "public face" where your organization can receive the public.
- In some instances, some states might require this place to be accessible to the public and not in a private abode.
- Morally, the place must be of social repute and not a brothel.
- As of 1986 the tax code was revised in an effort to curtail protest by certain nonprofit community organizations of certain specific policies.

These lobbying efforts must be confined to no more than 5 percent of its annual budget.

· The resources used to protest specific policies matters before the courts or legislation in question must not come from government sources.

· At the same time, a fiscal agent, normally an established public trust organization or institution, serving at the request of an organization seeking tax exemption as a 501(c)(3) nonprofit charitable organization has to have representation on the policy board of the said organization. With the IRS interpretation holding sway, the fiscal agent was to assume veto power over the applying organization, since 1986. The fiscal agent is the parent; the new or dependent organization is the child. The fiscal agent has a legal responsibility to serve in an *en loco parentis* relation on behalf of the government over the affairs of the dependent organization. If the parent organization does not adhere to these requirements, it could jeopardize its standing as a tax-exempt, nonpublic corporation (Wolf 1999).

This last circumstance can be devastating for emerging organizations with just causes which might have controversial conclusions or outcomes and representing militant, radicalized constituents, for it makes it difficult for emerging organizations to sustain these aims over a long haul.

In Chicago, since 1972, CBOs and CHDOs and CDCs have undergone restrictions to their freedom of action under local municipal governments. This was particularly the case if there were applicants and prospective recipients of public goods. These strictures were not always mere formalities; these were legalities to regulate agencies, though otherwise qualified and eligible to receive these funds. This process has a history. CBOs offering food programs could not recruit members or solicit participants through these food programs, lest they be accused of using government-purchased food items as a bribe. These groups were banned from withholding food to compel participation. From this understandable level of regulation, it escalated.

Worse than this, CBO members, officers, and volunteers could not benefit from government purchased food or other goods for which they were, otherwise, eligible, for fear of being accused of "organizational nepotism." One example of this occurred in 1985 to the *Kenwood Oakland Community Organization (KOCO)*. KOCO, through its spinoff development corporation, the *Kenwood Oakland Development Corporation* (KODC), had effected the development of seventy units of low-income and mixed-occupancy rental housing units. It received over four thousand area resident applications for those seventy units. So a lottery was held and an independent accounting firm was selected to manage the lottery.

KOCO at that time had a membership of over five hundred residents. Most were income eligible and longtime residents of the historical service area.The government administrative agency, the Department of Housing, under Mayor Harold Washington, ruled that neither its board representatives nor the membership and staff were eligible to participate in the lottery, citing HUD regulations. The consequence was traumatic; the need for decent, affordable housing was great. Many residents were KOCO members who had struggled long and hard; they had sacrificed much time and effort to secure and promote the housing development for nearly five years. The consequence of this ruling was that nearly 80 percent of the member base resigned, so that they could enter the lottery. Once the lottery was over, many rejoined. But the damage was done, politically.

Perhaps KOCO was able to regain about half of its lost or disaffected members back to the organization. That still amounted to a loss of 40 percent of the organization's base membership. Most of the disaffected members thought that KOCO had betrayed their struggle or had deliberately withheld knowledge of the ruling from them. KOCO had not. It took several years to gain back their trust.

Charitable Organizations and Foundations
Government is not the only agency that requires CBOs to jump through legal and civic "hoops." Foundations and charitable trust organizations require them also. As early as 1972, KOCO (which had been in existence since 1965) was a volunteer organization with a paid staff of as many as twenty persons. Most board members were active members of the young organization, and about a third of the board members, local residents, were paid staff who retained their voting privileges. When KOCO was first established in 1965, this was permitted by the State of Illinois laws. Again, this article presented no problems when the KOCO constitution was revised in 1968. But by 1972, nonprofit law had been revised to negate this provision. It required a separation between the policy-making board and an executive and support staff responsible for implementation. It was no longer possible to be a member and on the staff. Nor was it possible to be a "working chair" of the board of directors and paid executive staff personnel.

Also, when KOCO applied for *United Way* provisional membership as a community and human services agency, this statute had standing. So, before it could be admitted, KOCO had to revise its constitution and bylaws to reflect this change. KOCO board members who were staff had to give up their board seats or resign from the staff and staff members had to give up their positions. Mind you, the UW was one of the few charitable organizations also recognized by Mayor Daley that he recommended that city employees support.

This is an application of corporate laws governing conflicts of interests that need not be applied to smaller community-based (and community service) organizations. In small organizations, this is problematic because it suggests a conflict between the most skilled leaders and the most caring, supportive, and committed activists who might have similar roles to perform in small but effective grassroots organizations. In short, activist leaders, indigenous to the community, generally could not afford to join organizations or become officers without having to sacrifice material benefits of membership. This was due to applying for profit rules to nonprofits.

Political Delimiters
These were implicitly, if not explicitly, legal fetters that have the potential to obstruct communities from having the freedom and capacity to be self-defining and determining a radical course of societal transformation. These next requirements of government are more expressly political delimiters of transformative actions in Chicago politics and policy, since about 1991:

· Scofflaws regarding unpaid parking tickets and other unpaid city bills were efforts to restrict participation of activists or to undermine the stability of groups which were in opposition of the mayor's policies. This was inclusive of board members of CBOs.
· Anyone running for appointments to boards and commissions could not self-nominate if he/she had certain financial obligations to the city or if he/she was a litigant before civil courts and, certainly, a criminal court.

Other qualifiers were intent on restricting CBOs' degrees of freedom. First, after 2002, after the passage of the Patriot Act, CBOs and their leaders with a tradition of radical activism were more likely to be scrutinized.

These restrictions served to place barriers on the flexibility and options available to CBO potential and actualized leadership. By "barriers," I mean that it prevented the community's choice among their peers about which actors they selected could represent them to negotiate with policy-making bodies. By "options," this is to say that communities decide on the strategy and tactics to be deployed by CD activists. By "flexibility," it means that given a strategy, any road can get you there, dependent upon the tools available.

Other Qualifying Hoops and Loops

Economic Entanglements

The second major delimiter to CBO freedom is that of economic and financial mechanisms that bind community developers to the mainstream ideological and financially. CBOs take several forms; this overall economic social and ideological process of incorporation is discussed in Squires, Bennett, Nyden and McCourt (1987). However their treatment is on how growth ideology fosters the reproduction of racism and class inequality in urban life. I use these authors to show how growth ideology becomes ingrained in the unconscious practices of CD leaders and technical professionals. Further, I am suggesting that a progressive CD movement can militate against the uncritical application of development growth in the routine practices of CD practitioners and serve as a force of accountability.

CDOs need to participate within the market economy or otherwise gain access to market mechanisms. So, in addition to these politically salient requirements to gain access to public and foundation industry funding, there are economic and financial requirements as well. Among these are the following preconditions:

- CDOs must demonstrate that they can be trusted with other entities' money in the development process. The officers and executive officer must be bonded and/or carry bond insurance. Thus, CDOs must be creditworthy by meeting certain bank criteria.
- The organization must have the expertise, experience, or a track record that demonstrates that it can be successful as a developer within its board and staff.
- It must show evidence that it has an acceptable accounting system. It must show annual budgets and expenditures to ascertain whether or not it can manage money and other resources securely; moreover, it must show that it has filed withholding statements and paid taxes to the IRS. It must have a certified CPA statement to this effect.
- The organization must have a bank account that documents a history of transactions.
- It must show evidence that it pays its debts and creditors, in a timely fashion.

During the Harold Washington mayoral administration (1983–1987), the departments of housing, development and planning, and human services were all helpful in enhancing the organizational capacity of community development and service organizations, such that communities and neighborhoods otherwise eligible would have qualified agencies ready to receive funds targeted to low-income and disadvantaged communities, families, and individuals. This facilitative role of building the capacity of CBOs would be changed after 1989 at the end of Mayor Sawyer's term in office.

City departments had provided assistance in the form of capacity building grants so that existing new and emerging community groups could overcome these structural hurdles to their participation in the CD process as defined by the federal government and encouraged by the local government in Chicago. As a consequence, they were incorporated and *mainstreamed*. The local state was facilitative of this process. Yet, the state was not consistent. All this would be changed in less than seven years in Chicago.

Beyond these more general conditions to be met by all CBOs, when there is a development project proposed, the development organization must show the following:

- Compelling evidence that the project is marketable and feasible; a market feasibility study must be conducted at considerable cost.
- Predevelopment and social costs are usually not included in the business plan. These are the areas where the community is normally written off and excluded from the business and construction plans.
- A business development plan that demonstrates that sufficient revenues are available to pay: debt service; planned amenities; management; security and maintenance of the property. A payout schedule is available to show investors payout targets on their investments.
- A construction plan that shows how construction payouts will be managed and adjusted against change orders and waivers, and the construction site will be secured during specific phases of construction as well as postconstruction.
- Pro forma statements are provided which demonstrate that the debt service can be paid on a timely basis.
- A property management plan that shows that revenues generated by sales and rentals are sufficient to maintain the value of the property over the life of the loan.

Each finance mechanism further locks the CDC into an intricate web of private market relations from the covering of predevelopment costs—which includes building community support and community goodwill, to community planning, to marketing and public relations, to architecture renditions and support for other soft cost prior to construction. Then, there is also the cost of a construction management and payout inspectors during actual construction. If these costs are to be covered by grants from the public and foundation industry, it will take skillful and artful negotiations for these costs not to raise eyebrows or to be rejected out of hand.

Local Aldermen and Foundations

One other local actor becomes salient in redevelopment planning and implementation: the local alderman in whose jurisdiction a particular development project was being proposed and sited became "boss." By 1991, under negotiated arrangements between Daley and each alderman, the alderman was given freedom to manage development in his/her respective wards, in return for his/her support of Daley's budget and citywide development policies. Some local aldermen would intervene in these local community development initiatives. In most cases, they did not play a progressive role.

Over time, aldermen became the key decision-makers and presided over the course of local development. They decided what percentages of affordable housing would be contained in each project; they decided how many and who was hired on these projects. He or she had to be satisfied with minority and community "affirmative action" targets and for minority contractor set-asides. Over time, CDOs became less significant players in development initiatives, requiring public participation. Few CBOs/CDOs could build affordable housing developments strictly on foundation grants and low-interest loans alone. (WECAN—*Woodlawn East Community and Neighbors*—is the only CBO that has attempted this in the past two decades that I am familiar with.)

By 1995, CD practice in Chicago was in crisis. The foundation industry in Chicago, augmented by the *Local Initiative Support Committee* (LISC), had become the pivotal influence in local development policy and used its power to fund CD activities to become the primary player on the community side. Since 1988, LISC, as a quasi-intermediary in Chicago, had been playing the central role as gatekeeper for CDC performance requirements, using academic types, with limited practical experience in evaluation of CDCs and CHDCs performances; and, most importantly, for their continued operations through managing donor-supported funding.

LISC announced that CDCs, with few exceptions could no longer be the managing entity for LISC and National/Chicago Equity Fund sponsored properties. The bottom line on this maneuver was that CDCs could not be used as a medium and a "pass-through" mechanism to support soft development and social services of a host CBOs. This took any incentive out of doing development projects that would serve broader social purposes.

Furthermore, intermediaries such as LISC and foundations such as McArthur determined what are good practices for Chicago CDOs through the *New Communities Project*. Begun in 2004, the NCP is comprised of sixteen communities within Chicago where community development planning is being proposed and implemented. These initiatives were selected by LISC, in consultation with McArthur Foundation. The independence and initiative of CBOs has reached an all-time low.

THINGS THE CD MOVEMENT HAS DONE TO ITSELF

The public/private partnership was dangerous and undermined the organized CD. It was introduced under HW and was given a pass. If anyone else had pronounced such a partnership, it would have been banned on arrival. The idea that community development actors were considered by private sector development actors as anything other than "junior partners" was naïve. The city had the public subsidy dollars and an incentive to get underdeveloped property on the tax rolls; to private developers, all CD actors had was the capacity to disrupt the development deal and the ear of progressive mayoral administrations. Although in most cases the subsidy dollars were federal in nature, they were not about to get embroiled in "local community matters."

Note the federal administration's posture toward the conflict over governance of Empowerment Zone funds (Herring Bennett, Gills and Temaner 1998). The presence of money, available land, and flexible mobility were keys to the effective partnership between the public and private development sectors. For any other big-city administrations, save for Harold Washington and Eugene Sawyer in Chicago, the idea of a tripartite, balanced development partnership that gave equal billing to communities was farcical.

There are several ways in which CDOs have contributed to their own demise. What follows represents a few of the most significant factors:

- Detachment from the grassroots. CDCs have oriented their practices to the mainstream, so much so that they have become isolated and

detached from their constituencies. They no longer have very much organizational or mobilizing capacity.
- Reliance on external resources. CDOs and CBOs have become too reliant on external sources of funds for operational and capital initiatives. This has led them into a dangerous, harmful set of practices, where they have been encouraged to jettison their organizing capability and to jettison their advocacy and service capacity to focus on development niches that cannot and should not be pursued by CDOs in isolation from their constituencies.
- Forsaking legacies of struggle: Few CDOs, as well as CBOs in general, understand and can apply the lessons of their histories and the histories of community struggles. They have forgotten them. There has been too much thinking that suggests: that's old-school thought. They will be destined to repeat this history but less prepared to do so.
- Buying into the ideology of growth: Too much of our thought is uncritically driven by individualism and enterprise development and the spirit of entrepreneurialism. The spirit of collective work and social responsibility has been lost on professionals and those with careerist pursuits who believe that their skills and expertise can overcome the lack of community/collective activism.
- Building coalitions led by grassroots are linked broadly: There will be occasions to join in broad, cross-community coalitions. However, they are likely to be led by these same professional practitioners. This class is not capable of leading struggles of the poor and marginalized against the forces of oppression. The history of the CD movement suggests that they are no longer capable, if they ever were. The CD movement must be rebuilt, again from the bottom – up!

ENTER PRIVATIZATION

The concept of balanced development between the downtown business district and the neighborhoods and with a public, private, community partnership was later supplanted by Mayor Daley's endorsement of privatization, by 1991, and its subsequent deployment throughout local government, replacing work performed by public sector personnel by 2000. Such, then, is the demise in the relationship of community development and the rise of privatism in local development policy. The thought was that if real estate developers could compete competently and more efficiently with community developers in the production of low-income housing property, then why not supplant CD organizations altogether? Those same for-profit interests, who are more likely to cry "foul" about too much public regulation, are all too willing to receive public subsidies in the forms of interest write-downs, subsidies for charter schools (taking away monies from poorer kids who cannot afford to attend schools with more affluent kids) and many others. Moreover, these neoliberals see nothing wrong with receiving no-bid contracts to become sole source (monopoly) service providers.

The academic construct advanced by Michael Porter (1995) of the global, urban "competitive advantage" of private sector providers argues that the market is a more efficient provider of development goods and services than CDOs. Porter received a broader, more receptive hearing than was previously suspected that he would get when considering the source. In addition, just twenty years earlier, this same market had been failing black and brown communities miserably. This construction had come out of the academy, mind you; and, therefore, community activists and development practitioners usually have shunned the theories born in the academy. They were usually devoid of social practice and action. In this case they did not. We shall be paying for this a long time into the future unless a movement is built within urban communities, which is aimed at radical change of the context in which community development is practiced.

RECOMMENDATIONS

Principally, a movement must be built to radicalize the populace and heighten the critical conscience and radicalize the consciousness of the most advanced sectors of the population. In the meantime, there are certain things that seem appropriate to do. What follows is a list of the things which should be pursued to reinvigorate the community development movement within urban communities. This recognizes the basic fact that there is no social movement presence that can create opportunities for advancing within the crevices of the system.

First, the organic connection between community constituents and the CDO must be reestablished. Most CDOs exist as a detachment, separated from their natural constituents. There are various methods by which this relation can be rebuilt. Primarily, this is a question of community organizing around the felt concerns of community members. Heretofore, these concerns within communities of place, with large, overlapping concentrations of blacks and Latinos, have been the following: a) afford-able housing targeting multifamily rental units; b) jobs and employment development; c) building/rebuilding viable schools through which quality education can be attained; and d) building safe communities and resisting the forced criminalization of black and brown youth.

Second, and related to the first, the connection between the CDOs and the broader social movement should be maintained and extended by bringing activist leaders who know the facts of the issues around commu-nity needs for housing, employment, and training; education and, after school, constructive, alternative activities for children, youth, and young adults and the relationship to the criminalization process as affecting them and serving as barrier to restoring positive relations within high-impact communities.

Third, the building and reconstruction of a strategic orientation of the development group towards a vision of social change and the assurance of an adherence to a mission designed to maximize benefits to the core constituents and optimize opportunities must be fought for with all vigor and determination –if the models to be used in building development initiatives are to be promoted through CDOs.

Fourth, the concept of "social cost accounting" must be factored into development projects. Framing development initiatives without consider-ing the overall costs of resources used and exhausted must not continue. The tendency is for CDOs to end up subsidizing market development agents when this is done, and the true cost of development does not include predevelopment costs. CD initiatives must be pursued with a consideration to the social resources, including political resources expended in support of development projects. This is the best way to restore community building efforts and process the hidden cost of devel-opment that is absorbed into the project units as a subsidy and no return is made to the community. There must be a collective, community return on social investments, represented by development initiatives.

Fifth, for the poorest of the poor, present political, economic, and housing finance mechanisms do not deliver affordable rental housing, appreciably targeting low-income housing. Moreover, multifamily rental housing production might be the best, although not the preferred option for most poor people. This should be pursued, with a view toward certain step-up housing occupancy models that combine sequenced, rental-to-cooperative and equity-based ownership models which provide certain options in ownership classes.

Sixth, community activists, CD practitioners, and community constituent leaders should consider actively the demand for certain community development initiatives and not worry about what mechanism actually delivers the benefits. In this way, community development leaders and its representatives are not entangled into intricate market relations, which tend to lead to compromising positions vis-à-vis the state and market, in juxtaposition to one's relationship of accountability to community constituents. It is an adage in community development praxis that you can't serve two masters.

Finally, we need to build a movement around low-income housing affordability, jobs and income that are tied to the current mortgage housing crisis. It would unite a broad segment of the population around legitimate demands. However, this movement must have the leadership of grassroots activists at its helm.

CONCLUDING REMARKS: IMPLICATIONS AND RAMIFICATIONS

CDCs had gone through a golden age in Chicago in terms of their status and influence between the late 1970s and the mid- to late 1980s. They had a major set of community-directed coalitions and networks through which they worked to influence, challenge, and shape local development policy. CD activists, practitioners, and community leaders aligned to them had led a wing of a broad mobilization that: a) went into the Chicago electorate and successfully opposed Mayor Jane Byrne, driving her from power; b) thwarted and deterred the mayoral ambitions of Richard M. Daley, son of the former mayor Richard J. Daley, the machine boss; and c) was a major force in the election of anti-patronage, machine, reform Mayor Washington. Though shortened by his death, his tenure catapulted the community-driven wing of the movement to a place of prominence in shaping local development policy in the city and throughout the country.

By 1990, no less than seven functioning, community-directed development coalitions were formed in Chicago. The oldest was the *Chicago Rehab Network* (formed in 1976), a network of thirty-five housing advocacy and development organizations representing nationality diverse, low-income neighborhoods. The *Community Workshop on Economic Development* was formed in 1982 as a community directed multinational coalition of housing, industrial, commercial, and venture development organizations targeting low-income communities.[9]

The successes of these coalitions, which had great range and influence on promoting a balanced development agenda, were partly responsible for the ultimate unraveling of them all. The Chicago foundation industry was not committed to funding the plethora of CDOs which had emerged by the mid- to late 1980s in Chicago, although they remained committed to their ends. There emerged a process to winnow down the number of eligible groups doing development activities at the neighborhood level. Many of the coalitions were not able to find a niche while some merely duplicated efforts of others. Many of the latter networks were disconnected from struggles and the causes of their constituents. These were self-imposed limitations.

Also, earlier staff and leaders were radicalized by the social movements in which they had participated. More recently, academies and institutes had produced a growing number of highly skilled staff personnel rather than persons who saw CD as a vocation. Yet these professional hires became leaders of CBO staff. Over the past two decades, a growing number of CDO and CD coalitions consist of persons who have been professionalized as development specialists of all sorts; but they have not acquired or retained a community-based orientation toward their position and their aim toward these struggles. Thus, they were not sensitive to the conditions under which community members lived and experienced life, or they were indifferent to them. They saw themselves as merely doing a job.

Related to the factors above, there has become a clear disaffection between the staff of CDOs and the constituents whom they say that they serve. While some organizations typically brought members of their constituents to community and or coalition functions, too many leaders and staff heads showed up alone. Too few delegates to coalitions engaged in community leadership development. As early as 1982, many coalition representatives saw the networks as a place for them as leaders of CDOs to

---

[9] These two citywide groups played influential roles in the formation of other community coalitions: the *Community Economic Development and Law Project*, the *Statewide Housing Action Coalition*, the *Neighborhood Capital Budget Group*, the *Chicago Jobs Council*, and the *Neighborhood Action Agenda*. The Neighborhood Agenda was the only special purpose organization formed to effect national level community and local economic development policy but without being formally organized. Principally, it was formed as an umbrella development coalition to protest the Bush policies of privatization and the undermining of CDBG and other pro-city urban development policies.

hang out and share fluffy stories outside the presence of their constituents. Although one of the purposes of CRN and CWED was for the sharing of development experiences and engagement in exchanges that led to innovative approaches to community problem-solving, it certainly was not a venue for the leadership to "destress."[10]

At a time when poor communities could best use progressive CBOs/CDOs as vehicles in the fight for transparency and openness, the fight against big development growth, we no longer have them. To the extent that there is no progressive CD movement, no radicalized leadership with a vision of change and, to the extent there is no favorable political environment for the effective operation of CDOs, it is expected that there will be no successful CDOs on the ground. For there is no set of favorable political conditions where constituents of CDOs can press their demands and thereby expand the degrees of freedom within which these CD mechanisms have to operate. The slide to the right, toward conservatism, began with the lure of market mechanisms and finance tools and instruments which were creatively used for the advantage of constituents of` CDOs, initially. It has now bulldozed over local communities, especially among the poor.

Over the past two decades, CD practices have done more to benefit private actors in development than they have benefitted members of developing communities, especially with respect to housing access and occupancy by low-income groups. The best that can be hoped for in these instances is that there will be an overproduction of housing products, which would lead to devaluation—a reduction of housing prices and rentals. Given the savings-and-loan crisis of the decade of the 1980s, developers elected to destroy thousands of new housing units rather than feed further devaluation in the market, so there is little likelihood of this at present.

CD practices were good things; yet, left to themselves, they turned into their opposites. There are no political vacuums for, rather than working for disadvantaged constituents, these activities work better for the development growth consortium. How? The CD movement's leadership has become middle class professionals and careerists, which means, maybe

---

[10] I had proposed as early as 1993 that the citywide coalition might consider expanding its board and committee representation to include at least one indigenous leader from each member organization. This was proposed as a mechanism to secure an organic connection to those constituents back on the frontlines and at or near ground zero.

we should *consult* with CDCs rather than occupy decision-making positions, making decisions about matters in which we have no real stakes in the outcome. After all many of us go home at the end of a work day and no longer think about the job. Rather than being in a job, perhaps we should look upon our tasks as a vocation.

The CDC organization is too connected to finance development interests who think about *things* rather than the effect of things on people. CDOs are under the hegemony of development growth dynamics, instruments and values. It is ideological, permeating virtually every aspect of community life.

The CD movement has not resolved the question of local governance and power and of democracy/ accountability. CD researchers and academics have failed to provide radical, strategic ideas to the broader movement; we are too impressed with our academic discourses. CD has forgotten its radicalized roots. CD practitioners have abandoned and forgotten its roots in the radicalism of the 1960s and '70s. It needs to rekindle the fire.

We have lost our way. We need to recapture our vision. It may mean first deciding on who or what we are against and who are our enemies before deciding what we are for, in this period. The system—the political economy, its government, and its market—continually fails too many people. Most CD groups, including CDCs, have abandoned their mission and purposes, and it has been a period of development as if poor communities—mainly composed of working-class tenants of color—do not matter. We must contribute to building a countermovement to unregulated capitalism, especially finance capitalism, by building efforts to take back communities, our city, and our government.

Finally, we must contribute to rebuilding local struggles through augmenting theory, method, and practice around the issues of everyday life and link these matters to the challenge of transformative social change. A first step in doing this is to see ourselves as servants and resources rather than leaders in the community contexts.

REFERENCES

Alexander, Stephen. 2000. "Black and Latino Coalitions: Means to Greater Budget Resources for Their Communities." Chapter 10, pp.197–214. In Betancur, John and Douglas Gills, eds. 2000. *The Collaborative City: Opportunities and Struggles for Blacks and Latinos in US Cities*. New York: Garland Publications.

Alkalimat, Abdul and Doug Gills. 1989. *Harold Washington and the Crisis of Black Power* Chicago: Twenty-first Century Books.

Anderson, Alan and George Pickering. 1986. *Confronting the Color Line: the Broken Promises of the Civil Rights Movement in Chicago*. Athens: University of Georgia Press.

Allen, Robert 1970. *Black Awakening in Capitalist America*. New York: Doubleday Anchor.

Betancur, John J. and Douglas Gills, eds. 2000. *The Collaborative City: Opportunities and Struggles for Blacks and Latinos in US Cities*. New York: Garland Publications.

—— 2000. "Introduction," chapter 1, pp. 1–16. In Betancur, John and Douglas Gills, eds. 2000. *The Collaborative City: Opportunities and Struggles for Blacks and Latinos in US Cities*. New York: Garland Publications.

—— 2000. "The Restructuring of Urban Relations: Challenges and Dilemmas for African Americans and Latinos in US Cities," chapter 2, pp. 17–40. In Betancur, John and Douglas Gills, eds. 2000. *The Collaborative City: Opportunities and Struggles for Blacks and Latinos in US Cities*. New York: Garland Publications.

—— 1993. "Race, Class and Community Development." Chapter 9, pp. 191–212. In Bingham, Richard and Rob Mier, eds. 1993. *Theories of Local Economic Development: Perspectives from Across the Disciplines*. Newbury Park, CA.: Sage Publications

Bingham, Richard and Rob Mier, eds. 1993.*Theories of Local Economic Development: Perspectives from Across the Disciplines*. Newbury Park, CA.: Sage Publications

Bonilla-Silva, Eduardo 2003. *Racism Without Racists: Color-Blind Racism and the Persistence of Racial Inequality in the United States*. New York: Rowman Littlefield

Boston, Thomas and Catherine Ross, eds. 1997. *The Inner City: Urban Poverty and Economic Development in the Next Century*. New Brunswick, NJ: Transaction Publishers.

Boty-Gendrot, Sophie. 2000. *The Social Control of Cities*. Malden, Mass.: Blackwell Publishers.

Chenais, Francois. 1998. Le Monde Diplomatique. www.mondediplo.com /1998/02/ 03deflation-3.

Chicago Works Together. 1984. Department of Economic Development, City of Chicago.

Clavel, Pierre. 1986. *The Progressive City: Planning and Participation*. New Brunswick, N.J.: Rutgers University Press.

—— Wim Wiewel. 1991. "Introduction,"pp.1–33. In Clavel, Pierre and Wim Wiewel eds. 1991 *Harold Washington and the Neighborhoods: Progressive City Government in Chicago, 1983–1987*. New Brunswick, NJ: Rutgers University Press.

Coleman, Walter "Slim" and George Atkins. 1989. *Fair Share: the Struggle fro the Rights of the People*. Chicago: Justice Graphics.

Davis, John. 1991. *Contested Ground: Collective Action and the Urban Neighborhood*. Ithaca NY: Cornell University Press.

Edwards, Richard. 1979. *Contested Terrain: the Transformation of the Work Place in the Twentieth Century*. New York: Basic Books.

Ferguson, Ronald and William Dickens, eds. 1999. *Urban Problems and Community Development*. Washington D.C.: Brookings Institution Press.

Ferman, Barbara. 1996. *Challenging the Growth Machine: Neighborhood Politics in Chicago and Pittsburgh*. Lawrence: University Press of Kansas.

Giloth, Robert. 1996. "Social Justice and Neighborhood Revitalization in Chicago: the era of Harold Washington, 1983–1987." Chapter 6, pp. 83–96 in Dennis Keating, Norman Krumholz and Philip Star eds. 1996. *Revitalizing Urban Neighborhoods*. Lawrence: University Press of Kansas.

Gills, Doug. 1991. "Chicago Politics and Community Development." Chapter 2, pp. 34–63. In Clavel, Pierre and Wim Wiewel eds. 1991 *Harold Washington and the Neighborhoods: Progressive City Government in Chicago, 1983–1987*. New Brunswick, NJ: Rutgers University Press.

—— and Wanda White. 1998. Community Involvement in Chicago's Empowerment Zone. In Herring, Cedric, Michael Bennett, Doug Gills and Noah Temaner 1998. *Empowerment in Chicago: Grassroots Participation in Economic Development and Poverty Alleviation*, pp. 14–70. Great Cities Institute. Chicago: University of Illinois Press.

——1997. "Chicago's Empowerment Zone and Citizen Participation."In Nyden, Philip, Anne Figert, Mark Shibley and Darryl Burrows; *Building Community: Social Science in Action* pp. 211–219.Thousand Oaks CA: Pine Forge Press.

Harris, Leonard. 1992. "Agency and the Concept of the Underclass," pp. 33–56. In Bill Lawson, ed. 1992. *The Underclass Question*. Philadelphia: Temple University Press.

Hart-Landsberg, Martin and Paul Burkett 1999. "Capitalism and Asian Crisis a Critique and Rejoinder." *Bulletin of Concerned Asian Scholars*, vol. 31

Harvey, David. 2001. *Spaces of Capital*. New York: Routledge Publishers.

Kotz, David. 1992. "The Business Cycle: Growth and Crisis Under Capitalism." Review author *Journal of Economic Literature*. American Economic Association

Herring, Cedric, Michael Bennett, Doug Gills and Noah Temaner. 1998. *Empowerment in Chicago: Grassroots Participation in Economic Development and Poverty Alleviation*. Great Cities Institute. Chicago: University of Illinois Press.

Keller, Suzane. 2003. *Community: Pursuing the Dream, Living the Reality*. Princeton: Princeton University Press.

Landry, Bart. 1987. *The New Black Middle Class*. Berkeley and LA: University of California Press.

Logan, John and Harvey Molotch. 1987. *Urban Fortunes: the Political Economy of Place*. Berkeley: the University of California Press.

McAdam, Doug. 1982. *Political Process and the Development of Black Insurgency, 1930–1970*. Chicago: University of Chicago Press.

McMillian, John and Paul Buhle. 2003. *The New Left Revisited*. Philadelphia: Temple University Press.

Mier, Robert. 1993. *Social Justice and Local Development Policy*. Newbury Park, CA.: Sage Publications.

Mier, Rob and Kari Moe1991. "Decentralized Development From Theory to Practice." pp. 64–99." In Clavel, Pierre and Wim Wiewel eds. 1991 *Harold Washington and the Neighborhoods: Progressive City Government in Chicago, 1983–1987*. New Brunswick, NJ: Rutgers University Press.

Mills, Charles. *The Racial Contract*. Ithaca, NY: Cornell University Press.

Monkonnen, Eric. 1995. *The Local State: Public Money and American Cities*. Stanford, CA.: Stanford University Press.

Newman, Katherine. 1999. *No Shame in My Game. The Working Poor in the Inner City*. New York: Alfred Knopf and Russell Sage.

Ofari, Earl. 1970. *the Myth of Black Capitalism*. New York: Modern Reader.

Pattillo, Mary. 2007. *Black on the Block: The Politics of Race and Class in the City*. Chicago: University of Chicago Press.

——1999. *Black Picket Fences: Privilege and Peril Among the Black Middle Class*. Chicago: University of Chicago Press.

Petras, James. 2006. "Crisis of US Capitalism or the Crisis of Wage and Salaried Workers." *Dissident Voice* www.dissidentvoice.org

Piven Frances Fox and Richard Cloward. 1977. *Poor Peoples' Movements*. New York: Pantheon Books.

Porter, Michael E. 1995. "The Competitive Advantage of the Inner City" " *Harvard Business Review* (May/June), pp. 55ff.

Ralph, James R., Jr. 1973. CORE: A Study in the Civil Rights Movement, 1942–1968

Rubin, Herbert and Irene Rubin 2008. *Community Organizing and Development*. New York: Pearson Publishing.

Shlay, Anne and Robert Giloth. 1987. "The Social Organization Of A Land-Based Elite: The Case Of The Failed Chicago 1992 World's Fair."*Journal of Urban Affairs* 9 (4), pp.305–324

Smith, Neil 1996. *The New Urban Frontier. Gentrification and the Revanchist City*. New York: Routledge Press.

Squires, Gregory, ed. 1992. *From Redlining to Reinvestment: Community Responses to Urban Disinvestment*. Philadelphia: Temple University Press.

—— 1994. *Capital and Communities in Black and White: the Intersection of Race, Class and Uneven Development*. Albany: State University of New York Press.

—— Larry Bennett, Kathleen McCourt, Phil Nyden. 1987. *Chicago: Race, Class and the Response to Urban Decline*. Philadelphia: Temple University Press.

—— ed. 1989, 1991. *Unequal Partnerships: The Political Economy of Urban Redevelopment in Postwar America*. New Brunswick NJ: Rutgers University Press.

Stoecker, Randy. 1994; 1995a. "The Community Development Corporation Model of Urban Redevelopment: A Political Economy Critique and an Alternative." comm-org.wisc.edu/papers96/cdc.html

Suttles, Gerald. 1990. *The Man Made City: the Land Use Confidence Game in Chicago*. Chicago: University of Chicago Press.

Varady, David and Jeffery Raffel. 1995. *Selling Cities: Attracting Homebuyers Through Schools and Housing Programs*. Albany: State University of New York Press.

Walsh, Lynn. 1998. "Capitalism's Economic and Political Crisis." *Socialism Today*, 32 October.

Wilson, James Q. 1995 edition. *Political Organization*. Princeton: Princeton University Press.

Wilson, William and Richard Tabb. 2006. *There Goes the Neighborhood*. New York: Alfred Knopf/ Random House.

Winant, Howard. 1994. *Racial Conditions*. Minneapolis: University of Minnesota Press.

Wiewel, Wim and David Perry, eds. 2008. Global Universities and Urban Development: Case Studies and Analysis New York: ME Sharpe Publishers.

Wolf, Thomas. 1999. *Managing a Nonprofit in the Twenty-first Century*. New York: Fireside/ Prentice Hall Press.

CHAPTER EIGHT

FAIRNES ON THE JOB: SKIN TONE, THE BEAUTY MYTH, AND THE TREATMENT OF AFRICAN AMERICAN WOMEN AT WORK

N. Michelle Hughes and Cedric Herring

Introduction

Increasingly, beauty and its gendered effects are the subject matter of social science research (e.g., Wolf 1991; Craig 2002; Banks 2000; Wallace-Sanders 2002; Hunter 2004; Watson and Martin 2004). Undoubtedly, this is the case because physical attractiveness or "beauty" is a key element of how women are judged. For example, in the Miss America beauty pageant, the largest scholarship-granting organization for women, the winner's merit is largely determined by her physical appearance as beautiful (Watson and Martin 2004).

In *The Beauty Myth*, Naomi Wolf (1991) argues that Western images of beauty—found on television and in advertisements, women's magazines, and pornography—are detrimental to women, as well as to the men who love them. She demonstrates that the concept of "beauty" is a weapon used to make women feel badly about themselves; after all, so few can live up to the ideal. Although Wolf acknowledges that beauty plays a legitimate role in our lives and in our attractions to one another, she suggests that the problem is when beauty is defined as thinness, pertness, and youthfulness taken to extremes that are unattainable for most healthy women.

Wolf also argues that beauty is an important form of capital for women in the labor market. She indicates that as women have gained access to power structures through employment, "the power structure used the beauty myth to undermine women's advancement" (Wolf 1991: 9). "The job market refined the beauty myth as a way to legitimize employment discrimination against women" (Wolf 1991: 10).

But beauty is not only gendered, it is also racialized (Banks 2000; Kinloch 2004). Recent research suggests that hegemonic ideals about beauty as whiteness abound within communities of color as well as within society at large (e.g., Hunter 1998, 2004; Thompson and Keith 2001; Thompson and Keith 2004).

Given the racialized nature of beauty and the importance of beauty to securing employment, the questions are: How does the beauty myth affect the workplace treatment of women of color? Is there a systematic bias in favor of women who more closely approximate the traditional European standard of beauty? Specifically, do those with lighter complexions or more physical attractiveness receive better treatment? Are they more likely to be hassled at work? Are those with darker complexions more likely to be unfairly fired or denied promotions?

This study examines the effects of physical appearance and skin color on the treatment of African American women, especially in the work setting. Using data from African American women in the 1995 Detroit Area Study, this chapter seeks to determine whether skin tone and other aspects of physical appearance are related to reports of being unfairly fired or denied promotions, being harassed at work, or being treated badly by whites or blacks.

THEORETICAL CONSIDERATIONS

Women are often referred to as the "fair" sex. According to Webster's dictionary, the primary meaning of "fair" is "pleasing to the eye or mind." In this expression, the word "fair" denotes that women are the visually pleasing members of our species. In addition, this understanding coincides with how women are evaluated in society. By the dictates of patriarchy, women are judged by their appearance. Dion, Bersheid, and Walster (1972) argue that in American culture, that which is considered beautiful is also considered good. Attractiveness was found to be linked to qualities such as intelligence, sociability, and virtue. Women who are deemed beautiful fare better in society (Webster and Driskell 1983).

The word fair also means "not dark." The multiple meanings of the word "fair" suggest the Western construction of feminine beauty as lightness and connect the concept of beauty to colorism. So, for women of color, the coincidence of the meanings of the word "fair" has personal as well as social, political, and economic consequences. According to Freedman (1986: 1), "good looks are a prerequisite for femininity." Moreover, because beauty ideals are based on Eurocentric standards, many women of color are often judged as not beautiful. The notion of femininity and the cult of true womanhood developed in the United States within a highly racialized and class-conscious context (Palmer 1983). Womanliness, and thus femininity, was achieved through race and the ability to avoid hard labor. Thus, race, femininity, and a woman's rightful place within the labor market are linked in the United States.

But the word fair also means "unbiased." It suggests that one is impartial and reasonable. When applied to the labor market, it suggests that one will not encounter discrimination based on factors that are not relevant to ability and productivity. It implies that two people who have equal capabilities to perform a task are equally likely to be hired, compensated, and retained to perform that task, irrespective of their appearance.

How and why does beauty matter? According to Hunter (2004: 31), "beauty is a crucial resource for women because it operates as a form of social capital. It is transformable into other types of capital, through access to high-status occupations, higher educational attainment, and even higher incomes." As she points out, beauty as capital operates similarly to whiteness as property (Harris 1995). Because beauty is privileged socially, culturally, and economically in society, we expect African American women with more attractive physical appearances to experience favorable treatment relative to their less-attractive counterparts.

But why study skin color? Hunter (2002, 2004) builds on previous work establishing that light skin is perceived as beautiful and, as a result, also functions like social capital. Light skinned African American women are able to use this capital (in the form of beauty) to secure higher education, higher incomes, and more prestigious husbands. Beauty, it seems, functions like other social capital characteristics, much like networks for men (Hunter 2002, Bourdieu 1986). Because attractive individuals are perceived as more successful in employment (Dion et al., 1972), this raises questions about how skin tone operates in the labor market as a form of capital, especially for women of color.

Evelyn Nakano Glenn found that within the United States, race and gender have been constructed and maintained within two main institutions, citizenship and labor (Glenn 2002). The social construction of womanhood includes ideas about beauty, femininity, and fragility. Historically, racism and patriarchy defined women of color primarily as physical laborers (Hurtado 1996). "Blacks and certain Latina women came to the United States through slavery or conquest of their native land" (Hurtado 1996). According to Angela Davis, in order to extract the greatest labor from black women during the slave era, they had to be recast as unfeminine (Davis 1983). A similar discounting process took place among other women of color where they were assigned the dirty labor and physical labor as household domestics (Glenn 1992: 606). According to Glenn (1992), the notion that inherent traits made women of color well suited for certain types of work supported occupational segregation among women by race: "Racial characteristics effectively neutralized the racial-ethnic woman's womanhood" (1992, p. 630). Glenn points to historical patterns of racial specialization in employment wherein white women are preferred in positions requiring physical and social contact and women of color are preferred in dirty back-room jobs (Glenn 1992: 618).

So, the preference for fair skin is not simply aesthetically linked to beauty, but also to femininity. Darkness is associated with masculinity. Since beauty is defined on the basis of Eurocentric standards, characteristics such as light skin, light colored or long hair, thin lips, and an aquiline nose are perceived as beautiful. Race as a stratifying mechanism helps determine life chances. In American society, it is also established, at least in part, by visual markers such as skin color, hair texture, shape of nose, and lips. Skin color is the primary determinant of race (Brown, Dane, and Durham 1998). Privileges are allocated through the perceptions attached to skin color for African American women.

Skin color stratification is not a new phenomenon in the United States. It has historically played a significant role in determining the life chances of African Americans and other people of color (Freeman et al. 1966; Ransford 1970; Telles and Murguia 1990; Hughes and Hertel 1990; Keith and Herring 1991; Herring 2002). It has also been important to our understanding of race and the processes of racialization. The legacy of colonialism, racial oppression during slavery, legalized discrimination in the Jim Crow era, and de facto segregation in the post-civil-rights era have all functioned to create and perpetuate skin color stratification in communities of color. But the nature and extent of these effects have changed over time.

"Colorism" is the discriminatory treatment of individuals falling within the same "racial" group on the basis of skin color. It operates both intraracially and interracially. Intraracial colorism occurs when members of a racial group make distinctions based upon skin color between members of their own race. Interracial colorism occurs when members of one racial group make distinctions based upon skin color between members of another racial group. Colorism in the United States dates back at least to the colonial era (Cooper 1892; Du Bois 1903). It is a poisonous legacy of slavery and reflects the persistent Eurocentric bias in U.S. culture. Black people with lighter skin tones were born as a result of various forms of miscegenation since colonial times (Smith et al. 1999). For the most part, it has often been overshadowed by or subsumed within more general issues of racism and race relations.

Colorism—much like the notion of race itself—is historically contingent and based on supremacist assumptions. In the United States, color preferences are typically measured against putative European (i.e., white) standards. These preferences have involved physical features, including skin color, hair color and texture, thickness of lips, eye color, nose shapes, and other phenotypical features. For centuries, African Americans with European features have been exalted above those with dark or black complexions. People with straight or "good" hair have been admired above those with nappy, kinky, or "bad" hair.

Several early studies by scholars such as Drake and Cayton (1945) and Myrdal (1944) documented the importance of light skin tone in obtaining prestige within the black population. These studies demonstrated that higher-status blacks tended to be of lighter skin tone than lower-status blacks. Moreover, they demonstrated how lighter-skinned blacks were extended more social and economic amenities than the dominant group, and how this translated over successive generations into the black elite being of fairer complexion. In *The Black Bourgeoisie*, Frazier (1957) argued that lighter-skinned blacks (i.e., mulattoes) enjoyed a privileged status that was far beyond the reach of their darker-skinned counterparts. Although the initial origin of this preferential treatment is in dispute, Gunnar Myrdal (1944) suggested that whites probably found mulattoes more attractive, as they often possessed some European characteristics. He also suggested that since whites were believed to be intellectually superior, those blacks who were of mixed heritage would be at an advantage.

But these patterns are also historically contingent. For example, among blacks during the 1960s and 1970s, dark skin coloring lost its negative connotations and associated stereotypes. The term "black" became a unifying description of the entire race rather than a divisive term used in a derogatory manner, and slogans such as "Black is beautiful" were in vogue.

Unlike most studies that have only focused on the advantages of light skin tones, Hunter (2004) also discloses the often hidden disadvantages of light skin. She shows that light skin is associated with whites, assimilation, and a lack of racial consciousness, and thus some light-skinned people of color are judged as lacking loyalty and lacking racial consciousness. Because they are seen as not ethnically authentic enough, they may be ostracized from community organizations and gatherings. Although these disadvantages may not necessarily be economic in nature, the social, psychological toll it takes on light-skinned people of color can be quite high.

There is a growing literature on the effects of skin tone on mate selection and the marriage market (e.g., Udry, Bauman, and Case 1971; Hughes and Hertel 1990; Ross 1997; Hunter 2004; Edwards, Carter-Tellison, and Herring 2004). Few studies, however, have focused on the effects of colorism on the employment of women of color. In the current study, we focus on the experience of African American women, especially in the labor market. Generally, we posit that darker-skinned African American women are penalized in the labor market. In particular, we believe that skin color functions through racism based on value systems that developed during the slavery era. Because whiteness is privileged socially, culturally, and economically in society, we expect African American women with lighter complexions to experience privilege (relative to their darker counterparts) on the basis of their association with whiteness. We examine these issues below. First, however, we provide some basic information about our data and methods of analysis.

Data and Methods

The data source for this chapter is the 1995 Detroit Area Study. The 1,139 respondents in the 1995 Detroit Area Study were asked about their employment status, type of job, and other job-related questions. Respondents were also asked a battery of questions about race relations, and they were also asked for demographic information. In addition, interviewers recorded their observations about respondents' physical appearances, such as their skin complexion, their physical appearance, their height, and weight. We use only the data from the 393 African American women for whom information about their skin complexion, physical appearance, and labor-market-related information was collected. This data source makes it possible to examine the relationship between skin tone, beauty, and employment among African American women. These operationalizations and the variable labels (in all capital letters) are presented below.

Key Independent Variables

SKIN TONE was determined in two ways. African American respondents were asked: "Compared to most black people, what skin color do you believe you have? (1=very dark brown, 2=dark brown, 3=medium brown, 4=light brown, or 5=very light brown)." In addition, survey interviewers made observations and coded them using the same rating system.

The values for these two ratings were combined. Thus, skin tone was coded as ranging from 2 (very dark brown) to 10 (very light brown).

Skin color is not the only physical characteristic used to define phenotype. Other traits, such as hair color and texture, size of nose and lips, and eye color (Piza and Rosemburg 1999; Tumin and Feldman 1971) are also used. Thus, we take advantage of the existence of such traits in the 1995 DAS and make use of such traits in our analysis. When respondents have blue, green, hazel, or gray eyes, or when they have blond or red (strawberry-blond) hair, they were dummy variable coded 1 as having EURO TRAITS and 0 otherwise.

In order to measure BEAUTY, interviewers were instructed to assess respondents' physical appearance on a scale from 1 (physically attractive) to 7 (physically unattractive). Scores were reverse coded so that BEAUTY ranges from a low of 1 to a high of 7.

Finally, survey interviewers made observations about respondents' WEIGHT and coded their observations on a scale ranging from (1) underweight to (7) overweight.

Dependent Variables

In order to assess treatment, especially at work, we included several dependent variables. To determine whether respondents were the objects of harassment, they were asked whether they had been HASSLED AT WORK: "Please tell me whether or not you were HASSLED AT WORK in the past month or so." Responses were coded 1 if the respondent had been HASSLED AT WORK and 0 otherwise.

To assess respondents' treatment in terms of retention and promotion, they were asked, "Do you think you have ever been UNFAIRLY fired or denied a promotion?" Those who responded yes were coded 1, and others were coded 0.

Respondents were also asked about their TREATMENT BY WHITES, i.e., their treatment because of their appearance. Specifically, they were asked, "Because of the shade of your skin color, do you think white people treat you a lot better, somewhat better, no different, somewhat worse, or a lot worse than other blacks?" Responses were coded in five categories: (1) treated a lot better, (2) treated somewhat better, (3) treated the same, (4) treated somewhat worse, and (5) treated a lot worse.

To measure TREATMENT BY BLACKS, they were also asked, "Because of the shade of your skin color, do you think black people treat you a lot better, somewhat better, no different, somewhat worse, or a lot worse than other blacks?" Responses were coded in five categories: (1) treated a lot better, (2) treated somewhat better, (3) treated the same, (4) treated somewhat worse, and (5) treated a lot worse.

Control Variables

EDUCATION was measured by responses to the question: "What is the highest grade of school or year of college you have completed?" Categories ranged from 0 (none) to 17 (graduate study).

Marital status was dichotomized between those who were currently MARRIED (coded 1) and others (coded 0).

Respondents were asked: "What was the month, day, and year of your birth?" AGE was measured in years from 18 through 96.

The survey also asked respondents about the racial type of their jobs: "Do you think your job is one that people of your ethnic or racial group tend to get more than people of other groups?" Those who said that they worked in predominantly BLACK JOBS were coded 1, and others were coded 0.

Respondents were also asked about the racial composition of their work groups: "Is your work group all black, mostly black, about half black and half white, mostly white, or all white?" Those who said they worked in groups that were mostly or all BLACK WORKGROUPS were coded 1, and others were coded 0.

ANALYSIS AND RESULTS

Is there a relationship between skin tone, appearance, and the treatment of African American women at work? Figure 8.1 illustrates the relationship between African American women's skin tone and reports of treatment by whites, treatment by blacks, being hassled at work, and being unfairly fired or denied a promotion. The first row of this diagram shows that among African American women, the lighter their skin tone, the less likely were they to say that they were treated worse by whites. In particular, more than one in five (23 percent) of those with dark complexions say they are treated worse by whites. This compares with 7 percent of those with medium complexions and 3 percent of those with light complexions. The second row of this diagram shows a substantially different relationship between skin tone and treatment by blacks. In this case, women with light complexion (27 percent) are the most likely to report worse treatment by blacks, and those with medium complexions (7 percent) are the

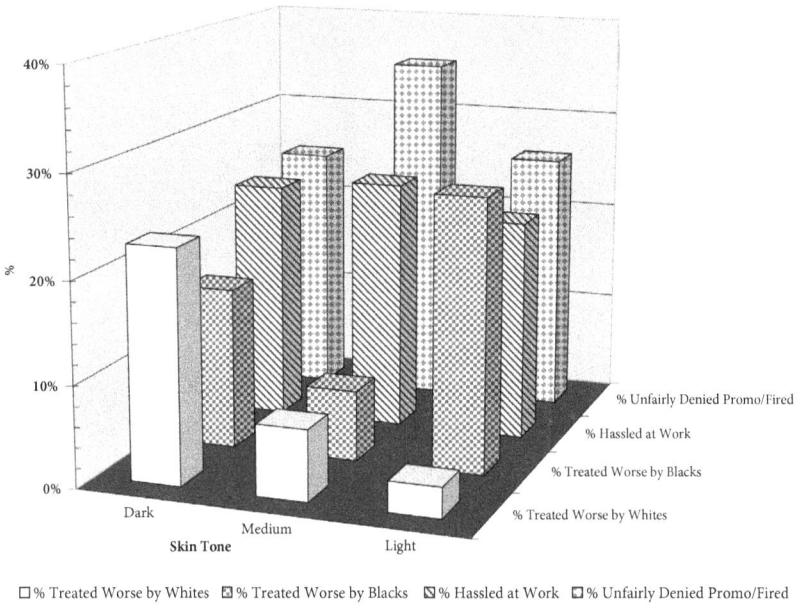

Figure 8.1: Treatment of African American Women at Work by Skin Tone.

least likely to say that they are treated worse by blacks. The third row suggests that there are few differences in being hassled at work by skin tone, as 24 percent of those with dark complexions, 25 percent of those with medium complexions, and 22 percent of those with light complexions say that they are hassled at work. The fourth row presents the relationship between skin tone and reports of being unfairly denied promotion or being fired. In this case, women with medium complexions are most likely to report being unfairly denied promotion or being fired, as 35 percent of those with medium complexions report such unfair treatment, and 25 percent of those with dark complexions and 26 percent of those with light complexions report being treated unfairly in their employment situation.

Figure 8.2 shows the relationship between African American women's beauty and reports of treatment by whites, treatment by blacks, being hassled at work, and being unfairly fired or denied a promotion. The first row of this diagram shows that among African American women, 15 percent of those with below average appearances say that they are treated

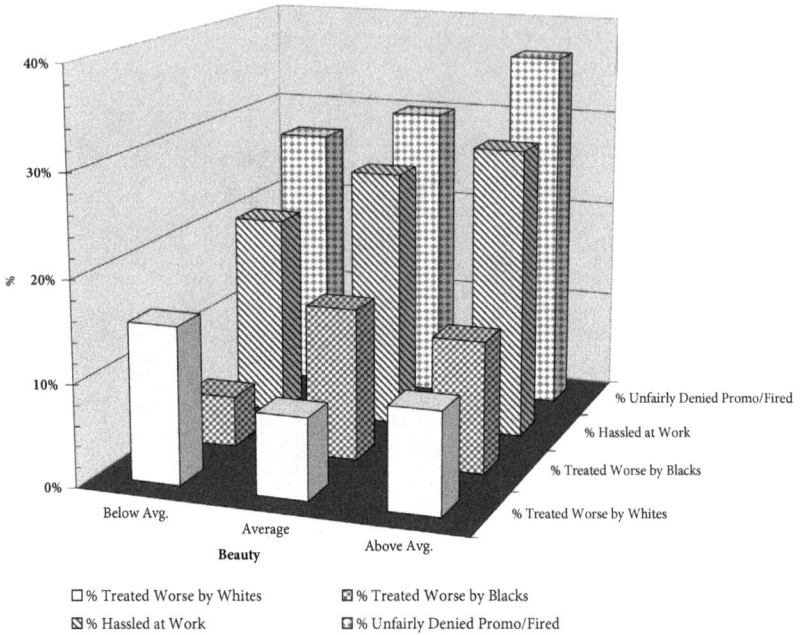

Figure 8.2: Treatment of African American Women at Work by Beauty.

worse by whites compared with 8 percent of those with average appearances and 10 percent of those with above-average appearances. The second row of this diagram shows that 15 percent of African American women with average appearances report being treated worse by blacks compared with 5 percent of those with below-average appearances and 10 percent of those with above-average appearances. The third row suggests that the more attractive a woman is judged to be, the more likely she is to report being hassled at work, as 20 percent of those with below-average appearances, 26 percent of those with average appearances, and 29 percent of those with above-average appearances report being hassled at work. The fourth row presents the relationship between appearance and reports of being unfairly denied promotion or being fired. Again, the results suggest that the more attractive a woman is judged to be, the more likely she is to report being treated unfairly at work, as 27 percent of those with below-average appearances, 30 percent of those with average appearances, and 37 percent of those with above-average appearances report being unfairly denied a promotion or being fired.

Table 8.1 presents two sets of relationships simultaneously: it summarizes the relationship between skin tone and African American women's treatment at work, controlling for beauty. It also displays the relationship between beauty and African American women's treatment at work, controlling for skin tone. Thus, for each cell in the table, there are at least two important comparisons: (1) across columns within a given panel (to examine the effects of skin tone) and (2) across panels but within columns within a skin tone (to examine the effects of beauty). Among women with below-average appearances, skin tone does not appear to have a systematic relationship to whether African American women report being hassled at work, as roughly one in five African American women with below-average appearances reports being hassled at work (20–21.7 percent), irrespective of her skin tone. Among those with average appearances, there appears to be a modest pattern such that those with dark complexions (29 percent) are more likely than those with medium complexions (27 percent) and those with light complexions (19 percent) to report being hassled at work. And among those with light complexions, this pattern appears to be a bit more pronounced, as 38 percent of those with dark complexions, 31 percent of those with medium complexions, and 22 percent of those with light complexions report being hassled at work. In addition, there is a general tendency for reports of being hassled to increase with more attractive appearances even when controlling for skin tone. For example, 20 percent of those with below-average appearances and dark skin report being hassled at work compared with 29 percent of those with average appearances and dark skin tone, and 38 percent of those with above-average appearances and dark skin tone.

Table 8.1 also presents the percentage of African American women reporting that they have unfairly been denied a promotion or been fired by skin tone and level of beauty. Within levels of beauty, there are no systematic patterns with respect to being unfairly denied a promotion or being fired by skin tone. Within various skin tones, however, there do appear to be links between levels of beauty and being treated unfairly. In particular, among those with dark complexions, the more attractive African American women are judged to be, the more likely they are to report being unfairly denied promotions or being fired unfairly. This same basic pattern also holds true for African American women with medium complexions or light complexions.

When controlling for skin tone variations, it is more difficult to discern any "beauty effects" when examining African American women's treatment by whites. There are, however, rather evident skin tone effects within

Table 8.1: Treatment of African American Women at Work by Skin Tone and Beauty.

| | Beauty | | | | | | | | | | | |
| Treatment of African American Women | Below Average Skin Tone | | | Average Skin Tone | | | Above Average Skin Tone | | | Overall Skin Tone | | |
	Dark	Medium	Light	Dark	Medium	Light	Dark	Medium	Light	Dark	Medium	Light
% Hassled at Work	20.0%	20.0%	21.7%	28.6%	26.9%	18.8%	37.5%	31.3%	21.7%	23.8%	24.9%	21.9%
% Unfairly Denied Promo/ Fired	13.3%	32.8%	21.7%	25.0%	33.3%	25.0%	44.4%	38.0%	30.4%	25.0%	35.3%	26.0%
% Treated Worse by Whites	26.7%	4.9%	0.0%	14.8%	3.2%	0.0%	12.7%	10.6%	8.7%	23.2%	7.2%	2.8%
% Treated Worse by Blacks	26.7%	9.8%	13.1%	10.7%	4.3%	25.0%	33.3%	8.0%	38.1%	16.2%	7.5%	26.8%

levels of beauty. For example, among those who are judged as having below-average appearances, 27 percent of those with dark skin tones, 5 percent of those with medium skin tones, and 0 percent of those with light skin tones report that they are treated worse by whites. Among those with average appearances, 15 percent of those with dark complexions, 3 percent of those with medium complexions, and 0 percent of those with light complexions report being treated worse by whites. And among those judged as having above-average beauty, 13 percent of those with dark complexions, 11 percent of those with medium complexions, and 9 percent of those with light complexions report being treated worse by whites.

Finally, Table 8.1 shows that African American women with medium complexions appear to be less likely than their darker and lighter counterparts to report worse treatment by blacks, irrespective of their level of beauty. Moreover, those with average appearances are generally less likely to report worse treatment by blacks than those judged as better looking or worse looking, irrespective of skin tone.

Although interesting, the descriptive statistics presented thus far do not provide much information about the net impact of skin tone and beauty on the treatment of African American women at work. In order to address these issues more rigorously, Tables 8.2–8.5 present the results from multivariate analysis. Table 8.2 presents four logistic regression models that predict the log odds of being hassled at work. Model I presents the bivariate relationship between skin tone and being hassled at work. Model II presents the bivariate relationship between beauty and being hassled. Model III estimates the effects of skin tone and beauty simultaneously and adds additional control variables. And model IV includes an interaction term for skin tone and beauty. Model I of Table 8.2 indicates that there is no systematic relationship between skin tone and being hassled at work for African American women. Model II, however, suggests that the more attractive a woman is, the more likely she is to report that she is hassled at work. This relationship is marginally significant ($p < .1$) but becomes non-significant when other factors (such as education, age, marital status, having European features, racial type of one's job, and racial composition of one's work group) are taken into consideration (in model III). Model IV tests the possibility that skin tone and beauty interact to affect the degree to which African American women are hassled at work. In this particular case, however, there is no significant effect of this interaction, and neither skin tone nor beauty has an effect on being hassled, net of other factors. We should also note that in both models III and IV, having more education, working in a predominantly black job, and working in a

Table 8.2: Logistic Regression Models Predicting the Log Odds of Being Hassled at Work with Skin Tone and Beauty, Net of Sociodemographic and Workplace Characteristics.[a]

Independent Variables	Hassled at Work			
	Model I	Model II	Model III	Model IV
Constant	-1.241***	-1.741***	-2.175***	-2.228
Skin Tone	.016		.028	.006
Beauty		.134*	.107	.080
Skin Tone by Beauty				.005
Weight			$-.014$	.029
Education			.109**	.109**
Age			$-.033$***	$-.033$***
Married			$-.627$**	$-.632$**
Euro Traits			$-.242$	$-.245$
Black Job			.559**	.554**
Black Work Group			1.221***	1.224***
R^2 Analog	.001	.004*	.148***	.148***
N	393	393	393	393

* $p < .1$ ** $p < .05$ *** $p < .01$

[a] Coefficients are unstandardized. For the dummy (binary) variable coefficients, significance levels refer to the difference between the omitted dummy variable category and the coefficient for the given category.

[b] The R^2 Analog statistic is the proportion of reduction in a baseline model X^2 (a model fitting only the constant term) attributable to the model shown. It is calculated as follows: $R^2 = $ (Baseline model X^2 − Selected model X^2)/ Baseline model X^2.

predominantly black work group all significantly increase the likelihood of being hassled at work, and being older and married significantly decreases such prospects.

Table 8.3 puts forward four logistic regression models that predict the log odds of being unfairly fired or denied a promotion. Model I suggests that there is no systematic relationship between skin tone and believing that one has been unfairly fired or denied a promotion. Model II, however, suggests that there is a marginally significant relationship between beauty and the belief that one has been unfairly fired or denied a promotion (p < 0.1): the more attractive a woman is, the more likely she is to report that she has been unfairly fired or denied a promotion. Model III shows, however, that this relationship is reduced to non-significance when other factors are taken into consideration. But the apparent relationship between

Table 8.3: Logistic Regression Models Predicting the Log Odds of Being Unfairly Fired or Denied a Promotion With Skin Tone and Beauty, Net of Sociodemographic and Workplace Characteristics.[a]

Independent Variables	Unfairly Fired or Denied a Promotion			
	Model I	Model II	Model III	Model IV
Constant	$-.556^*$	-1.255^{***}	-1.690^{**}	-3.476^{**}
Skin Tone	$-.034$		$-.068$	$.216$
Beauty		$.110^*$	$.089$	$.489^*$
Skin Tone by Beauty				$-.063$
Weight			$-.112$	$-.052$
Education			$.125^{***}$	$.123^{***}$
Age			$-.009$	$-.009$
Married			$-.327$	$-.305$
Euro Traits			$-.329$	$-.314$
Black Job			$.049$	$.068$
Black Work Group			$.364^*$	$.350^*$
R^2 Analog	$.001$	$.004^*$	$.036^{**}$	$.039^{**}$
N	393	393	393	393

* p < .1 ** p < .05 *** p < .01

[a] Coefficients are unstandardized. For the dummy (binary) variable coefficients, significance levels refer to the difference between the omitted dummy variable category and the coefficient for the given category.

[b] The R^2 Analog statistic is the proportion of reduction in a baseline model X^2 (a model fitting only the constant term) attributable to the model shown. It is calculated as follows:

$$R^2 = (\text{Baseline model } X^2 - \text{Selected model } X^2)/ \text{ Baseline model } X^2.$$

beauty and unfair treatment returns when the skin tone by beauty interaction term is added in model IV. Having more education and working in a predominantly black work group increases the likelihood of being unfairly fired or denied a promotion.

Table 8.4 provides four Ordinary Least Squares (OLS) regression models that predict whites' treatment of African American women by skin tone and beauty, net of sociodemographic and workplace characteristics. Model I indicates that the lighter a woman's complexion, the better is the treatment she receives from whites (p < 0.01). Model II shows that the more attractive an African American woman is, the worse she is treated by

Table 8.4: OLS Regression Models Predicting Worse Treatment by Whites with Skin Tone and Beauty, Net of Sociodemographic and Workplace Characteristics.[a]

Independent Variables	Treated Worse by Whites			
	Model I	Model II	Model III	Model IV
Constant	3.769***	2.789***	3.624***	3.637***
Skin Tone	-.142***		-.146***	-.159***
Beauty		.029*	.053***	.035
Skin Tone by Beauty				.003
Weight			-.035	-.006
Education			.010	.010
Age			-.001	-.001
Married			-.105*	-.106**
Euro Traits			-.051	-.053
Black Job			.097	.098
Black Work Group			-.120**	-.121**
R^2	.143***	.004*	.168***	.168***
N	393	393	393	393

* $p < .1$ ** $p < .05$ *** $p < .01$

[a] Coefficients are unstandardized. For the dummy (binary) variable coefficients, significance levels refer to the difference between the omitted dummy variable category and the coefficient for the given category.

whites at work ($p < 0.1$). When the effects of African American women's skin tone and beauty are considered simultaneously and net of sociodemographics and workplace characteristics, their relationship to treatment by whites becomes stronger: women with lighter complexions generally receive better treatment ($p < 0.01$) and women who are more attractive receive worse treatment ($p < 0.01$). Nevertheless, the interaction term in model IV does not significantly improve the fit of the model.

Table 8.5 presents four OLS regression models that predict blacks' treatment of African American women by skin tone and beauty, net of sociodemographic and workplace characteristics. Model I-III suggests no significant relationship between skin tone and treatment by blacks nor beauty and treatment by blacks. Model IV, however, indicates that the lighter a woman's complexion and the more attractive she is, the better is

Table 8.5: OLS Regression Models Predicting Worse Treatment by Blacks with Skin Tone and Beauty, Net of Sociodemographic and Workplace Characteristics.[a]

Independent Variables	Treated Worse by Blacks			
	Model I	Model II	Model III	Model IV
Constant	2.968***	2.996***	2.842***	3.847***
Skin Tone	.010		.009	−.131**
Beauty		.008	.019	−.181**
Skin Tone by Beauty				.031***
Weight			.055*	.030
Education			−.010	−.009
Age			.002	.002
Married			−.125**	−.138**
Euro Traits			.094	.091
Black Job			.029	.024
Black Work Group			.003	.006
R^2	.009	.004	.026*	.035**
N	393	393	393	393

* $p < .1$ ** $p < .05$ *** $p < .01$

[a] Coefficients are unstandardized. For the dummy (binary) variable coefficients, significance levels refer to the difference between the omitted dummy variable category and the coefficient for the given category.

the treatment she receives from blacks ($p < 0.05$). In addition, there is a significant interaction between skin tone and beauty such that women who are both lighter and considered more beautiful will receive somewhat worse treatment by blacks ($p < 0.01$).

In general, the results suggest that skin tone and beauty are related to how African American women are treated at work. For example, the more attractive an African American woman is, the more likely she is to report that she is hassled at work. This pattern disappears, however, when other factors are taken into consideration. Similarly, when we take into consideration the interaction between skin tone and beauty, the more attractive an African American woman is considered to be, the more likely she is to report that she has been unfairly fired or denied a promotion. The results also suggest that the treatment accorded to African American women differs depending on whether they are interacting with whites or blacks. When interacting with whites, African-American women with lighter complexions generally receive better treatment, and those who are considered more attractive receive worse treatment. When interacting with blacks, the lighter an African-American woman's complexion and the more attractive she is, the better is the treatment she receives from blacks (although this is offset to some degree among those who are both lighter and considered more beautiful).

CONCLUSIONS

This chapter began with a discussion about the potentially detrimental effects of the "beauty myth." It examined Wolf's (1991) argument that beauty is an important form of capital for women in the labor market that can be used to undermine women's advancement and to legitimize employment discrimination against women. The chapter also pointed out that beauty is not only gendered, but that it is also racialized. Given the racialized nature of beauty and its potentially important role in the workplace, the chapter posed the following questions: How does the beauty myth affect the workplace treatment of African American women? Is there a systematic bias in favor of women who more closely approximate the traditional European standard of beauty? Specifically, do those with lighter complexions or more physical attractiveness receive better treatment? Are they more likely to be hassled at work? Are those with darker complexions more likely to be unfairly fired or denied promotions?

This study used data from African American women in the 1995 Detroit Area Study to determine whether skin tone and other aspects of physical appearance are related to reports of being unfairly fired or denied promotions, being hassled at work, or being treated badly by whites or blacks. Generally, the results suggest that skin tone and beauty are related to how African American women are treated at work. In particular, we found that when we take into consideration the interaction between skin tone and beauty, the more attractive an African American woman is considered to be, the more likely she is to report that she has been unfairly fired or denied a promotion. The results also suggest that the treatment accorded to African American women differs depending on whether they are interacting with whites or blacks. When interacting with whites, African American women with lighter complexions generally receive better treatment and those who are considered more attractive receive worse treatment. When interacting with blacks, the lighter an African American woman's complexion and the more attractive she is, the better is the treatment she receives from blacks.

Consistent with Hunter's (2004) formulation of skin color as a form of capital, light skinned African American women are able to use this characteristic to secure more favorable treatment from whites and blacks. Curiously, though, light skin tone and beauty tend to reinforce each other in terms of the kind of treatment they elicit from blacks, but they appear to counterbalance each other in terms of the kinds of treatment they bring forth from whites. In other words, the effects of intraracial colorism and beauty appear to differ somewhat.

Also, similar to Hunter's (2004) insights about light skin tone presenting both advantages and disadvantages, our analysis discloses that beauty also has some disadvantages for attractive African American women. They report higher rates of being hassled at work, and they are more likely to report that they are unfairly denied promotions and fired. These disadvantages appear to point to a "beauty effect," but not quite in the way suggested by Wolf's (1991) "beauty myth." That is, although skin tone and beauty appear to be important to African American women's treatment on the job, it is not always the "fairest" women who receive the most favorable treatment in terms of being hassled on the job or in terms of job retention and promotion. Still, it is lighter complexioned and more attractive African American women who also report more favorable treatment both from whites and blacks generally. Future research will need to specify the conditions under which light skin tone and physical attractiveness lead to better treatment and when it leads to worse treatment. Researchers will also want to determine whether these patterns hold true for other racial and ethnic groups.

REFERENCES

Banks, Ingrid H. 2000. *Hair Matters: Beauty, Power, and Black Women's Consciousness*. New York: New York University Press.

Bourdieu, Pierre. 1986. "Forms of Capital." Pp. 241–258 in *Handbook of Theory and Research for the Sociology of Education*. edited by John G. Richardson. Westport, Conn.: Greenwood Press.

Brown, Terry D, Jr, Francis C. Dane and Marcus D. Durham. 1998. "Perception of Race and Ethnicity." *Journal of Social Behavior and Personality* 13: 295–306.

Cooper, Anna Julia. [1892] 1988. *A Voice from the South*. New York: Oxford University Press, in collaboration with the Schomburg Center for Research in Black Culture.

Craig, Maxine Leeds. 2002. *Ain't I A Beauty Queen?: Black Women, Beauty, and the Politics of Race*. Oxford University Press.

Davis, Angela Y. 1983. *Women, Race & Class*. New York: Vintage Books.

Dion, K., E. Bersheid, & E.H. Walster. 1972. "What is beautiful is good." *Journal of Personality and Social Psychology*. 24: 285–290.

Drake, St. Clair and Horace R. Cayton. 1945. *Black Metropolis*. Harcourt Brace.

Du Bois, W.E. Burghart. 1903. "The Talented Tenth." Chapter 2 of *The Negro Problem*. New York: James Pott and Company.

Edwards, Korie, Katrina Carter-Tellison, and Cedric Herring. 2004. "For Richer, For Poorer, Whether Dark or Light: Skin Tone, Marital Status, and Spouse's Earnings." Pp. 65–81 in *Skin Deep: How Race and Color Matter in the "Color-Blind" Era*. C. Herring, V. Keith, and H.D. Horton (eds). Chicago and Urbana-Champaign, IL: IRRPP and University of Illinois Press.

Frazier, E. Franklin. 1957. *The Black Bourgeoisie*. New York: Free Press.

Freeman, Howard E., J. Michael Ross, David Armor, and Thomas F. Pettigrew. 1966. "Color Gradations and Attitudes Among Middle-Income Negroes." *American Sociological Review* 31: 365–374.

Glenn, Evelyn N. 2002. *Unequal Freedom: How Race and Gender Shaped American Citizenship and Labor*. Cambridge, Mass.: Harvard University Press.

———. 1992. "From Servitude to Service Work: Historical Continuities in the Racial Division of Paid Reproductive Labor." *Signs: Journal of Women in Culture and Society*. 18: 599–641.

Harris, Cheryl. 1995. "Whiteness as Property." Pp. 126–142 in *Critical Race Theory*. K. Crenshaw, N. Gotanda, G. Peller, and K. Thomas (eds.). New York: The New Press.

Herring, Cedric. 2002. "Bleaching Out the Color Line?: The Skin Color Continuum and the Tripartite Model of Race." *Race and Society* 5: 17–31.

Hughes, Michael and Bradley Hertel. 1990. "The Significance of Color Remains: A Study of Life Chances, Mate Selection, and Ethnic Consciousness Among Black Americans." *Social Forces* 69: 1105–1120.

Hunter, Margaret L. 2004. "Light, Bright, and Almost White: The Advantages and Disadvantages of Light Skin." Pp. 22–44 in *Skin Deep: How Race and Color Matter in the "Color-Blind" Era*. C. Herring, V. Keith, and H.D. Horton (eds). Chicago and Urbana-Champaign, IL: IRRPP and University of Illinois Press.

Hunter, Margaret L. 2002. " 'If You're Light You're Alright': Light Skin Color as Social Capital for Women of Color." *Gender & Society* 16: 175–193.

Hunter, Margaret L. 1998. Colorstruck: Skin Color Stratification in the Lives of African-American Women. *Social Inquiry* 68: 517–535.

Hurtado, Aida. 1996. *The Color of Privilege: Three Blasphemies on Race and Feminism*. Ann Arbor, MI: University of Michigan Press.

Keith, Verna M. and Cedric Herring. 1991. "Skin Tone and Stratification in the Black Community." *American Journal of Sociology* 97: 760–779.

Myrdal, Gunnar. 1944. *An American Dilemma: The Negro Problem and Modern Democracy* New York: Harper and Row.

Palmer, Phyllis Marynick. 1983. "White women/black women: the dualism of female identity and experience in the United States." *Feminist Studies* 9: 151–170.

Piza, Edith and Fulvia Rosemburg. 1999. "Color in the Brazilian Census." Pp. 37–52 in *Race in Contemporary Brazil,* edited by Rebecca Reichmann. University Park, PA: Pennsylvania State University Press.

Ransford, Edward H. 1970. "Skin Color, and Life Chances, and Anti-White Attitudes." *Social Problems* 18: 164–178.

Ross, Louie E. 1997. "Mate Selection Preferences Among African-American College Students." *Journal of Black Studies* 27: 554–569.

Smith, Barbara, Gloria Steinem, Gwendolyn Mink, Marysa Navarro, and Wilma Mankiller (Eds.). 1999. *Reader's Companion to U.S. Women's History*. New York: Houghton Mifflin Company.

Telles, Edward E. and Edward Murguia. 1990. Phenotypic Discrimination and Income Differences Among Mexican Americans." *Social Science Quarterly* 71: 682–96.

Thompson, Maxine S. and Verna Keith. 2004. "Copper Brown and Blue Black: Colorism and Self-Evaluation." Pp. 45–64 in *Skin Deep: How Race and Color Matter in the "Color-Blind" Era*. C. Herring, V. Keith, and H.D. Horton (eds). Chicago and Urbana-Champaign, IL: IRRPP and University of Illinois Press.

Thompson, Maxine S. and Verna Keith. 2001. "The Blacker the Berry: Gender, Skin Tone, Self-Esteem, and Self-Efficacy." *Gender & Society* 15: 336–357.

Tumin, Melvin M. and Arnold S. Feldman. 1971. *Social Class and Social Change in Puerto Rico*. Indianapolis: Bobbs-Merrill.

Udry, J. Richard, Karl E. Bauman and Charles Case. 1971. "Skin Color, Status and Mate Selection." *American Journal of Sociology* 76: 722–733.

Wallace-Sanders, Kimberly Gisele (Eds.). 2002. *Skin Deep, Spirit Strong: The Black Female Body in American Culture*. Ann Arbor: University of Michigan Press.

Watson, Elwood and Darcy Martin (Eds.). 2004. *There She Is, Miss America: The Politics of Sex, Beauty, and Race and America's most Famous Pageant*. New York: Palgrave MacMillan.

Webster, Jr., Murray and James E. Driskell, Jr.1983. "Beauty as Status" *American Journal of Sociology* 89: 140.

Wolf, Naomi. 1991. *The Beauty Myth: How Images of Beauty are Used Against Women*. New York, NY: Doubleday.

CHAPTER NINE

TRAINING BLACK MEDIAMAKERS AFTER KERNER: *THE BLACK JOURNAL* WORKSHOP

Devorah Heitner

They [the news media] have not communicated to a majority of their audience—which is white—a sense of the degradation, misery, and hopelessness of living in the ghetto. They have not communicated to whites a feeling for the difficulties and frustrations of being a Negro in the United States.
Report of the National Commission on Civil Disorders, 1968

This chapter focuses on the history of black media training programs created in the wake of the Kerner Commission Report. Together with the movement toward Black public affairs television, the initiation of training programs and other new avenues to media careers constitutes a powerful and lasting result of the struggle for Black media representation. The regularity of uprisings each summer during the 1960s made clear that the "War on Poverty" sponsored by President Lyndon Johnson was not enough to stem the tide of black discontent. In 1967, President Johnson appointed a committee led by Illinois governor Otto Kerner to investigate the civil disorders that rocked American cities from Los Angeles to Newark in the years from 1964 to 1968. The Kerner Commission's report (1968) offered an analysis of a racially polarized country in which black discontent was growing.[1] The report found that the uprisings were the result of racism that created poor living conditions for African Americans and recommended broad changes in federal policy to improve schools, health care, housing, and employment outlooks for black people.

Chapter 15 of the report focused on the mass media, calling for change in clear terms. The Kerner Commission took print and broadcast media to task for exacerbating the riots by sensationalizing them and ignoring their root causes. They also criticized media outlets for sending poorly prepared

---

[1] Henceforth, referred to as the Kerner Report.

reporters into riots with no real understanding of the issues that caused the "civil disorders." The report's recommendations for hiring black journalists and for community collaboration, such as meetings between journalists, community residents, and police continue to reverberate in the media industries, despite a significant backlash. It is a testament to the impact of the uprisings and the fear they engendered that so many in positions of power were willing to consider the recommendations and criticisms of the Kerner Report.

Producing Black Media Workers

The history of pervasive anti-Black discrimination in the television unions made training programs vital as alternative credentialing sites. The emergence of numerous tuition-free, minority-oriented broadcast training programs in this era presented interested students with the opportunity to join a burgeoning field that had previously been almost completely inaccessible to them. The training programs gave hundreds of black media workers (and a significant number of Latinos as well) the skills they would need to enter media professions. In New York City alone there were numerous other training programs, from the film-oriented Third World Film Institute and Community Film Workshop to the journalism-oriented Michele Clark Institute[2] and several other programs that offered workshops and classes in broadcast or print media to African Americans. There were also training programs in Boston,[3] Chicago, Los Angeles, and other cities.[4] Some universities and television stations offered tuition-free television training programs specifically to train "minority" journalists, producers and technicians. Many of these workshops focused on preparing students for specific jobs in the film and television industries from editors to cinematographers. Support for these programs came from

---

[2] Named for a young graduate of the program who died tragically, the Michele Clark program trained black journalists at Columbia University and offered guaranteed placement to graduates. Al Deleon, "Showdown in Morningside Heights," *Black Enterprise* (1974).

[3] Kay Bourne, "A New Film School to Begin April 1 at Tubman House," *Bay State Banner* (March 9, 1978). Earlier in the decade, probably around 1970, a consortium of stations in Boston put together a thirty-three-week training program for thirteen black technicians. Undated memo in Corporation for Public Broadcasting Archives, College Park, Maryland.

[4] Merritt, "Black Efforts for Soul in Television." See also: "Black Filmmakers Work Under O. Davis," *Chicago Daily Defender* (March 13, 1970). This article describes an innovative mentorship program that sent three young media makers to Africa. One of them, Topper Carew, later became the executive producer of *Say Brother* in the early 1970s.

governmental agencies and private foundations, with the Ford Foundation offering major funding for several of these programs.

One of the most prominent training programs among the many that Black media activists demanded and created in this era was the Black Journal Workshop (later called the National Educational Television Training School), which was affiliated with the national television program, *Black Journal. Black Journal,* as the first national Black public affairs television program, had a strong interest in creating a pool of trained graduates to hire to work on the show, and they employed many graduates of the school. Additionally, being in the midst of a radical black production contributed to students' political consciousness and offered an embodiment of the possibility for transforming television from the inside out. Graduates describe an aura of possibility permeating the workshop. Despite the *Black Journal* Workshop's small size (relative to some of the other programs) and minimal funding, it fostered the careers of many individuals who have made their mark in television and film careers.[5] The workshop produced an exceptional number of long-standing and prolific media makers, creating a network of Black media professionals who were able to hire, train, and collaborate with one another.

Among these schools, the *Black Journal* Workshop is notable for graduating a number of directors and producers in addition to many successful cinematographers and other production and technical workers. Whether trained on the job at or in a training program such as *Black Journal* Workshop, Third World Film Institute, or Community Film Workshop, black media workers who began their careers between 1968 and 1978 contributed to an unprecedented period of opportunity for "minority" media workers. Their shared experiences at black television shows and in training programs fostered a sense of critical community that continues to nurture their careers. The veteran media makers interviewed for this volume continue to make an impact through their own productivity and by their mentorship of other media makers. The interviews survey the conditions that shaped, encouraged, and discouraged the careers of the interviewees, offering context crucial to understanding both the history and the present for African American media makers.

---

[5] Notably, the program was much smaller in scale than the Community Film Workshop, which at its height had seven sites nationally and is still in existence. Some of the funding for *Black Journal* Workshop came from the Corporation for Public Broadcasting and the New York Foundation. (See Fritz Jacobi, "NET Press Release," Wednesday, February 18, 1970.).

The history of the *Black Journal* Workshop shows that the workshop served as more than a technical training ground for black producers, directors, cinematographers, technicians, and journalists, but also a political and intellectual foundation to life as a black media maker in a frequently hostile environment. The fact that film and television training programs received funding from the Department of Labor signals that federal employment antidiscrimination measures had an effect on the world of media employment. This context of affirmative action created new opportunities both for creating training programs and for employment of the graduates of those programs.

Black Journal Workshop—Boot Camp for Media Makers

The students at the *Black Journal* Workshop were participants in a much larger set of changes in training and hiring practices in the broadcast industry. In the decade following 1968, minority employment in broadcast professions grew at an unprecedented rate—a rate of growth that the industry has not seen since that era. For example, the percentage of African Americans working in local television almost doubled between 1971 and 1981, moving from 5.9 percent of total staff members to 10.2 percent.[6] However, the following decade saw this percentage rise only from 10.2 percent to 10.4 percent. In 1997, the percentage had grown only to 10.9 percent.[7] Thus, the 1970s were the period of the most rapid growth in "minority" employment in the field of American broadcasting. Tuition-free, specialized training programs for black and Latino media workers, such as the *Black Journal* Workshop, facilitated this growth.

This community of alumni continues to foster collaborations among its members, who have created feature films, documentaries, and television programs such as *Let the Church Say Amen*, 1974; *Watermelon Man*, 1969; *Hill Street Blues*, 1981–1987; *Eyes on the Prize*, 1987; *Good Morning America*, 1975–present; *Making Do the Right Thing*, 1989; *Martin*, 1992; *Dave Chappelle: Killin' Them Softly*, 2000; and *Let the Spirits Dance Mambo*, 2003.[8] Many graduates worked for NET's black programs, *Black Journal* and *Soul!*, and several graduates went to work at other black public-affairs programs, such as ABC's *Like It Is* and NBC's *Positively Black*.[9]

---

[6] Ibid.

[7] Ibid.

[8] Jacobi mentions recent *Black Journal* Workshop graduate Jim Morris, who worked on Melvin Van Peebles' *Watermelon Man*.

[9] This graduate was Vernon West. See Jacobi, p. 2.

The impact of this cohort extends beyond their long list of production credits, as many of them have trained and mentored other media makers. They have taught on the job in film studios and television programs, as well as by starting independent production companies that employed and trained other media makers. Additionally, several graduates of the *Black Journal* Workshop teach at university film programs, including New York University's Cinema Studies Department, as well as community-based programs.[10]

The pedagogy of the *Black Journal* Workshop nourished a sense of community among its students that sustained some of its members through encounters with the racism in the broadcast industry. Many of the workshop alumni who confronted racial barriers and hostility in the industry responded by starting their own production companies or creating alternative career networks. These new workers challenged broadcast and film industries to expand and change, and simultaneously were politicized by their experiences.[11] According to numerous graduates, the curriculum of empowerment and resistance at the school was as important as the technical curriculum. The workshop fostered the leadership potential and talent that it sought in its applicants. These newly minted black media workers challenged television hierarchies from the inside: transforming genres, challenging industry racism, and fighting or circumventing union hegemony.

Historical Exclusions and New Regulations

While union membership would later provide some African Americans with good pay and benefits in the broadcast industry, in the 1960s the unions were perhaps the single greatest barrier to black participation in media careers. Known for a history of racism and insularity, they effectively prevented African Americans from entering these "father-son" organizations.[12] They also excluded daughters of any race, as Madeline

[10] For example, Ronald Gray is currently on the faculty at New York University's film school.

[11] The changes that the school brought about, as well as the larger climate of black media activism and affirmative action made in the lives of its students, became apparent to me after conducting oral history interviews with eight graduates of the NET school, including Ronald Gray, Danny Dawson, Bahati Best, Bobby Shepard, and Angela Fontanez.

[12] For an exploration of the ways in which unions excluded African Americans and women, see MacLean. MacLean's account of exclusionary tactics by unions in industries such as construction has strong parallels to the kinds of barriers union members constructed to exclude women of all ethnicities and African American men from

Anderson, who fought her way into the editors' local union earlier in the 1960s, points out.[13] They were gatekeepers to broadcast professions, and few stations could or would hire nonunion workers.

Jessie Maple, who successfully sued the New York cinematographers' union to gain entry in 1973, wrote: "For minorities, the union has been more harmful than helpful in terms of this group's getting behind the camera jobs. This is true because of the union's method of excluding women and other minorities by maintaining a 'closed' union situation."[14,15]

In addition to enabling aspiring media workers to circumvent union discrimination, training programs also answered a significant increase in demand[16] for African American workers in the industry following the Kerner Commission Report's criticism of the absence of minority points of view in mass media. A number of pressures contributed to this dramatic upward swing in demand for black television workers at the end of the 1960s. The broadcast industry was affected by a national climate of affirmative action, as well as being subject to its own, specific pressures to hire African Americans following the assassination of Dr. Martin Luther King Jr. The urban uprisings of the 1960s had already caused stations to scramble to find black newscasters, often because white journalists were unwilling or unable to enter African American communities during uprisings.[17] Stations were also motivated to change their racist hiring policies by activist boycotts and other protest tactics, negative publicity, and new regulatory pressures.[18] Regulatory investigation increased somewhat in this period, against both racist hiring practices and racist exclusions in program content. The well-publicized censure of several stations for racist practices added to the stations' concern about regulation, although the FCC's actual affirmative-action requirements remained weak, and their enforcement even weaker.[19] The release of the Kerner Report caused some stations to hire African Americans, yet this hiring was often tokenistic,

---

membership. For a personal account of this treatment, see Jessie Maple, *How to Become a Union Camera Woman* (New York: LJ Film Productions, 1977).

[13] Interview with author, 2004. Madeline Anderson's career is also documented in Yvonne Welbon's documentary film *Sisters in Cinema*, as well as in Frances Gateward's chapter "Documenting the Struggle, African American Women as Media Artists, Media Activists," in *Still Lifting, Still Climbing*.

[14] Maple, p. 1.

[15] "Mrs. Mastermind" *Ebony*, May 1972, pp. 12–17, pp. 102–104.

[16] "Mrs. Mastermind," 1972.

[17] Kerner Commission.

[18] See Merrit, "Black Efforts for Soul in Television."

[19] See Classen, *Watching Jim Crow*.

or even exploitive (i.e., sending unprepared workers with minimal train-ing to do riot coverage). While the seeds of change were sown by these events, it is the training programs (also catalyzed by the assassination of Dr. Martin Luther King, Jr. and urban uprisings) that built a community of black media workers that has had a lasting impact.

Black Journal Workshop Produces a Black Vanguard of Media Makers

The *Black Journal Workshop* was developed to train black workers not just for the *Black Journal*, but also for the industry as a whole. The program would be free, comprehensive, and very pragmatic. The workshop hired a number of well-known media makers, a few black but mostly white, to train the students. The eight-week, intensive, pragmatically oriented cur-riculum presented a lot of information in a short time. Motivated students worked hard to keep up with the brisk pace, and those who could not left the program. Some talented students found jobs before finishing the program.

The students at the *Black Journal* Workshop were a diverse group that included both black and Latino students of different ages and experience. Recent Vietnam veterans, clerical workers, high school and college students, and graduates took advantage of free film and television training in order to enter broadcast professions. Because of the growth in black programming and the changes in hiring practices due to regulatory and activist pressures described earlier, the graduates of the training program entered a labor market that was eager to hire them, despite their lack of union cards. Angela Fontanez began at *Black Journal* shortly after the strike, possibly as part of an effort to bring in more women. The staff saw her Puerto Rican identity as adding desirable diversity. This training, along with her ambition and talent, was central first to her promotion to associ-ate producer of the *Black Journal* and ultimately to a career that would earn Fontanez several Emmy Awards.[20]

Fontanez's experience demonstrates how working at the first national black public-affairs program and participating in that program's self-invention was politicizing. Fontanez was from a left-leaning Puerto Rican family and became more politicized through work at the *Black Journal*. She cited meeting activists such as Angela Davis as one of the most influ-ential and exciting experiences of her life. Experiences like these led Fontanez to consider herself "black" rather than "Spanish" (the label her mother insisted on.) She felt it was important to identify explicitly with the black movement. Although it distressed her mother, Fontanez wore

20 See Fontanez, interview by author. 2004.

an Afro in those years. "I started identifying with my black roots...it was powerful...it was coming hand in hand at a time when I really saw television as a tool to politicize and educate people."

Furthermore, Fontanez points out, as a woman, she was breaking two boundaries with her television career: "Women were not in television in any droves: white, black, or otherwise...a handful of women of color on or off the screen." Like several other people I interviewed, Fontanez attributes her initial opportunity to work in television to the critiques of the Kerner Commission Report, reflecting: "The Kerner report...that's why I was hired...."

The logo for the school, designed by Fontanez, featured a silhouetted figure with an Afro, holding a film camera. In addition to street encounters and word of mouth, some students learned of the school through newspaper advertisements. Others saw film crews from the school in action and inquired. In 1968, a film crew involved large cameras and lights; for the most part, the school predated the proliferation of video. Since so few African Americans held cinema jobs, an all-black crew shooting film could have been a very unusual and striking site, an exciting vision to encounter for an aspiring media maker.

The workshop expanded over time, but initially survived on few resources, shutting down several times in 1968 and 1969 and reopening.[21] Using borrowed equipment and laboratory facilities, teachers initially volunteered (but were soon paid) to teach an innovative, pragmatic curriculum to eager students. Interest in the workshop was very high, and the first year the program was overwhelmed with applications. In order to be considered for admission, students had to write an essay about their career goals. Many were turned away. Despite excellent press in the *New York Times, Ebony,* and other publications, those working on the program felt that NET could have done more to publicize the workshop's offerings and the accomplishments of its students. Furthermore, the inconsistent funding from the Corporation for Public Broadcasting kept school director Peggy Pinn and her successor, Geri Feagans, under persistent stress and kept the school under constant threat of closure. Later in 1969, the Corporation for Public broadcasting contributed $20,000 and the school expanded from a short "crash course" to a longer, several-nights-per-week program that taught cinematography, editing, scriptwriting, directing,

---

[21] "Black Woman in Television Is a Real Go Go Go Girl," *New York Amsterdam News* (March 7, 1970). Jacobi Describes the school closing in September 1969 for "lack of money" and resuming in February of 1970.

film aesthetics, sound recording, and mixing over a twelve-week semester. At the height of funding and size, the NET school paid a small stipend plus carfare for its full-time students.

The workshop's technical and aesthetic curriculum was beneficial for students; equally important, if not more so, was the formation of a critical community and consciousness building about being a black media worker in a white-dominated field. One instructor, Roland Mitchell, would sabotage student productions intentionally if students were not paying attention. He did this explicitly to prepare them for the racism they would find in the field. One student remembers:

> Roland Mitchell was, like—the man.... He would tell you in the beginning— "If you don't love it get out now." "If it's an 8 o'clock call—be there 10 minutes early or we'll leave without you. And he was serious. He knew the problems black folks faced being in the industry. If the assistant camera wasn't by his camera, Roland would sabotage the shoot to mirror sabotage in the field that you might expect because you were black or whatever."

Both white and black teachers at the school recognized the racism that their students would experience in the field. In a sense the workshop was a "boot camp" environment, seeking to foreshadow the challenges that lay ahead. For some students, this type of training was quite familiar. Like a good number of the *Black Journal* Workshop/NET School alumni, Bahati Best was a recent armed forces veteran. Thus, the physical and psychological rigors of the workshop were not difficult to adapt to.[22] As of this writing, Best is a successful cinematographer at ABC. At the time of the workshop, Best had heard that television jobs were hard to get, that television was a "closed shop" to African Americans.[23] Despite his interest in the field, he did not seek out work in the industry after getting out of the Air Force in 1970. However, when a friend told him about the *Black Journal* Workshop, he applied and was accepted.

> I knew John Wise—who was in the *Black Journal* program—he was really a gung-ho kind of independent-minded filmmaker—and he invited me to watch a class project in action. It spurred my interest. Around that time, after I got out of the Air Force, I was looking through a magazine on careers. The article said that television was a very closed shop [to minorities].

Bahati Best recalls, "Based upon how you performed in the class—it was up to your peers. That has proven out—some of the people did become

---

22 Bahati Best, telephone interview by author, September 24, 2004.
23 Ibid.

producers—people asked to recommend people for a shoot. Your future employment depended—on how well, how interested you were, and how much you absorbed."

The school equipped African American students with skills necessary to enter and survive in the industry, but it also provided a revolutionary pedagogy—encouraging young media workers of color to anticipate and surpass racist expectations in the burgeoning and competitive field of television. Students knew that their voices and the voices of their families and communities had never been heard and that television and film offered powerful representational opportunities, as well as class mobility. All of the alumni interviewed reiterated this sense of community that the school offered. These personal and professional colleagues extended critical personal support as well as professional networking.

Reflecting on this history, we must ask ourselves, "Where is the new generation of black media makers going to come from?" The film school route to a media career is prohibitively expensive, and few inexpensive or free training options exist. As the vanguard generation of black media makers retires, who will take their places? We need to consider the impact of the Kerner Report in the wake of the tremendous backlash to affirmative action, and the decline in the real dollar value of federal financial aid. Furthermore, the economic basis for media jobs is changing. Whereas media jobs were a ticket to working- or middle-class life, will aspiring journalists and media makers today from working-class or poverty-class families have the same experience? Community-based training programs are an important alternative to university credentialing, but universities also must consider their responsibilities. Otherwise, we will continue to be, to paraphrase Robert McChesney, a "poor democracy" with a "rich media."[24]

---

[24] Mchesney, 1999 (Rich Media, Poor Democracy, Communication Politics in Dubious Times).

CHAPTER TEN

"ILLEGALS UNDER FIRE":
ANALYZING U.S. NEWS FRAMES OF LATINA/O
IMMIGRATION AND IMMIGRATION RIGHTS (1997–2007)

Isabel Molina-Guzmán

On the same day as the National Day of Action for Immigrant Justice, "La Marcha," the largest national immigration rights mobilization in US history, *Newsweek* magazine published a cover story headlined "Illegals under fire: Who deserves to stay?" The news magazine cover featured a grainy, darkly lit caution road-sign familiar to drivers in California and the Southwest depicting a man and woman running while dragging along a female-child, presumably across a highway (Newsweek 2006). The cover image and its lead story tapped into and reaffirmed a racialized understanding of contemporary immigration discourses by subtly calling forth established metaphors of Latina/o threat and invasion (Chavez 2008; Molina-Guzmán 2005; Ono and Sloop 2002; Santa Ana 2002). *Newsweek* similar to other news publications dehumanized undocumented immigrants by reducing them to a darkly lit traffic sign and describing them as "illegals." In doing so, it reinforced the social status of undocumented immigrants as perpetual foreigners and outsiders to the United States. Ironically, activist groups would reappropriate the same traffic sign in materials for the marches, and the stark cautionary image would come to stand-in for the rights of immigrants as it became recirculated in front-page news accounts, newscasts, and journalistic photographs of the record-setting marches.

Taking up the challenge of the 1967 report by National Advisory Commission on Civil Disorders commonly known as the Kerner Commission, which in response to the civil unrest that swept across the United States called upon news organization and the unique ethical responsibilities of journalists to consistently and exhaustively report on the concerns of society's most poor, marginalized, and vulnerable populations. While the original report focused on understanding and addressing the tensions between white and black US Americans, the largest racial minority at the time, this essay takes up the ethos of the Kerner Commission by examining the role of the news media in shaping public understanding of the largest ethnoracial minority demographic group today, Latinas/os. In particular, the essay documents how immigration was covered from 2005–2007, a time of increasing national and local tensions over issues of immigration and the changing ethnic and racial demographics of the United States that bore witness to Latinas/Latinos becoming the largest minority group. Because immigration from Latin America drew the most public attention during this period, I analyze a selective sample of *the New York Times* coverage of Latino immigration. During this time frame the Republican controlled Senate attempted to pass the politically moderate Comprehensive Immigration Reform Act of 2006, while the House of Representatives attempted to pass the restrictive immigration legislation, HR 4437. Immigration rights activists who wanted comprehensive reform inclusive of a path to citizenship responded to both pieces of legislation by launching the largest set of protest and marches around these issues in U.S. history. Both bills failed to get out of Congress and ultimately died in 2007 handing President George W. Bush who was supportive of comprehensive immigration reform a legislative defeat.

The essay engages in an analysis of news coverage of immigration by asking the following questions: What were the news frames surrounding immigration during this period? What role did Latinas/os play in news coverage about immigration? Finally, how are these news frames informative of social conflict and tensions resulting from shifts in US ethnic and racial demographics? Studying the journalistic news framing of important social issues, such as immigration, provides an opportunity to revisit the role of journalism in informing public understanding of ethnic and racial relationships in the United States more generally and for the Latina/o community more specifically.

FRAMING IMMIGRATION IN THE NEWS

This project uses discursive framing analysis to situate itself at the intersection of humanistic and social scientific approaches to the study of ethnicity, race, gender and the media. A critical discursive approach to the study of mediated representations positions the media as a text informative of and embedded within broader social, political and cultural currents (Fairclough 2010; Van Dijk 2008). Such a methodology contributes to understanding the relationship between the social construction of knowledge, formation of ethnic and racial identity, and the symbolic status of marginalized groups within the public imaginary.

Additionally, the study builds on media studies scholarship on agenda-setting and framing. Agenda-setting theory suggests that the news media influence what issues the public identifies as politically salient (Bennet and Iyengar 2008; McCombs 2004). Most of the media studies scholarship on agenda-setting has focused on news coverage of military conflicts and the presidency to illustrate that there is a correlation between the amount of news coverage about an issue and the likelihood that the issue will be identified as an important issue by likely voters (McCombs and Reynolds 2008). In other words, agenda setting scholars suggest the news media does not tell its audiences "how to think" but it does signal to audiences who consume high amounts of news content "what to think about" as a salient or important political issue.

In 2006 at the height of news coverage about the immigration legislation and the immigrant-rights marches, the US public identified immigration as a significant political issue. Although 2005 actually regis-tered a decline in national television news coverage about Latina/o immigration (Montalvo and Torres 2006, 2007) such coverage saw a sharp increase with immigration becoming the most reported story in the US media for the first time since the Pew Research Center's Project for Excellence in Journalism began tracking news stories.[1] Agenda setting sug-gests that the increase in news coverage should result in an increase of the US public identifying the issue as an important one, and according to the Gallup Poll News Service it did. The Gallup Poll News Service reported that 24 percent of the US public in 2007 identified immigration as one of the top five issues of concern (Saad 2007). The previous high of 23 percent occurred in 2006 following the April-May immigration rights marches.[2]

Given the established role of the news media in influencing what the public thinks about as significant, this analysis seeks to study the news framing of Latina/o immigration in the general-market news. Within the theory of agenda setting, a framing analysis of news examines how journalists describe a topic, person or event and how those descriptions may reinforce particular cognitive associations. McCombs and Reynolds argue, "An important part of the news agenda and its set of objects are the attributes that journalists and, subsequently, members of the public have

---

[1] Excellence in Journalism News Coverage Index. New twist in immigration fight is big news, June 10–15, 2007 [accessed November 26 2011]. Available from http://www.journalism.org/node/6107.

[2] According to Gallup Poll News Service, the average number of US residents ranking immigration as an important issue is 12 percent (Saad 2007).

in mind when they think about and talk about each subject" (2008: 10). Journalists are social actors and do not live or work in isolation from the world around them. The interpersonal contacts, lived experiences, and ideological beliefs journalists have about an issue implicitly inform story selection, source selection, word choice, and other elements of how they tell the story (Zelizer and Allen 2010). How a story is told and delivered will resonate or be perceived as dissonant with how news audiences come to understand that issue (Entman 2002; Entman and Rojecki 2003; Edy and Meirick 2007). News audiences who are immigrants, for instance, will read a story differently than audiences who have never met an immigrant. The news media's role in the creation of a discourse about ethnicity, race, Latina/o identity and culture is particularly significant because most audiences live and play in highly racially segregated spaces. The Cultural Indicators Project reported decades ago that most of what audiences learn about people who are different from them is through the popular media (Morgan, Shanahan, Signorielli 2010). Audiences rely on entertainment and news media to teach them about ethnic and racial communities with whom they do not regularly interact. Consequently, the media behave as a broad and accessible repository of cultural and social knowledge for audiences. Likewise, I argue, the omnipresent circulation of media images about Latinas/os becomes part of the cultural ecology that influences general attitudes and beliefs about Latinas/os (Molina-Guzmán 2010). Thus, news both informs and is informed by the hegemony of a particular society helping publics to narrate complex issues through story frameworks that speak to them in familiar and uncomplicated ways. By foregrounding some elements of a story or news narrative while eliding others, journalists create a frame through which audiences can look through to understand their world.

Methodology

The analysis for this paper is based on an examination of *New York Times* (NYT) articles published from January 1, 2005 to December 30, 2007. The NYT was selected for analysis, because it is generally considered to be one of the most prestigious newspapers of record for the United States. In other words, the NYT generally influences the news agenda for other news organizations and is considered an important national public forum for politicians and policy makers attempting to influence public opinion.

Using the Lexis-Nexis online database, all news stories and editorial opinion columns containing the search term "Latina/o/Hispanic and immigration" were collected. A total of 366 texts were initially identified. In 2005, the NYT published 71 items; 164 stories in 2006; and, 131 in 2007. Film and book reviews, and news stories dealing with Latina/o entertainment figures or announcements of community events were removed from the initial stories collected. Also removed from the analysis were editorials, columns and other opinion-pieces. Thus, out of the initial 366 files only 268 texts were analyzed (97 stories from 2007; 126 from 2006; and 45 from 2005). Of 268 stories analyzed, 24 stories focused on the immigration rights marches with 8 stories published in 2007 and 16 stories published in 2006. The remaining stories ranged from news coverage of immigration raids to human-interest features about Latina/o immigrants.

For this essay, the framing analysis focuses on the language used in news headlines and the lead paragraph. Headlines generally indicate the most important elements of the story and the significance of the event as perceived by journalists (reporters, staff writers, editors, copyeditors). The first paragraph or lead paragraph of an event or issue news story provides the readers with the most important piece of information regarding the article often described as the who, what, why, when, and how of the story, while the lead paragraphs of human-interest stories are generally more provocative statements designed to catch the reader's attention for a more in-depth coverage of an issue or event. The analysis in this essay is not meant to be exhaustive or generalizable, but rather a thoughtful preliminary interrogation of journalistic discourses about Latina/os and immigration during an important historical moment and at a time when Latina/os have become the largest ethnoracial minority demographic group in the United States (US Census 2011).

Defining Immigration as Latina/o American

According to the US Census (2011) immigrants from Latin America make up less than 50 percent of the foreign-born population. Indeed, immigrants from Asia have grown steadily and now comprise more than 40 percent of the foreign-born in the United States (ibid). Latinas/os in the United States are more likely to be US-born than foreign-born (Pew Hispanic Center 2009). Nevertheless, Latinas/os and immigrants from Latin America remain the face of news coverage about immigration reifying the status of Latina/os as always outsiders and perpetually foreign-born (Del Rio 2007). Scholars of race and news framing have long documented that news coverage of ethnic and racial minorities often positions white and female bodies as victims and brown and black masculine bodies as criminals (Dixon 2008; Dixon, Azocar and Casas 2003; Dixon and Linz 2000). News coverage about immigration is not only defined by Latin American immigration, but is also embodied through the criminalization of masculine immigrant bodies.

News coverage of immigration sets up the following association: immigrant → Latino → Mexican → illegal. Latinas/os are perpetually conflated as immigrants and immigrants are perpetually conflated as Mexicans (Del Rio 2006). By discursively linking immigration with Latin America and undocumented immigrants as Latino (usually male and Mexican), mainstream news coverage of immigration throughout this period uneasily aligns black and white bodies along the socioeconomic axis of normative citizenship while simultaneously marginalizing Latina/o bodies through the language of illegality, criminality and more recently terrorism (DeGenova and Peutz 2010). Although the demographics of undocumented immigration are difficult to attain, the Pew Hispanic Center estimates that there are less than 8 to 10 million undocumented immigrants from Latin America out of more than 50 million Latinos in the United States each year (Passel 2005). Undocumented immigrants from Latin America are a relatively small segment of the US immigrant and Latina/o population, but a significant element of how immigration is covered in the news media and imagined by the US public.

For instance, similar to other news organizations the NYT often published photographs of the April immigration rights marches that featured a diversity of immigrants from Latin America, Asia and Africa as was evident through the use of national flags and signs. However the focus of the actual news texts often emphasized immigration from Latin America and Mexico in particular. Stories that often led with images of diversity, such as "Waving American flags and blue banners that read 'We Are America,' throngs of cheering, chanting immigrants and their supporters converged on the nation's capital and in scores of other cities on Monday calling on Congress to offer legal status and citizenship to millions of illegal immigrant," worked against a notion of multiplicity by exclusively citing immigrants from Latin America (Swarms 2006b). Additionally, stories such as "21 immigrants fired after missing work for rally" (Ruethling 2006) and "Latina/os Protest in California in Latest Immigration March" (Archibold 2006) further reinforce the association of Latina/os as immigrants and immigrants as undocumented Latina/os. Latina/os are thus journalistically constructed as a threat to US citizenship and both white and black identity, such as in this headline "Bridging a Racial Rift That Isn't

Black and White" (Swarms 2006c). Coverage of immigration in the mainstream U.S. media reinforces a dominant construction of authentic US citizenship and racial identity as black and white and shifts groups who fall out of that binary to non-citizenship.

Conflict Frame

Central to journalistic framing of news coverage about immigration is the "conflict frame." In the conflict frame, Latino/Mexican immigration is constructed as a threat to cultural, political, and economic interest of (white and black) US society. Within the US media, general-market news conventions, the rules and social norms by which journalists produce stories, often favor stories that can be narrated and framed through notions of human conflict. Michael Schudson argues that "News tend to simplify complex social processes in ways that emphasize melodrama, that turn a complex set of phenomena into a morality tale of battle between antagonists, often between good guys and bad guys" (2003: 48). US news coverage of Latina/o immigration and immigration policy likewise becomes reduced to conflict.

Approximately 106 of the 268 analyzed had headlines or leads that exhibited the conflict frame, and it was the dominant frame in 2005 and 2007 (See Table 10.1). The conflict frame was further broken down into three subsets (political conflict, legal conflict, ethnic/racial conflict). Political conflict is defined by disagreement within the US political system over public policy and legislation, such as conflict between Democrats and Republicans over immigration reform. Legal conflict is defined by tensions created by the law or legal policies surrounding immigration, such as raids by Immigration Control Enforcement or Visa application rules. The most prevalent conflict covered in immigration news, however, is the conflict between ethnic and racial groups. News stories defined by ethnic/racial conflict center on the tense relationships between Latinas/os and white or black residents. In the conflict frame Latin American immigrants and by association Latinas/os are often positioned as the "bad guys," the cultural outsiders, criminals by virtue of ethnic identity and country of birth.

Throughout all three years examined, ethnic/racial conflict was a central element of journalistic coverage about Latina/o immigration. While 2007 saw an equal amount of ethnic/racial and political conflict framing due to the presidential primaries and the debate over dueling federal immigration bills, ethnic/racial conflict was by far the dominant

Table 10.1: NYT Conflict News Frames.

Conflict Frame Type	2005	2006	2007
Political	3	12	16
Legal	7	13	11
Ethnic/Racial	11	21	15
Total	21/45	46/126	42/97

focus of much of the news (See Table 10.1). Ethnic/racial conflict stories emphasized a binary construction of citizenship and nation that situated Latina/o bodies as perpetually foreign – outsiders who threaten the United States' established racial hierarchy and melting pot ideology of cultural assimilation. Within the ethnic/racial conflict frame, Latin American immigrants were usually positioned as competing for scarce resources with established US minorities, such as black Americans, or as polluting nostalgically white rural communities.

In the wake of Hurricane Katrina and the massive displacement of poor and working-class black communities, Latina/o immigrants became constructed as a source of conflict in the competition for jobs and debates over the economic recovery of the South. Post-Katrina NYT news stories, such as "Study Sees Increase in Illegal Hispanic Workers in New Orleans" (Eaton 2006); "Katrina Begets A Baby Boom By Immigrants" (Porter 2006), and "In Louisiana, Worker Influx Causes Ill Will" (Eaton 2005) affirm the underlying ideological associations created by the ethnic/racial conflict frame that positions Latina/o immigrant population growth as unstoppable and harmful to established minority populations and the dominant racial binary of the United States. During this period, news coverage of the immigration rights marches also led to stories about the declining economic and political power of black communities. For example, stories such as "For Blacks, A Dream in Decline" (Uchitelle 2005); "A nation divided on immigration" (Ponson 2006) and "Growing unease for some Blacks on immigration," (Swarms 2006a) affirmed the status of Latinas/os as foreigners and outsiders who threaten the racial hierarchies and destabilize the economic order.

The NYT reporters often turned to small towns in the Midwest, South and Southwest to document the impact of Latina/o immigration on spaces nostalgically perceived as white. News features such as "In this Small Town in Iowa the Future Speaks Spanish" (Grimes 2005) and "For Latina/os in the Midwest a Time to be Heard" (Archibold 2006) reaffirm the sense that a massive tide of undocumented Latin American immigration is unsettling established ways of life. Idealized white spaces in US popular culture, news coverage of Latinas/os in the Midwest and South often highlighted increasing cultural and racial tensions created by the arrival of Latina/o immigrants, as indicated in this headline "In Immigrant Georgia, New Echoes of an Old History" (Downes 2006). The seemingly unstoppable "browning of America" is implicitly framed as a social problem, such as in this 2007 story:

> New immigration and the political reaction against it are nearly as old as the United States itself. Yet the immigration surge of the last decade has awakened tensions of unexpected intensity that have pervaded the presidential campaigns of both parties and stirred voter anger across the country (Preston 2007).

The ethnic/racial conflict frame foregrounds a sense of cultural and economic loss by highlighting white anger and hostility towards newly arrived Latin American immigrants, often perceiving this wave of immigrants as responsible for the moral and economic decline of its town.

The conflict frame ultimately defines Latina/o as immigrants and by association Latinas/os as a threat. Latinas/os are discursively integrated within the ongoing economic discourse of resentment that has informed ethnic and racial politics throughout the 1990s and 2000s (McCarthy 2003). The discourse of resentment mandates that difference (sexual, racial or linguistic) must be disciplined in such a way as to maintain hegemonic economic hierarchies by reifying the tropes of U.S. liberalism, the ideological narrative of the United States as a "colorblind" society that affords those with the skills and desire the ability to move to the top of the democratic marketplace. Such discursive disciplining is most efficaciously carried out through the interconnected gendering and racialization of Latina/o immigrant bodies in the mainstream media and the erasure of non-Latina/o ethnic/racial others (Molina Guzmán 2005; Vargas 2000).

The gendering of Latinidad builds on scholarship that recognizes gender as a socially constructed category of identity that derives its meaning from political, economic and social structures, such as the family and the media. However, it more explicitly connects gender with race and ethnicity (Molina-Guzmán 2010). In other words, gender derives its meanings not only from what is defined as masculine or feminine but also in terms of how feminine and masculine others are characterized racially and ethnically. Lucila Vargas extends the concept of media gendering by studying how the practices and technologies used in news production contribute to the feminization of the Latina/o community in North Carolina. Based on a quantitative and qualitative analyses of print news reporters, sources, genres and themes in regional newspaper coverage, Vargas contends that given the journalistic focus on personalized stories about extraordinary Latina/o individuals and the emphasis on Latina/o family issues, coverage about Latinas/os most often appears within the feminized domain of the private sphere. In other words, the lives of Latinas/os are dominantly coded within the stereotypically feminine realm of hearth and family and ascribed archetypical feminine characteristics, such as sexual fertility, domesticity and powerlessness.

Not surprisingly, an analysis of the news coverage about the immigration, from California's Proposition 187 to the 2006 debate about the U.S. House and Senate immigration bills, demonstrates the continuation of an economic discourse of resentment that uneasily unites the interest of working class white and black citizens against a homogenized, gendered, and racialized unstoppable wave of immigration (Ono and Sloop 2002; Santa Ana 2002). According to Leo Chavez (2008) within mainstream news coverage of immigration prior to and after the immigration rights marches, the wave is framed as driven by unruly Latinas who will not tame their sexuality and fertility ["Katrina begets a baby boom by immigrants" (Porter 2006)] and threatening brown men whose very bodies pose a physical and economic threat ["Coming to terms with the men on the corner," (Santos 2006)].

REDEFINING LATINA/O THREAT THROUGH A TROUBLED FRAME

Despite the dominance of conflict frames grounded in racially binary definitions of citizenship, the immigration rights movement produced an oppositional news frame, a frame that provides an opportunity to symbolically rupture the dominant discourse about Latina/os as threatening foreigners. In the spring of 2006, news coverage of the immigration rights marches and rallies led to the preponderance of the "Latina/o power frame." Because media culture is not homogenous and at times may contradict the demands of global capitalism, journalistic narratives about immigration actually result in texts and images that destabilize and decenter dominant constructions of citizenship and ethnic and racial identity (Molina-Guzmán 2010). News coverage of the immigration rights marches provided one such potential opportunity through the use of the Latina/o power frame (See Table 10.2).

Table 10.2: Ratio of Conflict Frames to Latina/o Power Frames.

Frame Ratio	2005	2006	2007
Conflict	21	46	42
Latina/o Power	19	61	30

Latina/o Power Frame

The Latina/o power frame foregrounds visible and numerical demonstrations of political and economic strength. It associates numerical strength with the potential to result in institutional transformations through political and legislative reforms. Focusing on numbers also serves the mandate for journalistic objectivity and provides journalists with an opportunity to reflect on the social or political impact of issues and events through a simplified narrative (Schudson 2003). Political impact can be measured in numbers: number of people, percentage of voters, strength of public opinion.

The NYT news coverage following the immigration rights mobilizations in April and May illustrate the circulation of this frame with stories of Latina/o Power outweighing news centered on conflict (See Table 10.2). Many of the stories focused simply on the large numbers of protestors. Headlines emphasizing the large numbers of people participating in the marches linked the numbers to the potential for increased political strength and the potential ability to influence congressional immigration legislation. Stories such as "Immigrants Take to U.S. Streets in Show of Strength" (Archibold 2006b); "Thousands Rally in New York in Support of Immigrants' Rights" (Confessore 2006); and, "In the Streets, Suddenly, An Immigrant Groundswell" (Bernstein 2006) focus on the visible, numerical demonstration of power and demands for comprehensive immigration reform. The unprecedented national news coverage surrounding these events produces an opportunity to re-frame public discussions of immigration. Such images have moved away from the perception of Latina/o immigrants as threatening to established US norms and toward images of Latina/os as politically organized and normative citizens.

However, the Latina/o power frame is double-edged. The frame demands conformance to white norms of social respectability. As Lisa Cacho (2008) illustrates, the news media coverage about the contemporary Latina/o immigrant movement creates discursive openings for immigrants to redefine themselves, but it does so by demanding that Latinas/os define themselves exclusively as economically productive, law abiding, and sexually normative. The effectiveness of the Latina/o power frame in redefining Latinas/os as non-threatening depends on the celebration of heteronormativity, socially appropriate domesticity, white norms of civil disobedience, and the perpetuation of ethnoracial minority victimhood. Thus, the Latina/o power frame found in news coverage of the immigration rights marches ruptures the conflict frame but at the cost of creating exclusions for some Latina/o communities.

Furthermore, the Latina/o power frame gains its ability to transform the public discourse about Latina/o immigration by engaging in a gendered discourse that makes Latina/os safe through their feminization. If the dominant construction of undocumented immigration as threat is embodied through the brown male body, then the alternative construction of Latina/o immigration as safe must be performed through the women and children. Indeed, it is often within the realm of the feminine that mainstream news coverage about the immigration rights is at its most favorable. For example, news coverage of the "National Day of Action for Immigration Justice" (April 10, 2006) often highlighted the presence of children, and the family atmosphere of rallies in Chicago, Dallas, Los Angeles, New York, Washington, D.C., among other places constructing the political protest as a safe family affair:

> The demonstrators marched under mostly clear blue skies with Spanish-language music blaring, street-vendors selling ice cream and parents clinging to mischievous toddlers and the banners of their homelands.

> The rallies, whose mood was largely festive rather than angry, were the latest in recent weeks in response to a bill passed in the House that would speed up deportations, tighten border security and criminalize illegal immigrants (Swarns 2006b).

The visuals tell a similar story. Journalistic photographs prominently feature women and children laughing and waving flags, playing with water, and consuming food. These marches are not evocative of the violent civil rights protests of the 1960s or the civil disorder of the 1970s; the immigration rights marches of the 2000s are safe, festive, family-friendly affairs. The visual iconography creates an emotional link between woman and child and associates both with the familial and domestic constructions of immigrants as normative, as similar to other US families. The photographs and stories evoke safe associations by encoding the political practices of Latina/os within the domestic sphere of home and family.

The Latina/o power frame and the gendering of Latina/o immigration embedded within these stories troubles the frame in a second way. By gendering Latina/o bodies through stereotypically feminine characteristics, such as intimate, familial, and normatively domestic, the political power of the mobilizations is subtly undercut. The journalistic emphasis on women, children and family taps into popular narratives about the sexuality, fertility and heteronormative domesticity of Latina border-crossers (Ruiz 2002). Latina/o political identity and power are coded through a feminizing narrative. Lucilla Vargas (2000) argues that such gendering produces a complex set of associations:

> This womanish construction of Latino news is achieved not only by downplaying strong masculine Latino voices, but also by relying on "common sense" associations and metaphors that link Latinos to woman as sign, and thus to qualities that a patriarchal capitalist culture regards as unworthy (285).

The gendering of the immigration rights movement frame may limit its transformative potential. As Cacho (2008) suggests, Latina/os gain political power by becoming the right type of ethnoracial minority – heteronormative, domestic, passive, non-threatening.

Concluding Thoughts

Thus, this chapter posits that the news frames surrounding Latina/o immigration in the mainstream U.S. media contribute to the construction of a binary definition of racial identity and citizenship where citizenship is always aligned with whiteness (sometimes black) and non-citizenship is associated with Latina/os. When Latina/o immigrants are framed as having power, it is a safely contained and socially acceptable power. Both the conflict frame and the Latina/o power frame reinforce the problematic association of immigration as Latina/o, as Mexican, as illegal. Consequently, the mainstream news coverage of immigration throughout this period uneasily aligns black and white bodies along the socioeconomic axis of normative citizenship while simultaneously marginalizing Latina/o bodies through the language of illegality, criminality, and domesticity.

Contemporary news coverage of immigration is occurring in a social and political climate that seeks to marginalize immigrants and immigrant communities to protect nativist notions of the imagined nation (Inda 2002). In other words, the nostalgic construction of an U.S. melting pot driven by ethnic assimilation is increasingly dissonant with many US journalists and a US public preoccupied with the "Browning of America" created by the presence of foreign languages, culture and often racially unclassifiable hybrid bodies. Public support for decreasing immigration to the United States peaked in 2006 with 51 percent of the public stating that levels should decline and remains steady at 43 percent since then (Jones 2011). Throughout 2005–2007 a majority of the public supported enforcing current immigration laws more strictly in addition to passing new immigration laws (Carroll 2007). At the same time, the past 10 years have seen an increase in hate crimes against sexual, ethnic, and racial minorities in the United States indicating a growing intolerance for difference (FBI Hate Crimes Statistics 2010). Citizenship and national identities are under political and cultural contestation throughout the globe and, as a result, majority (often racially white) communities are working out anxieties about their changing status by disciplining those who embody racialized ethnic difference. In January 2009, *The New York Times* reported on a grisly story of Suffolk County teenagers (most of them white) engaging in a pastime they called "beaner hopping." The teenagers specifically hunted Latina/o immigrants, or at least people assumed to be Latina/o immigrants, violently attacking them, which in one instance resulted in murder. Many of the victims were too afraid to report the crimes to the police because of their immigrant status. Hate crime incidents draw into focus the importance of journalism and the continuing ethical responsibility of journalists to a US civil society defined by multiplicity.

How the news media covers immigration contributes to the ongoing disciplining of citizenship and ethnic and racial difference by the US public. The narratives of cultural and economic threat circulated through the conflict frame are more compelling than the safe gendering of news stories through the Latina/o power frame. Both frames and the overall coverage of immigration write out the multicultural coalition of immigrant activists who took the streets across the nation – Asian, Latina/o and African immigrants who were often joined by white and black civil rights activists. As consumers of the media, we have a responsibility to ask for more and better of today's journalists, to demand that complex stories about immigration be told and the diversity of the Latina/o community and its issues be fully represented.

REFERENCES

Alvarez, L. and Broder, J. 2006. "More and more, women risk all to enter U.S." *The New York Times*. 19 January: p. A1.

Archibold, Randal C. 2006a. "Latinos Protest in California In Latest Immigration March." *The New York Times*. 2 April: A24.

——. 2006b. "For Latinos in the Midwest, A Time to Be Heard." *The New York Times*. 25 April: P. A1.

Bennet, W. Lance and Shanto Iyengar. 2008. "A New Era of Minimal Effects? The Changing Foundations of Political Communication." *Journal of Communication*, pp. 707–731.

Bernstein, Nina. 2006. "In the Streets, Suddenly an Immigration Groundswell." *The New York Times*. 27 March: p. A14.

Cacho, L. 2008. "The Rights of Respectability: Ambivalent Allies, Reluctant Rivals, and Disavowed Deviants." In *Immigrant Rights in the Shadows of United States Citizenship*, edited by Rachel Ida Buff. New York: New York University Press.

Carroll, Joseph. 2007. "Americans Divided on Need for New Immigration Laws: View that immigration should be one of top government priorities is at high point in last year." *Gallup Poll*: 16 July.

Chavez, Leo. 2008. *The Latino Threat: Constructing Immigrants, Citizens, and the Nation.* Stanford University Press.

Confessore, Nicholas. 2006. "Thousands Rally in New York in Support of Immigration Rights." *The New York Times*. 2 April: p. A29.

De Genova, Nicholas and Nathalie Peutz. 2010. *The Deportation Regime: Sovereignty, Space, and the Freedom of Movement.* Duke University Press.

Del Rio, Esteban. 2006. "The Latina/o Problematic: Categories and questions in media communication research. In C. Beck (ed) *Communication Yearbook 30*. Lawrence Erlbaum, pp. 387–429.

Dixon, Travis. 2008. Crime news and racialized beliefs: Understanding the relationship between local news viewing and perceptions of African Americans and crime. *Journal of Communication*, 58, 106–125.

Dixon, Travis, Azocar, D. and M. Casas. 2003. "The portrayal of race and crime on television network news." *Journal of Broadcasting and Eletronic Media*, 47, 495–520.

Dixon, Travis. and Daniel Linz. 2000. 'Overrepresentation and Underrepresentation of African American and Latina/os as Lawbreakers on Television News', *Journal of Communication* 50(2): 131–154.

Downes, Lawrence. 2006. "In Immigrant Georgia, New Echoes of an Old History." *The New York Times*. 6 March: p. A20.

Edy, Jill and Patrick Meirick. 2007. "Wanted Dead or Alive: Media Frames, Frame Adoption and Support for the War in Afghanistan," *Journal of Communication*. 57, 1, pp. 119–141.

Entman, Robert. 2003. *Projections of Power: Framing News, Public Opinion, and U.S. Foreign Policy*. University of Chicago Press.

Entman, Robert and Andrew Rojecki. 2000. *The Black Image in the White Mind: Media and Race in America.* Chicago: University of Chicago Press. ISBN: 0-2262-1075-8.

Federal Bureau of Investigations. 2010. "Hate Crime Statistics 2010." Report available online at http://www.fbi.gov/ucr/01hate.pdf.

Fairclough, Norman. 2010. *Critical Discourse Analysis: The Critical Study of Language*. Pearson Publishers, 2nd Edition.

Grimes, William. 2005. "In This Small Town in Iowa, The Future Speaks Spanish." *The New York Times*. 14 September: P. A6.

Inda, Jonathan X. 2002. Biopower, reproduction, and the migrant woman's body. In *Decolonial Voices: Chicana and Chicano Cultural Studies in the 21st Century*, ed. Arturo J. Aldama and Naomi Quiñonez, 98–112. Bloomington, Ind.: Indiana University Press.

Jones, Jeffrey. 2011. "Americans' Views on Immigration Holding Steady: Plurality continues to prefer decreased immigration levels." *Gallup Poll*: June 22.

McCombs, Maxwell. 2004. *Setting the Agenda: The News Media and Public Opinion*. Polity Press.

McCombs, Maxwell and Amy Reynolds. 2008. "News Influences on Our Pictures of the World." In J. Bryant and Dolf Zillmann (eds) *Media Effects: Advances in Theory and Research*," 1–16.

Molina Guzmán, Isabel. 2005. Gendering Latinidad in the Elián news discourse about Cuban Women. *Latina/o Studies*, 3, 179–204.

——. 2010. *Dangerous Curves: Latina Bodies in the Media*. New York University Press.

Montalvo, Daniela and Joseph Torres. 2007. *Network Brownout Report 2006: The Portrayal of Latina/os and Latina/o Issues in Network Television News*. Association of Hispanic Journalist.

Morgan, Michael and James Shanahan, Nancy Signoreilli. 2008. "Growing up with television." In In J. Bryant and Dolf Zillmann (eds) *Media Effects: Advances in Theory and Research*," 39–49.

Ono, K. and Sloop, J. 2002. *Shifting Borders: Rhetoric, Immigration and California's Proposition 187*. Philadephia: Temple University Press.

Passel, J. 2005. *Unauthorized immigrants: Number and Characteristics*. Washington, DC: Pew Hispanic Center.

Pew Hispanic Center. 2011. "Tabulations of 2000 Census (5% IPUMS) and 2009 American Community Survey," February 17 (accessed November 26, 2011). Retrieved from http://pewhispanic.org/factsheets/factsheet.php?FactsheetID=70.

Preston, Julia. 2007. "Tough Question for a New Test: What Does "American" Mean?" *The New York Times*. 28 September: P. A1.

Ruiz, M. 2002. Border Narratives, HIV/AIDS, and Latina/o Health in the United States: A Cultural Analysis. *Feminist Media Studies* 1: 37–62.

Saad, Lydia. 2007. "Iraq Still Tops Policy Agenda, but Immigration, Gas Prices Gain. Percentage citing immigration is highest in a year," June 1 (accessed November 26, 2011). Available from http://www.gallup.com/poll/27742/Iraq-Still-Tops-Policy-Agenda-Immigration-Gas-Prices-Gain.aspx?utm_source=email-a-friendandutm_medium=emailandutm_campaign=sharingandutm_content=titlelink.

Sandoval, C. 2000. *Methodology of the oppressed*. Minneapolis: University of Minnesota Press.

Santa Ana, Otto. 2002. *Brown Tide Rising: Metaphors of Latina/os in Contemporary American Public Discourse*. Austin, Texas: University of Texas Press.

Swarns, R. 2006a. "Growing unease for some Blacks on immigration." The New York Times, 4 May 2006. Retrieved from http://www.nytimes.com/2006/05/04/us/04immig.html on 4 May 2006.

Swarns, R. 2006b. "Immigrants rally in scores of cities for legal status." *The New York Times*.11 April: P. A1.

Swarns, R. 2006c. "Briding a Racial Rift That Isn't Black and White." *The New York Times*. 3 October. P. A1.

U.S. Census Reports. 2010. "American FactFinder: Demographic/Ethnicity/Race."

Van Dijk, Teun, 2008. *Discourse and Power*. Palgrave MacMillan.

Vargas, L. 2000. Genderizing Latina/o News: An Analysis of a Local Newspaper's Coverage of Latina/o Current Affairs. *Critical Studies in Media Communication* 3: 261–293.

Walters, Nathan and Edward Trevelyan. 2011. The Newly Arrived Foreign-Born Population of the United States: 2010. *American Community Survey Briefs*, US Census.

Zelizer, Barbie and Stuart Allen. 2010. *Keyworks in News and Journalism Studies*. Open University Press.

CHAPTER ELEVEN

MUSLIMS IN THE GLOBAL CITY: RACISM, ISLAMOPHOBIA, AND MULTIRACIAL ORGANIZING IN CHICAGO

Junaid Rana

INTRODUCTION

Cities in the global economy have come to serve specific purposes. From economic and financial markets to cultural, political, and social patterns and processes, some urban spaces have come to be called quintessential global cities. In this essay, I argue for an understanding of Chicago, often referred to as the Second City, as a specific kind of global city that can potentially offer alternative models to understand the rapid changes taking place within these urban spaces. Here I refer to the challenges of racism and combating anti-immigrant rhetoric through the emergent social movements based in Chicago's history of radical organizing, the consequence of which is an important model of multiracial organizing that is forging a new path to contest racism and other forms of systematic oppression through the platform of faith-based organizing and the recognition of immigrant rights. Central to this congruence is the complex migration history of domestic and immigrant people of color. And herein lay many of the contradictions, conflicts, and potential of organizing paralysis that is brought forth in contesting racism, particularly in its anti-immigrant form, while also dealing with an internalized racism that pits anti-black against anti-immigrant forms of racism. That is to say, competing forms of racism and anti-racism have called for multiple organizing strategies and tactics in the effort to find common cause. Specifically, I refer to the formation of the Muslim American community that has often pitted African American Muslims against Arab and South Asian American Muslims. Through various efforts and historical circumstances, a new paradigm of Muslim American organizing with the imperative of overcoming these divides has gained prominence.

In an important intervention in Muslim American history and theological thought, Sherman A. Jackson has called for the crafting of a third resurrection in which those he refers to as Blackamericans must find their

distinctive voice within the meta-tradition of historical Islam. This provocative and somewhat convincing argument lays the ground for the
dilemma of the crossed wires of religion and race in the larger Muslim
American community. As he argues, for Blackamericans Islam is part of
the pantheon of the "black religious tradition" that includes the church,
mosque, and other spaces and forms of religious organization and redefinition of American blackness. Formed in protest and in resistance to long-
standing forms of racism and the historical experience of American
slavery, religion became a source of acting and coping against a racial
formation that sought to dominate Blackamericans, making this history of
anti-racism a central aspect of historical analysis within the black religions. In contrast, for immigrant Muslims—mostly Arab and South Asian
Americans—the nemesis of an American Islam is not white supremacy
but a vague sense of "the West" that imagines this configuration in terms
of a religious and civilizational threat (Jackson 2005: 151–152). For Jackson,
then the problem is that the immigrant group that came to dominate the
institutions of American Islam no longer viewed racism as one of the
prevailing dividing lines of American society, but instead relied on a position that relegated religion to a cultural argument over competing value
systems. This latter configuration of Islam versus the West is more in line
with typical color-blind approaches that imagine a global civilizational
conflict without regard for its racialized underpinnings. Such arguments
are widespread with armchair and pop experts and media rhetoric that
constantly make claims over "the battle of soul of Islam" and claims to
"discovering moderate Islam" in confronting radical jihadism.[1]

While I agree with the general outlines of this argument, I think these
communal claims are not as disparate as Jackson claims them to be. Rather
than enclosed and separate spheres of theological and historical difference, this stand-off appears to be a case of limited vocabularies. This sense
of racism and religious persecution historically has more in common
in the United States than Jackson is willing to acknowledge. As I have
argued elsewhere, in the case of anti-Muslim racism, the concepts of race
and religion have a far more intimate relationship than is often understood going back at least to fifteenth- and sixteenth-century Spain and the
encounter with the New World (Rana 2007). In the contemporary Muslim
American context, these differing analytical contexts of the Blackamerican

---

[1] An entire media industry has been constructed out of this thought that is largely the
work of Samuel Huntington and Bernard Lewis.

and the immigrant Muslim are the result of a history of separation and isolation. The race concept itself has often been attributed to cultural and civilizational difference that was at times based on religious and biological difference. The history of the race concept is one of a malleable category used according to context and need. This is to say that although the Arab and South Asian Muslim American communities have not embraced the kind of anti-racism present in the black religious tradition, this does not mean that racism is not prevalent—one need not verbalize it as racism for it to be so. Indeed, as Jackson indirectly argues, developing further strategies to deal with anti-Muslim racism remains the challenge for the entire spectrum of the Muslim American community.

The historic relationship of Islam to America has increasingly placed Muslim communities in an ambiguous position within the U.S. racial formation and concomitantly the constantly expanding global racial system. The tragic events of September 11, 2001, and their aftermath demonstrate that regardless of this vague placement, these communities are racialized through a logic that connects them to multiple histories of racial violence and religious othering. Hence, in the contemporary moment when anti-terror is a substitution mechanism for anti-immigrant, Muslims are racialized as threats, criminals, foreigners, and outsiders. To examine these effects in Chicago, this chapter first surveys this racial landscape within an urban setting of a global city to understand how the language of race and racism is articulated both within this community and through external forces. A central component here is the examination of the impact of state violence on Muslims in theorizing the relationship of this growing population in the United States to the broad conception of rights and recognition associated with citizenship. Specifically, this refers to the tactics the U.S. state has deployed in Muslim communities to wage the War on Terror, which includes strategies of containment, control, and fear.

Second, this chapter examines the multiracial and cross-racial response of Muslims in the post-9/11 era to organize their communities across the lines of identity formation in an effort to create new conceptions of race, religion, class, and gender. Grassroots organizing efforts in Chicago have seen a revitalized relationship between domestic Muslim populations (African Americans and Latinos) and immigrant Muslims (Arab and South Asian Americans) due to the efforts of anti-racist organizers and the rearticulation of the Muslim community in the United States. The larger project is situated as an urban ethnography that examines the place of Chicago's Muslim population in relation to the impact of state and popular racism in everyday life and the effort to organize communities in this context. This chapter thus addresses the role of civic engagement in the contemporary moment in which the U.S. government's War on Terror directly affects the Muslim American community of Chicago, and the role of the emerging multiracial constituency of Muslim Americans that goes beyond traditional notions of black-white racial formation.

MUSLIMS IN AMERICA

In many ways the arrival of Islam in America parallels the construction of the notion of New World racism by European explorers. Islam did not come as part of the spread of religious freedom, but was a central aspect of religious prejudice, persecution, and enslavement. Indeed, some of the first explorers to the Americas not only had Arabic-speaking translators on board in anticipation of finding trade routes to India, but also individuals fleeing Catholic Spain that had purged itself of Jews and Moors. These crypto-Jews and crypto-Muslims, as they have come to be called by historians, hid their faith and religious conviction to escape persecution in Spain, but to also try their luck in the New World.[2] This history of religious and migration origins has led to a movement within the Latino community to convert back to Judaism and Islam, or, as it is now commonly referred to, revert.

In addition, through the history of slavery, the Americas received a large percentage of enslaved African Muslims. While estimates are inconclusive, the available evidence suggests that there were between 2.25 million and 3 million Muslims out of the approximated 10 million to 15 million Africans brought to the Americas and the Caribbean Islands (Diouf 1998: 48). Michael Gomez has provided a fairly rigorous assessment of the North American population that estimates that out of 481,000 enslaved Africans during the slave trade, approximately 255,000 came from Muslim regions of Africa (2005: 166). For the North American population, this suggests the

---

[2] Stanley Hordes (2005) offers a remarkable ethnohistory of crypto-Jews with settlements throughout Mexico and important colonies in New Mexico. Many who were part of this population were collapsed within Roman Catholicism. While this history is convincing, it remains unclear what relationship crypto-Muslims had to this migration, if any. Recently, DNA technology has spurred interest in tracing religious and ethnic heritage for Latinos in the U.S. Southwest. While many chose to embrace a Jewish background, DNA testing suggests that an Arab or Muslim heritage as also just as likely. See "Hispanic's Uncovering Roots as Inquisition's 'Hidden' Jews," Simon Romero, *New York Times*, Oct. 29, 2005. Such testing requires further scrutiny into the replication of biological discourses of race placed onto notions of ethnicity and religion.

vastly significant influence of Islam among the enslaved populations. It was to these histories that many of the offshoots of nineteenth and early twentieth century Islam-inspired religious movements that included the Moorish Science Temple, the Nation of Islam, and others that created resonances with African Americans refer.

Simultaneously, the Ahmadiyya movement was making inroads in the urban industrial cities of the United States through the work of various evangelicals from India, such as Mufti Muhammad Sadiq. Ahmadidyya Movement in Islam, Inc., USA, was a force in cities such as New York, Philadelphia, Detroit, and was finally based in Chicago for its central location. The work of these evangelicals was responsible for creating early Muslim American models of multiracial Islam by bringing together groups from multiple backgrounds, including South Asian, African American, European, and Caribbean (Turner 2003). And although Arab and South Asian Americans had a presence in the United States from the late nineteenth into the twentieth century, it was not until the 1965 Immigration and Naturalization Act that large numbers of Muslim immigrants arrived from these parts of the world.

One of the counterintuitive paradoxes of the demographics of the Muslim American population is its makeup. Currently, the Muslim population of the United States appears to be a majority African American, with Arab Americans and South Asians coming up a close second and third. Although the predominance of African Americans is acknowledged by social scientists, there is great resistance to the purported size of the black Muslim population within the religiously dominant Arab and South Asian American community. This is largely due to undercounting the prison Muslim population and a lack of recognition of nontraditional Muslims, for example, the Nation of Islam and other black Muslim offshoots. A recent survey by the Pew Research Center estimated that the number of Muslims associated with a mosque was around 2.3 million, while other surveys have estimated the total population of Muslims to be between 5 million and 7 million (Pew 2007: 13). Estimates of the African American Muslim population hover between 1.5 million and 4.5 million and are rapidly increasing due to the long history of prison conversion that is often underestimated in many of these surveys (McCloud 1995). An earlier survey in 2001, conducted for the Council on American-Islamic Relations (CAIR), determined that an estimate of six to seven Muslims seemed reasonable given the number of 2 million Muslims associated with a mosque, of which they surveyed regular Sunni mosque atendees across the United States to be 33 percent South Asian American,

30 percent African American, and 25 percent Arab American (Bagby et al. 2001). Among the issues with the discrepancies in these surveys is the ability to count the category of the so-called unmosqued Muslims that do not attend a mosque or no longer readily identify as Muslim although they may come from such a background. Suffice it to say that African Americans, Arab Americans, and South Asian Americans make up a large majority of the American Muslim population that is most likely divided in percentages that are close thirds of the community.

This complex multiracial history of Muslim America raises several significant issues as to the organization and institutionalization of American Islam. Through this complex history and through longstanding divisions within these communities, there remain separate places of worship and institutionalized practices between the domestic and immigrant populations. As mentioned above, the approach to racism is also an important pivot around which the communities remain divided. The crisis of 9/11 and its role in the Muslim American community broadly provided a platform and opportunity to critically examine the makeup of the community and many of its internal issues alongside a critique of the racist and stereotypical representations of Muslims rampant in U.S. society from popular practice to the use of media images and the impact of the policing of the U.S. Muslim community by the U.S. state. Discussions and debate around racism and Islamophobia have taken important steps in bringing formerly distant and separate Muslim communities closer together. In large part, this is also due to the work of the U.S.-born generation of immigrant Muslims who understand the status of Islam and Muslim in America from a different vantage point. The beginning of this conversation across communities in the post-9/11 era begins with the analytical use of the concepts of racism, and in particular Islamophobia as a particular form of racism.

Islamophobia as a concept of racial violence has received much attention in European literature of race relations that has also incorporated theories of multiculturalism more thoroughly. In North American academic scholarship, the predominant mode of understanding Muslims is in terms of religious practice and difference to a dominant Christian identity. Such a classification, rather than making a process of racialization apparent, subsumes race under religious difference. This resistance to theoretically articulate the racialization of Muslims can be read through the incoherence of an ethnically diverse religious category that is complex in terms of national and ethnic origins. Yet Islam and Muslims have historically been racialized through an Orientalism that functions simultaneously through domestic and international spheres. Asian American studies scholars have also pointed out that this process of racialization has often been placed in groups deemed foreign and unassimilable. For example, the terms of the "heathen Chinee" and the "Hindoo" in nineteenth-century Asian America similarly treated the "Mohammadan" in contrast to notions of a self-defining white Christian America.[3] This is a relationship of religion to race that uses the logic of difference to translate cultural differences into biological and phenotypic ones. Thus power translates through a white Christian America against both religious and racial difference.

The concept of Islamophobia, then, allows an analysis of how religious practice is connected to the logic of racialization. Indeed, the fear of Islam connects cultural (i.e., religious) signifiers to racial ones. Thus, xenophobic attitudes to Muslim immigrants are not only based on religious difference, but are also interpreted through racial difference. Islamophobia in the United States is then a product of race making, or, in the terms of Omi and Winant, a racial project (1994). As a racial project, the placement of Muslims within the U.S. racial formation seeks to assign cultural and biological characteristics to this group in terms of the racial history of the United States. From immigration law to the Patriot Act, Muslim communities have become a target of infiltration and surveillance under the War on Terror. This has created a new relationship to civic life for Muslims who feel they are under duress, are made to fear the threat of potential detention, deportation, and incarceration, and are constructed through notions of criminality, terror, fundamentalism, and as perpetual foreigners and outsiders.

MUSLIMS IN CHICAGO, THE GLOBAL CITY

As Saskia Sassen defines it, the global city is a specific entity in which urban space takes on a specific function in the global economy. In this economic and financially dominated schema, a global city is intimately entangled with the complex flows of people, ideas, and commodities at a planetary level. Global cities such as New York, London, and Tokyo are those that ultimately come to dominate the global economy through economic, social, and political means (Sassen 2001). As command centers of the global economy, the changes required of these cities entail financial,

---

[3] For example, Takaki 1989 and Lee 1999.

economic, and social shifts within urban space in parallel with other global cities. In this sense, Chicago is a global city because of the combination of resources to service the global operations for corporations and of markets. It has a highly internationalized professional class, which is crucial for these services. It has world-class cultural institutions and events. And by virtue of its waves of immigration it has a historically internationalized social environment—a global culture and global worldview that are common to all global cities and give them many advantages in today's world (Sassen 2004: 16).

This sense of worldly cosmopolitanism that Sassen defines as the global city from a social and cultural perspective involves complex histories and a constantly shifting sense of globality. This definition of Chicago as a global city is one that relies upon economic functions to imagine the needs of specific urban spaces but also points to a need to situate social migration history alongside the development of a global and international outlook in opposition to the parochialisms that such a forward-progressive modernity depends upon. Alongside these economic flows are the particular patterns of social migration that bring specific groups of people within the confines of economic necessity. That is to say, global cities must have migration to feed their growth and maintain their dominance in the competitive world of globalization. It is the workers of globalization that are caught within the confines of social, economic, and political structures of particular urban histories. The exact confines of these structures are constantly shifting, to be sure, and are dependent on historical and urban context. Yet, the challenge of the city in this self-consciously defined modernity is to find ways of operating in efficient and productive ways through the structures that define it.

Chicago has historically been a migrant-receiving city. Long referred to as the Second City in relation to New York, Chicago has emerged as a central global city of the Midwest region of the United States. Since the early nineteenth century, Chicago has been a major destination for immigrants. Beginning with European immigrants and the great migration of African Americans in the latter part of the 20th century, Latino and Asian immigrants were soon to follow. These historical patterns led to the particular formation of Chicago as predominantly a city of immigrants and communities of color divided along a north-south and west axis. The privilege of being closer to the waters of Lake Michigan is procured for Chicago's wealthy and middle class, while the Southside and parts of the Westside are the historic communities of Chicago's black residents. Immigrants, although they are present throughout Chicago, are found mostly in the

Far Northside, Westside, Southwest side, and the suburbs. According to the 2000 U.S. Census, Chicago is home to 1.4 million immigrants, of which 628,000 live in the city and 787,000 live in the suburbs. From this population, Mexico, Poland, and India are the leading countries represented in the metropolitan area. Chicago ranks as the fifth largest immigrant population nationally. Many Chicago neighborhoods that have seen vast growth include diverse populations from Africa, Asia, Latin America, and the Middle East.[4]

Simultaneous to this rapid growth in immigration demographics, race continues to be a salient and important characteristic of residency patterns that demonstrate extremely high isolation for African Americans and less so for Latinos and Asian Americans.[5] Sociological and anthropological studies of Chicago have often examined racialized communities and immigrants of color in terms of racial conflict.[6] As a counterpoint to the idea of racial conflict, multiracial and cross-racial organizing offers a different insight into the complex strategies of social change and the dynamics of uniting multiple racialized communities around similar shared issues. The continued significance of race and racial separation in relation to population growth in immigration is dependent on the divisions within Chicago's racial politics. It is in this urban context that multiracial and cross-racial organizing is forging new strategies and tactics in relation to identities, social practices, and political processes.

Chicago has one of the largest African American Muslim populations in the country, in addition to large South Asian American, Arab American, and a small but significant Latino and European Muslim population. Indeed much of the work done on Islam in Chicago has focused on the African American experience and the Nation of Islam.[7] This diversity offers a vast array of possibilities to understand how multiethnic communities work both in conflict and toward common goals. Indeed, many such

---

[4] *Metro Chicago Immigration Fact Book*, Institute of Metropolitan Affairs, Roosevelt University, http://www.roosevelt.edu/ima/publications.htm#Immigration.

[5] For example, see James Lewis et al., "Race and Residence in the Chicago Metropolitan Area, 1980–2000." Institute of Metropolitan Studies, Roosevelt University and Northern Illinois University. 2002. See also the recent ethnographies of Pattillo 2007 and Perez 2004.

[6] This idea of racial conflict in many ways draws from the Chicago School of Sociology, led by Robert Park and others; see Park et al. 1925; and Park (1921). For examples in much of the classic literature on the African American community see Drake and Cayton (1962); Spear (1967); Pattillo (2007). And recently, on Chicago's Latino community, De Genova and Ramos-Zayas (2003).

[7] See McCloud 1995. Schmidt 2004 is one of the first major treatments of Chicago's Sunni Muslim population.

diasporic Muslim populations have been experiments in crafting democratic models of community support and belonging. Nonetheless these
communities are often highly segregated according to religious sect,
nationality, and gender. Such conflicts speak to the necessity to compli-
cate what some commentators have labeled a transnational *umma*, or
community of believers.[8]

Muslim Americans and Multiracial Organizing

The post-9/11 era for Chicago's Muslim American community offered some
specific challenges in confronting hate crimes, hate speech, and other civil
rights abuses. Although many of these acts also predated 2001, the surge in
racism is remarkable.[9] Specific communities of Chicago's Muslims, namely
Arab American and South Asian Americans, have been drastically affected
by the events that followed September 11, 2001. After this tragedy, the U.S.
wars in Afghanistan and Iraq have led to large changes within these communities.[10] These communities have seen a dramatic rise in hate crimes as
well as anti-terror sweeps by the U.S. government. For many of these communities, the post-9/11 era has lead to greater policing, surveillance, suspicion, and increased danger from hate crimes. The stakes for the Muslim
community are based on calculations of risk and fear. On the one hand is a
fear that various state and popular forms of intimidation create for Muslim
citizens and noncitizen immigrants alike. From this fear emerges a certain
level of risk that involves the possibility of detention, deportation, and

---

[8] The actual existence of a singular umma is a historical debate that is encapsulated in
many of the arguments concerning contemporary Muslim politics, community, and
migration.

[9] The Council of American-Islamic Relations has produced reports for over the last ten
years on the civil rights of American Muslims. The most recent report, called "The Status of
Muslim Civil Rights in the United States: Presumption of Guilt," released in 2007, showed
that since 2001 there has been an extraordinary growth of civil rights complaints by Muslim
Americans, with a 25 percent increase from 2005 to 2006. This report, and each annual
report, is available at http://www.cair.com/CivilRights/CivilRightsReports.aspx.

[10] The *Chicago Tribune* printed a special issue on Muslims mainly from Chicago titled
"Tossed Out of America" from November 16 to 18 that covered these changes from deportations to illegal detentions to demographic shifts due to the mass exodus of Muslims fleeing
potential deportation. A majority of those interviewed were Pakistani in origin, demo-
graphically the group hit hardest by the threat of deportation. Many Pakistanis are recent
immigrants as opposed to other Muslim groups in Chicago, such as Arab Americans, that
are more established. Estimates by human rights groups in Pakistan place the returnee
figure from the diaspora in Europe and North America at around one hundred since
September 11, 2001.

incarceration through selective immigration and police enforcement. Although this is a generalized threat, it most readily affects a certain sector of the Muslim immigrant population that is vulnerable to attacks, hate crimes, and potential arrest.

In the context of the post-9/11 era, several Chicago-based national Islamic organizations have consistently called for a greater understanding of moderate Muslims in opposition to the Islamophobic stereotypes of terrorism and fundamentalism in an effort to create an image of mainstream Islam.[11] For example, for the last several years at the annual conference of the Islamic Society of North America (ISNA), calls for this sort of tolerance have repeatedly been made.[12] Simultaneous to this is a more complicated analysis of discrimination and prejudice that has emerged in terms of religion-based racism. This comes in an era when this realization of religious and racial persecution has required greater understanding across the multiracial constituency that is a large part of the Muslim community in the United States. After years of isolation, and even the irony of separate black Muslim and immigrant Muslim conferences, the ISNA annual conference has become a de facto meeting ground for the Muslim leadership to address their differences and plot a forward path. This conflict is part of an apparent clash between a black exceptionalism and the idea of immigrant assimilation. For many African American Muslims, Islam is a point of difference from the dominance of white Christian racism, whereas for immigrant Muslims the desire to combat such racist discrimination has led to a model of multicultural assimilation. That is to say that many Muslim immigrants and the generations that have followed them are more interested in claiming an American identity as Muslims as opposed to other national and hyphenated identities.[13] The clash of exceptionalism and assimilation has lead to different anti-racist strategies and importantly a starkly different approach to identity formation regarding questions of race.

This dilemma has given rise to new approaches to imagining the broader Muslim American community and their needs. In the context of Chicago, this challenge has led to the formation of new models of

---

[11] See Alsultany (2007) for an analysis of how this sort of diversity is produced through nonprofit advertising.

[12] See "Abandon Stereotypes, Muslims in America Say." Neil MacFarquhar, *New York Times.* Sept. 4, 2007.

[13] On this see "Between Black and Immigrant Muslims, An Uneasy Alliance." Andrea Elliott. *New York Times.* March 11, 2007; and Naber 2006.

multiracial organizing that are influenced by the Alinsky model of community organizing.[14] Many of these organizations combine professional style community based organizing with issue-based themes and an approach of accessible democracy toward social justice causes. These organizations vary from national umbrella groups such as ISNA (discussed above) that are based in Chicago to others that operate in relationship to specific issues and form alliances and coalitions with organizations with parallel goals.

The lone example of a neighborhood-specific community-based organization that operates as a Muslim-run service organization for a broad constituency is the Inner-City Muslim Action Network (IMAN). Formed in 1995 and officially incorporated in 1997, IMAN was formed in the Southwest side of Chicago to address issues of poverty, social abandonment, gang violence, and social justice. As a community-based nonprofit, IMAN seeks to provide a space for Muslim Americans to engage in social justice work and spiritual community service work that goes beyond religious or racial background. The organizing model is based around the three central issues of direct service, organizing and social justice, and arts and culture. As part of their direct service work they provide essential services such as food distribution, medical care, and career development. IMAN is also involved in several social justice initiatives that engage in comprehensive immigration reform, criminal justice reform, and education organizing. Additionally, they run several campaigns that provide programs for the expression of Muslim arts and culture that engages in contemporary popular forms such as a bimonthly Community Café and a biannual concert series called "Takin' it to the streets." As they state in their vision, IMAN works

> to foster a dynamic and vibrant space for Muslims in Urban America by inspiring the larger community towards critical civic engagement exemplifying prophetic compassion in the work for social justice and human dignity beyond the barriers of religion, ethnicity, and nationality. Our services, organizing and arts agenda stem from our spiritual convictions about community service, human compassion, and social justice, particularly for marginalized people of color.

---

[14] Much of Chicago organizing has been heavily influenced by the Alinsky activist handbook *Rules for Radicals* (1989) and has creatively combined this with the ideas of direct democracy and many of the theme-based approaches of the new social movements that organized around identity politics.

Grounded in a language of what might be referred to as a Islamic liberation theology, IMAN has used religious language of compassion and justice in spiritual service of communities of color that are on the margins of society. Through the social justice language of disadvantage and empowerment, IMAN has cultivated a service model of incorporation and outreach.[15]

Additionally, organizations such as CAIR-Chicago are important sources of activism on behalf of Muslim Americans in Chicago and the Midwest region. CAIR, in particular, has taken on the role of civil rights and legal representation, a governmental relations liaison, and media activism for Muslim Americans. CAIR-Chicago is a watchdog of civil rights abuses but also an important source of legal aid. Other organizations such as the Interfaith Youth Core (IFYC) are Chicago-based international nonprofits that empower youth to serve others.[16] Targeting interfaith youth through a shared value system rather than the differences of their faith, IFYC seeks to build a pluralist youth movement based in equality and diversity not only in the United States but at an international level. Arguing for a parallel in American society between racial difference and religious difference, IFYC borrows from anti-racist organizing methods of coalition and alliance building. This is not merely a substitution but a parallel development in which religious diversity is imagined as a parallel model of multiracial coalition. Calling it the faith line in reference to W.E.B. Dubois's famous reference to the color line as the dividing line of the twentieth century, founder Eboo Patel claims that the world is now divided between religious totalitarians and religious pluralists in the twenty-first century. Hence, it is a multiracial religious pluralist model that the IFYC ascribes to in its social justice initiatives as part of service and commitment to religious faith.

The overlap of several of these organizations has also resulted in cross-membership and coalition building with important immigrant rights

---

[15] IMAN has garnered relatively high attention from academics and journalists for its social justice model. Recently Geneive Abdo (2006) devoted several chapters of her book on Muslims in America to the work of IMAN and its founder, Rami Nashishibi. Earlier IMAN was included in one of the few monographs on sunni Muslims in Chicago by Garbi Schmidt (2004).

[16] Executive director of IFYC Eboo Patel describes his path to creating this movement in his book *Acts of Faith* (2007).

organizations in Chicago. In particular the Illinois Coalition for Immigrant and Refugee Rights (ICIRR) and the Coalition of African, Arab, Asian, European, and Latino Immigrants of Illinois (CAAAELII) have been instrumental in organizing and building around immigrant rights issues and providing services and advocacy to Chicago's broad immigrant community. These important alliances demonstrate a broad political vision that includes multiracial approaches with faith-based organizing and immigrant rights initiatives.

THE MULTIRACIAL MUSLIM MODEL:
BRINGING COMMUNITIES OF COLOR TOGETHER?

In the post-9/11 era the Muslim American community has been broadly challenged to reconfigure its organization and embrace a larger constituency. Given the history of divisions within Islam that are reflected in regional differences—say between Arabs and South Asians—it would appear reasonable to follow Sherman Jackson's call for a third resurrection for African American's that I began this chapter with. The importance of such a call is the need to claim a space of authority and specificity within the multiple traditions of Islam. The danger however is a continued isolation and a preponderance of a black exceptionalism against a notion of immigrant assimilation. The greater challenge is the ability to transcend such divisions in creating new formations of Muslim Americans that imagine this through a multiracial model, as is widely being created by Muslim American youth.

The test of such an approach is its sustainability. The remaining question of the multiracial Muslim organizing model is whether such an approach can continue to impact the communities it serves. Additionally, the question of addressing a wide spectrum of needs from discrimination and civil rights abuses to housing, medical care, and educational access are important issues at the forefront of the concerns of many of these organizations. The ability to map faith-based organizing onto an anti-racist platform also speaks to the shape that such activism will take. The role of immigrant rights within this narrative of organizing and activism is also an important aspect of the future of many of those in the Muslim American community. The future, however, lies in the ability to cross racial and faith lines to craft modes of solidarity that challenge all communities of color.

References

Abdo, Geneive. 2006. *Mecca and Main Street: Muslim Life in America after 9/11*. Oxford; New York: Oxford University Press.

Alinsky, Saul David. 1989. *Rules for Radicals: A Practical Primer for Realistic Radicals*. Vintage Books ed. New York: Vintage Books.

Alsultany, Evelyn. 2007. "Selling American Diversity and Muslim American Idenity through Nonprofit Advertising Post 9/11." *American Quarterly* 59, no. 3: 593–622.

Bagby, Ihsan, et al. 2001. "The Mosque in America: A National Portrait." Report from the Mosque Study Project. *Council of American-Islamic Relations*. April 26. Available at http://www.cair.com/AmericanMuslims/ReportsandSurveys.aspx.

De Genova, Nicholas, and Ana Y. Ramos-Zayas. 2003. *Latino Crossings: Mexicans, Puerto Ricans, and the Politics of Race and Citizenship*. New York: Routledge.

Drake, St Clair. 1945. *Black Metropolis; a Study of Negro Life in a Northern City*. New York: Harcourt.

Hordes, Stanley M. 2005. *To the End of the Earth: A History of the Crypto-Jews of New Mexico*. New York: Columbia University Press.

Jackson, Sherman A. 2005. *Islam and the Blackamerican: Looking toward the Third Resurrection*. Oxford; New York: Oxford University Press.

Lee, Robert G. 1999. *Orientals: Asian Americans in Popular Culture*. Philadelphia: Temple University Press.

McCloud, Aminah Beverly. 1995. *African American Islam*. New York: Routledge.

Naber, Nadine C. 2006. "Muslim First, Arab Second: A Strategic Politics of Race and Gender." *Muslim World* 95, no. 4: 479–95.

Park, Robert Ezra, Ernest Watson Burgess, Roderick Duncan McKenzie, and Louis Wirth. 1928. *The City*. Chicago, Ill.: The University of Chicago press, 1928.

Park, Robert Ezra, and Herbert Adolphus Miller. *Old World Traits Transplanted, Americanization Studies*. New York, London: Harper.

Patel, Eboo. 2007. *Acts of Faith: The Story of an American Muslim, the Struggle for the Soul of a Generation*. Boston: Beacon Press.

Pattillo, Mary E. 2007. *Black on the Block: The Politics of Race and Class in the City*. Chicago: University of Chicago Press.

Pew Research Center. 2007. "Muslim Americans: Middle Class and Mostly Mainstream." http://pewresearch.org.

Rana, Junaid. "The Story of Islamophobia." *Souls: A Critical Journal of Black Politics, Culture, and Society* 9, no. 2 (2007): 148–61.

Sassen, Saskia. 2004. "A Global City." In *Global Chicago*, edited by Charles Madigan, 15–34. Urbana: University of Illinois Press.

Sassen, Saskia. 2001. *The Global City: New York, London, Tokyo*. 2nd ed. Princeton, N.J.: Princeton University Press.

Schmidt, Garbi. *Islam in Urban America: Sunni Muslims in Chicago*. Philadelphia: Temple University Press, 2004.

Spear, Allan H. 1967. *Black Chicago; the Making of a Negro Ghetto, 1890–1920*. Chicago: University of Chicago Press.

Takaki, Ronald. 1989. *Strangers from a Different Shore: A History of Asian Americans*. New York: Penguin.

CHAPTER TWELVE

NEW CONFIGURATIONS OF RACISM AFTER 9/11: GENDER AND RACE IN THE CONTEXT OF THE ANTI-IMMIGRANT CITY

Elizabeth L. Sweet

Racism is a Gender Specific Phenomenon
(Patricia Hill Collins 2004: 7)

INTRODUCTION

In the forty years since the Kerner report's definitive account of the extent to which racism is embedded in contemporary U.S. society, the complexities of the problem have become increasingly apparent. One example is the tangle of difficulties that brown women, particularly Latinas and immigrant Latinas, struggle with in the United States, as a consequence of the combination of race, gender, and a perceived "illegal" immigrant status. In this chapter, after theorizing the new "anti-immigrant city," I use Patricia Hill Collins's concept of "intersectional paradigms" to argue that since 9/11, a combination of racism, sexism, and multileveled anti-immigrant bias has uniquely burdened brown women in immigrant communities in their role as wives/partners as well as through their characterization as undocumented producers of anchor babies and carriers of a perceived cultural threat, the browning of America.

The aggregation of these amplified racisms or triple racism has justified inflicting a range of misfortunes on them: the rape of women who cross the border without documents, traumatic family separations, and dehumanized treatment in detention centers and deportation processes. While the "illegal status" of brown women is used as justification for these unacceptable behaviors, the effects of intersectional racism are felt by the members of immigrant brown communities, whether documented or not, and by native-born Latina U.S. citizens as well. For example, the profiling of brown people by police and white citizens at day labor sites as "illegals" is a common occurrence (Tambini and Sandoval 2004) and negatively impacts all brown people regardless of legal status. This chapter explores the nature and dimensions of the contemporary intersection of race, gender, and perceived immigrant status.

First, I sketch out contemporary experiences of immigrants in the United States. Then I explain the phenomenon of the anti-immigrant city. I use the term "city" not in a literal sense, since this new form of racism is not bound to the formal limits of a city and often spreads into rural and suburban areas, but more as a concept to frame the context of contemporary relationships within societies in the United States. I then explore how Collins's intersectional paradigm might help us to understand the gendered implications of the anti-immigrant city. Finally, I use data from Chicago to explore the ramification of post 9/11 racism on women's lives in the anti-immigrant city. Health issues, economic well-being, violence, reproduction, and motherhood emerged as specific spheres wherein brown immigrant women are impacted but also the areas where they are actively challenging the anti-immigrant city.

CONTEMPORARY IMMIGRANT EXPERIENCES

At the turn of the twentieth century, Mexican, Chinese, Irish, and other immigrants, the majority of whom were men, were treated badly and often met physical violence. Currently, a majority of migrants to the United States are brown and from Mexico, and include more women and children than men (Passel 2006: 1). With the browning and the feminization of the immigrant population, there has been an increasingly racialized and gendered response to new U.S. residents.

The displacing of race bias and using instead gender-specific or anti-immigrant phenomena are part of what Bonilla-Silva (2006) suggests is a cover up of racism. Similarly, language difference is exploited as a nonracial characteristic that can be used to discriminate (Galindo and Vigil 2006: 427) without explicitly using race. Another, perhaps well-meaning strategy for sweeping racism under the rug is the infamous saying "can't we all just get along," which may seem innocuous but implicitly urges submission to "Anglo conformity" (Littlefield, 2008: 682). The movement in the United States toward a colorblind discourse is really a movement toward an Anglo norm, which helps to perpetuate the myth that racism has vanished. Hunter (2005) points out the implications:

> The United States is going through a racial Latin Americanization because its discourse has changed in this post-civil rights era to one that denies difference, denies inequality, and insists on a unified, monolithic American designation for all. This colorblind discourse makes it possible to ignore racial discrimination and to criticize those who name it as racist for doing so. (p. 112)

The media significantly shapes these attitudes. In the current intersection of understandings about race, gender, and immigration, media outlets often "present hegemonic ideologies that claim that racism is over, while at the same time stereotyping women of color, often as sex objects and as promiscuous" (Littlefield 2008: 676). "The mainstream media work to obscure the racism that does exist, and they undercut antiracist protest" (Collins 2004: 54). We clearly see this process in action in the media's conventional and poor coverage of the 2006 pro-immigrant marches across the country. The numbers reported were grossly misrepresented, the message was obscured, and some commentators suggested the Immigration Customs Enforcement (ICE) agents could have simply gone to the marches and arrested everyone (Coulter 2007).

The racialization of brown immigrants also emerges through the focus on law enforcement. Racial profiling, a longstanding practice of police in African American communities and towards blacks venturing into white neighborhoods, is now a common experience for Latinos, documented or not. Romero (2007) writes,

> "Mexicanness" becomes the basis for suspecting criminality under immigration law. Mexican American and other racialized Latino citizens and legal residents are subjected to insults, questions, unnecessary stops and searches. (p. 449)

The 2010 passage of SB 1080 in Arizona and Alabama's 2011 passage of an even tougher anti-immigrant bill have been criticized for actually legalizing and mandating racial profiling by requiring law enforcement officers to stop and question anyone who looks like they may be illegal (Preston 2011).

The reproductive role of brown women immigrants has been a primary target of hate groups and also of some academics, for example, Huntington (2004). He writes,

> In this new era, the single most immediate and most serious challenge to America's traditional identity comes from the immense and continuing immigration from Latin America, especially from Mexico, and the *fertility rates* of these immigrants compared to Black and White American natives. (p. 32) [emphasis added]

There have also been proposals by elected officials in several states to challenge the Fourteenth Amendment, which makes anyone born in the United States an American citizen. These officials explicitly reference "illegal" *women* who come to the United States to have their babies and take advantage of the generous welfare state and taxpayers' money

(Lacey 2011). The intersection of racialization and feminization of hostile responses to Latina immigration is a key element in anti-immigrant cities in the United States.

DEFINING THE ANTI-IMMIGRANT "CITY"

Defining the anti-immigrant city necessitates rethinking the "city," especially from the perspective of immigrants. Immigrants were attracted to cities by industrial and other job prospects along with community ties and information about opportunities. In the context of globalization, new information technology, the expansion of agribusiness, and industrialization, such as meatpacking, moving to more rural and suburban areas, immigrant destinations have expanded. The geography of immigrant-attracting activities, formerly associated almost exclusively with cities, began to sprawl. Rethinking the city in line with Castells' formulation of network societies applies here. Castells (2000) argues we have seen a change from an industrial organization of society to a network society. The network structure of contemporary economic and social society forces us to change our conceptualization of the city. As networks cross from cities to suburbs to rural areas and back again, boundaries blend and make it difficult to define precise frontiers in terms of land use, social use values, and mobility among these previously differentiated spaces. So, while I use the term "anti-immigrant city," I am not exclusively intending to conceptualize a traditional urban form of density but rather a social and spatial place that spans traditional boundaries of cities, suburbs, and rural areas in its use and function. For example, there are places like Beardstown, Illinois, that have an anchor industry (meat packing plant). The population is about six thousand people, more than half of which are immigrants from West Africa and Mexico, as well as a growing Puerto Rican population. Beardstown has a dual language school system (Spanish and English), garage sale signs in French, Spanish, and English, a robust *Cinco de Mayo* celebration. Further, they have been able to break the traditional exclusion of blacks living in the town, which had been in place since the early twentieth century. While this would be considered a rural area by traditional definitions, the activities of labor and diversity make it more like a city.

In addition, regional governance structures such as:

> ... annexation, merger or consolidation; proposals to establish *supra-* or inter-municipal agencies, councils, administrative districts or planning

bodies; legal measures imposed by higher levels of government (such as the federal government or the states) to regulate urban expansion; and a variety of intergovernmental and inter-organizational strategies to enhance cooperation and coordination among government agencies as well as between public and private institutions and actors (Brenner 2002: 5)

have emerged and influenced the way we experience cities. For example, the collaborative ways in which law enforcement and other agencies work together, produce more confused boundaries between cities, suburbs, and rural areas. With computer systems in police cars, police in rural counties are in direct contact with urban police and are able to share visual and other data immediately. Furthermore, the movement of people, products, and services transgresses traditional urban boundaries with such regularity as if the boundaries were not there. It is often hard to say where the city begins and where it ends. The combination of these factors suggests that the notion of a city can no longer be limited to conventional boundaries or population distinctions, but that the essence of the city has expanded; therefore, this formulation of the anti-immigrant city also includes suburban and rural areas. The anti-immigrant city crosscuts space and geography while bunching systems of power that reach into rural and other non-city places.

I suggest that the contemporary form of the anti-immigrant city has four components: (1) sharper enforcements of anti-immigrant federal policy, (2) new local anti-immigrant policies and ordinances, (3) expanded and diversified rosters of officials able to enforce immigration policies, a whole new category of enforcers and (4) an increasingly anti-immigrant social climate across the United States which has inspired aggression toward immigrants.

While there have been anti-immigrant sentiments directed toward previous immigrant groups, the current anti-immigrant climate is different and more intense. The advent of talk radio shows where callers are free to express opinions to a wide audience and twenty-four-hour news shows on TV where hosts like Lou Dobbs and numerous others spread anti-immigrant rhetoric contribute to the climate of fear in Latino communities and beyond (Shih 2005). While the intensity of the anti-immigrant fervor has been ratcheted up by these types of groups, especially in the aftermath of September 11, 2001, there were three U.S. congressional acts passed in 1996 that set the stage for what was to come. The first, the 1996 Personal Responsibility and Work Opportunity Reconciliation Act, a.k.a. Welfare Reform Act, repealed the sixty-year-old social safety net for the poor and required welfare recipients to work. Since jobs were unavailable in the "new economy"[1] to people without high skills, some women who were forced off welfare rolls were forced into "illegal" activity for survival (McMurrer, Sawhill, and Lerman 1997).

In the second measure, under the Antiterrorism and Effective Death Penalty Act of 1996, the definition of crime expanded. The act was supposed to deter terrorism, provide justice for victims, and provide for an effective death penalty. It had a tremendous impact on the law of *habeas corpus* in the United States (a legal action or writ by means of which detainees can seek relief from unlawful imprisonment). What it actually did was to effectively foreclose the power of federal courts to remedy unjust convictions, thus intensifying local control of criminal punishment. Section 287(g) of the act permits designated local officers to perform immigration law enforcement functions; however, this section was not implemented until 2002. This point is particularly important, because it seems to be in direct contradiction to the plenary power of the federal government over immigration policy. While the federal government made provisions in the 1996 act to allow this, some have argued that the new local acts and use of 287(g) are illegal and headed to the Supreme Court for decisions (Varsanyi, 2008).

The third act of 1996, the Illegal Immigration Reform and Immigrant Responsibility Act, intensified punishment for crime. Previously, immediate deportation was triggered only for offences that could lead to five years or more in jail. Under this act, minor offenses such as shoplifting could deem an individual eligible for deportation. The act also applied to residents who married American citizens and had American-born children. These three acts combined to create an environment where poor communities were further destabilized, courts were restricted in their ability to respond to injustice, and immigrants were more vulnerable to deportation, and they provide the context where the anti-immigrant city could thrive.

Since 2001, the enforcement of these acts has intensified in an effort to respond to the 9/11 attacks. The number of raids and deportations in Latino neighborhoods and workplaces has dramatically increased. From 2003 to 2007 the number of deportations annually has risen from 1,901 to 30,408 (U.S. ICE, December 4, 2007) with 392,862 deported from October

---

[1] See Elsie L. Harper-Anderson (2008), "Benchmarks and Barriers: African American Experiences in the Corporate Bay Area's New Economy Sector of the 1990s, *Journal of Planning Education and Research*, 27(4): 483–498, for an excellent explanation of the new economy and issues of racial disparities.

of 2009 to September of 2010 (Bennett 2010). The sharp increase has created havoc for children of undocumented parents and for those in mixed-status families (ones whose members have different immigration status) because families suffer profound disruption when one member is arrested and deported. A recent study (Capps et al. 2007) demonstrated that the effects are both psychologically and physically devastating in Latino communities.

Second, new local anti-immigrant laws and policies have skyrocketed. As of November 2007, 1,562 anti-immigrant local ordinances and state bills had been proposed, and of those 244 had passed (Lucero 2008: 48). Various groups are challenging the constitutionality of such ordinances; in the meantime, their negative effects on the Latino community persist. Policies enacted in the anti-immigrant city, particularly raids and deportations, not only have traumatized the deported individuals and their families but have generated widespread fear and stress among community members, with resulting emotional and physical ills.

Third, many cities and towns have authorized the local police through 287(g), mentioned earlier, to initiate deportation procedures, which had been the exclusive domain of the ICE agents. New local enforcement can turn parts of the community against each other. In a disagreement, those with documents or who are citizens can use the threat of police and deportation to abuse or take advantage of others. In addition, the current focus on community policing strategies becomes impossible in Latino communities if the same police are charged with immigration enforcement.

Finally, a general anti-immigrant sentiment and aggression toward immigrants in the U.S. is now more visible in multiple ways: e.g., the rise in anti-immigrant groups such as the Minute Men, and the renewed growth of the Ku Klux Klan with a focus on brown immigrants and their families (Anti-Defamation League 2006). Vazquez (2009) points to how in anti-immigrant cities, "...groups like the Minute Men and SOS organize their constituencies to undermine the incorporation and integration of immigrants, ignoring the destructive consequences for the local and state economy" (p. 13). Local public displays of private hostilities to immigrants (often using incorrect information) exemplify an anti-immigrant climate. A sign on the Route 66 Hotel and Conference Center in Springfield, Illinois, for example, said read in February 2008, "Illegals cost $90B a year in welfare." Since undocumented immigrants cannot access welfare, the sign was incorrect but accomplished its aim of feeding anti-immigrant fervor. The number of Web sites that ooze such anti-immigrant fervor with references to "anchor babies" and to immigrants as "animals" has increased dramatically (Anti-Defamation League 2006). In the 2009 health crisis surrounding the swine flu, more anti-immigrant rhetoric developed, intensifying the climate of hate.

> No contact anywhere with an "illegal alien!" conservative talk show host Michael Savage advised his U.S. listeners this week on how to avoid the swine flu. "And that starts in the restaurants," where, he said, you "don't know if they wipe their behinds with their hands! (Alexander, 2009)

Research on the implications of this hostile climate for Latino communities is still limited, but, "hate crimes targeting Latinos increased... in 2007...a 40 percent rise in the four years since 2003, according to FBI statistics" (Potok 2008). The gendered effects are even less well understood. Using Collins's "intersectional paradigm" will help to tease out the proliferating intersections of race, gender, and perceived immigrant status.

INTERSECTIONAL PARADIGMS: RACE, GENDER, AND IMMIGRATION

I use what Patricia Hill Collins describes as an "intersectional paradigm" to frame the discussion here. She asserts, "[I]ntersectional paradigms view race, class, gender, sexuality, ethnicity, and age, among others, as mutually constructing systems of power" (Collins, 2004: 11). When Collins (1998) describes the need for such a paradigm, she anatomizes the ways in which the social sciences have treated the subject of black women, including

> ...general absences of Black women from social-science consideration; a treatment of Black women via a social problems framework, especially female identity and the construction of Black women as matriarchs; the tendency to discuss Black men and to generalize the findings to Black women; a parallel tendency to conduct studies on White women and generalize the findings to Black women; the use of social science methodologies generally biased against black people, women and working people; and a generally limited list of topics that shaped social-science research on Black women, for example studying women only in relation to their families roles especially their relationship with males. (p. 114)

Collins argues that since black women are situated at the intersection of race, class, and gender, intersectional analysis can achieve more productive and authentic understandings of how racism affects them.

Many of Collins's critiques of social science research are also applicable to the research about Latinas. An intersectional analysis offers a fruitful approach to understanding the contemporary intersection of race, gender and citizenship or the lack or perceived lack thereof, as it affects both undocumented and documented Latinas in the anti-immigrant city. Drawing here primarily on my fieldwork in Chicago and also on relevant articles, I examine the intersection of race, gender, and perceived immigrant status, and the consequences for the health, economic stability, and safety of Latinas in the United States. I am interested in how power structures (economic, social, racial, and gendered), violence, and reproduction interact to produce a post-9/11, gender-specific (i.e., misogynistic) racism. What are the dimensions of this new racism—how is it manifested in daily life? How are Latinas oppressed by and/or reacting to their encounters with this new racism?

Achieving acknowledgment of how gender complicates manifestations of racism has been a struggle. When, in the civil rights movement of the 1960s and other social justice movements, sexism has influenced members' behavior, women have tried to challenge it but have often been made to feel that if they pressed issues of gender equity they were turning their backs on the battle against racism. A generation later, Chicanas in the National Association for Chicano Studies sponsored a 1982 special session addressing sexism and the next year developed a Chicana caucus called *voces de la mujer* (Cordova 1999). Nonetheless, twenty-six years later at a national pro-immigrant activist meeting in a Chicago suburb in August 2006, only men sat on the panels making presentations, while only women were working in the registration booth. By midday on that occasion, a group of young Latinas stormed the podium, proclaimed the arrangement unacceptable, and organized a women's caucus, "women 4 immigrants." By the end of the day a unanimous vote had authorized equal numbers of women and men on all panels and organizational posts for this and future conferences/meetings of the group, and in its organizational structures. The women had not only contested traditional male dominance in public action, but had made clear that women had different things to say about the challenges of racism and different ways of presenting their experiences of it. The problem here was no resolution was made to include men at the registration booth, in effect adding to the *doble jornada* (double shift) of women.

In the 1982 Chicano studies meeting, the consideration of gender was made to point out how Chicanas had different or additional concerns than Chicanos. They certainly faced racism in the academy, but also sexism, both from the academy as a whole and within the Chicano studies association. Women at the 2006 pro-immigrant conference added the identity of immigrant to the challenges of gender and race in their expression of an intersectional paradigm. In this context we see the need for intersectional analysis. It gives access to a more complete picture of this new post 9/11-racism. A labyrinth of factors culminates to produce and support the construction of systems or bunches of power that oppress women immigrants, especially Latinas.

Several contexts appear germane to contemporary gendered racism. Collins (2004) views responses to globalization and transnationalism, the proliferation of the media, and sexual violence as new ways in which racism is manifested in contemporary society, particularly toward African American women. The same phenomena may be driving the racism encountered by Latinas. In addition, the concentration of capital and economic power in the hands of fewer people has increased poverty, which continues to be racialized and gendered (Collins 2004: 54). Globally, brown and black people are poorer, and among those poor, women and children constitute the greatest proportion. Using intersectional analysis including perceived immigrant status helps us to understand this new configuration of racism and the ways power structures that support it intersect and compound in the lives of brown women.

The Case of Chicago

From 2006 to 2010, I worked with two groups of Latinas in Chicago who organized to act on issues of economic self-sufficiency and gender violence. In addition to participant observation, I conducted in-depth interviews with twelve women from these groups about their day-to-day experiences. My participant observation comprised meetings in Chicago, phone conversations, conferences, e-mail correspondence, and shadowing women in their daily activities, sometimes for twelve hours. The most intense work was carried out from September 2006 to September 2009. During this period I made an average of two trips per month to Chicago and had numerous weekly e-mails and phone conversations. While the stories I describe here are the experiences of specific persons, similar stories are found on the women4immigrants listserve and in public media from across the country. These stories yield common patterns of experiences in the anti-immigrant city that demonstrate a new kind of racism embedding gender bias and targeting perceived illegal immigrant status.

The gender specific consequences of post-9/11 racism include health care problems, sudden changes in or elimination of income streams, increased vulnerability to violence from the state or society and from intimate partners, and challenges to reproductive roles. These harms affect not only undocumented immigrants, but also the larger Latino population of documented immigrants and U.S.-born citizens of Latino ancestry through the essentialized common view of all Latinas/os as "illegals" (Hamill 2008).

Health Issues

Policies enacted in the anti-immigrant city, particularly raids and deportations, have not only traumatized the deported individuals and their families but have generated widespread fear and stress among community members, with resulting emotional and physical ills. Stories about increased depression and its unhealthy side effects abound. For example, one woman whom I interviewed in Chicago described her sixty-pound weight gain in just a matter of months. She worried about being caught in a raid in the factory where she worked; she worried about whether her two undocumented children attending college might get caught in a raid or be vulnerable to expulsion because of their immigration status. "I would wake up in the morning with food stains on my pajamas without remembering having eaten during the night." Through a friend whose sister is a psychologist in Mexico, she had received phone therapy, and her friend had brought medication from Mexico. While her health was impacted negatively in the context of the anti-immigrant city, she used networks and transnational connections to get help and regain her health. Other women also described their emotional health issues as they related to their fear in their communities. One woman said she felt like she needed to use the church as a refuge, as a place to take care of what she called posttraumatic distress syndrome. She explained that when there is a traumatic event in a community, the government comes in and provides counseling for community members. But since the government is causing the event, the community is left to "cure itself." These health issues have real impacts on economic well-being, as well.

Economic Well-Being

Women who are left behind when a partner is deported can suffer great hardship as they are left to fend for themselves, often without income and with no way to generate it. Men represent about 85 percent of deported immigrants (Hagan, Eschbach, and Rodriquez 2008: 71), and women often become the sole supporters of the families left behind. Sometimes women are unaware of the whereabouts of bank accounts or where money is kept. Often they themselves have no waged labor experience. If they find work, childcare can be elusive. The kinds of jobs or income-generating activities that are available to immigrants can be dangerous or degrading. One woman described how she had finally turned to prostitution to support her U.S.-born children, because employers in the anti-immigrant city have become reluctant to hire undocumented individuals. She was extremely depressed, facing domestic violence, and worried about her children's safety. Here intersectional analysis demonstrates that the combination of her identities as a woman, brown, and immigrant compound to put her in an extremely dangerous and vulnerable position. If any one of these identities were different, she might not be in such a susceptible position.

Violence against Immigrant Women

Abraham (2000) concludes "...through male-centric immigration policies, the state indirectly ensured that minority women were subject to the racist patriarchal order and thus were made more vulnerable to the power exercised by an abusive spouse" (p. 50). In cities and towns where 287(g) has been implemented, where police also enforce immigration laws, we see more vulnerability of women as undocumented victims of violence who normally would call for help or report violence to the police but now may hesitate and so put their lives in danger (Brennan 2003, Fanlund 2008). Furthermore, immigrant victims of violence might be deterred from applying for U visas.

U visas were created by the Victims of Trafficking and Violence Prevention Act, which passed in October 2000. They are available to noncitizens who 1) have suffered substantial physical or mental abuse resulting from a wide range of criminal activity and 2) have been helpful, are being helpful, or are likely to be helpful with the investigation or prosecution of the crime. The U visa allows eligible immigrants to legally stay in the United States and provides employment authorization. The woman described above who had turned to prostitution should have been able to apply for a "U" visa, but when I asked her if she had applied, she said she did know of the U visa but was afraid to apply for it. Also, even though the U visas were established in 2000, no regulations for implementation were established; therefore, victims of violence could only apply for one-year work permits and interim protection from deportation (Bernstein 2007). Each state had different implementation rules for U visas, but generally women were able to renew without any problems.

In 2007, however, responding to the anti-immigrant climate, all fifty states embarked on an effort to make the U visa process the same across the states and even suggested that the U visa conflicted with federal and local anti-immigrant legislation. Then, while they were debating the issue, U visa applications were not processed, and no temporary protection or work permits were issued, essentially preventing victims from access to formal work or protection from abusers. Finally, in August of 2008 regulations were established and U visas were granted again. But during the almost yearlong period without any permits or protection, women in particular were forced into alternative and unregulated economic activities. New configurations of racism emerge that are painfully complicated in the anti-immigrant city; the three factors—race, gender, and perceived or real immigrant status—combine to construct a more intense and dangerous existence for these women.

Reproduction and Motherhood

The consequences of the anti-immigrant environment are grave for the men, who more often face deportation, but the consequences for women are also severe. Since women are the usual primary childcare providers, it is even more profoundly traumatic for women and for their children when mothers are deported and their children remain. (Nossiter 2008)

Indeed, the separation of children from their mothers can entail disastrous consequences, such as abrupt cessation of breastfeeding. In New Bedford, Massachusetts, in 2007, a raid at a leather factory making vests for the U.S. Army resulted in the arrest of over 350 workers, mostly women (Abraham and Ballou 2007). Many of the women, including some who were lactating, were flown to a Texas prison, far from their children. Several of the babies, U.S. citizens, were hospitalized for dehydration, which in infants can be fatal. Furthermore, there are videotaped testimonies (http://www.youtube.com/watch?v=2qG6FZbr9rM) of the women's humiliation and abuse in the Texas prison: they were forced to expose their breasts and express milk in front of a large group of laughing and teasing police officers. Again, in this instance, vicious behaviors arose from a mixture of race, gender, and immigrant identities.

Sexual violence has become an increasingly prominent and sinister component of brown women's experiences of racism, as seen in the New Bedford women's nightmare in the Texas prison. The entertainment media have glorified violent rape of women (though not of men), and we must recognize that problem as structural in society – not simply a matter of individual acts and individual victims (Collins 2004: 243). The militarization of the U.S.-Mexican border combined with allowing local police to initiate deportation proceedings has made brown women particularly vulnerable to sexual violence (Falcon 2001: 31). Recently, a police officer in Cobb County, Georgia, was convicted of raping an undocumented woman at gunpoint while threatening to deport her if she did not cooperate (Nill 2011). The ACLU attributes the implementation of 287(g) as the driving force behind the rape. Along the border, patrol agents have raped also Latinas. The message that rape in the context of "borderlands"[2] sends is of the "systematic degradation of women" (Falcon 2001: 32).

A study in Switzerland suggests how, in another aspect of the anti-immigrant preoccupation with sexual violence, the immigrant other's own culture is essentialized to be violent as well as sexist (Roux and Perrin 2007): the immigrant man as violent and sexist and the immigrant woman as submissive. In the case of Latinas, whether immigrants or citizens, that stereotyping exhibits a duality. According to Hondagneu-Sotelo (1999), women are constructed simultaneously as the "problem" but also as "victims" in the context of their culture and their gender. Latinas' non-Anglo culture and language signify to Anglos that they are a problem, but their gender stereotypes them as victims of stereotyped Latino machismo (Villenas 2001: 8). Immigrant women are presumed to encounter violence as part of their culture, which is distinct from Anglo culture and presumed to be therefore inferior.

The new racism that targets Latinas embodies hostility toward their citizenship status (Michalowski 2007) but also toward their childbearing functions, viewed as a threat to pass on an alien culture (Villenas 2001, Inda 2002). Immigrants from Mexico and Central America are dehumanized by being viewed as illegal, alien, and the justified quarry of the present-day "Minute Men" (Michalowski 2007: 64). Even those Latinas/os who are citizens or permanent legal residents are seen as "noncitizens... undeserving of American democracy" (Villenas 2001: 6) or the right to have babies (Inda 2002). The dehumanization of Latinas is particularly vicious in reducing them to "breeders" whose bodies are the loci for policing against the demonized "anchor babies."

At the same time, post-9/11 racism takes the misogynistic form of what some have called benevolent racism (Villenas 2001: 9) or microaggression

---

[2] Moreover, we may think of the borderlands as extending some relatively small distance from the border, but Rosas (2006) argues that the activities of recent immigration enforcement officers and others call for expanding the notion of borderland to include cities like Chicago and New York.

(Romero 2006: 435). Latina motherhood skills are denigrated and the dominant culture is called on to benevolently correct them in order to halt the transmission of their "alien" culture and ensure assimilation of their children. For example, Villenas describes a newspaper article titled "Program Enables Hispanic Women to Become Better Mothers" (2001: 7). An even more forthright example of the intersection of race with culture and gender bias was the attempt by ICE to deport an Asian immigrant woman from Seattle before she could give birth there to twins (Rebugio, Novakowski, and Timbang 2007: 4). Brown immigrant women are seen as inevitably mothers and nothing else.

It is ironic that along with the demonizing of Latinas' maternity, the bond between mother and child is callously ruptured by such ICE actions as the New Bedford raid and later a raid in Potsville, Iowa, in May of 2008. In other such instances, in California there have been raids near the schools where parents, mostly mothers, drop off their children (Martinez 2008). What kinds of decisions face Latinas about keeping their families intact as they try to facilitate education for their children?

DISCUSSION AND AVENUES FOR FURTHER RESEARCH

A new, post-9/11 racism has emerged, which encompasses, race, gender, and perceived immigration status. The repercussions differ for brown men and women, being directly related to their gender roles and identities. The discourse that enables this new racism centers on brown immigrant women's physical and cultural reproductive roles. The high proportion of women immigrants, their roles in their communities and their image as childbearers have made them targets for racists and rapists. It is the immigrant men who are more often deported, since brown man's bodies are criminalized on the basis of their race, gender, and perceived immigrant status. The women who stay behind, however, face oppression also on the basis of their race, gender, and perceived immigration status. Moreover, in their case, the intersectional paradigm also reveals their stigma as less than human through terms like "breeders" and "anchor babies" applied to their gender.

Understanding post-9/11 racism in terms of gender and immigrant status as well as race may not provide immediate solutions to racism, but it should lead us to converse about the problem in more nuanced ways. From such dialogues, strategies may arise to counter the gender-specific onslaughts of the latest racism in the United States. More research as well as prompt action is badly needed to document, understand, and untangle post-9/11 racism and the gender components that work together to oppress women. We cannot address those without first recognizing how greatly Latinos/as' educational advancement, housing opportunities and health are put at hazard risk by the new forms of racism. How are the obstacles to attending college or even finishing high school affecting future generations? How is the presence of ICE agents at schools affecting children's performance and their parents' decisions about school attendance? Are long-term public health problems generated by the high stress levels in Latino communities in anti-immigrant cities? What are the gender aspects of public health in the anti-immigrant city? Age is another unknown variable; Latinos are a very young population. The ways in which age will influence the situation of Latinos should be explored in the new understanding of post-9/11 racism. Using an "intersectional paradigm" is a productive way to examine these questions.

References

Abraham, Margaret. 1998. Immigration Policies and Practices in the United States: Gender, Ethnicity, Race and Class, Implications. International Sociological Association.

Adler, Rachel H. 2006. "But they claimed to be police, not la migra!": The Interaction of Residency Status, Class, and Ethnicity in a (Post-PATRIOT Act) New Jersey Neighborhood. *The American Behavioral Scientist*. Vol. 50, Iss. 1: 48.

Benjamin-Alvarado, Jonathan, Louis DeSipio, and Celeste Montoya. 2007. Immigrant Outrage as a National Phenomenon: Anti-HR 4437 Protests Beyond the Traditional Cities of Immigrant Reception. faculty.washington.edu/mbarreto/courses/398 _Alvarado_et_al.pdf (retrieved March 16 2008).

Chavez, Leo R.F. Allan Hubbell, Shiraz I. Mishra and R. Burciaga Valdez. 1997. Undocumented Latina Immigrants in Orange County, California: A Comparative Analysis. *International Migration Review*, Vol. 31, No. 1 (Spring): 88–107.

Coleman, Matthew. 2007. Immigration geopolitics beyond the Mexico-U.S. border. *Antipode*. Vol. 39, Issue 1: 54–76.

Deren, Sherry et al., 1997. Dominican, Mexican, and Puerto Rican Prostitutes: Drug Use and Sexual Behaviors. *Hispanic Journal of Behavioral Sciences*, 19: 2 (May): 202–213.

Falcon, Sylvanna. 2001. Rape as a Weapon of War: Advancing Human Rights for Women at the U.S.-Mexico Border. *Social Justice*, vol. 28, no. 2: 31–50, summer.

Galindo, René and Jami Vigil. 2006. Are Anti-immigrant Statements racist or nativist? What difference it makes? *Latino Studies*, Vol. 4: 419–447.

Gilbert, M.R. 1998. 'Race' space, and power: the survival strategies of working poor women. *Annals of the Association of American Geographers*. Volume 88, Issue 4: 595–621.

Grosholz, Emily. 2007. Black Sexual Politics: African Americans, Gender, and the New Racism. *Hypatia*, Vol. 22, Issue 4: 209–212.

Hagan, Jacqueline, Karl Eschbach and Nestor Rodriguez. 2008. U.S. Deportation Policy, Family Separation, and Circular Migration. *International Migration Review*. Vol. 42, No. 1: 64–88.

Hagan, John and Alberto Palloni. 1999. Sociological Criminology and the Mythology of Hispanic Immigration and Crime. *Social Problems*, Vol. 46, No. 4 (Nov.): 617–632.

Hill Collins, Patricia. 2004. *Black sexual politics: African Americans, gender, and the new racism*. New York: Routledge.

Hondagneu-Sotelo, Pierrette and Ernestine Avila. 1997. "I'm here, but I'm there". The Meanings of Latina Transnational Motherhood. *Gender and Society*, Vol. 11, No. 5: 548–571.

Hondagneu-Sotelo, Pierrette. 1999. *Women and Children First New Direction in Anti-immigrant Politics in American Families: A Multicultural Reader*, Edited by Stephanie Coontz with Maya Person and Gabrielle Raley. New York, Routledge.

Hunter, Margaret Lily. 2000. The Lighter the Berry? Race, Color, and Gender in the Lives of African American and Mexican American Women. Dissertation Abstracts International, A: The Humanities and Social Sciences, vol. 60, no. 7, 2690, Jan.

Hunter, Margaret L. 2005. *Race, gender, and the politics of skin tone*. New York: Routledge.

Huntington, Samuel P. 2004 The Hispanic Challenge. *Foreign Policy*, 141: 30–45.

Karjanen, David. 2008. Gender, Race, and Nationality in the Making of Mexican Migrant Labor in the United States. Latin American Perspectives, Vol. 35, No. 1: 51–63.

Kilty, Keith M. and Maria Vidal de Haymes. 2000. Racism, Nativism, and Exclusion: Public Policy, Immigration, and the Latino Experience in the United States. *Journal of Poverty*, Vol. 4, Issue 1/2: 1–25.

Littlefield, Marci Bounds. 2008. The Media as a System of Racialization: Exploring Images of African American Women and the New Racism. *American Behavioral Scientist*, January, Vol. 51 Issue 5: 675–685.

Malkin, Victoria. 2004. "We go to Get Ahead": Gender and Status in Two Mexican Migrant Communities. *Latin American Perspectives*, Vol. 31: 75.

Martinez, Elizabeth. 1993. Beyond Black/white: The Racisms of Our Time. *Social Justice*, Vol. 20, Issue 1–2.

Michalowski, Raymond. 2007. Border militarization and migrant suffering: a case of trans-national social injury. *Social Justice*, Vol. 32, Issue 2: 62–77.

Padín, José Antonio. 2005. The normative mulattoes: the press, Latinos, and the racial climate on the moving immigration frontier. *Sociological Perspectives*. Vol. 48, Issue 1: 49–75.

Pessar, Patricia R. 1999. Engendering Migration Studies: The Case of New Immigrants in the United States. *American Behavioral Scientist*, Vol. 42, No. 4: 577–600.

Powers, Mary G., William Seltzer and Jing Shi. 1998. Gender Differences in the Occupational Status of Undocumented Immigrants in the United States: Experience before and after Legalization. *International Migration Review*, Vol. 32, No. 4 (Winter): 1015–1046.

Pulido, Laura. 2007. A Day without Immigrants: The Racial and Class Politics of Immigration Exclusion. *Antipode*. Vol. 36, No. 1: 154–157.

Robinson, William I. 2006. 'Aquí estamos y no nos vamos!' Global capital and immigrant rights. *Race & Class*. Vol. 48, Issue 2: 77–91.

Romero, Mary. 2006. Racial Profiling and Immigration Law Enforcement: Rounding Up of Usual Suspects in the Latino Community. *Critical Sociology*. Vol. 32, Issue 2–3: 447–473.

Roux, P., Gianettoni, L., Perrin, C. 2007. The instrumentalization of gender: A new form of racism and sexism. *Nouvelles Questions Feministes*. Volume 26, Issue 2: 92–108.

Sánchez, George J. 1997. Face the Nation: Race, Immigration, and the Rise of Nativism in Lare Twentieth Century America. *International Migration Review*. Vol. 31, No. 4: 1009–1030.

Taylor, Janette Y. 2005. No resting place: African American women at the crossroads of violence. *Violence Against Women* 11.12 (Dec.): 1473–1489.

Villenas, Sofia. 2001. Latina Mothers and Small-Town Racisms: Creating Narratives of Dignity and Moral Education in North Carolina. *Anthropology & Education Quarterly*, Vol. 32, No. 1: 3–28.

Weinberg, Sydney Stalhl. 1992. The Treatment of Women in Immigration History: A Call For Change. *Journal of American Ethnic History*, (11) 4 Summer: 25.

Weis, Lois. 2001. Race, Gender, and Critique: African-American Women, White Women, and Domestic Violence in the 1980s and 1990s. *Signs: Journal of Women in Culture & Society*, Autumn, Vol. 27 Issue 1: 139.

CHAPTER THIRTEEN

GANG MEMBERS, JUVENILE DELINQUENTS,
AND DIRECT DEMOCRACY

Lisa Marie Cacho

Proposition 21, California's "Gang Violence and Juvenile Crime Prevention Initiative," passed easily (62 percent to 38 percent) in 2000. The amendments to adult and juvenile criminal law were both extensive and indiscriminate, imposing harsher penalties on crimes considered "gang" related, increasing penalties for certain violent or serious offenses, and requiring that more juveniles be tried as adults.[1] While Proposition 21 was unforgiving and overly punishing, its amendments were not new for youth of color in California. Youth of color were overrepresented in transfers to adult court even before the passage of Proposition 21. For instance, in 1996, 95 percent of the juvenile cases transferred to adult court in Los Angeles were those of youth of color.[2] When compared to white youth in Los Angeles, youth of color were 2.8 times more likely to be arrested for a violent crime, 6.2 times more likely to be transferred to adult court, and 7 times more likely to be imprisoned.[3] After implementing Proposition 21, circumstances worsened for adolescents of all colors. Only nine months after Proposition 21 went into effect, about 30 percent of all teenage offenders in California were charged in adult court.[4]

This attack on youth did not go unchallenged. Soon after Proposition 21 was implemented, lawyers persuasively, but unsuccessfully, argued for

---

[1] Proposition 21 also required that juveniles be held in state correctional facilities and that convicted gang members register with law enforcement. Confidentiality protections and probation programs were also significantly altered. The measure was preceded by Proposition 184, the "three-strikes-and-you're-out" initiative that mandated life sentencing for three felonies. Proposition 184 passed in 1994.

[2] Mike Males and Dan Macalliar, "The Color of Justice: An Analysis of Juvenile Adult Court Transfers in California" (Washington, D.C.: Building Blocks for Youth, January 2000), 5.

[3] Mike Males and Dan Macalliar, "The Color of Justice: An Analysis of Juvenile Adult Court Transfers in California" (Washington, D.C.: Building Blocks for Youth, January 2000), 7–8.

[4] Jennifer Taylor, "California's Proposition 21: A Case of Juvenile Injustice," *Southern California Law Review* 75 (2002): 991.

its repeal. But although the legal battles often referenced racial bias in the criminal justice system, the high-profile lawyers whose cases received the most media attention did not have clients of color. As Denise Ferreira da Silva contends, "The most insidious and pervasive manifestation of race injustice is not the masking of racism under said universal principles. The most vicious form of race injustice is that which usually does not make it to the courts."[5] Silva reminds us not to forget that much of the violence, brutality, and murder—by the state and its neglect—never becomes a news story or makes it to a trial by jury. And for those that do, "it always-already ensures that the black or Latino perpetrator will receive a guilty verdict because the blackness and brownness of the accused or victim and the place where she or he lives is read as the indigenous locus of violence."[6] Manuel Ortega, Carlos Martinez, Carlos Sanchez, and Jesus Miranda were among the first youth tried as adults after Proposition 21. These youths not only did not receive much media attention, but their trials (those who had them) were also not able to convey legitimate injury or genuine innocence.

This chapter examines how one of the legal challenges to Proposition 21 was presented to the public in print media, paying particular attention to how race, criminality, and whiteness have been "reinvented," or rather resignified for the twenty-first century. As mentioned, youth of color were unable to be representative victims of Proposition 21 legally or in media, so I will analyze representations of white ethnic gang members' legal challenges to the initiative. Following Silva's critique of the logic of racial exclusion, I apply the way in which she reads race as an analytic and as a political strategy to demonstrate how 1) race does not need to be invoked when people and places are already marked as criminal and illegal and 2) criminality is racialized and spatialized even when the bodies referenced do not neatly correspond. In other words, most racial analyses see race as an arbitrary marker of human difference that perpetuates or exacerbates class exploitation; through this framework, race excludes people of color not only from economic opportunities and social resources, but also from the democratic principles of freedom and equality. This reading

---

[5] Denise Ferreira da Silva, "Towards a Critique of the Socio-logos of Justice: The Analytics of Raciality and the Production of Universality," *Social Identities* 7, no. 3 (2001): 448.

[6] Denise Ferreira da Silva, "Towards a Critique of the Socio-logos of Justice: The Analytics of Raciality and the Production of Universality," *Social Identities* 7, no. 3 (2001): 448.

of race needs racial difference to be invoked in order to prove racial discrimination, but as Silva explains, focusing our attention on the moments of racial exclusion from the ideals and practices of universality fails to realize that "the primary effect of the power of race has been to produce universality itself."[7] When race does not need to be invoked, these moments are often misunderstood as evidence that race no longer matters or that class has become more salient than race, which is both an inaccurate and dangerous misreading of how race functions in U.S. society and through U.S. global politics. What Silva's re-reading of the racial and the cultural helps us to understand are the ways in which the structures, institutions, and principles of the United States have been constituted, designed, and sustained by the deeply ingrained, but never recognized conviction that *"whiteness* and only *whiteness* signifies *universality.*"[8] My analysis of how young Armenian gangsters were represented by print media illustrates how race and culture operate to render "other" people and places of color irrevocably illegal while enabling legal escape mechanisms for non-targeted whites.

In Glendale, a suburb of Los Angeles, two months after Proposition 21 passed, seventeen-year-old Raúl Aguirre died from a stabbing. The suspects were three teenagers; two were under eighteen. Aguirre was stabbed four times in the chest by one of the boys while the other beat him with a crowbar; a young girl drove the attackers to and from the scene. Karen Terteryan (eighteen years old), Rafael Gevorgyan (fifteen years old), and Anait Ano Msryan (fourteen years old), allegedly members of an Armenian gang, were some of the first youths tried after Proposition 21 was passed and implemented. Their trial, covered by the *Daily News of Los Angeles*, provides us a concrete example of the ways in which racial masculinity, gang membership, and criminal activity were rendered as interchangeable signifiers by print media even though the actual (white ethnic) bodies of the gang members did not neatly or easily invoke "race."

Armenians occupy an ambiguous position in Los Angeles' current racial hierarchies as white ethnics, but not necessarily European. They have not all emigrated from Armenia, but also from the former Soviet Union, Iran,

---

[7] Denise Ferreira da Silva, "Towards a Critique of the Socio-logos of Justice: The Analytics of Raciality and the Production of Universality," *Social Identities* 7, no. 3 (2001): 427.

[8] Denise Ferreira da Silva, "Towards a Critique of the Socio-logos of Justice: The Analytics of Raciality and the Production of Universality," *Social Identities* 7, no. 3 (2001): 447.

Lebanon, and other parts of the Middle East. Historically, Armenians have been considered legally white in the United States but, as relatively recent immigrants, they are also marked by geopolitical difference, and consequentially, they have been victimized by white supremacist groups.[9] Glendale, a fairly diverse suburb of Los Angeles, has the largest population of Armenians in the United States with 26.2 percent of the city claiming Armenian ancestry, according to 2000 census data.[10] In this suburb, Latinas/os constituted the next largest group at 17.2 percent (primarily Mexican and Central American), and Asians made up 13.4 percent (mostly Filipino and Korean).[11] The racial, economic, and social characteristics of Glendale cannot be considered representative of the United States, California, or even Los Angeles; however, as Natalia Molina suggests, we do need to be cognizant of how race is not only nationally produced, but also locally constructed: people "see" race differently in different locations and during different time periods.[12] Even so, for the purposes of my analysis, I will not be focusing on the ways race or ethnicity is relationally and locally constructed in Glendale, but rather on how "the racial" and "the cultural" are used as signifiers (whether race is or is not invoked) to render certain people and places as either potentially recoverable or categorically criminal.

Coverage of the case reveals how gang membership is represented as both identity and motive; it describes who they are *and* explains what they do, so that bodies are indistinguishable from behaviors. The reading audience was offered only two possible motives for Aguirre's murder—gang violence or racial hatred: "Police and school officials acknowledged there are racial tensions between Armenian and Latino students at Hoover, but said they believe the slaying was the result of gang violence, not ethnic hatred."[13] In addition to explicitly equating "racial" with "ethnic," staff writer Donna Huffaker provided us two motives that only have one source:

---

[9] Janice Okoomian, "Becoming White: Contested History, Armenian American Women, and Racialized Bodies," *MELUS* 27, no.1 (Spring 2002): 221.

[10] http://www.epodunk.com/ancestry/Armenian.html, accessed May 26, 2008.

[11] http://www.epodunk.com/cgi-bin/genealogyInfo.php? locIndex=10208 <accessed May 26, 2008> http://factfinder.census.gov/servlet/ACSSAFFFacts?_event=Search&geo _id=&_geoContext=&_street=&_county=glendale&_cityTown=glendale& _state=04000US06&_zip=&_lang=en&_sse=on&pctxt=fph&pgsl=010, accessed May 26, 2008.

[12] Natalia Molina, *Fit to Be Citizens?: Public Health and Race in Los Angeles, 1879–1939* (Berkeley and Los Angeles: University of California Press, 2006), 6.

[13] Donna Huffaker, "Teens Charged in Gang Slaying; Girl, 14, Treated as Adult under Prop. 21," the *Daily News of Los Angeles*, May 10, 2000: N3.

racialized, masculine identities, limiting and linking interpretations of Terteryan, Gevorgyan and Msryan's violent actions as either/both racist or/and gang related. Not only are structural conditions—such as deindustrialization, chronic unemployment, increased immigration, under-funded schools, racial segregation, political disenfranchisement, or racial profiling—not mentioned as possibly affecting the suspects' states of mind, but even personal circumstances, such as depression or family problems, are not offered as potentially influencing the youths' behaviors. Without (even the pretense of) motive, racial masculinity functions to describe both the suspect and the reason for his behavior; it is both the cause for and the effect of his (alleged) crime.

But besides the slip of writing "racial" as synonymous with "ethnic," how do these Armenian bodies come to stand in for racial masculinity? They do not. These Armenian bodies do not signify gang membership—but rather gang membership signifies racial masculinity, criminality, and economic dispossession. Gang membership marks these particular Armenians *and entire urban areas of color* as beyond ethical consideration and moral obligation. After Aguirre's murder, Armenian gangs are not represented as the new target for increased surveillance, further research, or more investigation.[14] Rather, *the neighborhood* where the crime was committed was put under surveillance, and that became the primary news story of Aguirre's murder. Rather than searching for motive or psychologizing the suspects, Huffaker's sources were law enforcement, which functioned to structure identification with the police: "Admittedly targeting gangs, Sgt. Rick Young, spokesman for the Police Department, said patrol officers will stop and question anyone who looks like a gang member for even the smallest of infractions."[15] Young justified taking legal action against anyone who "looks like a gang member" by saying: "People are going to say we're harassing the kids, that it's a violation of their civil rights. Well, (they should) stop dressing like gang members. I'm sorry, but there comes a point in society where the line has to be drawn. If you want to be a gang

---

[14] The collapse of the Soviet bloc spurred immigration to the United States in the 1990s. These new immigrants invoked anxieties that Russian and other Eastern Europeans gangs would form organized crime groups, like the 1930s. In Los Angeles, Armenians were depicted as gangs from two angles: 1) as organized crime brought over from their former countries and 2) as the necessary response of Armenian youth who had to live alongside Mexican and Salvadoran gangs.

[15] Donna Huffaker, "Slaying, Shooting Trigger Sweeps; Suspected Gang Members Targeted," the *Daily News of Los Angeles,* May 13, 2000: N3.

member, then you pay the consequences."[16] Young's justification for racial profiling exposes that gang members are positioned beyond the law, outside of the realm of civil rights because they are rendered criminal regardless of whether or not they commit crimes. Therefore, the semblance of a gang aesthetic was enough to establish guilt. As illustrated by Young's line of argument, youth in this neighborhood, who are not gang members, have one basic civil right: to dress appropriately or to dress inappropriately. If such youth exercise their civil right to dress like a gang member, then they forfeit all other civil rights. Young continued with equating public safety with more police: "This should be one of the safest weekends we've had in a while. We will target anyone on the street who appears to be a gang member."[17] Again, these articles structure identification with the police, rather than with the youth under intensified surveillance or their families. For youth wearing the wrong (skin) color, the streets will not necessarily be safer.

This example is indicative of what Silva terms "a rearrangement of the analytics of raciality."[18] In *Toward a Global Idea of Race*, Silva traces how race has become (come into being as) a signifier for the supposedly "affectable consciousness" of racialized, gendered subalterns. She defines "affectability" as "the condition of being subjected to both natural (in the scientific and lay sense) conditions and to others' power."[19] Subjected to their natural and man-made environments, people of color were represented as *products* of their environments. They were not imagined as able to actualize the principles of self-determination or universality, which are guided by one's interior consciousness. In other words, when rendered intrinsically affectable, people of color are denied interiority where reason, rationality and ethicality reside. Furthermore, they become products of environments that are identified as the cause, rationale and evidence for not only their inability to access political and economic equality, but also for their vulnerability to state sanctioned violence.

The "rearrangement of the analytics of raciality" refers to the recent resignifications of race both within U.S. borders and globally in the

---

[16] Donna Huffaker, "Slaying, Shooting Trigger Sweeps; Suspected Gang Members Targeted," the *Daily News of Los Angeles*, May 13, 2000: N3.

[17] Donna Huffaker, "Slaying, Shooting Trigger Sweeps; Suspected Gang Members Targeted," the *Daily News of Los Angeles*, May 13, 2000: N3.

[18] Denise Ferreira da Silva, *Toward a Global Idea of Race* (Minneapolis: University of Minnesota Press, 2007), 265.

[19] Denise Ferreira da Silva, *Toward a Global Idea of Race* (Minneapolis: University of Minnesota Press, 2007), xv.

contemporary moment. These current resignifications reveal how "affect-ability"—while still intimately connected to race—is no longer signified by race alone. In the *Daily News* articles, it is *gang membership*, not Armenian bodies, that signifies "affectability," which is how poor Latino, African American, and Southeast Asian neighborhoods are still rendered categorically criminal by these representations even though their particular racialized bodies are not invoked. As Silva explains, "What the prevailing strategy of racial subjection in the United States indicates is not that the racial explains class subjection but that the association of criminality and material (economic) dispossession has become the new signifier of the affectability of the racial subaltern."[20] Because gang members are represented as products of poor urban environments (as affectable consciousness), then criminal activity signals that the environment is not under enough regulation and repression, which justifies increasing police surveillance and suspending civil rights.

The news articles represented the young Armenian suspects as disconnected from family, friends, teachers, and classmates, which depersonalized the initiative's legal and moral ramifications. Reporters chose sources who confirmed their personal beliefs about gangs and reaffirmed their preconceived scripts of gang violence. Journalists did not, for instance, seek to interview the parents of the suspects to find out whether their teenagers' behaviors were atypical or whether the offenders had suffered from recent traumatic experiences. They did not interview school counselors to figure out if the youth were good students or whether they were often the victims of bullying. They did not interview students who had witnessed acts of violence to tell us whether it was provoked, whether the suspects seemed to be in control or under the influence of drugs or alcohol, or whether tensions had been building between the victims and perpetrators. These other/ed sources would have personalized not just the consequences of Proposition 21, but also the people affected by it. Personalizing the stories of the suspects would require framing the news stories in ways to structure identification with the alleged offenders, their relatives, their social networks, and their communities. But instead reporters appealed to readers' civic sensibilities, desire for law and order, and collective disdain for law breaking. Readers were primed to identify with the police, district attorneys, and defense lawyers, all of whom were

---

20 Denise Ferreira da Silva, *Toward a Global Idea of Race* (Minneapolis: University of Minnesota Press, 2007), 265.

the primary sources in articles about these youth of color's legal challenges to Proposition 21.

But journalists also did not personalize the stories of gang violence victims, who are almost always youth of color. Victims, too, seemed to be disconnected from family, friends, and social networks. It was not Aguirre's death that made the news; rather his death set the stage to tell the story about lawyers' challenges to Proposition 21. His death was part of the background, a minor detail. Huffaker quoted Deputy District Attorney Darrell Mavis, who said,

> This crime happened to have occurred shortly after the statute had been enacted and it is the type of crime [murder of nongang member by gang violence] that the voters wanted to stop...The public wanted them [gang members and underage criminals] to be treated as adults. All we're trying to do is carry out the will of the people.[21]

As with the articles about Terteryan, Gevorgyan, and Msryan, the reading audience (represented as "the public" and "the will of the people") is structured to identify with the lawyers, law enforcement, judges, and jurors.

Aguirre's family was interviewed and quoted by the *Daily News of Los Angeles* when Huffaker reported that Aguirre's funeral would be able to proceed because the battle over his body as evidence would not continue. Glendale Court Commissioner Steven Lubell ruled that Aguirre's already released body would not be returned to the coroner's office for Gevorgyan and Msyran's attorney, Andrew Flier, to have it independently examined. Although Aguirre's mother and sister were both quoted in this article, the quotes merely contextualized why it would be morally suspect to return the body to the coroner's office. Aguirre's mother, Leticia Aguirre, was quoted as saying, "I just want him to rest in peace. I'm hurting a lot and I don't want to hurt anymore."[22] Hurt and tired and only wanting her son's spirit to rest, Leticia Aguirre's statement is juxtaposed against Flier's heroic commitment to his client, who argued for the return of Aguirre's body "in front of nearly two dozen family members, friends and neighbors of the deceased youth."[23] Leticia Aguirre was quoted to be the representative spokesperson of her son's friends and family, but the story was not about

---

[21] Donna Huffaker, "Murder Case Tests New Law on Trying Juveniles," the *Daily News of Los Angeles*, November 26, 2000: N3.

[22] Donna Huffaker, "Dead Boy's Funeral Will Proceed," the *Daily News of Los Angeles*, May 11, 2000: N3.

[23] Donna Huffaker, "Dead Boy's Funeral Will Proceed," the *Daily News of Los Angeles*, May 11, 2000: N3.

their collective loss because the role they played in the narrative was only as Flier's audience for his inappropriate, yet brave and audacious, arguments. The victim in this news story is Flier, not Leticia or Raúl's sister Lorena, not even Raúl. Aguirre's mother and sister were only cited to help explain the understandable, yet unfortunate, circumstances for Flier's loss over Raúl Aguirre's body.

Although this article gave a voice to Aguirre's family, it did little to differentiate Aguirre from those who murdered him. In fact, Huffaker reported that "Flier likened Aguirre's body to a weapon."[24] Of all the metaphors Flier could have used to illustrate that he believed Aguirre's body was evidence in a murder case (such as fingerprints, DNA, or clothing), he chose to liken the dead body of a victim of gang activity to a "weapon." Even in death and even as victim, the bodies of youth of color were imagined as "weapons," reiterating that racial masculinity signifies criminal conduct. Murdered bodies of color were only evidence for the senselessness of gang members' indiscriminate brutality and inhumanity—their affectable consciousness and irrepressible immorality. But even in the last story of their lives, youth of color were not elevated to the status of protagonists. Rather, reporters represented the racialized dead as akin to unfortunate casualties of a war that happens only in foreign, faraway zip codes where bodies by themselves are dangerous weapons and where safety can only be acquired through increased police surveillance and a little leniency with civil rights. In these articles, the lives of youth of color, whether gang member or gang victim, were portrayed as dispensable and expendable. Victims and perpetrators were undifferentiated, rendered equivalent and interchangeable, all immutable products of poor, violent environments.

Only by apprehending and applying the current "rearrangement of the analytics of raciality" are we able to uncover such urgent and devastating consequences of how race works with economic dispossession and criminalization without ever having to be directly invoked.

> Neither the liberal argument (nonsystemic or institutional discrimination) nor the critical field of racial and ethnic studies' focus on institutional racism touches on the most dramatic consequences of economic dispossession, nor can they apprehend recent resignifications of raciality. While recognizing that media-produced terms such as "gang banger" and "welfare queen" refer to the racial/gendered subalterns, they read them as codes for racial

---

[24] Donna Huffaker, "Dead Boy's Funeral Will Proceed," the *Daily News of Los Angeles,* May 11, 2000: N3.

> difference that mask the racially exclusionary aims of the legislation and policy initiatives these terms are deployed to support.... The problem, however, is that the "gang banger" and the "welfare queen" do not participate in the U.S. economy, and the legislation (mid-1990s welfare reform and crime bills) and the public policies they enable displace them from the juridical moment as well.... (264)

Investments in reading racial exclusion can only read the figure of the gang member as merely a code that stands in for racial difference and "falsely" ascribes criminality to the bodies of young men of color, thus, legitimizing the economic exclusion of people of color and justifying current and future exclusionary laws and policies. But if the gang member is read as only a code for racial, gendered difference, then analytical and political efforts are too often spent de-linking masculine bodies of color from criminality, re-inscribing "innocence" and "respectability." In this vein, racialized criminality as "false" ascription is differentiated from racialized criminality as "true" embodiment. But proving that the racial representation of criminality is primarily "false" cannot assess how criminalized populations and places—the "true" embodiments that needs to be disavowed in order to make ethical appeals—are rendered "affectable," which positions them (literally and legally) outside state protection and beyond ethical obligation. As unable to be incorporated into U.S. notions of ethicality and morality, criminalized and impoverished populations and places cannot activate discourses of innocence or injury, upon which the logic of exclusion relies.

At the same time, it is still important and significant to note that although recent resignifications of race register representations of Armenian gang members as evidence for the need to contain and surveil poor people of color and their neighborhoods, these white ethnic gang members were not subjected to the racialized state repression for which their crimes were a catalyst. All, for instance, were able to hire lawyers, which is why their legal challenges to Proposition 21 could even be represented within print media. Terteryan's lawyer was even the high-profile lawyer Mark Geragos, from Court TV, who also represented Scott Peterson. As gang members, these three young adults are represented in media as absolutely unable to evoke even the most reluctant sense of ethical obligation to give them a fair trial, but as white ethnics able to activate discourses of injury and innocence, their legal battles in the court-room can evoke a sense of moral obligation to give them a second chance. Geragos, like Flier, drew upon Raúl Aguirre's racial body as a signifier for affectablity and criminality: "[Geragos] will tell jurors that Terteryan was only protecting himself when he knifed Aguirre. 'Our defense is self-defense and that this is manslaughter not murder,' he said."[25] While receiving long sentences for voluntary manslaughter, neither Terteryan (who received a twenty-three-year sentence) nor Gevorgyan (who was sentenced to eighteen years) were convicted for murder. Msryan pled guilty to attempted murder, receiving seven years in the California Youth Authority as part of her plea bargain to testify for the prosecution.

[25] Harriet Ryan, "Peterson not the only murder suspect banking on Geragos: The high-profile defense attorney will spend the next month on another murder case, this one low-profile," *Court TV*, September 17, 2003. http://www.courttv.com/trials/peterson/gangcase_ctv.html. Accessed Sunday, May 25, 2008.

CHAPTER FOURTEEN

RACIAL DISADVANTAGES AND INCARCERATION: SOURCES OF WAGE INEQUALITY AMONG AFRICAN AMERICAN, LATINO, AND WHITE MEN

Kecia R. Johnson and Jacqueline Johnson

According to the Bureau of Justice Statistics, the incarceration rates for African American men are five to seven times greater than those for white men in the same age cohorts, while Latino men's rates of incarceration are nearly twice those of whites (Harrison and Beck 2006). Because prior incarceration can result in an ex-offender experiencing long-term unemployment or low-wage employment, African American and Latino men who have been incarcerated are more likely than whites to experience careers characterized by economic instability. Removal from the labor force limits the possibility for ex-offenders to develop the level of human and social capital and job- or firm-specific skills that allow them to aggressively compete with non-offenders in the open labor market (Holzer, Raphael and Stoll 2001, 2002, 2003; Pager and Western 2005; Waldfogel 1994; Western, Kling, and Weiman 2001). The reputation or "mark" associated with a criminal record also disrupts the earnings potential of ex-offenders when employers read incarceration history as symbolic of low productivity when screening job candidates (Pager 2003).

Yet, incarceration is not the only factor that contributes to the economic instability of African American and Latino men. Supply-side studies, which examine the characteristics of workers, argue that racial differences in wages are a function of human-capital deficits among racial minorities that are debilitating in contemporary labor markets characterized by racially neutral shifts in labor demands towards better skilled workers (Becker 1964, 2003; Rodgers 2006). Poorly qualified racial minorities are left to scramble for jobs at the lower end of the wage pool, especially in the early stages of their careers. Some arguments link low human-capital investment to minority men's disproportionate preferences for income-producing, illegal activities since their limited skills are not highly valued in legitimate labor markets (Freeman 1996). Others argue that race is not a significant determinant of low skills, as much as

African American men's acceptance of countercultural values that lead them to choose illegal income-producing activities over legitimate work outcomes (Murray 1984; D'Souza 1995; McWhorter 2000).

Sociological perspectives argue that human capital differences explain some but not all of the racial differences in earnings among workers. They argue that continuing sex and race segregation (England et al. 1988; Tomaskovic-Devey 1993), differences in social capital (Bridges and Villemez 1986; Granovetter 1985; Royster 2003), and racial discrimination factor prominently in the employment and wages of African American and Latino men across their careers (Grodsky and Pager 2001; Pager 2005a; Pager 2005b; Royster 2003; Tomaskovic-Devey, Thomas, and Johnson 2005; Thomas, Herring, and Horton 1994). When incarceration factors into the wage equation, racial disparities are magnified by the effects of imprisonment (Western and Pettit 2005; Western, Kleykamp, and Rosenfield 2006). The main problem for ex-offenders seems to be denied access to employment. Yet, African American and Latino men are not always crowded into jobs at the low end of the wage scale because they are often denied access to even these jobs. Audit studies reveal that employer preferences for white workers, regardless of their former incarceration status, are commonplace, especially in low-wage labor markets (Pager 2005a; Pager and Western 2005; Pager 2003). Interestingly, incarceration status seems to be more problematic for the post-incarceration employment of ex-offenders who are African American or Latino than for white men. White ex-offenders are also preferred over African American men with no records of incarceration (Pager and Western 2005; Pager 2003).

Does incarceration exacerbate existing racial inequality in wages among men? This article examines the effect that incarceration has on wages by examining the wage trajectories of formerly incarcerated and never-incarcerated African American, Latino, and white men. While we draw heavily on prior research that studies the impact of incarceration on employment (Uggen 1999; Western 2002; Western and Pettit 2004), we extend this research in several ways. First, we go beyond research that focuses on hiring practices (see Pager 2003, 2005a. 2005b) to examine the wage trajectories of ex- and non-offenders who do manage to secure employment. When the barriers to employment are not a factor, are racial differences in earnings among men explained by human capital differences? Second, we conceptualize incarceration as a supply-side factor that African American, Latino, and white men may bring to the labor market along with other individual characteristics. If incarceration is the outcome of a bad career choice, we are interested in how this factor functions as a wage-depreciating mechanism on earnings across the career in comparison to wage-appreciating mechanisms, such as human capital. Finally, if patterns of racial disadvantage are revealed among ex-offenders, how do they compare to racial differences in wages among African American, Latino, and white men who were never incarcerated? Our analysis examines within and across racial group comparisons to estimate the degree to which incarceration may affect the wage trajectories of African American, Latino, and white men.

INCARCERATION AND WAGE DEPRECIATION OVER TIME

When considering the impact of imprisonment, the depreciative effect of incarceration on wages may vary by frequency and length of time served by inmates over the course of their career. It is easy to imagine that longer prison stays may contribute to the erosion of a former inmate's labor market attractiveness and earning potential, in terms of the devaluation of work skills, lack of on-the-job training and work experience, and diminished contact with lucrative social networks. Freeman (1992) found this to be the case for a survey of ex-offenders who experienced substantial, long-term employment barriers and reduced earnings in direct proportion to increases in the amount of time they served. On the other hand, Grogger's (1995) study found that the effects of multiple arrests and longer jail terms on men's wages are moderate and short-lived. He attributes any long-term earnings penalties experienced by ex-offenders to unobserved characteristics of workers that are correlated with both crime and labor market success, such as increased criminal opportunities in a growing drug trade and declining wages for youth who are concentrated in low-wage labor markets. Similarly, Kling's (2006) study found no negative effect of incarceration length on earnings for ex-prisoners in Florida and California. He contends that the depreciative effects of longer incarceration spells on wages are short term, limited to only one or two years after release, especially when the prison reentry programs are available to help ex-offenders make the transition to work. While these jobs may pay higher starting salaries upon entry, their long-term stability or wage growth is not clear from Kling's analysis. Ideally, even if the jobs attained by ex-offenders in this study are transitory rather than stable, any reentry employment opportunity would place them in a better position to search for other employment and to demand higher wages over time. This is particularly the case if workers gain valuable skills and work experience and are able lose some of the stigma associated with their former incarceration status. Perhaps the mixed results reveal that the long-term effect of incarceration on earnings is less likely attributed to variations in the frequency and length of time served among inmates and more likely related to other individual factors, such as human capital.

INCARCERATION ERODES HUMAN CAPITAL

Depressed wages may result from the depreciation of human capital characteristics, such as education and skills that can occur with spells of unemployment. According to some estimates, about 70 percent of current inmates and ex-inmates are high school dropouts, which means that their average pre-incarceration earning potential was well below what it might have been in the absence of incarceration (Travis, Solomon, and Waul 2001; Freeman 1994; Holzer et al 2003). The time spent out of legitimate labor markets may be particularly erosive to vocational or job-specific skills that often deteriorate when they are not used and/or are subject to rapid change, such as computer technology (Irwin and Austin 1987). Others point out that incarceration is, itself, an often unaccounted form of unemployment. Because African American men in the United States are disproportionately incarcerated, their rates of absence from labor markets is underestimated, but their average wages are exaggerated in traditional employment and unemployment reports that do not consider incarceration as a form of joblessness (Western and Beckett 1999, Pettit and Western 2004). Western (2002) and Holzer et al. (2003) contend that because incarceration removes ex-inmates from private sector labor markets, they are not able to gain work experience, job skills, or develop work habits that may be attractive to employers. Western, Pettit, and Guetzkow (2002) argue that African American men's significantly higher rates of incarceration only amplified existing racial gaps in earnings and estimate that the black-white earnings gap among men aged thirty or younger could be reduced by as much as 6 percent if African Americans and whites were incarcerated at the same rate.

While diminished human capital characteristics are a consequence of incarceration, former incarceration status also reduces wages over time by interrupting potential patterns of stable employment. According to Nagin and Waldfogel (1993; 1995), ex-offenders are often limited to employment in spot market jobs that are highly vulnerable to labor market fluctuations and are subject to low wage growth over time. Likewise, the ex-offenders in Pettit and Western's (2004) study experienced patterns of unstable employment and flatter wage trajectories across their careers. In both cases, it is not just the individual ex-offender who is unstable, but also the types of jobs they are able to secure upon release are less likely to offer economically stabilizing opportunities.

INCARCERATION ERODES RELATIONSHIPS

Relationships also deteriorate over time when individuals spend time in prison. Researchers argue that imprisonment undermines the development of social networks that provide job referrals and employment opportunities (Sullivan 1989; Hagan and Dinovitzer 1999; Western 2002). Ex-offenders' networks are more likely to be criminogenic rather than beneficial for legitimate job seeking, largely because these relationships are developed within prison contexts (Irwin and Austin 1987; Sullivan 1989). Many ex-offenders return to communities where their social contacts have few connections to secure, well-paying jobs. This is particularly the case for African American men, whose social networks are limited because they are more likely than whites to live in communities characterized by high rates of unemployment and crime (Sampson and Wilson 1985; Young 1999). Social contacts have proven to be more advantageous to white than African American men for access to highly paid jobs, even when both groups are nearly identically matched on work experience and human-capital attributes (Braddock and McPartland 1987; Royster 2003).

In addition, incarceration weakens relationships that ex-offenders may have with past or future employers because of the stigma associated with former incarceration status (Schwartz and Skolnick 1962; Boshier and Johnson 1979; Finn and Fontaine 1983, 1985; Freeman 1992; Sampson and Laub 1993; Holzer 1996; Needels 1996; Nagin and Waldfogel 1995; Pager 2003, 2005; Western and Pager 2005). Incarceration stigma limits wage potential by decreasing the desirability of ex-offenders to employers. Using data from surveys of employers, Holzer et al. (2001) found that ex-offenders are undesirable job candidates for most employers. Citing concerns of safety, trust, and legal liability, employers were less likely to hire job seekers with criminal records than other groups of disadvantaged workers.[1] In some cases, the extent to which employers may seriously

---

[1] Only 38 percent of employers in this study stated that they would "definitely or probably hire" an ex-offender, while 92 percent said that they would consider a former or current welfare recipient, 96 percent would consider an applicant with a GED in lieu of a high school diploma, 83 percent would consider an applicant who had been unemployed for a

consider candidates with criminal records is beyond their personal discretion. Guidelines for particular professions, including law, real estate, medicine, physical therapy, and education, are subject to both federal and state guidelines that restrict the employment opportunities for ex-offenders. Six states permanently bar ex-offenders from public-sector employment, and most states also impose restrictions on employment for ex-offenders with felony convictions[2] (Petersilia, 2000; Travis et al. 2001; Western et al. 2001; Bushway 2004).

African American men's dominant presence within state and federal prisons means that they are more likely than whites or Latinos to be subjected to incarceration stigma. Pager (2003) found this to be the case in audit studies of Milwaukee, where matched pairs of African American and white male job applicants with and without criminal records for drug possession applied for 350 advertised entry-level jobs. The callback rate for whites was 17 percent with a criminal record and 34 percent without, while for African Americans the call back rate was 5 percent with a criminal record and only 14 percent for those who had no criminal record. Interestingly, the callback rates for African American men both with and without criminal records are lower than those of all white men. This finding is consistent with Holzer et al.'s (2002) study, which found that employers' perceptions and the fear of black criminality were more likely to influence racialized hiring patterns than job seekers' actual records of criminal involvement. In a more recent study of job seekers in New York City, Pager and Western find that "...black job seekers are only two-thirds as successful as qualified Latinos and little more than half as successful as equally qualified whites. Indeed, black job seekers fare no better than white men just released from prison." (2005: 12).

Racial differences in callback rates mean that African American men, regardless of their former incarceration status, are experiencing longer spells of unemployment, gaining less work experience, and earning less than white or Latino men.

Wage patterns and barriers to employment among Latinos are similar to those of African Americans, although their rates of incarceration are much lower (Kirschenman and Neckerman 1991; Moss and Tilly 1991; Waldinger 1995; Harrison and Beck 2006). Common stereotypes argue that

---

year or more, and 59 percent would consider an applicant with a spotty employment history (Holzer 1996).

[2] These states are Alabama, Delaware, Iowa, Mississippi, Rhode Island, and South Carolina.

Latinos benefit financially over African Americans and whites because they underbid the wages of other workers and use network connections to effectively secure employment for each other. If the demand for the lowest-wage worker is a driving factor in labor markets and Latinos accept the lowest wages, studies should reveal a preference among employers for Latinos over whites and African Americans. However, research shows that discrimination by employers and job segregation continue to be significant factors that plague the employment and wage histories of Latinos (Kirschenman and Neckerman 1991; Ong and Valenzuela 1996; Valenzuela and Gonzalez 2000; Catanzarite and Aguilera 2002; Bonilla Silva 2003). A study by Pager and Western (2005) found that Latinos with no criminal records are more likely to be called back for jobs than white ex-prisoners and African American ex- and non-offenders, but have no hiring advantages over white non-offenders. If hiring patterns are any indication of wage patterns, this means that Latino ex- and non-offenders are likely to see higher wages than African Americans, yet still earn less than comparable whites.

While incarceration has a depreciative effect on earnings over time for all ex-offenders, there are significant racial differences. Due to African American men's disproportionate involvement in the criminal justice system, higher rates of incarceration mean that they are more likely to experience incarceration-based unemployment, skill depreciation, human-capital deficits, and stigma in labor markets than whites or Latinos. Therefore, we expect to see the lowest earnings among African American ex-offenders. Since African American non-offenders do not seem to receive any employment or wage benefits to their non-offender status when compared to white men, we also expect their wages to be lower than white ex-offenders, as well as white and Latino non-offenders. While Latino men face discriminatory practices that are similar to those experienced by African American men, we predict that Latino ex- and non-offender wages will be lower than whites but slightly higher than African Americans.

When comparing the wage gap between ex- and non-offenders, we expect to find the smallest wage penalty associated with incarceration among African Americans, a slightly higher penalty among Latinos, and the most severe wage penalties among whites. Our rationale is based on the idea that whites have more to lose, economically, from spending time in prison. This is evident when you consider white men earn higher wages across the career than African American or Latino men. Yet, because of employers' illustrated preferences for white male, post-incarcerated labor over all African American and most Latino men's labor (Pager 2003; Pager and Western 2005), we do not expect this wage penalty to grow exponentially and depress white men's long-term career earnings relative to other men. We expect white men, regardless of their former incarceration status, to maintain an earnings advantage over African American and Latino ex-offenders across their careers. We also suspect that African American, Latino, and white men are not operating within labor markets that equally value their labor, whether or not incarceration is a factor in their employment history.

DATA AND METHODS

The National Longitudinal Survey of Youth (NLSY) is a panel sample of young men and women ages fourteen to twenty-two in 1979 (Bureau of Labor Statistics 2002). These respondents were interviewed annually over a fifteen-year period and biennially since 1996. We restrict our analyses to the career dynamics of men who were twenty years or older in an observation year and compare three racial/ethnic groups: African Americans, Latinos, and whites (N=6,403). Individuals enter the analysis in any year in which they have employment earnings. This means the typical sample-selection problem (that in any given year, some individuals are out of the labor market) in cross-sectional research is solved by following people across the career.

Since we think the consequences of incarceration and race/ethnicity unfold in a career-based process, the panel nature of these data is a huge advantage. We have created a pooled cross-section in which the unit of analysis is an individual in a particular year. By following this sample over time, we can track human-capital and earnings inequality and other characteristics as they emerge across the career.

A useful method for analyzing longitudinal data with continuous outcome variables is the fixed effects model. The main purpose of using the fixed-effects model for this research is to derive estimates of effects of individual characteristics that are free from the sort of selection bias that results from misspecifications involving omitted variables. The fixed effect captures the influence of omitted variables that may be correlated with the observed predictors. Only time-varying explanatory variables are included in the estimation of fixed-effects models. This statistical tool controls for fixed demographic characteristics such as race or gender (Allison 1994). Thus, using fixed effects models enables us to focus on how changes in covariates affect wage growth from 1979 to 2002.

Our analytic strategy is twofold. First, we estimate fixed effects models that allow us to examine whether incarceration has an impact on earnings by comparing the wage trajectories of ex-offenders and non-offenders. To see whether the effect of incarceration on earnings varies among African Americans, Latinos, and whites, we estimate separate models for each racial group and conduct a series of z-tests to assess whether the betas for prior incarceration are significantly different across race.[3] For this analysis main effects and interaction models are estimated. In the main effects model, earnings are predicted to be a function of incarceration, net of a host of other factors. The incarceration coefficient generates a shift in log wages and provides the percent change in the wage gap between ex-offenders and non-offenders at the mean age. The interaction model estimates the age-earnings profile of ex-offenders and non-offenders by including an interaction between log age and prior incarceration. A negative coefficient for the interaction term suggests that ex-offenders experience slower wage growth than non-offenders. This predicted flatter wage trajectory might be the result of ex-offenders working in the secondary labor market where jobs are unstable and pay low wages.

Measures

Earnings, the dependent variable, are measured as the hourly wage reported by the respondent in the calendar year preceding the interview. Reported values for hourly wages are logged because they are skewed toward the higher end of the distribution. To adjust for inflation, we standardized the hourly wage data by using the Consumer Price Index deflator to calculate earnings in 1983 constant dollars. This practice is similar to other studies using the NLSY data. Outlying observations at the low end of the wage distribution, less than $1.00 per hour and observations greater than $80.00 per hour were removed (see Western 2002; Tomaskovic-Devey et al. 2005).[4]

Race/ethnicity of the respondent is based upon the respondent's self-identification, as Hispanic, non-Hispanic black, or non-Hispanic

---

[3] Following the suggestion of Paternoster, Brame, Mazerolle, and Piquero (1998), we use z-tests, with the equation $z = (\beta_1 - \beta_2)/[(se\beta_1)^2 + (se\beta_2)^2]^{1/2}$

[4] We also estimated models that did not have an upper wage restriction. The conclusions from these models were substantively consistent with the results reported in this article.

white. Age is measured in years, as the respondent's current age at the time of the interview. We model the log of age to capture the nonlinear nature of the age-earnings profile. Since our cohort consists of young workers, this nonlinear functional form fits the distribution better (see Western 2002).

The NLSY includes an annual residence item, which addresses the time-varying nature of incarceration for respondents. This question identifies whether respondents are being interviewed in prison or jail. This item measures incarceration status of the respondents with error because it only obtains the respondent's residence status at the time of the interview. Therefore, some prison or jail sentences of less than twelve months are underobserved. However, since most prison sentences typically exceed twelve months, they are observed with certainty. Following Western (2002), we created two dummy variables that capture current and prior incarceration within the NLSY. Current incarceration equals 1 if the respondent was interviewed in prison or jail in year t, and 0 otherwise. Likewise, prior incarceration is a dummy variable that records whether the respondent has ever served time in prison or jail. The prior incarceration variable equals 1 if the respondent recorded an interview in a correctional facility in year t-1 or earlier, and 0 otherwise. This measure of prior incarceration permits an assessment of the effect of incarceration after release from prison.[5]

Education is measured as respondents' highest grade completed, which ranges from 0 to 20 (college degree). Cumulative job search length measures the total number of weeks respondents searched for employment. Cumulative work experience is measured as the sum of the number of weeks respondents reported working during the survey years. Job tenure measures the total number of weeks a respondent has worked in their current job. These measures of job search length, work experience, and tenure are more sensitive than those typically available in cross-sectional research (see Tienda and Stier 1996), and they can vary across the career. Since the NLSY data allows us to track a person's status on a week-by-week basis, the measure of experience is not an age-education proxy, but is a direct observation of employment spells over time.

---

[5] Similar to Western (2002), a count variable based upon the total number of correctional interviews given by a respondent was used as an alternative measure of prior incarceration. Using a count variable might identify serious offenders who have served multiple spells in prison. However, only a few respondents would be considered chronic.

Control Variables

Since there are a variety of traits that would predict both incarceration and weak labor market involvement, the issue of selection is important for this analysis. The advantage of estimating a fixed-effect model is that it controls for stable, unmeasured individual characteristics. Thus time-invariant characteristics, such as intelligence, preferences developed during early socialization, socioeconomic background, social skills learned before labor force entry, underlying criminal propensity, as well as fixed demographic traits such as race/ethnicity that might influence both getting into prison and getting a job are absorbed by the fixed-effect model (Kilbourne, England, and Beron 1994; Uggen and Thompson 2003; Western 2002).

Fourteen time-varying variables are included to control for selectivity pertaining to imprisonment and participation in the labor market: hours worked per week, marital status, suburban residence, city residence, current school enrollment, local unemployment rate, health problems, union membership, military service, and five industry variables. Since ex-offenders tend to have low levels of labor force participation and tend to work in secondary sector jobs, controlling for the total number of hours that a respondent works per week is important in determining wages and the slope of the wage profile throughout the career. According to Sampson and Laub (1993), a social attachment such as marriage is important for ex-offenders, because as an institution marriage is a type of informal social control. Marital status is a dummy variable that equals 1 if the respondent reports being married during the survey year, 0 otherwise. There is a tendency for wages to be higher in large central cities than rural areas and the suburbs (Holzer 1996). As a result, the geography of the labor market may influence respondents' wage profiles. The dummy variable suburb is equal to 1 if the respondent reports living in a suburban area. The dummy variable central city is equal to 1 if the respondent reports living in the central city. The reference category for both of these variables is rural residence. If the respondent is attending some type of education or vocational program, this program may potentially limit the amount of time they can participate in the labor force and subsequently may affect the observed earnings reported. Current school enrollment is measured as 1 if the respondent is enrolled in college or vocational school and 0 otherwise. Controlling for the local unemployment rate provides information about the difficulty of securing employment in areas where the respondents reside. Local unemployment rate reports the percentage of people unemployed in the respondent's county of residence at the time of the interview. Health problems reports whether or not the respondent has any health limitations that would prevent them from obtaining work. Union membership is measured by determining whether the respondent has a job in which the wages or salary are set by a collective bargaining agreement. The variable military service indicates whether the respondent has served in any branch of the armed forces since the last interview. Finally, detailed census industry codes corresponding to the industry in which the respondent was employed in a given year were merged onto the person-year observations. These industry codes were collapsed into several categories: agriculture, transportation, sales/financial, business/service, construction/manufacturing, and professional/management. The dummy variables (agriculture, transportation, sales/financial, business/service) are equal to 1 if the respondent has been employed in any of these industries, with professional/management as the reference category.

RACE, INCARCERATION, AND WAGE INEQUALITY

We examine descriptively wage and human capital disparities between ex- and non-offenders within the data. The means and standard deviations of hourly wage and human capital variables by race/ethnicity and offender status are presented in Table 14.1. The discussion of the descriptive results will focus on the following comparisons: 1) ex-offender and non-offender differences, 2) racial/ethnic differences among non-offenders and 3) racial/ethnic differences among ex-offenders. These comparisons allow us to discuss three foci of substantive interest: 1) the impact of incarceration on labor market opportunities for individuals, 2) the impact of racial disadvantage on labor market processes for men who have never been incarcerated, and 3) the impact of incarceration and racial disadvantage on the labor market opportunities of men who have been incarcerated.

Impact of Incarceration on Individuals

Ex-offenders have fewer opportunities to accumulate human capital than their non-offender counterparts. The stigma associated with spending time in prison affects the supply-side factors that employers typically find attractive when hiring workers. When compared to non-offenders, ex-offenders have lower hourly wages, educational attainment, cumulative work experience and job tenure. However, ex-offenders do report

Table 14.1: Means and Standard Deviations of Hourly Wage and Human Capital Variables by Race/Ethnicity and Offender Status

	All Non-offenders	All Ex-offenders	White Non-offenders	White Ex-offenders	Latino Non-offenders	Latino Ex-offenders	African American Non-offenders	African American Ex-offenders
Hourly Wages (1983 Dollars)	13.16 (7.51)	9.87 (4.25)	13.59 (9.08)	10.90 (6.03)	12.41 (4.30)	10.23 (3.39)	10.70 (4.31)	8.92 (3.08)
Education (years)	13.05 (1.74)	11.21 (1.03)	13.20 (2.05)	11.06 (1.45)	12.11 (1.17)	11.03 (0.76)	12.56 (1.05)	11.47 (0.76)
Cumulative Work Experience (weeks)	395.66 (167.83)	308.87 (113.55)	404.10 (199.34)	319.73 (157.33)	380.23 (98.07)	315.05 (78.67)	346.55 (112.83)	292.00 (91.53)
Job Tenure (weeks)	178.37 (145.30)	70.46 (62.45)	184.13 (175.10)	77.24 (91.53)	166.25 (82.00)	71.82 (47.84)	145.71 (89.60)	60.56 (43.03)
Cumulative Job Search Length	34.04 (34.98)	88.73 (43.87)	30.46 (38.29)	75.88 (56.86)	39.44 (21.95)	85.97 (28.61)	55.43 (31.92)	100.18 (38.53)
Person Years	61,303	2,848	35,812	849	10,643	545	14,848	1,454

Note: Total person years for non-offenders= 61,303. Total person years for ex-offenders = 2,848. Total Men = 6,403.

Means (standard deviations) reflect the weighted sample. Non-offender/Ex-offender and Race mean differences are statistically significant (p <.001).

spending more weeks searching for work than their non-offender counterparts. This suggests that being incarcerated has an influence on the labor market prospects of these men.

Impact of Racial Disadvantage for Non-offenders

When examining differences in human-capital accumulation for men who have never been incarcerated, we find similar patterns that are consistent with findings from cross-sectional studies. Latinos and African Americans have lower hourly wages than their white counterparts. Latino men earn $1.18 less per hour than whites, while African American men earn $2.89 less per hour. The racial/ethnic differences in the patterns for cumulative work experience and job tenure are similar to the hourly wage relationship. Although African American men have a slightly higher level of education than Latinos, they still spend a significant amount of time searching for work than Latinos and whites. This suggests that there is not a high economic return to educational investment for these men.

Impact of Racial Disadvantage for Ex-offenders

African American, Latino, and white ex-offenders report fewer years of education, fewer weeks of cumulative work experience, and less job tenure than non-offenders. These ex-offenders spend more weeks looking for work across their careers than non-offenders. The hourly wages reported by African American, Latino, and white ex-offenders are lower than the wages reported by their non-offender counterparts. This pattern suggests that incarceration has a negative effect on earnings.

Across racial groups, there are differences in the acquisition of human capital. African American and Latino ex-offenders spend more weeks looking for work and have fewer weeks of cumulative work experience and job tenure across their careers than white ex-offenders. Interestingly, among ex-offenders, African Americans have slightly more education than Latinos and whites, but still manage to have lower levels of human capital, such as work experience and job tenure, than their Latino and white counterparts. One way to explain the pattern of lower returns to education regardless of incarceration status for African American men is that employers may devalue the human-capital attributes of these men when making hiring decisions.

When examining hourly wage differences across racial groups, white ex-offenders report higher hourly wages than both Latino and African American ex-offenders. Based upon the descriptive data, we observe that incarceration decreases the hourly wages of minority ex-offenders relative to whites. Surprisingly, white ex-offender's wages are higher than those of African American non-offenders. This result suggests that even whites with a criminal record may maintain an earnings advantage over young law-abiding African American men. While the mark of a criminal record is clearly affecting African Americans more than white or Latino ex-offenders, these findings show that their longer time out of the paid labor market is due to factors other than incarceration.

To test whether prior incarceration has an impact on wage inequality across the career, we turn to Table 14.2, which reports models of hourly wages as a function of prior incarceration and various controls. In Table 14.2, three models are presented for the full sample. The first model includes prior incarceration and the substantive variables of interest along with the controls. The second model adds the interaction between log age and prior incarceration on hourly wages. Model 3 adds human capital variables, job search length, and cumulative work experience and job tenure to determine whether they mediate the prior incarceration-wage relationship. These models isolate the influence of prison experiences on hourly wages.

The first model shows that there is indeed a significant relationship between prior incarceration and earnings. The model indicates that incarceration reduces wages, controlling for current incarceration, educational attainment, hours worked per week, marital status, city residence, suburban residence, school enrollment, local unemployment rate, health problems, union membership, military, and employment in the following industries: agriculture, transportation, sales/financial, business/service, and construction/management. Model 2 introduces an interaction term between age and prior incarceration. Here the main effect of prior incarceration is positive, but the interaction effect is negative and statistically significant. Note that the main effect of prior incarceration in model 2 represents the influence of incarceration at age 0. Yet, the data points for this sample begin at age 20. The incarceration effect on hourly wages calculated for a 20-year-old man equals: (Incarceration effect= Prior Incarceration – (Age *Prior Incarceration) *Age which is 2.70-0.84(20) = –14.10). This means that 20-year-old men who have been incarcerated experience a 14.1 percent reduction in hourly wages. From age 20, the effect of incarceration is negative and the interaction coefficient shows the gap in log hourly wages between ex- and non-offenders grows increasingly negative over time. Thus, when these men reach age 41, they experience a 31.7 percent reduction in hourly wages across the career.

Model 3 includes the human-capital variables cumulative job search length, cumulative work experience, and job tenure. The human capital variables have the expected relationship with wages; more weeks spent searching for work leads to lower wages, and higher levels of experience and tenure lead to higher wages. The addition of these variables reduces the association between prior incarceration and log hourly wages from (14.1 percent to 11.7 percent at age 20) and from (31.7 percent to 26.4 percent at age 41). However, the prior incarceration coefficient remains significant, which means that the association between incarceration and wages is only partially mediated by human capital factors.

Table 14.2: Mean Differences of Incarceration Effect on Wages, by Race.

	All Non-Offenders $13.16	All Ex-Offenders $9.87	White Ex-Offenders $10.90	African American Ex-Offenders $8.92	Latino Ex-Offenders $10.23
All Non-Offenders $13.16	0	– 3.29 (25%)	– 2.26 (17.2%)	– 4.24 (32.24%)	– 2.93 (22.26%)
All Ex-Offenders $9.87	– 3.29 (25%)	0	+ 1.03 (9.4%)	– .95 (9.6%)	+ .36 (3.5%)
White Non-Offenders $13.59	.–.43 (3.16%)	– 3.72 (27.4%)	– 2.69 (19.8%)	– 4.67 (34.4%)	– 3.36 (24.7%)
African American Non-Offenders $10.70	+ 2.46 (18.7%)	– .83 (7.8%)	+ .20 (1.8%)	– 1.78 (16.6%)	– .47 (4.4%)
Latino Non-Offenders $12.41	+ .75 (5.7%)	– 2.54 (20.5%)	– 1.51 (12.2%)	– 3.49 (28.1%)	– 2.18 (17.6%)

To address whether ex-offenders from different race/ethnic groups are differentially disadvantaged pertaining to hourly wages, we estimated separate earnings models for African Americans, Latinos, and whites. The results for the total sample and the racial/ethnic samples are similar in that ex-offenders have significantly flatter wage trajectories than their non-offender counterparts, with the wage gap growing across the career.

For white, Latino, and African American ex-offenders, including the human-capital variables reduces the main effect of prior incarceration and the interaction between log age and prior incarceration on wages. The findings suggest that at age 20, whites who have been incarcerated experience a 12.5 percent reduction in hourly wages, Latino hourly wages are reduced by 13.3 percent, and African American hourly wages for those formerly incarcerated are reduced by 7.5 percent. This reduction in hourly earnings increases for all ex-offenders. When these ex-offenders reach age 41, whites who have been incarcerated experience a 28.2 percent reduction in hourly wages, Latino hourly wages are reduced by 30.1 percent, and African American hourly wages for ex-offenders are reduced by 17.0 percent. This finding suggests that the impact of incarceration on the wage trajectories of ex-offenders grows across the career. The magnitude of the hourly wage reduction for each group illustrates how the racial disadvantage associated with earnings is reproduced among the ex-offender population.

We also test to see whether the coefficients in these models are significantly different across racial groups. The coefficients for prior incarceration, log age, education, log age*prior incarceration, log cumulative work experience and job tenure are statistically different for whites and African Americans. The coefficients for prior incarceration, education, log age*prior incarceration, cumulative job search length and log cumulative work experience are statistically different for Latinos and African Americans.

To visually depict group earnings trajectories, Figure 14.1 presents the predicted values of log hourly wages across the career for Latino and white ex- and non-offenders with controls for each group.[6] Figure 14.1 illustrates that Latino and white ex-offenders have flatter age-wage profiles than their non-offender counterparts. However, the wages of both Latino and

---

[6] All predicted values are calculated at the sample mean for all variables in the model, with the exception of married and currently enrolled in school. These two variables are strongly related to age and earnings. Therefore, age specific means for current enrollment and currently married are used in the estimation of predicted wages (see Tomaskovic-Devey et al. 2005).

whites regardless of incarceration status are similar in magnitude. The within group predicted wage gap between Latino ex-offenders and non-offenders at age 20 is 11.5 percent and decreases to 4.9 percent when these men reach 41 years of age. Similarly, the within group predicted ex-offender/non-offender wage gap for white men at 20 years of age is 8.1 percent and decreases to 5.8 percent at age 41. When we examine the between group earnings differences, we find that at age 20, Latino ex-offenders wages are 6.5 percent less than their white counterparts. By age 41, the Latino/white ex-offender wage gap decreases to 1.2 percent. The same pattern exists for non-offenders.

Figure 14.2 presents the incarceration-wage relationship for whites and African Americans. When examining the pattern within racial groups, the wage trajectory of white ex-offenders is not as steep as the white non-offender trajectory. The wage difference for white ex- and non-offenders increases slightly across the career. At age 20, there is an 8.1 percent difference in the wages of these groups. By age 41, this gap is reduced to a 5.8 percent difference in the predicted log hourly wages of white ex- and non-offenders. For African Americans, the wage trajectories for ex- and non-offenders are nearly identical, except at age 35, the ex-offender trajectory is slightly flatter than the non-offender trajectory. For 20-year-olds, there is a 6.6 percent difference in the predicted log hourly wages for African American ex- and non-offenders. As these men age, the wage gap is reduced to 3.7 percent.

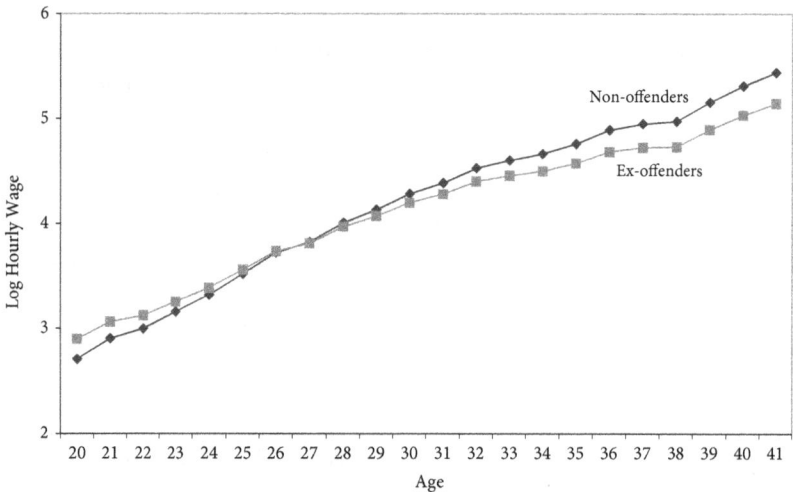

Figure 14.1: Predicted Log Hourly Wages by Offender Status for Whites and Latinos.

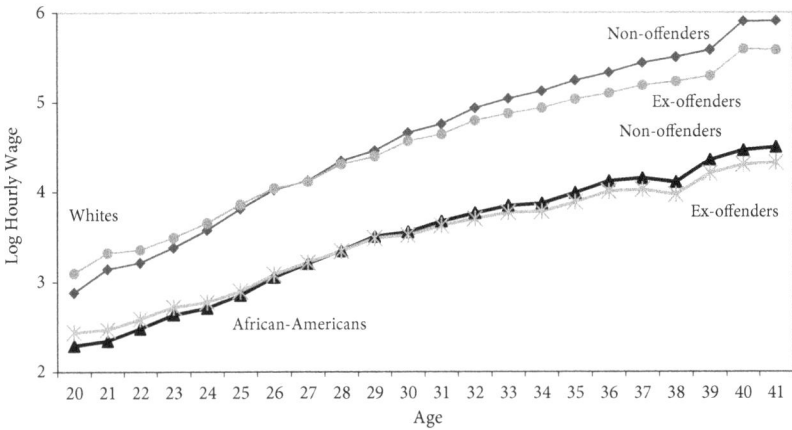

Figure 14.2: Predicted Log Hourly Wages by Offender Status for Whites and African Americans.

When we examine earnings trajectories across racial groups, we discovered that both white ex- and non-offenders have higher age-wage profiles than African American ex-offenders and non-offenders. At age 20, African American ex-offender wages are 17.1 percent less than those of their white counterparts. This large wage gap remains constant across the career. Interestingly, African American non-offenders earn 22.2 percent *less* than white ex-offenders. This large wage disparity is reduced to 13.1 percent by the time these men turn 41 years old. Perhaps this wage difference suggests that the stigma associated with incarceration is more salient and contributes to depressing wages for all African American men regardless of whether they have ever been to prison.

Figure 14.3 presents the age-wage profiles by incarceration status for Latinos and African Americans. Looking at wage trajectories within racial groups, the earnings of Latino ex-offenders are similar to Latino non-offenders. The wage difference between Latino ex- and non-offenders increases slightly across the career. For African Americans, the wage trajectories for ex- and non-offenders are virtually identical. Among 20-year-olds, there is a 6.6 percent difference in the predicted log hourly wages for African American ex-offenders and non-offenders. When these men reach age 41, the wage gap is reduced to 3.8 percent. When examining between group earnings, we discovered that both Latino ex- and non-offenders have higher age-wage profiles than African American ex-offenders and non-offenders. At age 20, African American ex-offender wages are

22.1 percent less than their Latino counterparts. This wage gap decreases to 18.3 percent across the career. Interestingly, African American non-offenders earn 27.0 percent *less* than Latino ex-offenders. This large wage disparity is reduced to 12.1 percent by the time these men turn 41 years old. Note here, the wage gap between Latino ex-offenders and African American non-offenders are quite similar to the wage difference between white ex-offenders and African American non-offenders. Overall, African American men, regardless of human capital, job search history, or even their incarceration status, experience significant wage disadvantages relative to whites and Latinos.

Conclusion

This study contributes in several ways to the literature on the consequences of incarceration on earnings and research on African American disadvantage in the labor market. We examined racial variation in wage penalties associated with incarceration by comparing the earnings of African American, Latino, and white men who have never been incarcerated with those who were formerly incarcerated. We were not surprised to find that men who were formerly incarcerated earn less than those who were never incarcerated, or that African American and Latino men earn less than whites. Yet this study reveals a pattern of significant racial differences in the impact of incarceration on wage trajectories. We found support for the hypothesis that white ex-offenders would suffer a higher wage penalty to their former incarceration status than African American or Latino men. White men have higher wage trajectories across the career,

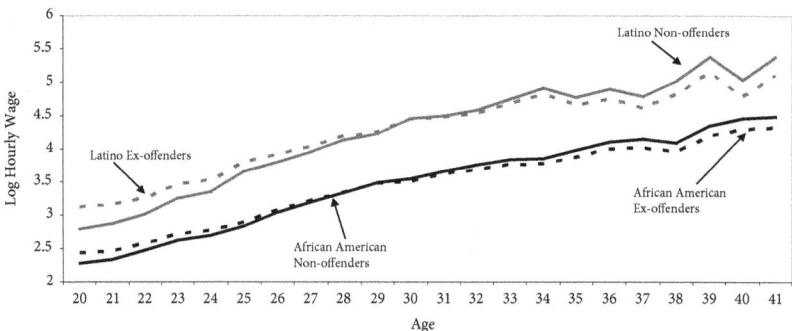

Figure 14.3. Predicted Log Hourly Wages by Offender Status for Latinos and African Americans.

which means that they have more to lose economically from spending time in prison. White ex-offenders even manage to maintain an earnings advantage over African American non-offenders across their careers. This may point to the relative power of white men's network ties to higher-wage employment. The average job search length for white men is much shorter than Latinos and African Americans, regardless of their prior incarceration status. Perhaps white men's network ties are strong enough to endure stints of incarceration that weaken their wages in comparison to white non-offenders, yet sustain their earnings advantages over African American men.

We found evidence to support the hypothesis that the earnings gap between Latino non-offenders and ex-offenders is smaller than the gap between comparable whites, but larger than that among African Americans. Given the popular idea that Latinos in low-wage labor markets will accept the lowest wages, we were surprised to see such a large difference between the wage trajectories of African Americans and Latinos. We were especially surprised by the fact that Latino ex-offenders see wage advantages over African Americans who were never incarcerated. While this particular pattern does decrease as the men age, Figure 14.3 shows that the wage gap between Latino and African American men continues across their careers and increases sharply after age 40 among non-offenders. We attribute Latino's wage advantages relative to African Americans to their higher rates of work experience and job tenure, which produce an economic payoff that proves to be particularly salient as the men age. Figure 14.1 shows that Latino ex-offenders even occasionally earn as much as white non-offenders across their careers. Although prior research shows that Latinos are disadvantaged economically when they are ghettoized in Latino-dominated job sites (Catanzarite and Aguilera 2002), employers are sometimes willing to offer higher wages to Latinos if they have more work experience than whites. Since this pattern is sporadic across their careers, we suspect that employer preference for Latino labor is more likely linked to jobs that may feature higher hourly wages but are also likely to be temporary, low-status jobs that offer no medical benefits, no opportunities for advancement, or may even be dangerous, as is the case for many construction, agriculture, and service-sector jobs.

The smaller wage gap among African Americans means that African American men who were never incarcerated do not earn much more across their careers than African American men who were formerly incarcerated, in comparison to their white and Latino counterparts. As predicted, African American men have the lowest wages of any group.

The wage penalty for incarceration is smaller among young African American non- and ex-offenders than comparable whites or Latinos. The wage gap between African American ex-and non-offenders does not increase at the same rate as that seen by whites or Latinos. Yet, this smaller wage penalty does not translate into any earnings advantages for African American non-offenders.

Previous research has shown that African American men who were never incarcerated are commonly subject to the kind of discriminatory practices that are usually reserved for ex-offenders (Pager and Western 2005). In fact, employers often prefer white ex-offender's labor to any African American men's labor. Though an empirical examination of employer's perceptions and preferences are beyond the scope of this study, there are several reasons why we maintain that such hiring processes and practices of statistical discrimination have a significant effect on the patterns of African American disadvantage in wages found in this study. First, we were struck by our finding that the wage gap between African American ex- and non-offenders was significantly smaller than the wage gap among white or Latino ex- and non-offenders. One might expect that incarceration would trump race in terms of the depression of wages across the life course, and result in a wage penalty that is much more consistent across the groups of men, especially men of color. Yet, African American and Latino men do not appear to hold the same types of jobs.

Second, we are surprised by the pattern of depressed wages for African American non-offenders in comparison to Latino and white ex-offenders. White ex-offenders suffer higher earnings penalties, but their wages are never reduced to the lower status of African American ex- and non-offenders. While some argue that white men's earnings are a function of their human capital characteristics, African American non-offenders average more education, cumulative work experience and job tenure than white ex-offenders. Although, white ex-offenders search for jobs longer than African American non-offenders, their incarceration status and lower human capital attributes do not diminish their wage potential relative to African American men who were never incarcerated. Studies that focus on access to employment (Holzer 1996; Holzer et al. 2003; Pager 2003; Pager 2005a; Pager 2005b; Pager and Western 2005) talk about how African Americans are economically disadvantaged by employers' preferences for white labor. This racial preference is so strong that sometimes employers prefer to hire whites who were formerly incarcerated over African Americans and Latinos who were never incarcerated. Yet, this story of racial disadvantage is not just about denied access to employment. The reduced value assigned to African American labor relative to whites is also reflected in the wage trajectories of African American men who do manage to secure employment.

Given the very high rates of incarceration among African American men in the United States relative to whites and Latinos, many employers assume that criminality is a common feature in the history of most young African American men whether or not that information is disclosed on their job applications or in interviews. We know from previous research that employers are more likely to evaluate gaps in a job candidate's work history as a signal for possible hidden records of imprisonment when they consider African American candidates than when they evaluate comparable white candidates for the same jobs (Holzer 1996). Holzer even recommends the use of criminal background checks among employers in low-wage labor markets to adjust for the pervasiveness of inaccurate incarceration biases that inform employers hiring practices and limit African American men's employment opportunities. Kling (2006) hypothesizes that employer perceptions of incarceration can negatively affect earnings when employers are less likely to associate the subgroup of job candidates with a record of criminal activity, such as whites who served long prison sentences. If white ex-offenders, as exceptions to the rule of black incarceration, are subjected to harsher wage penalties, one might conclude that African American non-offenders, who are also exceptions to the rule, will experience wage benefits relative to ex-offenders. This study does not support such ideas about exceptionality in the case of African American men. Racial disadvantage remains a consistent factor even when white men bring highly stigmatizing characteristics to the labor market.

Fourth, while Latino men may also be subjected to discriminatory hiring practices, our study reveals that this does not deter them from securing and keeping higher wage jobs for longer periods of time. Perhaps their lower overall rates of incarceration than African American men means that Latinos are simply more available for work and/or employers are not as likely to make group generalizations about their past or future criminality. Latinos are such an ethnically and racially diverse group that practices of statistical discrimination based on averages of group productivity may prove to be more difficult for employers. Regardless of their former incarceration status, Latinos maintain earnings advantages over African Americans across their careers. With significantly less education, Latino men see more average work experience, more job tenure, and spend fewer weeks searching for work than African Americans. Perhaps, Latinos' human capital and wage advantages over African Americans are reflective of employers' preferences for Latinos to occupy particular kinds of jobs. At any rate, men of color are not equally disadvantaged by incarceration in labor markets.

In conclusion, we suspect that the stigma associated with incarceration and discriminatory hiring practices results in African American men's common experiences of employment isolation and low-wage employment, regardless of their incarceration status. The source of racial disadvantage for African American men is not limited to their former incarceration status. Incarceration stigma translates into wage inequality differently across racial and ethnic groups. Whites and Latinos suffer harsher earnings penalties to incarceration but never see the low level wages earned by African American ex-offenders or non-offenders. Perhaps white and Latino earnings advantages are made possible by the mass removal and devaluation of African American men's labor, which reduces the size of the labor pool and the amount of competition that whites and Latinos have for jobs. Future research should more closely examine the employment and wage benefits that whites and Latino ex- and non-offenders experience as a direct or indirect result of the mass incarceration of African American men.

References

Allison, Paul. 1994. "Using Panel Data to Estimate the Effects of Events." *Sociological Methods and Research*, 23: 174–99.

Becker, Gary. 1964. *Human Capital.* New York: National Bureau Economic Research.

Becker, Gary 2003. "How to Level the Playing Field for Young Black Men." *Business Week.* 3844: 24.

Bonilla-Silva, Eduardo. 2003. *Racism Without Racists: Color-Blind Racism and the Persistence of Racial Inequality in the United States.* Lanham, MD: Rowan & Littlefield.

Boshier, Roger and Derek Johnson. 1979. "Does Conviction Affect Employment Opportunities?" *British Journal of Criminology*, 14: 264–69.

Braddock, Jomills and James McPartland. 1987. "How Minorities Continue to be Excluded from Equal Opportunities: Research on Labor Markets and Institutional Barriers." *Journal of Social Issues*, 43: 5–39.

Bureau of Labor Statistics, U.S. Department of Labor. 2002. National Longitudinal Study of Youth 1979 cohort, 1979–2002 (Rounds 1–20) {Computer File}. Produced and Distributed by the Center for Human Resource Research, The Ohio State University. Columbus, OH.

Bushway, Shawn. 2004. Labor Market effects of Permitting Employer Access to Criminal History Records. *Journal of Contemporary Criminal Justice*, 20: 276–291.

Catanzarite, Lisa and Michael Bernabe Aguilera. 2002. Working with Co-Ethnics: Earnings Penalties for Latino Immigrants at Latino Jobsites." *Social Problems*, 49: 101–27.

D'Souza, Dinesh. 1995. *The End of Racism: Principles for a Multicultural Society.* New York: Free Press.

Finn, R.H. and Patricia A. Fontaine. 1983. "Perceived Employability of Applicants Labeled as Offenders." *Journal of Employment Counseling,* 20: 139–44.

Finn, R.H. and Patricia A. Fontaine. 1985. "The Association between Selected Characteristics and Perceived Employability of Offenders." *Criminal Justice and Behavior,* 12: 353–365.

Freeman, Richard. 1992. "Crime and the Employment of Disadvantaged Youth." In *Urban Labor Markets and Job Opportunity,* edited by George Peterson and Wayne Vroman, Washington, DC: Urban Institute.

Freeman, Richard. 1994. "Crime in the Labor Market." In *Crime,* edited by James Q. Wilson and Joan Petersilia. San Francisco: ICS Press.

Freeman, Richard. 1996. "Why Do So Many Young American Men Commit Crimes and What Might We Do About It?" *Journal of Economic Perspectives,* 10: 25–42.

Grogger, Jeffrey. 1995. "The Effect of Arrests on the Employment and Earnings of Young Men." *Quarterly Journal of Economics,* 110: 51–71.

Hagan, John and Ronit Dinovitzer. 1999. "Collateral Consequences of Imprisonment for Children, Communities and Prisonsers." In *Prisons,* edited by Michael Tonry and Joan Petersilia. *Crime and Justice Review of Research,* Volume 26. Chicago: University of Chicago Press.

Holzer, Harry. 1996. *What Employers Want: Job Prospects for Less-Educated Workers.* New York: Russell Sage Foundation.

Holzer, Harry, Steven Raphael, and Michael Stoll 2001. "Will Employers Hire Ex-Offenders? Employer Checks, Background Checks, and Their Determinants," Working Paper Series W01-005, Berkeley Program on Housing and Urban Policy.

Holzer, Harry, Steven Raphael and Michael Stoll 2003. *"Employment Barriers Facing Ex-Offenders."* Paper presented at the Urban Institute Roundtable on Prisoner Reentry. Urban Institute. May 19–20.

Holzer, Harry, Steven Raphael and Michael Stoll 2006. "Perceived Criminality, Criminal Background Checks and the Racial Hiring Practices of Employers." *Journal of Law and Economics,* 49: 451–480.

Irwin, John and James Austin. 1997. *It's About Time: America's Imprisonment Binge.* 2nd ed. Belmont, CA: Wadsworth.

Jensen, Walter Jr. and William C. Giegold. 1976. "Finding Jobs for Ex-Offenders: A Study of Employers'Attitudes." *American Business Law Journal,* 14: 195–226.

Kirschenman, Joleen, and Kathryn M. Neckerman. 1991. "We'd Love to Hire Them But..." The Meaning of Race for Employers." Pp. 203–34 in *The Urban Underclass,* edited by C. Jencks and P. Peterson. Washington, DC: Brookings Institution.

Kilbourne, Barbara, Paula England, and Kurt Beron. 1994. "Effects of Individual, Occupational, and Industrial Characteristics on Earnings: Intersections of Race and Gender." *Social Forces,* 72: 1149–76.

Kling, Jeffrey R. 2006. "Incarceration Length, Employment and Earnings." *American Economic Review,* 96: 863–76.

Mauer, Mark and Meda Chessney-Lind. 2003. *Invisible Punishment: Collateral Consequences of Mass Imprisonment.* New York: New Press.

McWhorter, John. 2000. *Losing the Race: Self-Sabotage in Black America.* New York: The Free Press.

Moss, Philip, and Chris Tilly. 1991. *"Why Black Men Are Doing Worse in the Labor Market: A Review of Supply Side and Demand Side Explanations."* Working paper. New York, NY: Social Science Research Council.

Murray, Charles. 1984. *Losing Ground: American Social Policy 1950–1980.* Jackson, TN: Basic Books.

Nagin, Daniel and Joel Waldfogel. 1995. "The Effects of Criminality and Conviction on the Labor Market Status of Young British Offenders." *International Review of Law and Economics,* 15: 109–26.

Nagin, Daniel and Joel Waldfogel. 1998. "The Effect of Conviction on Income Through the Life Cycle." *International Review of Law and Economics,* 18: 25–40.

Needels, Karen. 1996. "Go Directly to Jail and Do Not Collect? A Long-Term Study of Recividism, Employment and Earnings Patterns among Prison Releasees." *Journal of Research in Crime and Delinquency*, 33: 471–96.

Ong, Paul and Abel Valenzuela, Jr. 1996. "The Labor Market: Immigrant Effects and Racial Disparities." Pp. 165–192 in Roger Waldinger and Mehdi Bozorgmehr (eds.) *Ethnic Los Angeles*, New York: Russell Sage Press.

Pager, Devah. 2003. "The Mark of a Criminal Record." *American Journal of Sociology*, 108: 937–75.

Pager, Devah. 2005a. "Walking the Talk? What Employers Say Versus What They Do." *American Sociological Review*, 70: 355–80.

Pager, Devah 2005 b. "Double Jeopardy: Race, Crime, and Getting a Job." *Wisconsin Law Review* (2): 617–60.

Pager, Devah and Bruce Western. 2005. *Race at Work: Realities of Race and Criminal Record in the NYC Job Market*. Report for the NYC Commission on Human Rights Conference, December, 2005. Schromburg Center for Research in Black Culture.

Pager, Devah. 2007. Marked: Race, Crime and finding work in an era of mass incarceration. Chicago. Chicago University Press.

Pager, Devah, Bruce Western and Naomi Sugie. 2009. "Sequencing Disadvantage: Barriers to Employment Facing Young, Black and White Men with Criminal Records." *Annals of the American Academy of Political and Social Science*, 623: 195–213.

Paternoster, Raymond, Robert Brame, Paul Mazerolle and Alex Piquero. 1998. "Testing for the Equality of Maximum Likelihood Regression Coefficients Between Two Independent Equations." *Journal of Quantitative Criminology*, 14: 245–61.

Petersilia, Joan. 2000. Prisoners Returning to Communities: Political, Economic and Social Consequences. In *Sentencing and Corrections: Issues for the 21st Century*. National Institute of Justice: Washington, D.C.: U.S. Department of Justice.

Pettit, Becky and Bruce Western. 2004. "Mass Imprisonment and the Life Course: Race and Class Inequality in U.S. Incarceration." *American Sociological Review*, 69: 151–69.

Rodgers, William M. 2006. Male White-Black Wage Gaps, 1979–1994: A Distributional Analysis. *Southern Economic Journal*, 72: 773–793.

Royster, Deirdre A. 2003. *Race and the Invisible Hand: How White Networks Exclude Black Men from Blue-Collar Jobs*. Ewing, NJ: University of California Press.

Sampson, Robert and John Laub. 1993 *Crime in the Making: Pathways and Turning Points Through Life*. Cambridge, MA: Harvard University Press.

Sampson, Robert and William Julius Wilson. 1995. "Toward a Theory of Race, Crime and Urban Inequality." Pp. 37–54. in *Crime and Inequality* edited by John Hagan and Ruth Peterson. Stanford, CA: Stanford University Press.

Schwartz, Richard and Jerome Skolnick. 1962. Two Studies of Legal Stigma. *Social Problems*, 10, 133–42.

Sullivan, Mercer. 1989. *"Getting Paid": Youth, Crime and Work in the Inner City*. Ithaca: Cornell University Press.

Tienda, Marta and Haya Stier. 1996. "Generating Labor Market Inequality: Employment Opportunities and the Accumulation of Disadvantage." *Social Problems*, 43: 147–165.

Tomaskovic-Devey, Donald, Melvin Thomas and Kecia Johnson. 2005. "Race and the Accumulation of Human Capital across the Career: A Theoretical Model and Fixed Effects Application." *American Journal of Sociology*, 111: 58–89.

Travis, Jeremy, Amy Solomon, Michelle Waul. 2001. *"From Prison to Home: The Dimensions And Consequences of Prisoner Reentry."* Washington, DC: The Urban Institute.

Uggen, Christopher. 1999. "Ex-Offenders and the Conformist Alternative: A Job Quality Model of Work and Crime." *Social Problems*, 46: 127–51.

Uggen, Christopher and Melissa Thompson. 2003. "The Socioeconomic Determinants of Ill- Gotten Gains: Within-Person Changes in Drug Use and Illegal Earnings." *American Journal of Sociology*, 109: 146–85.

Valenzuela, Abel, and Elizabeth Gonzalez. 2000. "Latino Earnings Inequality: Immigrant and Native-Born Differences." Pp. 249–278 in *Metropolis: Inequality in Los Angeles*, edited by Lawrence D. Bobo, Melvin Oliver, James H. Johnson, Jr., and Abel Valenzuela, Jr. Russell Sage Foundation.

Waldfogel, Joel. 1994. "Does Conviction have a Persistent Effect on Income and Employment?" *International Review of Law and Economics*, 14: 103–19.

Waldinger, Roger. 1995. *"Black/Immigrant Competition Reassessed: New Evidence from Los Angeles."* UCLA Department of Sociology. Unpublished paper.

West, Heather C. 2010. "Prison Inmates at Midyear 2009." Bureau of Justice Statistics Bulletin, NCJ 230113. Washington, DC: U.S. Department of Justice.

Western, Bruce. 2002. "The Impact of Incarceration on Wage Mobility and Inequality." *American Sociological Review*, 67: 526–46.

Western, Bruce and Katherine Beckett. 1999. "How Unregulated is the U.S. Labor Market: The Penal System as a Labor Market Institution." *American Journal of Sociology*, 104: 1030–60.

Western, Bruce, Jeffrey Kling, and David Weinman. 2001. "The Labor Market Consequences of Incarceration." *Crime and Delinquency*, 47: 410–27.

Western, Bruce. 2000. "Incarceration and Racial Inequality in Men's Employment." *Industrial and Labor Relations Review*, 54: 3–16.

Western, Bruce, Becky Pettit, and Josh Guetzkow. 2002. "Black Economic Progress in the Era of Mass Imprisonment." Pp. 165–80 in *Invisible Punishment: The Collateral Consequences of Mass Imprisonment*, edited by Meda Chesney-Lind and Marc Mauer. New York: New Press.

Western, Bruce, Meredith Kleykamp, and Jake Rosenfeld. 2006. "Did Falling Wages and Employment Increase U.S. Imprisonment?" *Social Forces*, 84: 2291–2310.

Young, Alford. 1999. The (Non) Accumulation of Capital: Explicating the Relationship of Structure and Agency in the Lives of Poor Black Men." *Sociological Theory*, 17: 201–227.

CHAPTER FIFTEEN

CASUALTIES OF WAR:
THE WAR ON DRUGS, PRISONER RE-ENTRY
AND THE SPREAD OF HIV/AIDS AND HEPATITIS C
IN CHICAGO'S COMMUNITIES

Cedric Herring

Since the beginning of the HIV/AIDS epidemic, the disease has struck incarcerated populations extraordinarily hard (Doll and Gaiter, 1996). The War on Drugs has produced a prison population overwhelmingly dependent on illicit drugs. The combination of drug use and national drug arrest policies has made HIV and related infections rampant in the nation's prisons and jails. Even more troubling, however, are the possible effects that incarceration have, not only on inmates, but also on the communities to which they return.

This chapter focuses on the connection between incarceration for illegal drugs, prisoner re-entry into Chicago's communities, and the spread of infectious diseases such as HIV/AIDs and Hepatitis C. It examines the link between incarceration and increased need for access to health care. It also provides basic information about procedures and programs that could assist former inmates in their reintegration into their communities upon release.

THE WAR ON DRUGS, MASS INCARCERATION, AND INFECTIOUS DISEASES

According to the United States Bureau of Justice Statistics, by the end of 2010 more than 7 million people were in prison, jail, on probation, or on parole—about 3.1 percent of adults in the United States (U.S. Bureau of Justice Statistics, 2011). More than 2.2 million people are currently in jail or prison in the United States. This constitutes an increase of more than 100 percent in 20 years. Since 1980, the number of incarcerated drug offenders has increased twelvefold. More than 1 in 5 of those in federal and state prisons were convicted on drug charges (Arriola and Braithwalte 2003). These figures indicate the country's devotion to a policy of imprisonment, and they suggest that the central tactic of the United States' War on Drugs has been incarceration.

The millions of intermittently incarcerated people in America, many of whom are illicit drug users, are among the most difficult people to reach with critical health information and adequate health services (Khan 1996; and Kaplan and Merson 2002). As a consequence, the HIV/AIDS rate is estimated to be seven times higher in state and federal prisons than in the general United States population (Auerbach and Coates 2000). Nationally, health officials estimate that about 17 percent of people who have HIV were previously in a correctional facility. In addition, one in three Hepatitis C (HCV) cases in the United States occurs in people who were previously incarcerated.

Several activities known to occur among prisoners pose a risk for HIV infection. Several studies have identified transmission of HIV in prison (e.g., Doll and Gaiter 1996; D'Aunno, Vaughn, and McElroy 1999; DiFranceisco, et al. 2000; Ehrmann 2002; and Arriola, and Braithwalte 2003). Sexual activity between inmates is not uncommon in prisons and jails. A Federal Bureau of Prisons study reported that 30 percent of federal prison inmates engaged in sexual activity while incarcerated. Incidents of interpersonal violence (including fights involving lacerations, bites, and bleeding in two or more participants) present some risks for HIV transmission (Federal Bureau of Prisons, 2010). These risk activities in prisons and jails do not involve *consenting* participants; therefore, condoms or educational programs alone are not likely to prevent HIV transmission in these situations. Sharing of syringes also increases during imprisonment, as does less effective methods of syringe cleaning. Tattooing is widely practiced in prisons and is usually performed without fresh or sterile instruments. It involves multiple skin punctures with recycled, sharpened, and weaponized products such as staples and paper clips. Since HIV and Hepatitis C (HCV) have similar modes of transmission, co-infection is quite common.

Prisoners infected with HIV or HCV face obstacles to care that do not usually exist in the general community. HIV and HCV have placed an enormous fiscal burden on prisons which are already financially stressed. When populations are high, bed space and staffs short, budgets shrinking, and the incidence of HIV and HCV disease among prison populations constantly on the rise, most correctional facilities and institutional officers will have different priorities than medical care for their inmates. Prisoners in hospitals require the additional expense of 24-hour guards. Many prisons are far from the urban centers where HIV and HCV are most common, and practitioners at prisons and local hospitals are not usually familiar with diagnosis and management of HIV and HCV. Standard treatments now accepted as commonplace in HIV and HCV care are available to only a minority of prisoners, and only when practitioners have the current information, are willing to go through detailed procedures to prescribe the medication, and believe the incarcerated patients will comply and continue treatment once released from custody. Relatedly, doctors drawn to prison practice often have little or no first-hand experience in treating HIV and HCV in their communities. Often, medical professionals working in correctional settings lack experience in the philosophy, program design, implementation, management, and standards of care. And prison pharmacies often fill orders with delays that create gaps in treatment that are detrimental to the efficacy of prescribed drugs.

Most correctional systems rely on voluntary testing, testing based on clinical indications, or prisoner involvement in accidents. This makes tracking the actual rate of infection difficult. Stigmatization, the potential threat of violence, poor HIV and HCV education, and lack of confidentiality cause many prisoners to avoid voluntary testing even when they know that they are at risk for infection. If a prisoner knows that he is HIV positive before entering prison and does not receive needed HIV specific medical care during the course of the sentence, he can escape identification as HIV positive.

The high rates of incarceration and low rates of appropriate treatment are not only endangering inmates but also individuals in the communities to which they return. More than 2 million people are released each year from jails and prisons to American communities. According to the Centers for Disease Control and Prevention (CDC), there are between 800,000 and 900,000 United States residents who are living with HIV infection (Centers for Disease Control and Prevention, 2011). One-third of those infected are unaware of their infection. Approximately 40,000 new HIV infections occur each year in the United States. Overall, the CDC says that 774,467 Americans have been diagnosed with AIDS and 448,060 have died from AIDS since the first cases were reported in 1981.

It is estimated that 30 to 40 percent of the nation's inmate population is infected with Hepatitis C (Centers for Disease Control and Prevention, 2011). There are many possible reasons for the high rate of infection in the inmate population. The link between IV drug use, Hepatitis C infection, and incarceration is an obvious culprit. Prison itself, however, poses unique risk factors to inmates. The sharing of personal care items such as electric razors and razor blades can be common in prison situations.

Something as mundane as getting a haircut becomes a risk factor in a prison setting when the barber does not sterilize shears between cuttings. Tattooing and body piercing take place with needles that have not been sterilized. IV drugs and the snorting of drugs also take place within prison walls. The blood-to-blood contact men can have when fighting is another concern.

Complications from HCV are becoming one of the most important medical issues facing HIV positive individuals. In the United States it is estimated that 4,000,000 people are infected with HCV and as many as 240,000 to 300,000 people (up to 40 percent of people with HIV) are infected with both HIV and HCV (Centers for Disease Control and Prevention, 2011).

The implications of these patterns are enormous. HIV/AIDS and Hepatitis C are now in their second wave, and are assailing drug users, their partners and families. That means that large percentages of the people who go through the prison system are in this high-risk category; yet, there is little opportunity to take the message to where it is most needed. There are too few attempts to reach the incarcerated population with information about prevention, harm reduction or outside services in either short-term jails, where the turn-over is so high, or longer term prisons, where there is the time for in-depth education. There are also few discharge services that are being targeted for HIV positive and Hepatitis C carrying ex-offenders in need of health related services.

So, if inmates do not receive sufficient information and proper care while they are incarcerated, not only will they continue to be at-risk, but also they will continue to place their communities at-risk. Left undetected, sick inmates pass disease to each other and in turn carry HIV/AIDS as well as other communicable diseases such as Hepatitis C back into their communities.

HIV/AIDS, Hepatitis C and Ex-Offenders in Illinois

There were more than 22,000 confirmed AIDS cases in federal, state and local correctional facilities in 2008. Nationally, at the end of 2008, 1.5 percent of male prisoners and 1.9 percent of female prisoners were known to be HIV positive. Even more disturbing is the fact that a study of infectious diseases among people passing through correctional facilities in 2008 found that 17 percent of those being released from prison and jail were HIV positive.

The Illinois Department of Corrections operates 27 adult correctional centers as well as various work camps, boot camps and adult transition centers statewide. These facilities incarcerate more than 45,000 inmates. In an average week, 1,000 inmates may be shifted between facilities, and 500–600 new inmates may enter the system. In 2009, more than 26,000 inmates were released. If rates of HIV infection of ex-offenders in Illinois are similar to those nationally (cited above), more than 4,400 of those released in 2009 will be found to have been infected with HIV. In general, the larger the jail is, the higher is the percentage of inmates with HIV infection. Jails in large metropolitan areas like Chicago have higher preva- lence rates of HIV infection. According to the CDC, in 2010, more than 17,000 residents of Illinois were known to be living with AIDS. Of these, more than 80 percent lived in the Chicago metropolitan area.

Hepatitis C is classified as a silent killer; no recognizable signs nor symptoms occur until severe liver damage has occurred. As mentioned above, nearly 4,000,000 Americans, carry the HCV virus that causes Hepatitis C. Nationwide, it is estimated that 30,000 acute new infections occur each year, and only 25 to 30 percent of those are diagnosed. Current data sources indicate that 8,000 to 10,000 Americans die from Hepatitis C each year. Studies also indicate that inmates in correctional facilities have a higher incidence of Hepatitis C than the general population. Upon their release from prison, these inmates also present a significant health risk to the general population.

In Illinois, as many as 200,000 individuals may be carriers and could develop the debilitating and deadly liver disease associated with Hepatitis C in their lifetime. Undeniably, HIV/AIDS and HCV infections are prob- lems among prison inmates in Illinois. But why should the rest of the state's population care about inmates sequestered away from the general public? Most inmates get paroled from prison. Illinois Department of Corrections statistics show that 47 percent of offenders who are released have been in the agency's custody for six month or less (Illinois Department of Corrections, 2010). If they do not learn how to manage their disease while they are incarcerated, they will continue to practice unsafe behav- iors and infect others once they are released. Additionally, the financial implications of a growing HIV-positive and HCV prison population are great. As more inmates become infected with HIV and develop AIDS or become co-infected with HCV, the expenses for their medication and health care can reach into the hundreds of thousands of dollars in excess of the $25,000 average cost of housing an inmate for one year.

Who Is At-Risk?

More than 80 percent of those released from Illinois prisons lived in the Chicago metro area, and they are concentrated in communities with low income, especially on the south side of Chicago. According to data from the Health and Economic Conditions Survey conducted by the Illinois Department of Public Health, the formerly incarcerated are more likely than their counterparts to be African American, male, younger than 35 years old, to have less than a high school education, to be unemployed, and to earn less than $10,000 per year. All of these are risk factors for being HIV positive and HCV positive. In addition, the formerly incarcerated are more likely than their counterparts to have piercings, tattoos, to have shared intravenous needles, to use alcohol, to use illicit drugs, and to be men who have sex with men. Again, these are risk factors for being HIV positive and HCV positive.

In addition, this survey found that 62 percent of those ex-offenders with Hepatitis C reported that they were disease-free before their incarceration. Similarly, 60 percent of ex-offenders with HIV reported that they were disease-free before their incarceration. In short, when most offenders entered the prison system, they were not infected with HIV nor Hepatitis C. Upon exiting the system, however, more than 30 percent were infected with HIV and/or Hepatitis C.

Strategies to Meet Ex-Offender and Community Needs: Some Recommendations

There are several strategies that can be employed to make the state's efforts better known, more widely used, and more effective in prevention efforts directed at ex-offenders at-risk of spreading HIV/AIDS and HCV in their communities. For example, we can take some steps that are not currently being taken to slow down this infection where it is occurring. Access to the most basic prevention measures–condoms, clean needles and syringes–remains nonexistent in most correctional systems. The numerous obstacles discussed above lead to increased stress levels, more rapid disease progression, shorter life expectancy and a depressed quality of life. In the incarcerated population, only a dramatic shift in preventive measures and public policy will result in the changes necessary to bring about meaningful improvements in education, testing, and access to treatment.

Pre-Release Testing

Perhaps the most important role that corrections play in the AIDS crisis is the role of testing and educating HIV-infected individuals. It is still clear that many HIV-infected subjects do not know their status. Clearly, because there are so many individuals who are unaware of their infection, it is important to continue to test individuals for HIV and HCV. This is particularly true in corrections, a setting with which many people at high risk for HIV and HCV infections come into contact. While the patient may not see the benefit of getting tested for HIV, the correctional health care provider must continue to encourage testing of individuals at risk for infection. While pre-release testing is better than no testing, testing of inmates upon their arrival for incarceration would make it easier to identify those in need of HIV/AIDs and/or HCV treatment while they are incarcerated. This would also do much to slow the spread of infectious diseases within prisons, and this would also serve to slow the spread of such diseases in communities once those incarcerated are released.

In addition, all imminent parolees should be required to obtain confidential HIV and HCV tests prior to release. It is easy, and at no cost to the inmate within the institution. Once within the community, there are often long waits and substantial fees. Inmates will often forget, find several reasons not to seek a test, and an important opportunity to significantly impact the public health is lost. Disease can be spread. This will assists in halting the inadvertent spread of the disease from prison to community.

Education, Prevention, and Early Intervention

Education is very important for both infected and non-infected to prevent possible infection and to minimize the stigma caused by misinformation. In prison, HIV is primarily transmitted through unprotected sex or injection drug use with shared needles. The most successful method of getting inmates to listen to health messages is to use peer educators or counselors—someone like themselves who understands their backgrounds and particular pressures. Peer counselors, whether matched to the inmate population by gender, race, ethnicity, or circumstances, have a much better chance of breaking through barriers that may exist between teachers and students. When designing health programs for inmates, one has to consider the messenger as well as the message. Inmates tend to listen, and to remember these messages when they are delivered repeatedly at regular intervals, and by other inmates or from volunteers from the community who were previously incarcerated.

These efforts could stop the rising incidence of disease, ameliorate the seriousness of the disease among inmates while in prison, reduce the rate of HIV- and HCV-related recidivism, while lessening the impact on health care services within the parolee's receiving community and saving money. HIV/AIDS and HCV education and prevention programs are important component parts of any agency or institutional approach to these diseases.

Support after Release

Returning inmates trying to provide care for themselves and their families will typically find that they have lower wages, unstable employment, discrimination, and marital problems. Thus, former inmates, especially those infected with HIV/AIDS and HCV, have many needs: health, financial, employment, family support, etc. Services that could be offered to them include public benefits counseling, eligibility and application assistance, referral services, mentoring programs, coping and support groups and counseling, substance use and other 12 step programs, access to housing, hospice and community living, public housing, SSI, Medicare and Medicaid programs, referrals to physicians, clinics, and assistance programs specializing in employment, nutrition, and household goods. All of these programs would assist former inmates in their reintegration into their communities upon release.

It is crucial to the long-term viability of the state's efforts at combating HIV/AIDS and HCV in post-release populations that it assesses the impact of its interventions. This will, by definition, require careful, systematic, and ongoing collection and analysis of data about who is served and what impact the services they receive have on them and their communities.

Determining what efforts are working and what might be improved will provide insights necessary for enhancing the quality and quantity of services being provided. Such assessments are closely related to understanding the impact of services. They are, however, somewhat different in that they point to the internal operations and procedures that might be changed to make interventions more resource-efficient and capable of expanding to cope with more users with various needs as the post-release HIV/AIDS and HCV populations continue to expand.

Illinois will likely need to offer a wide range of services to the ex-offender population at-risk for infection with HIV/AIDS and HCV. It will have greater success in meeting the needs of this population by working in conjunction with other organizations and entities that may have closer proximity, greater contact, or more complementary areas of specialization for a given clientele. The state, therefore, will need to devise effective strategies for generating referrals to other organizations and entities that may act as additional points of contact or resource bases for providing direct services to this population. The state will need to become somewhat clearer in terms of what kinds of working relationships it will have with others such as local community health organizations, health providers, and other community-based organizations and agencies located in the same city or region as former inmates.

Raising Public Awareness of the Problem

Despite the fact that the incidence of HIV/AIDS and HCV is growing, and the fact that the size of the former inmate population at-risk for infection with these viruses is growing, the scope of this public health challenge is not as well known as it needs to be, nor is it as well known as it must be to be successful. The state will need to expand its social marketing and public education efforts to generate more awareness of these problems and understanding of the services that it is (and will be offering) to combat these public health threats.

Building Greater Trust of Potential Clients

There is reason to believe that some ex-offenders who are at-risk for HIV/ AIDS and HCV are unfamiliar with the services the state provides, and therefore, are not fully trusting that it will be able to help them. Until this issue is confronted successfully, it will be extremely difficult for the state to be truly effective in helping those who are suspicious of many agencies. These are issues that will require more than standard marketing and conventional promotions.

Remaining Innovative

While the State of Illinois may find that many of its current practices and efforts are effective in improving the timeliness and delivery of services, it will find that there will be those who will attempt to thwart its efforts and challenge the legitimacy of its services. It is likely that some potential supporters will refrain from lending their support precisely because they question the legitimacy of agencies dedicated to improving the conditions of those formerly incarcerated. The state may also find that those supporters who have initial levels of enthusiasm for its efforts may become less excited about the goals or methods over time. For these reasons, the state will need to remain abreast of emerging service delivery practices, innovative methods of meeting challenges to its efforts, and new breakthroughs that will aid it in fulfilling its mission.

Generating Community Support

Currently, Illinois has limited efforts directed at the ex-offender population that is at-risk for HIV/AIDS and HCV infection, per se. Relatedly, there is little public resistance to its efforts. As the profile of these issues becomes higher and as the state's efforts become greater, support may be fickle or difficult to renew, especially if taxpayers question this as a priority in times of budget cuts. For these reasons, the state will want to be ready to answer the following kinds of questions for potential supporters: (1) What are the demonstrated needs of the community as the community members define them, and why are they important? (2) What problems would appear if the state's efforts were not instituted, and who would be affected? (3) Who are the constituencies of the proposed efforts? (4) Who benefits directly and indirectly? (5) How does the state know that it is successful in its efforts? (6) Who speaks for the communities? and (7) Why are the proposed activities a good investment? Although public support does not appear to be a pressing concern at this point, the state needs to be poised to answer these questions as they arise in the future.

The detrimental effects of elevated rates of incarceration on former inmates are clear. It is also clear that incarceration has affected the health and well-being of the families and communities to which ex-offenders return. There are many issues that the state will want to monitor as it pursues its goal of coordinating efforts to improve the quality of life for ex-offenders at risk of spreading HIV/AIDS and HCV to their communities.

The spread of AIDS in the white community has been largely contained. Still, AIDS infections continue to grow in communities of color, especially among Latinos and African Americans. The high rates of incarceration of these communities are related to racial disparities, and they make the issue particularly critical for these communities. Moreover, a high proportion of the youth of these communities is incarcerated for drug offenses. This sets of a serious chain reaction in these communities, as higher and higher percentages of their youth are disqualified from fully participating in society, and their communities are deprived of their contribution. This pattern is a clear manifestation of the disadvantages of race, inequities in the law enforcement, and an incarceration system that are critical parts of neoracism. As a society, we need to make these groups our priority (akin to affirmative action) so that the issues that confront them can be addressed comprehensively. It is only by doing so that we can begin to redress some of the racial inequalities that reproduce and accelerate *de facto* racism.

REFERENCES

Arriola, Kimberly R.J. and Ronald L. Braithwalte. 2003. "Male Prisoners and HIV Prevention: A Call for Action Ignored." *American Journal of Public Health* 93: 759–763.

Auerbach, Judith D. and Thomas J. Coates. 2000. "HIV Prevention Research: Accomplishments and Challenges for the Third Decade of AIDS." *American Journal of Public Health* 90: 1092–1095.

Centers for Disease Control and Prevention. 2011. Data and information retrieved from http://www.cdc.gov/hiv/topics/testing/resources/guidelines/correctional-settings/section1.htm.

D'Aunno, Thomas, Thomas E. Vaughn, and Peter McElroy. 1999. "An Institutional Analysis of HIV Prevention Efforts by the Nation's Outpatient Drug Abuse Treatment Units" *Journal of Health and Social Behavior* 40: 175–192.

DiFranceisco, Wayne J., et al. 2000. "Bridging the Gap Between the Science and Service of HIV Prevention: Transferring Effective Research-Based HIV Prevention Interventions to Community AIDS Service Providers." *American Journal of Public Health* 90: 1082–1088.

Doll, Lynda S. and Juarlyn Gaiter. 1996. "Editorial: Improving HIV/AIDS Prevention in Prisons is Good Public Health Policy." *American Journal of Public Health* 86: 1201–1203.

Ehrmann, Tanya. 2002. "Community-Based Organizations and HIV Prevention for Incarcerated Populations: Three HIV Prevention Program Models." *AIDS Education & Prevention* 14: 75–84.

Federal Bureau of Prisons. 2010. *State of the Bureau 2009*. Washington: U.S. Department of Justice, Federal Bureau of Prisons.

Illinois Department of Corrections. 2011. *Illinois Department of Corrections Annual Report FY2010*. Springfield, IL: Illinois Department of Corrections.

Kaplan, Edward H. and Michael H. Merson. 2002. "Allocating HIV-Prevention Resources: Balancing Efficiency and Equity." *American Journal of Public Health* 92: 1905–1907.

Khan, James G. 1996. "The cost effectiveness of HIV prevention targeting: How much more bang for the buck?" *American Journal of Public Health* 86: 1709–1712.

United States Bureau of Justice Statistics. 2011. Data and information retrieved from http://bjs.ojp.usdoj.gov/.

CHAPTER SIXTEEN

MARCHING IN MARCH: EARLY PARTICIPATION IN CHICAGO'S IMMIGRANT MOBILIZATION

Angela Mascarenas and Cedric Herring

INTRODUCTION

On March 10, 2006, Chicago was the site of a mass demonstration of more than one hundred thousand participants protesting in favor of immigrant rights. That demonstration for immigrant rights was the first of its kind, and it greatly exceeded the expectations of immigrant rights organizers. As events unfolded, however, it became evident that the March 10 Chicago demonstration was part of a growing tidal wave of immigrant protests across the country that were linked to the debate on immigration reform. The March 10 marchers were among the first to protest against the harshly punitive enforcement provisions of anti-immigrant legislation that were before the Congress. That historic demonstration sent shock waves throughout the country. Arguably, its success emboldened others who were sympathetic to the cause of immigrants' rights and blazed the trail for the larger-scale demonstrations in May.

But who were these early movement participants? And why did they participate in this early mobilization in March? Do they differ from the participants of later mobilizations? If so, what do the differences (or absence thereof) tell us in terms of participation in protest activities in general and in immigrant mobilizations in particular?

Since scholars began studying social movements, two enduring questions have remained the same: (1) who participates in social movements? and (2) why do people participate in such collective actions? During more than one hundred years of research, the ways in which these questions have been answered have gone through many changes. Among the factors that were identified to be linked with participation in collective action generally were individual characteristics, access to resources, and contextual factors, such as organizational affiliations.

Resource mobilization theorists (e.g., McCarthy and Zald 1973; McCarthy and Zald 1987), for example, argued that people with similar interests often pooled their limited resources and organized themselves into social movements to implement social change. In contrast to the classical collective behavior approach that viewed participants as irrational or structural/cultural deviants, the post-1960 resource mobilization theorists argued that participation in social movements and other forms of collective action were rational activities aimed at maximizing the limited resources of groups that could not achieve their goals otherwise. Resource mobilization theorists focused on how and why members of movement organizations acquired resources to advance their goals. They explained the motivation to participate in collective action in terms of rational analysis of the costs and benefits of participation (Oberschall 1973).

More recently, however, social movement researchers have argued that resource mobilization theorists may have overcorrected classical theory by underestimating the role of the individual's social psychological characteristics (Gamson 1992). "Political process" analysts, for example, argue that participation in social movement activities is an extension of political involvement, especially for those (indigenous) groups outside of the polity who lack routine, low-cost access to resources and decision making controlled by the government (McAdam 1982; Tilly 1978; Gamson 1975; Morris 1984). Collective political action, according to this view, is the vehicle for groups outside of the polity to pursue their group interests. This perspective explicitly links institutionalized politics with collective action. Much like resource mobilization theorists, scholars using this political process framework have focused on how and why organizations accumulate resources and mobilize those with similar interests. This framework, however, has been much more explicit in its focus on the political aspects (rather than the financial aspects) of movements, such as political opportunities, power differentials, demands for rights, and political conflicts among power holders and challengers.

The most recent theorizing on social movements suggests that contemporary movements are fundamentally different in character from "traditional" movements of the past. These "new social movements," the claim goes, require new theoretical lenses and tools to analyze and understand them. For example, unlike most traditional social movements, minority communities and others without full standing in the polity rarely participate in the new social movements. Rather, it is those with full citizenship rights, such as members of the white middle class, who typically engage in protest over the issues that are the focus of these new social movements. For some, what is unique about new social movements is that they are "extra-institutional phenomena rooted in civil society [that] point to a recovery of civil society" (Boggs 1986: 47). Thus, we see movements that are concerned with cultural questions (involving matters of identity, role definitions, and community) rather than expansion of the polity and extension of citizenship rights that are linked to quality of life issues.

This analysis hopes to shed some light on the participants of the 2006 immigrant mobilizations, in particular, their characteristics and reasons for participation. We argue that a more fact-based characterization of these mobilizations and their participants is a necessary and useful corrective to the many and often contentious, if not politically-motivated, characterizations of the media and various interest groups.

This chapter uses survey data from the May 1 immigrant mobilization in Chicago to assess competing formulations about participation in social movement activities. It uses propositions derived from competing social movement theories to generate hypotheses about the nature and characteristics of participants involved in the March 10 and May 1 immigrant rights demonstrations in Chicago. It compares the characteristics and behaviors of participants who were involved in both the March 10 and the May 1 mobilizations to those who were involved only in May. It uses quantitative methods to assess the determinants of early participation in the movement. In doing so, it hopes to gain insights into what distinguishes early adopters from others, and possibly what makes such early adopters unique. The chapter also hopes to contribute to a greater understanding of immigrant mobilizations in general.

IMMIGRANT MOBILIZATION

As Morris and Herring (1987) point out, in the 1960s when the contemporary civil rights movement emerged, it caught most social movement scholars off guard. They suggest that this was the case because existing theories of social movements were largely inadequate and focused on the wrong things. Similarly, it could be argued that the scope and scale of the immigrant rights movement in 2006 surprised most social movement scholars. Some analysts would suggest that we were again surprised because, in the twenty-first century, we are confronted with contemporary social movements that are fundamentally different in character from movements of the past. These differences are said to appear in the ideology and goals, tactics, structure, and participants of contemporary movements. Others would suggest that it is not so much that the movements are different as it is that scholars of social movements have been inaccurate in their predictions about who participates in social movements and why they do so.

In December of 2005, the U.S. House of Representatives passed HR 4437, the Borders Protection, Antiterrorism, and Illegal Immigration Control Act, or, as it is more commonly known, the Sensenbrenner Bill. That legislation would have made immigration without proper documentation a felony. It would have punished employers for hiring undocumented workers, and it called for the construction of hundreds of miles of fences along the U.S.-Mexico border.

In response to the passage of the Sensenbrenner Bill in the House of Representatives, millions of activists in dozens of U.S. cities participated in marches in support of immigrants. In May of 2006, for example, from Los Angeles to New York, Chicago to Houston, and Miami to Phoenix, the "Day Without Immigrants" demonstrations attracted widespread participation. Immigration activists organized the marches to challenge provisions of the legislation that would have criminalized undocumented immigrants and tightened the U.S.-Mexico border. While the goals of these mobilization efforts were numerous, the marchers had been urging lawmakers to help an estimated eleven million undocumented immigrants settle legally in the United States.

But as mentioned above, prior to the May 1 mobilizations, Chicago's downtown area was paralyzed on March 10 by an immigrant rights march of more than one hundred thousand people. We believe understanding who those early activists were and why they were participating will shed light not only on the larger-scale demonstrations for immigrant rights that occurred in May, but also on participation in social movements more generally. Below, we review the arguments of various theories of social movements that might be invoked to explain early participation in this movement.

Theories of Social Movements

Resource Mobilization I: The Organizational-Entrepreneurial Model

The resource mobilization approach has become central in the analysis of social movements and collective action. In particular, this approach suggests that there is no fundamental difference between movement behavior and institutionalized behavior; movement participants and their actions are rational; social movements pursue interests; movement mobilization occurs through an infrastructure or power base; outcomes of collective action are products of strategic choices made by participants; and either support or repression by elite groups can affect the outcomes of movements.

McCarthy and Zald's (1977) organizational-entrepreneurial variant of this approach became a central focus within the resource mobilization approach. Their model sought to explain modern American movements. According to their model, social movements are usually represented by several social movement organizations that compete for resources and participants to support the efforts of the movements. Also, social movement organizations usually represent groups with few of the discretionary resources needed to keep the organizations in business. Moreover, members of such groups are not likely to participate in collective action on their behalf because of the 'free rider" dilemma, i.e., the unwillingness of people to participate in collective action because (1) their individual contribution will not make a significant difference to the outcome, and (2) they will receive the same collective goods regardless of their level of participation. To overcome these problems, McCarthy and Zald argue that it is organizations and individuals from outside oppressed groups that make mobilization possible. Indeed, the organizational-entrepreneurial model argues that these movements are best conceptualized as professional movements that rely on the affluent middle class for funds, entrepreneurial leadership, and professional movement organizations from outside the oppressed groups. Rather than depend on members of the oppressed community for money, manpower, and leadership, "modern movements can increasingly find these resources outside of self-interested memberships concerned with personally held grievances." That is, these resources can be drawn from outside elites because it is they "who control larger resource pools" (McCarthy and Zald 1977: 1221). Therefore modern movements are led by professional movement organizations such that "it is increasingly possible that their financial support is totally separate from their presumed beneficiaries" (McCarthy and Zald 1973: 18). Even more, McCarthy and Zald (1973) argue that discontent and grievances are basically irrelevant in generating social movements. In short, the organizational-entrepreneurial model argues that movements among underdog groups do not rely on indigenous leadership, mass participation, and resources from grassroots sources. There has been research to support these claims (Bailis 1974 and Jenkins and Perrow 1977); however, Morris (1981, 1984) and McAdam (1982) have presented evidence to the contrary.

Resource Mobilization II: The Political Process and Opportunity Model

For proponents of the "political process and opportunity" model, the study of movements is the study of the political process and the collective action it generates (McAdam 1982; Tilly 1978; Gamson 1975; Morris 1984). For them, the different forms of collective action are part of the regular processes of struggle. Political actions are generated by interest groups. Such political activities have an orderly side (e.g., routine political activities like voting) and others are from a more disorderly side (e.g., social movement activities). The central process is a process of sets of people acting together on their interests. This framework tries to incorporate into a single theory both conventional political behavior and unconventional political behavior. Groups engage in social movement tactics such as demonstrations, boycotts, strikes, violence, riots, and sit-ins when they are excluded from the polity, i.e., when they lack routine, low-cost access to resources controlled by the government. Thus, the interests of challenging groups cannot be realized through "legitimate" means because governments respond to the interests of polity members only. Collective action and its accompanying tactics are the vehicles of groups who rationally pursue group interests. It is the struggle for power between polity members and challengers that give rise to collective action.

Focusing on the excluded interests of movement groups, this model investigates the social structures and processes enabling challengers to pursue power through collective action. The first requirement is that challenging groups have internal organization. Organization is the extent of common identity and unifying structure among members of the challenging group (Tilly 1978: 54). The relevant internal organization consists of various forms including established institutions, professional and informal networks, and formal movement organizations (Morris, 1981). Organization is important because, through it, movement groups are able to collectively plan and strategize, hold meetings, organize and coordinate demonstrations, raise money, and facilitate the mobilization process. In this approach, organization is crucial to both the emergence and success of movements. Though potential movement groups usually possess organizational structures and resources, they must be mobilized if challengers are to contend for power. Mobilization refers to the process by which challenging groups gain collective control over resources that make collective action possible (Tilly 1978: 84).

The political process model analyzes the link between the mobilization process of movement groups and their preexisting structures and resources. Unlike classical models which often portray new movement groups as having the tasks of creating new symbolic systems and constructing new organizations, political process theorists argue that the task is usually much easier because these groups already have many of these resources. Preexisting organization, rather than the absence of organization facilitates mobilization. The model predicts that individuals who are well integrated into preexisting community structures constitute the bulk of the early participants of collective action (Oberschall 1973). When preexisting social organization and the mobilization process are combined, they generate collective action.

As a variant of the resource mobilization theory, the political process and opportunity model shares some arguments and assumptions with the organizational-entrepreneurial model (e.g., no fundamental difference between movement behavior and institutionalized behavior; movement participants and their actions are rational; social movements pursue interests; movement mobilization occurs through organizations, etc.). These models part ways, however, on issues of the role and centrality of the beneficiary population, the role of political issues and grievances, and the degree to which the beneficiary (indigenous) population contributes resources to the social movement efforts.

Hence, using the different resource mobilization arguments, some of the hypotheses that will be tested are: (1) membership in the beneficiary population (i.e., being an immigrant) increases (decreases) the likelihood that one will be an early participant in the immigrant rights movement; (2) having grievances or explicitly political concerns increases (decreases) the likelihood that one will be an early participant in the immigrant rights movement; (3) having attended prior movement efforts and activities increases (decreases) the likelihood that one will be an early participant in the immigrant rights movement; (4) having higher income increases (decreases) the likelihood that one will be an early participant in the immigrant rights movement; and (5) being a member of the polity increases (decreases) the likelihood that one will be an early participant in the mobilizations.

New Social Movements Theory

"New social movement" theories have been developed to explain participation in new forms of social activism. New social movement theory states that "new social movements" are different from traditional social movements that tend to focus on the struggle for political power.

These new social movements generally concentrate on the role of culture and the relationship between the rise of contemporary social movements and the larger economic structure. This framework is concerned with how issues of identity and personal behavior are bound up in social movements. The theory offers a historically specific vision of social movements as associated with new forms of middle-class radicalism. It presents a distinctive view of social movements, the larger sociopolitical environment, and how individuals fit into, respond to, and change the system (Pichardo 1997).

This theory suggests that new social movement participants seek to create a new social paradigm that challenges the dominant goal structure of Western societies by advocating postmaterialist, anti-growth, libertarian, and populist themes (Buechler 1995). To achieve these goals, new social movements tend to emphasize symbolic action, self-determination, postmaterialist values, collective identities, grievance articulation, and self-referential organization instead of direct political confrontations (Buechler 1995).

The central claim of the new social movement theory is that new social movements are a product of the shift to a post-industrial economy and that they are unique and, as such, differ from social movements of the industrial age. New social movements are said to be a product of the post-material age and are seen as fundamentally different from class-based and interest-group-based movements of the industrial period (Olofsson 1988). New social movement demands are believed to have moved away from the instrumental issues of industrialism to the quality of life issues of postmaterialism (Buechler 1995; Burklin 1984; Inglehart 1990; Parkin 1968).

New social movements tend to draw from a constituent base that is not particularly class focused. Participants tend not to be bonded by a common class, but rather by a common ideology (Buechler 1995). Still, most members of new social movements are from the middle-class (Buechler 1995). These constituents do not tend to be individuals brought together by common grievances in their immediate lives (Buechler 1995). In fact, they can even be characterized as privileged middle-class people getting together to protest for fun and excitement. Instead of using either institutionalized politics or the unruly politics of traditional social movements, new social movement participants use apolitical introspection and emphasize "politically correct" lifestyles rather than political activity (Buechler 1995).

New social movement theory suggests that new social movements tend to be anti-materialist, anti-growth, and to have an anti-consumerist ideology. Therefore, the kind of material benefits that are believed to motivate participants in traditional social movements are not believed to hold much sway in such movements. As Melucci (1985) points out, "they do not fight merely for material goals, or to increase their participation in the system. They fight for symbolic and cultural stakes, for a different meaning and orientation of social action" (p. 798).

New social movements, thus, may rely on social solidarity and such "soft" (nonmaterial) incentives as collective identity, social prestige, or even merely joining for fun as social cohesion mechanisms to recruit participants. Hence, in addition to the hypotheses presented earlier, we will also test the hypothesis that being concerned with issues of solidarity and unity increases the likelihood that one will be an early participant in the immigrant rights movement. Finally, being concerned with tangible material benefits and political issues will also be hypothesized to increase the likelihood that one will be an early participant in the immigrant rights movement.

Structural Location and Biographical Availability

In addition to the variables identified with the various theoretical formulations discussed above, several other factors are believed to influence participation in activism. Herring (1989) and Pichardo and Herring (2004) incorporate the idea of "social structural location." "Social structural location" is a concept that takes into account the fact that people have multiple memberships in groups (e.g., race, gender, class, life stage, etc.) with varying levels of social, economic, and political power that simultaneously interact to determine life chances, world views, political beliefs, and behaviors (Herring 1989). The central idea is that a person's interests are shaped by his or her social structural location. Structural locations are also imbued with varying levels of influence and resources as well as kinds of power (social, political, and economic) that allow individuals to absorb, bear, or shift the risks/costs of high-risk/cost activism (Pichardo and Herring 2004). Because such factors can influence how an individual regards the goals of social movements and their ability to absorb or mitigate the costs of activism, they should be taken into account when attempting to understand participation in activism.

McAdam (1986) and Wiltfang and McAdam (1991) introduced the idea of "biographical availability" for participation in protest activity. "Biographical availability [is] defined as the absence of personal constraints that may increase the costs and risks of movement participation such as full-time employment, marriage, and family responsibilities" (McAdam 1986: 70). "The argument is that those with less time to engage in activism or more personal responsibilities constraining involvement will be less likely to participate" (p. 83).

We will include such factors in our analysis. Below, we use survey data from the May 1 immigrant mobilization in Chicago to assess competing formulations about why activists participate in social movement activities. We test hypotheses about the nature and characteristics of activists involved in the March 10 and May 1 immigrant rights demonstrations in Chicago. These hypotheses were derived from the competing social movement theories discussed above.

DATA AND METHODS

The data for the analysis come from the Immigrant Mobilization Project Survey. The study conducted face-to-face surveys of participants in the May 1, 2006, immigrants' rights march and rally that took place in Chicago. The Immigrant Mobilization Project survey used a multistage block sampling technique to give respondents an equal chance of being selected for the study. Interviewers were assigned "block numbers" within Union Park and Grant Park in Chicago. Within those blocks, interviewers were instructed to approach every tenth person as a potential respondent for the survey. Because of Institutional Review Board (IRB) restrictions, they were also told not to approach people who were clearly under age sixteen. This process yielded 410 surveys. The surveys focused on the immigrant mobilization and the political conditions, resources, and ideological frames that led to participation. We were interested in the role of different social, cultural, and political institutions in shaping and framing the movement and in mobilizing participants. We used these data to test the following hypotheses:

Hypothesis 1: Membership in organizations increases the likelihood that one will be an early participant in the immigrant rights movement.

Hypothesis 2: Membership in the beneficiary population (i.e., being an immigrant) increases the likelihood that one will be an early participant in the immigrant rights movement.

Hypothesis 3: Having grievances or explicitly political concerns increases the likelihood that one will be an early participant in the immigrant rights movement.

Hypothesis 4: Having attended prior movement efforts and activities increases the likelihood that one will be an early participant in the immigrant rights movement.

Hypothesis 5: Having higher income increases the likelihood that one will be an early participant in the immigrant rights movement.

Hypothesis 6: Not being a member of the polity increases the likelihood that one will be an early participant in the immigrant rights movement.

Hypothesis 7: Being concerned with issues of solidarity and unity increases the likelihood that one will be an early participant in the immigrant rights movement.

Hypothesis 8: Being concerned with tangible material and political issues increases the likelihood that one will be an early participant in the immigrant rights movement.

Figure 16.1 presents a summary of these hypotheses and the expectations associated with various theories of social movements.

Operationalizations

Dependent Variable

To measure EARLY PARTICIPATION, respondents were asked: "Did you happen to attend the March 10 march?" Those who said they had participated in the March 10 march were coded 1. Others were coded 0.

Independent Variables

In order to test the eight hypotheses listed above, there are several independent variables that need to be operationalized. To determine whether respondents were MEMBERs OF ORGANIZATIONs, they were asked (1) whether they had been convinced to come to the march by an organization, and (2) whether they had come to the march with an organization. Those who responded yes to either question were coded 1. Others were coded 0.

To determine whether respondents were members of the BENEFICIARY POPULATION (i.e., immigrants), they were asked, "In what country were you born?" Those who said any country other than the United States were coded 1. Those who said the United States were coded 0.

To measure the reasons for people's participation in the march, respondents were asked: "What is the most important reason you are marching today?" Those respondents who said they were marching against Senate Bill 4437, for justice, or against abuse were coded 1 (as participating in the march because of GRIEVANCES); others were coded 0. To measure the

Figure 16.1: Summary of Hypotheses and Expectations Associated With Various Theories of Social Movements

Hypotheses	Classical Collective Behavior	RMI: Organizational-Entrepreneurial	RMII: Political Process	New Social Movements
Hypothesis 1: Membership in organizations increases the likelihood that one will be an early participant in the immigrant rights movement.	No	Yes	Yes	N/A
Hypothesis 2: Membership in the beneficiary population (i.e., being an immigrant) increases the likelihood that one will be an early participant in the immigrant rights movement.	N/A	No	Yes	No
Hypothesis 3: Having grievances or explicitly political concerns increases the likelihood that one will be an early participant in the immigrant rights movement.	N/A	No	Yes	No
Hypothesis 4: Having attended prior movement efforts and activities increases the likelihood that one will be an early participant in the immigrant rights movement.	N/A	Yes	Yes	No
Hypothesis 5: Having higher income increases the likelihood that one will be an early participant in the immigrant rights movement.	N/A	Yes	No	Yes
Hypothesis 6: Not being a member of the polity increases the likelihood that one will be an early participant in the immigrant rights movement.	N/A	No	Yes	No
Hypothesis 7: Being concerned with issues of solidarity and unity increases the likelihood that one will be an early participant in the immigrant rights movement.	N/A	No	No	Yes
Hypothesis 8: Being concerned with tangible material and political issues increases the likelihood that one will be an early participant in the immigrant rights movement.	N/A	Yes	Yes	No

degree to which respondents were participating in the march because of POLITICAL CONCERNS, those who said they were marching for legalization, for rights, or for voice were coded 1; others were coded 0.

In order to determine whether respondents had previously ATTENDED ACTIVITIES in support of or contributed time to the social movement efforts, they were asked: "Not counting the March 10 march or today's march, have you attended any other political meetings, rallies, or speeches in the last year?" Those who said yes were coded 1; others were coded 0.

To measure whether respondents were POLITY MEMBERs, they were asked whether they had written a letter or telephoned a public official's office about a concern or problem; contributed money to a candidate, a political party, or some other political organization; or voted in the last presidential election. Those who said yes to any of these items were coded 1; others were coded 0.

Respondents were asked about their household INCOMEs. Amounts ranged from less than $5,000 to more than $150,000. Dollar amounts were coded as the midpoint of category ranges (e.g., 2500 for $0–$5,000). Those in the highest, open-ended category were coded 175,000.

To indicate whether respondents were CONCERNED ABOUT SOLIDARITY AND UNITY, those who said they hoped to accomplish immigrant awareness or were marching for immigrants, for "my people," or for unity were coded 1; others were coded 0. To indicate whether respondents were CONCERNED ABOUT MATERIAL BENEFITS, those who said they hoped to accomplish equality or were marching for workers, or to change government policy were coded 1; others were coded 0.

Control Variables

Respondents were asked about their race/ethnicity. Those who said they were LATINO were coded 1; others were coded 0. FEMALE respondents were coded 1, and males were coded 0. Respondents were coded 0–18 to indicate how many years of EDUCATION they had attained. Respondents were coded 12–72 to indicate their AGE. Respondents were asked about their marital status. Those who said they were MARRIED were coded 1; others were coded 0. Those who said they have at least one CHILD AT HOME who is younger than age 18 were coded 1; others were coded 0. Respondents who said they were currently enrolled as a high school or college STUDENT were coded 1; others were coded 0. And finally, those respondents who said that they had to MISS WORK in order to attend the march were coded 1; others were coded 0.

RESULTS

What factors help explain who the early immigrants rights social movement participants were and why they participated? Did early participants differ from later participants? How do these factors correspond to the hypotheses outlined above? What do they tell us about participation in immigrant mobilizations?

Table 16.1 presents comparisons of selected characteristics of early participants in the immigrant rights movement versus those of later participants. This table shows that 86 percent of early movement participants were Latino. This compares with 68 percent of later participants. The table also shows that early participants were slightly less likely to be female (44 percent) than were later participants (48 percent). Later participants had more education on average (12.8 years of education attainment versus 11.4 years of educational attainment). They also had higher incomes on average ($48,197 versus $41,588). Early participants were more likely than were later participants to have children at home (44 percent versus 28 percent), and they were more likely to be married (45 percent versus 36 percent).

Table 16.1 also shows that 68 percent of early activists were immigrants. This compares with 49 percent of later participants. There was not much difference in the average ages of early participants (31.9 years) versus later participants (31.1 years), nor was there much difference in the percentage of early participants who were students (29 percent) compared with the percentage of later participants who were students (28 percent). Finally, early participants were slightly more likely than later participants to report that they had to miss work in order to participate in the march (75 percent versus 70 percent). We take these differences into account in our multivariate analysis.

What do these patterns reveal? As Figure 16.2 shows, organizational membership is associated with a greater tendency to be involved as an early activist, as 58 percent of those who were members of organizations were early activists compared with 45 percent of those who were not members of organizations. In addition, more than half (51 percent) of those who had previously attended social movement activities were early activists. These findings support the arguments of the resource mobilization theories that organizations foster the development of interpersonal ties that in turn facilitate early participation in collective actions. It is also consistent with the findings of other studies that showed how

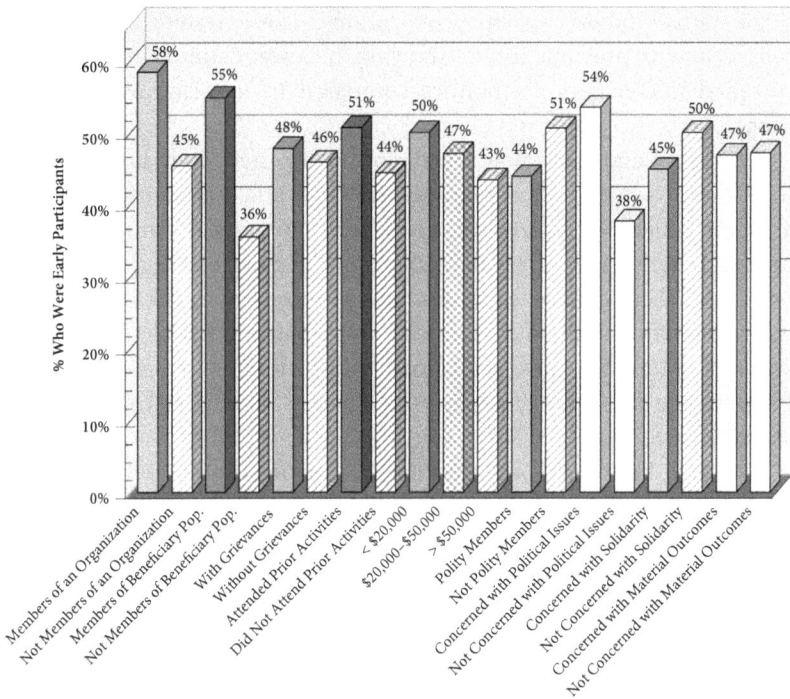

Figure 16.2: Percentage Who Were Early Participants by Attributes Associated with Various Social Movement Theories.

organizations serve as "development" grounds for political engagement (Flanagan 2003) and for acquiring organizational and civic skills that tend to increase participation in political mobilizations.

The graph also shows that a substantially higher percentage of those from the beneficiary population (i.e., 55 percent of immigrants) were among the early activists than those who are not part of the beneficiary population (i.e., 36 percent of non-immigrants). Similarly, grievances played a significant role in the participation of early activists and lower-income people were more likely to be early activists than were those with middle incomes and higher incomes (e.g., 50 percent of those with incomes below $20,000 were early participants versus 47 percent of those with incomes between $20,000 and $50,000, versus 43 percent of those with incomes above $50,000). These finding run counter to the expectations of the organizational-entrepreneurial model and the new social movements theory that emphasize the role of "professionals" or "high-status" individuals in mobilizations. These results are also *not consistent* with previous studies showing the lower Latino participation in so-called unconventional politics compared to non-Latinos (Martinez 2005).

A central claim of the new social movements theory is that movements have moved away from the instrumental issues and that their participants are more concerned with issues of solidarity and unity. The graph provides information that is contrary to these claims. In particular, it shows that 45 percent of those concerned with solidarity were among the early participants compared with 50 percent of those who were not concerned with solidarity. Moreover, those concerned with material outcomes and benefits were just as likely (47 percent) to be early activists as those without such concerns.

Although interesting, the descriptive statistics do not provide much information about the net relationship between these factors and early participation in the immigrant rights movement. In order to address this issue more rigorously, Tables 16.2–16.4 present the results from multivariate analysis. Table 16.2 presents the relationship between early participation in the immigrant rights movement and structural location and biographical availability. Model I shows that being Latino significantly increases that likelihood that one would be an early participant, net of gender, education, and age. It also shows that one's likelihood of being an early participant decreased as education increases. Model II adds biographical availability variables. This model shows that, in addition to the effects of education and of being Latino, having children at home and being a student also increase the likelihood that one would be an early participant in the movement. This "baseline model" with structural location and biographical availability variables account for a modest 6.3 percent of the variance.

The next column illustrates what happens when additional factors are added. The relationship between organizational membership and early participation in the movement becomes more robust and in the direction predicted by the organizational-entrepreneurial model. Contrary to the expectations of this model, however, is the finding that higher income is not associated with early participation.

The results in Table 16.3 show that when political process factors are taken into account, some of the previously discussed relationships change. In particular, organizational membership becomes non-significant, but membership in the beneficiary population becomes statistically significant in predicting early participation. Moreover, grievances become

Table 16.1: Selected Characteristics of Early Versus Later Participants in the Immigrant Rights Movement.

Selected Characteristics	Early Participants	Later Participants	Overall
% Latino	84.6%	68.3%	75.8%
% Female	43.6%	48.2%	46.2%
Mean Educational Attainment	11.4	12.8	12.2
Mean Family Income	$41,588	$48,197	$45,320
% with Children Younger than 18	44.1%	27.6%	35.5%
% Married	45.2%	35.8%	40.4%
% Immigrants	67.9%	49.0%	58.0%
Mean Age	31.9	31.1	31.5
% Students	28.7%	27.6%	28.0%
% Who Missed Work to Attend	74.6%	70.3%	72.4%
N	188	214	402

Table 16.2: Logistic Regression Models Predicting Early Participation in the Immigrant Rights Movement with Structural Location and Biographical Availability.

Independent Variables	Model I	Model II
Constant	.029	−.095
Structural Location Variables		
Latino	.680**	.518*
Female	−.101	−.074
Education	−.062**	−.083**
Age	.004	.005
Biographical Availability Variables		
Married		.119
Children at Home		.564**
Student		.546*
Missed Work		.084
R² Analog	.034***	.063***
N	329	252

* p < .1   ** p < .05   *** p < .01

a Coefficients are unstandardized. For the dummy (binary) variable coefficients, significance levels refer to the difference between the omitted dummy variable category and the coefficient for the given category.

Table 16.3: Logistic Regression Models Predicting Early Participation in the Immigrant Rights Movement with Factors from Various Theories of Social Movements, Net of Structural Location and Biographic Availability.

Independent Variables	Classical Collective Behavior	Organizational-Entrepreneurial Model	Political Process Model	New Social Movement Theory
Constant	-.052	-.401	-1.464*	-.003
Latino	.591**	.618*	.858**	.560*
Female	-.027	-.078	-.288	-.094
Education	-.089**	-.062	-.078*	-.074**
Age	.003	-.001	-.008	.004
Married	.108	.295	.253	.138
Children at Home	.593**	.271	.330	.556**
Student	.484*	.660*	.737**	.558*
Missed Work	.048	.073	-.058	.096
Member of Organization	.667*	.767**	.221	
Beneficiary Population (Immigrants)		.420	.771**	
Grievances		.233	.435*	
Income		-.00005	-.00005	
Political Concerns			1.073***	
Attended Prior Activities			1.473***	
Polity Member			.184	
Concerned about Solidarity and Unity				-.351
Concerned about Material Benefits				.056
R^2 Analog	.069***	.083**	.161***	.068**
N	252	224	224	252

* $p < .1$ ** $p < .05$ *** $p < .01$

[a] Coefficients are unstandardized. For the dummy (binary) variable coefficients, significance levels refer to the difference between the omitted dummy variable category and the coefficient for the given category.

marginally significant, and having political concerns and attending prior movement activities are highly significant factors in the directions predicted by the political process model. We should also note that including these political process factors almost doubles the amount of the variance explained.

The final column in Table 16.3 presents the relationship between factors such as emphasis on solidarity and nonmaterial concerns with early participation in the immigrant rights movement. Net of the effects of structural location and biographical availability, these variables highly emphasized by the new social movement theory are not statistically significant. Concerns about solidarity do not have the predicted facilitative effects, and concerns about material benefits do not have the predicted dampening effects on early participation in the immigrant rights movement. Also, it should be noted that this model accounts for the least amount of the variance.

Table 16.4 presents a model that incorporates factors that reflect the expectations of the different theories simultaneously. In order to make interpretation of these results more straightforward, we converted "log odds" into the more intuitive and accessible "predicted probabilities" of participation that can be compared to actual rates of participation. For example, the overall rate of early participation in the immigrant rights movement was .464 (i.e., 46.4 percent). Net of all other factors in the full model, those who were Latino had an early participation rate of .527 (i.e., 52.7 percent). Also, those who were members of organizations had higher than average early participation rates at 53 percent. Members of the beneficiary population also had higher early participation rates at .543 as well as those with grievances (i.e. 47.2 percent) and those with lower incomes (.546). These results also show that, consistent with the expectations of the political process model, those with political concerns (.579) and those who had attended prior movement activities (.523) had higher levels of early participation. Also consistent with the political process model is the finding that members of the polity (.443) had lower levels of early participation. Contrary to the predictions of new social movement theory, those concerned with solidarity had lower rather than higher rates of early participation. Consistent with new social movement theory, however, is the finding that those concerned about material benefits are slightly less likely to be early participants.

Generally speaking, these results are most consistent with the political process model. Indeed, while not all of the relevant factors achieve statistical significance, there are no results that are completely incompatible

Table 16.4: Logistic Regression Model Predicting Early Participation in the Immigrant Rights Movement with Factors from Various Theories of Social Movements.

Independent Variables	Factors from All Models	Predicted Probabilities
Constant	-1.474^*	.464
Latino	$.890^{**}$	.527
Female	$-.268$	.432
Education	$-.080^*$	<12 = .632 12 = .505 > 12 = .384
Age	$-.008$	< 30 =.455 30–50 = .476 > 50 = .438
Married	.257	.532
Children at Home	.311	.557
Student	$.719^{**}$	.511
Missed Work	$-.060$	.475
Member of Organization	.227	.530
Beneficiary Population (Immigrants)	$.775^{**}$	.543
Grievances	.313	.472
Income	$-.0005$	< $20K = .546 $20–50K = .479; > $50K =.400
Political Concerns	1.097^{***}	.579
Attended Prior Activities	1.505^{***}	.523
Polity Member	.164	.443
Concerned about Solidarity and Unity	$-.052$	.437
Concerned about Material Benefits	.216	.442
R^2 Analog	$.162^{***}$	
N	224	

* p < .1 ** p < .05 *** p < .01

[a] Coefficients are unstandardized. For the dummy (binary) variable coefficients, significance levels refer to the difference between the omitted dummy variable category and the coefficient for the given category.

with the predictions of that framework. This is not true for the organizational-entrepreneurial model or new social movement theory, however.

Discussion and Conclusions

This chapter began with a brief overview of the demonstrations in support of immigrant rights that took place in Chicago on March 10, 2006. It posed questions about who these early movement participants were and why they participated in this early mobilization effort. We argued that this March 10 mobilization was significant in that it paved the way for the larger mobilizations that followed. Hence, we found it just as important not only to describe who these early participants were but also to gain insights as to why they participated.

We used insights from theories of social movements to approach the task at hand. In particular, we tested hypotheses based on likely predictions of the organizational-entrepreneurial model, the political process model, and the new social movements model in order to highlight patterns in early participation. These theories suggest the importance of organization, resources, grievance, or solidarity—factors identified in previous studies to be significantly related to participation (or lack thereof) in collective actions.

The results show that early participants in the immigrants' rights movement differed from later participants. On average, early participants were more likely to be Latino, less likely to be female, had lower levels of educational attainment, lower incomes, were more likely to be married, were more likely to have children at home, were more likely to be immigrants, were slightly older, were about as likely to be students, and were slightly more likely to have missed work to attend the march.

These results are most consistent with the predictions of the political process model that argues that organization and resources are necessary for groups to advance their collective interests. Further, the results also render support for the model's arguments on the centrality of the beneficiary populations and the degree to which they contribute indigenous resources to the mobilizations as well as the significant role of political issues and grievances to participation. These results run counter to the predictions of the organizational-entrepreneurial model that suggests that because groups that benefit from social movements usually have few discretionary resources needed for mobilization, it is people from outside oppressed groups that make mobilization possible. These results also tend to be inconsistent with the predictions of the new social movements theories that predict that large participation would come from groups that are not particularly aggrieved but would tend to be brought together by a common desire for social solidarity and share nonmaterial incentives, such as collective identity or social prestige.

Based on the results, we argue that early participation in the immigrant rights movement was a form of political expression, especially for immigrants who lacked other avenues to voice their displeasure with the direction of immigration reform. These early activists used collective political action to pursue their group interests. Involvement for them was not just about solidarity nor about narrowly defined individual interests. Rather, it was about making political changes that would improve conditions for those who would be relatively powerless without collective action. Moreover, this was not a movement carried out by affluent middle-class people on behalf of immigrants; it was a movement *for* immigrants and *of* immigrants, often with limited means.

However, while the political process model provided the strongest support for the hypotheses in this study, we do recognize that the other approaches may be stronger in answering other questions pertaining to movement participation. For instance, the new social movement's emphasis on meaning and identity construction may be better in helping us understand how meanings emerge and become shared among movement participants. Thus, it is useful in analyzing how individual identities get transformed into collective identities or how participation is sustained over time.

Further, as the new social movements argue, the vast transformations in society ushered in by postindustrial conditions changed the field and forms of political life, and hence, of social conflicts and movements. The shift to the symbolic arena necessitates the shift to the study of social action that emphasizes the link between new technology, cultural orientations and social conflicts (Melucci 1995). Hence, it may be interesting to see, for instance, what role the internet played in increasing (or decreasing) the likelihood of movement participation.

Finally, we also recognize that much may be gained by finding complementarities among these approaches. As the more recent works in social movement literature indicate, the trend is towards more integration or synthesis among different perspectives (Meyer, Whittier, and Robnett 2002; Buechler 2000). This approach would focus, for instance, on the linkages between political processes, organizational structures and discourse and how these factors together (rather than separately) impact movement participation. Though not the approach taken in this study, a follow-up analysis may be conducted that can test concrete assumptions based on this synthesizing model.

The story of the immigrant rights movement is still unfolding. It is too early to tell what will happen or how events will play out. But it is clear that immigrants themselves will play a significant part in writing their own story and in shaping the course of their movement for full inclusion.

References

Bailis, Leonard. 1974. *Bread or Justice*. Lexington, MA: Heath.

Boggs, Carl. 1986. *Social Movements and Political Power: Emerging Forms of Radicalism in the West*. Philadelphia: Temple University Press.

Buechler, Steven M. 2000. *Social Movements in Advanced Capitalism*. New York: Oxford University Press.

Buechler, Steven M. 1995. "New Social Movement Theories."

Burklin, Wilhelm P. 1987. "Governing Left Parties Frustrating the Radical Non-Established Left: The Rise and Inevitable Decline of the Greens." *European Sociological Review* 3: 109–126.

Flanagan, Scott C. and Aie-Rie Lee. 2003. "The New Politics, Culture Wars, and the Authoritarian-Libertarian Value Change in Advanced Industrial Democracies." Comparative Political Studies 36: 235–270.

Gamson, William A. 1975. *The Strategy of Social Protest*. Homewood, IL: Dorsey Press.

Gamson, William A. 1992. *Talking Politics*. New York: Cambridge University Press.

Herring, Cedric. 1989. *Splitting the Middle: Political Alienation, Acquiescence, and Activism among America's Middle Layers*. New York: Praeger.

Inglehart, Ronald. 2000. "Globalization and Postmodern Values." *The Washington Quarterly* 23: 1 pp. 215–228.

Inglehart, Ronald. 1987. "Value change in industrial societies." *American Political Science Review 81*: 1290–1303

Jenkins, J. Craig, and Perrow, Charles. 1977. "Insurgency of the powerless: Farm worker movements, 1946–1972." *American Sociological Review* 42: 249–268.

Martinez, Lisa M. 2005. "Yes We Can: Latino Participation in Unconventional Politics." *Social Forces* 84: 135–155.

McAdam, Doug. 1982. *Political Process and the Development of Black Insurgency, 1930–1970*. Chicago: University of Chicago Press.

McAdam, Doug. 1988. *Freedom Summer*. New York: Oxford University Press.

McAdam, Doug. 1989. "The Biographical Consequences of Activism." *American Sociological Review, 54,* 744–760.

McAdam, Doug. 1986. "Recruitment to High-Risk Activism: The Case of Freedom Summer." *American Journal of Sociology* 92: 64–90.

McCarthy, John D., & Zald, Mayer N. 1973. *The Trends of Social Movements in America: Professionalization and Resource Mobilization*. Morristown, NJ: General Learning Press.

McCarthy, John D. and Mayer N. Zald. 1987. *Social Movements in an Organizational Society*. Transaction: New Brunswick.

McCarthy, John D. and Mayer N. Zald. 1977. "Resource Mobilization and Social Movements: A Partial Theory." *American Journal of Sociology* 82: 1212–1241.

Melucci, Alberto. 1995. "The Process of Collective Identity" In *Social Movements and Culture*, eds. Hank Johnston and Bert Klandermans. MN: University of Minnesota Press, 41–63.

Melucci Alberto. 1985. "The Symbolic Challenge of Contemporary Movements." *Social Research* 52: 789–815.

Meyer, David, Nancy Whittier, and Belinda Robnett. 2002. Social Movements: Identity, Culture, and the State. New York: Oxford University Press.

Morris, Aldon D. 1981. "Black Southern Student Sit-In Movement: An Analysis of Internal Organization." *American Sociological Review* 46: 755–767.

Morris, Aldon D. 1984. *Origins of the Civil Rights Movement*. New York: Free Press.

Morris, Aldon and Cedric Herring. 1987. "Theory and Research in Social Movements: A Critical Review." *Annual Review of Political Science* 2: 137–193.

Oberschall, Anthony. 1973. *Social Conflict and Social Movements*. Englewood Cliffs, NJ: Prentice Hall.

Olofsson, Gunnar. 1988. "After the Working-class Movement? An Essay on What's 'New' and What's 'Social' in the New Social Movements." *Acta Sociologica* 31: 15–34.

Parkin, Frank. 1968. *Middle Class Radicalism*. New York: Praeger.

Pichardo, Nelson A. 1997. "New Social Movements: A Critical Review." Annual Review of Sociology 23: 411–30.

Pichardo, Nelson A. and Cedric Herring 2004. "Sacrificing for the Cause: Another Look at High-Risk/Cost Activism." *Race and Society* 7: 113–129.

Tilly, Charles. 1978. *From Mobilization to Revolution*. Reading, MA: Addison-Wesley.

Wiltfang, Gregory, and Doug McAdam. 1991. "The Costs and Risks of Social Activism: A Study of Sanctuary Movement Activism." *Social Forces* 69: 987–1010.

CHAPTER SEVENTEEN

FROM POLITICAL NOVICE TO VETERAN: YOUTH PARTICIPATION IN THE IMMIGRANT MOBILIZATION

Loren Henderson

The 1960s were a period of social turmoil, political mobilization, and popular participation in collective action (Koffler 2005). Young African Americans, for example, were involved in social movement organizations such as the Student Nonviolent Coordinating Committee (SNCC). Such organizations, composed primarily of young activists, were involved in activities such as freedom rides, lunch counter sit-ins, and teach-ins that brought about a great deal of social change (Morris and Herring 1987; Pichardo and Herring 2004). Today, however, many commentators characterize young people as politically apathetic and extremely disillusioned about politics and political activism (Koffler 2005).

So how and why—in an era of declining political participation, especially among young people—did more than one hundred thousand young people come to take part in the immigrant rights marches that began in 2006? Along with more than half a million other participants in the May 1 march, these young activists marched in support of rights and amnesty for the estimated twelve million undocumented immigrants in the United States. Far from being disengaged, their participation in these marches was intense and deliberate. They were there to denounce current and proposed immigration laws as unfair, to exercise the constitutional right to protest, and to send a clear message to the government (Flores-Gonzales 2007). Their participation contrasts sharply with recent studies that show that youth have low levels of political participation. In particular, Latino youth who compose most of the youthful crowd at the marches, have the lowest levels of political participation, lagging well behind white and African American youth. If "political apathy" among Latino youth is so high, why did they march in such massive numbers, and what accounts for the different levels and types of participation among these young people?

Using data from the 2006 Immigrant Mobilization Project Survey, this chapter examines political activism among young participants (ages fourteen to twenty-eight) in the May 2006 Chicago immigrant rights marches. In particular, this chapter examines (1) how youth of various races differ in their levels of experience in unconventional political participation, and (2) how factors such as race/ethnicity, immigrant status, having immigrant family members, income, and work status affect their levels of experience in participation.

YOUTH POLITICAL ENGAGEMENT

According to Pichardo and Herring (2004: 127), African American students during the civil rights and Black Power movements

> were motivated to accept the risks and costs inherent in social movement activism because they placed a high value on the goals of movement events. That is, despite the fierce opposition and culture of intimidation African Americans faced they stepped forward and put their lives on the line because the cause of equality and justice was so highly valued. Regardless of the personal costs and risks involved an individual will accept the risks and costs even when a rational cost/benefit analysis may argue against participation. If the goal is "worth it" then the risks and costs of activism become somewhat irrelevant: they are willing to suffer for the cause.

Put simply, young people were the driving force of the civil rights and Black Power movements of the 1960s and 1970s. But today, youth are generally less engaged in politics. Research points to a trend of declining political participation among young people starting in the mid-1980s. In particular, there has been a tendency among African American and Latino youth who live in urban areas to remain inactive politically (Lopez 2003). Lopez (2003) reveals that, compared with their white and African American counterparts, Latino youth have the lowest rates of voter registration and voter turnout. In addition, they deem voting as less important, discuss it less with their parents, and view political candidates more negatively.

There are skeptics who counter the claim that low levels of political engagement are a reflection of youth apathy and pessimism. Despite their low levels of political engagement, youth tend to be civically active through volunteerism. These experiences are institutionally structured through the school system in that many high schools require at least forty hours of volunteer services within the community in order to graduate. Most schools go out of their way to avoid political engagement as part of these service-learning hours. In essence, they are channeling the energies of urban youth toward more passive social involvement rather than political engagement. Camino and Zeldin (2002) found that many youth lack the opportunity structure to employ or engage in political activities. Therefore, much of the perceived political apathy among youth may be the result of inadequate opportunities rather than simple cynicism.

Political engagement may also be a function of age. Scholars have found that youth become more politically active with age. There also is a correlation between levels of civic engagement during the teen years and political engagement in adulthood (Almond and Verba 1963; Andolina et al. 2003; and Youniss et al. 2002). It appears that those youth who tend to engage civically are more likely to engage politically as adults. Given that many youth are now required to engage civically, it is likely that there will be a generation of more politically active urban adults in the near future.

The lack of political engagement may also result from youth failing to find a link between themselves and current political issues. For example, Zurkin et al. (2006) found that those of the baby boom generation became immersed in civil rights and challenging military policy because they felt connected to the issues and such concerns united them as a group.

When race/ethnicity and economic factors are added to the equation, the picture looks bleaker. In addition to the variables identified with the various theoretical formulations discussed above, several other factors are believed to influence participation in activism. McAdam (1986) and Wiltfang and McAdam (1991) introduced the idea of "biographical availability" for participation in protest activity. "Biographical availability [is] defined as the absence of personal constraints that may increase the costs and risks of movement participation such as full-time employment, marriage, and family responsibilities" (McAdam 1986: 70). "The argument is that those with less time to engage in activism or more personal responsibilities constraining involvement will be less likely to participate" (Herring 1989: 83). Herring (1989) and Pichardo and Herring (2004) also include the concept of "social structural location." The main idea is that "social structural locations are also imbued with varying levels of influence and resources as well as kinds of power (social, political, and economic) that allow individuals to absorb, bear, or shift the risks/costs of high-risk/cost activism" (Pichardo and Herring 2004: 117). Social location and racial hierarchy are also related to a group's level of political engagement (Sanchez-Jankowski, 2002). As noted earlier, Latino youth have the lowest levels of political engagement among urban youth from all racial and ethnic groups. This leads to the question: why are Latino youth less likely to engage politically?

High levels of poverty in urban areas offer youth limited opportunities to engage either civically or politically. This decreases the likelihood that youth of color will engage politically, given that many of these youth live in such areas (Hart and Atkins 2002, 2003). Beyond those discussed already, structural factors such as family, Internet, and community organizations are also closely linked to civic and political engagement among youth (Almond and Verba 1963; Camino and Zeldin 2002; Hart and Atkins 2002; Youniss et al. 2002; Andolina et al. 2003; Atkins and Hart 2003; Sherrod 2003; Ginwright, Noguera, and Cammarota 2006; and Zukin et al. 2006).

Lopez (2003) found that there are regional differences in the amount of political engagement among Latino youth in the United States. He found that Latino youth in Chicago were more likely to engage politically than other Latino youth across the nation. Is there something unique to this population? This research examines this population more closely.

An additional issue that should be examined is that of citizenship. In 2006, the Immigrant Mobilization Project Survey found that the majority of the youth participants were citizens (Flores-Gonzalez et al. 2006). This survey also found that most of the youth had participated in some form of political engagement prior to the 2006 march. Therefore, citizenship will be an important factor to include in the analysis.

Finally, it is quite possible that another key factor that greatly differentiated young marchers from older ones is the role of the Internet, e-mail, and the media in the mobilization and political participation of young people.

But which of these factors are most important in getting young people involved in political activities? What was the relative role of friends and peers versus socialization by parents who have been involved in political activities? What, in particular, differentiates veterans, repeaters, and novices?

A great deal could also be learned about youth political participation by focusing on the idea of differential opportunities to participate in various *modes* of political activism. By definition voting as a means of participation is closed off to those who are under age as well as those who are not documented. So, does marching open up a mode of participation for would-be activists who do not have low-cost, routine access through such formal modes of political participation as voting or contributing to the electoral process?

NOVICES, REPEATERS, AND VETERANS: VARIATIONS IN POLITICAL
EXPERIENCE AMONG YOUTH

About a third of the young participants say that they had no previous involvement in politics. For these "novices," the marches were their first time as political activists. They went to the marches simply because they believed strongly in immigrant rights, and most of them had been affected directly or indirectly by immigration issues. The other two-thirds of young participants reported various degrees of involvement ranging from those who had previously attended "rallies and little marches and demonstrations" to the politically savvy and politically engaged youth activists.

Nearly half of the youth involvement fell between political novices and political veterans. These young people could be identified as "political repeaters" because they had experience in politics prior to the May 1 mobilization, but they were not long-term participants. What is interesting is that previous civic and political engagement tended to be connected to immigrant rights. Some mentioned volunteering for citizenship workshops or being part of youth organizations that focused on immigration issues. Many mentioned having attended previous immigrant rights marches, specifically mentioning one that took place the previous summer that had been organized by El Pistolero, a popular radio personality.

Almost half of the youth respondents in the survey say they attended the March 10 march (45 percent). Overall, the youth surveyed have much higher rates of previous political engagement than suggested by previous studies: 56 percent had voted in the last elections, 54 percent had attended public meetings, 44 percent had attended other rallies, 42 percent had signed petitions, 31 percent had placed campaign stickers, 28 percent had written letters or called elected officials, and 19 percent had contributed money to a political candidate.

"Political veterans" were those 20 percent of respondents who had multiple experiences of involvement in efforts to bring about political change. Some of these experiences were through the formal political process; others were through unconventional political behavior.

Conventional political behaviors are acts that are a part of the formal electoral political process and are viewed as legitimate and are meant to influence policy makers. Several studies have documented that racial and ethnic minority groups are less likely than are Anglo whites to participate in electoral politics (e.g., Paulsen 1991; Verba et al. 1995). In order to explain disparities in conventional political behavior, some studies focus on differential levels of political efficacy (e.g., Verba et al. 1995). These analysts suggest that individuals who think that they have little ability to influence outcomes in the political realm are far more likely to abstain from conventional political participation.

Other researchers point to differences in resources that account for lower levels of political participation among racial and ethnic minorities (e.g., Schlozman, Lehman, Burns, and Verba 1994). People who have resources such as education, money, time, and information are more likely to participate in conventional politics (Lipset 1960; McAdam and Paulsen 1993; Verba and Nie 1972; Verba et al. 1978; Martinez 2005).

If people who lack resources are less likely to participate in conventional political behaviors, they may be more likely to participate in unconventional political behaviors (e.g., Piven and Cloward 1979). These are political acts that are not part of electoral politics. Often, they are not viewed as legitimate, but they are still meant to bring about policy changes.

Below, the chapter tries to determine what factors are important in distinguishing among novices, repeaters, and veterans. It uses insights from the literature on unconventional political behavior and the literature on Latino political involvement to inform hypotheses about who is likely to be a political novice, a political repeater, and a political veteran. It tests the following hypotheses:

Hypothesis 1: Young Latinos are more likely than are other young people to be political novices. Young Latinos are no more likely than are other young people to be political repeaters. Young Latinos are less likely than are other young people to be political veterans. This prediction is consistent with Martinez's (2005) finding that Latinos are less likely than are other racial and ethnic groups to be involved in protest because a lower percentage of them are citizens, a higher percentage of them are immigrants, a high percentage of them are more concerned about political events in their homelands, they have lower levels of educational attainment on average, they tend to have lower levels of English-language proficiency, and they have lower incomes on average.

Hypothesis 2: Young immigrants are more likely than are other young people to be political novices. Young immigrants are no more likely than are other young people to be political repeaters. Young immigrants are less likely than are other young people to be political veterans. Although participation in protest marches is not particularly high-risk, as Martinez (2005: 140) points out, "they pose a moderate risk for immigrant populations who may not want to bring unwanted attention or trouble to themselves."

Hypothesis 3: Those young people who are college students are less likely than those who are not college students to be political novices. Those young people who are college students are no more likely than those who are not college students to be political repeaters. Those young people who are college students are more likely than those who are not college students to be political veterans. This expectation is consistent with McAdam's argument about biographical availability: "individuals must be biographically available for protest.... The argument is that those with less time to engage in activism or more personal responsibilities constraining involvement will be less likely to participate" (McAdam 1986: 83).

Hypothesis 4: Young people who are from mixed immigrant-citizen families are more likely than are other young people to be political novices. Young people who are from mixed immigrant-citizen families are no more likely than are other young people to be political repeaters. Young people who are from mixed immigrant-citizen families are less likely than are other young people to be political veterans. Immigration is particularly high risk for the young marchers, and especially for those who have undocumented family members who may be deported.

In addition to testing these hypotheses, the multivariate analysis includes statistical controls for other factors such as gender, educational attainment, age, how participants were contacted about the march, marital status, and language of one's interview.

Data and Methods

This analysis uses data from the survey conducted during the May 2006 immigrant march. The University of Illinois at Chicago conducted this survey for the Immigrant Mobilization Project. There were 410 completed surveys. Of these, 186 surveys were with respondents between the ages of fourteen and twenty-eight. The primary concern of the study was to examine survey participants' reasons for participating in the march (Flores-Gonzalez et al. 2006).

Operationalizations

Dependent Variable
All respondents, by definition, were participants in the May 1 march. To measure PARTICIPATION EXPERIENCE, respondents were asked, "Did you happen to attend the March 10 march?" In order to determine whether respondents had previously attended activities in support of or

contributed time to the social movement efforts, they were asked: "Not counting the March 10 march or today's march, have you attended any other political meetings, rallies, or speeches in the last year?" Those who had not participated in any previous marches or rallies were coded 1 for NOVICES. Those who said they had participated in the March 10 march or some other single rally or protest event were coded 2 for REPEATERS. Those who said that they had participated in multiple prior protest events were coded 3 for VETERANS. These categories were further dummy variable coded for the multivariate analysis.

Independent Variables

Survey participants answered questions about their demographic characteristics. They also answered questions pertaining to their familiarity with mobilizations through social networks, social media, family, friends, and community organizations. For more specific details about question wording, please contact the author.

RESULTS

What factors helped explain how experienced respondents were in the immigrants' rights movement? Did experienced participants differ systematically from those with less experience? How do these factors correspond to the hypotheses outlined above?

Table 17.1 presents a comparison of selected characteristics of novice participants, repeaters, and veteran participants. This table shows that 82.8 percent of novices were Latino. This compares with 82.2 percent of repeaters, and 51.0 percent of veterans. These results suggest that political veterans were less likely than were novices and repeaters to be Latino. This table also shows that veterans (13.9 years of education) were more highly educated than were novices (11.9 years of education) and repeaters (12.4 years). Moreover, veterans (55.2 percent) were more likely to be college students than were novices (29.0 percent) and repeaters (43.0 percent). Veterans (11.9 percent) were also less likely to be married than were novices (24.2 percent) and repeaters (22.5 percent). The table also indicates that novices (53.1 percent) were substantially more likely than were repeaters (32.1 percent) and veterans (31.8 percent) to come from mixed immigrant-citizen families. Veterans also came from families with somewhat higher incomes, as veterans had family incomes of $44,929 on average compared with novices ($41,550) and repeaters ($40,090). There was

Table 17.1: A Comparison of selected characteristics of Novices, Repeaters, and Veteran Participants.

Characteristic	Novices	Repeaters	Veterans	Overall
% Latino	82.8%	82.2%	51.0%	76.6%
Average Years of Educational Attainment	11.9	12.4	13.9	12.5
% Who are College Students	29.0%	43.0%	55.2%	40.8%
% Married	24.2%	22.5%	11.9%	21.7%
% From Mixed Immigrant-Citizen Families	53.1%	32.1%	31.8%	36.5%
Average Family Income	$41,550	$40,090	$44,929	$41,368
Average Age	21.7	22.0	22.6	22.1
% of Eligibles Who Voted in Last Election	50.0%	51.0%	66.7%	53.3%

less than one year's difference in the average ages of novices (21.7 years), repeaters (22.0 years), and veterans (22.6 years); yet, veterans (66.7 percent) were substantially more likely to report that they had voted in the last presidential election than were novices (50.0 percent) and repeaters (51.0 percent).

Figure 17.1 shows the relationship between political experience and whether the respondent was Latino. This figure shows that of those who identified as Latino, 34 percent were novices. In contrast, of those who did not identify as Latino, 22 percent of them were novices. This chart also shows that 51 percent of Latinos were repeaters compared with 35 percent of non-Latinos. Among those who are Latino, 14 percent were veterans compared with 43 percent of non-Latinos. These patterns are statistically significant at the p< .01 level with a X^2 of 18.2, and they are fully consistent with Hypothesis #1.

Figure 17.2 shows the relationship between political experience and whether the respondent is an immigrant. This figure shows that 25 percent of immigrants are novices. This compares with 37 percent of native-born

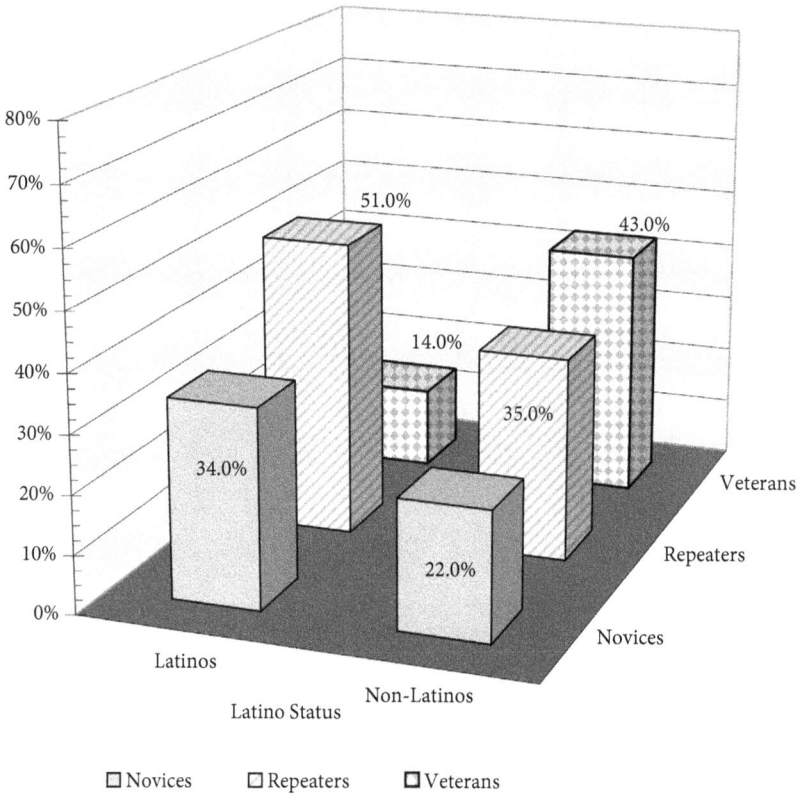

Figure 17.1: Level of political experience by Latino status.

respondents who are novices. In contrast, 59 percent of immigrants are repeaters, and 39 percent of native-born respondents are repeaters. And while 16 percent of immigrants are political veterans, 24 percent of U.S. natives are political veterans. These results are statistically significant at p< .05 level with a X^2 of 8.03, and they are fully consistent with Hypothesis #2.

Figure 17.3 shows the relationship between political experience and whether the respondent was a college student. The graph illustrates that while 23 percent of college students were political novices, 39 percent of others were novices. Half of college students were political repeaters and 46 percent of others were repeaters. And finally, the graph shows that 27 percent of college students were political veterans compared with 15 percent of others who were political veterans. These results are

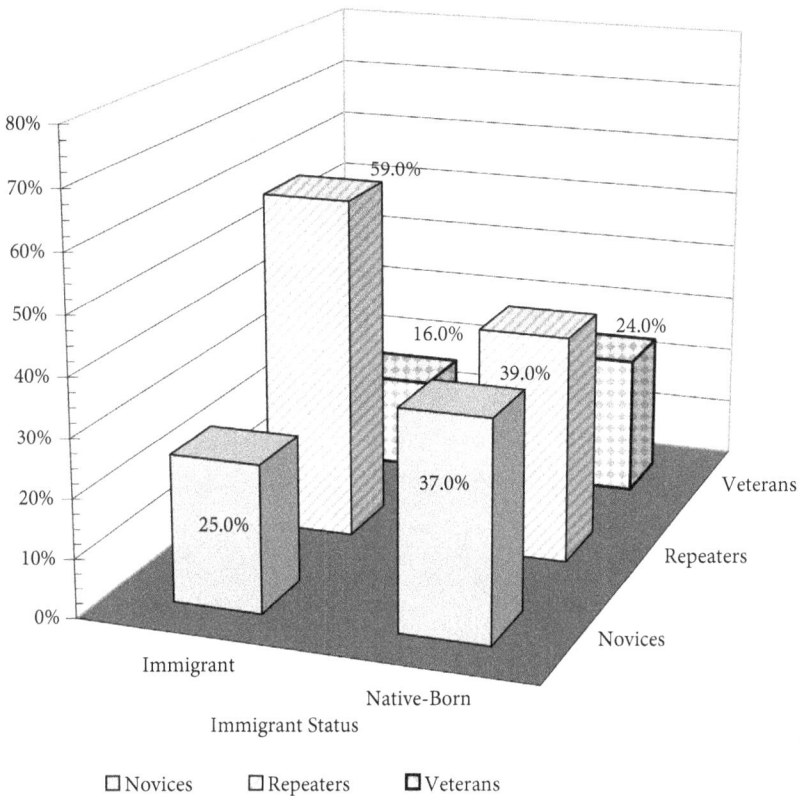

Figure 17.2: Level of Political Experience by Immigrant Status.

statistically significant at p< .1 level with a X^2 of 5.29, and they are generally consistent with Hypothesis #3.

Figure 17.4 shows the relationship between political experience and whether the respondent was from "mixed immigrant-citizen" family. This chart shows that 43 percent of those from mixed immigrant-citizen families are political novices. This compares with 23 percent of those from other kinds of families who are political novices. The chart also shows that while 39 percent of those from mixed immigrant-citizen families are political repeaters, more than half (53 percent) of others are political repeaters. The differences among political veterans are somewhat smaller, as 18 percent of those from mixed immigrant-citizen families and 23 percent of those from other kinds of families are political veterans. These results are statistically significant at p< .05 level with a X^2 of 9.0, and they are fully consistent with Hypothesis #4.

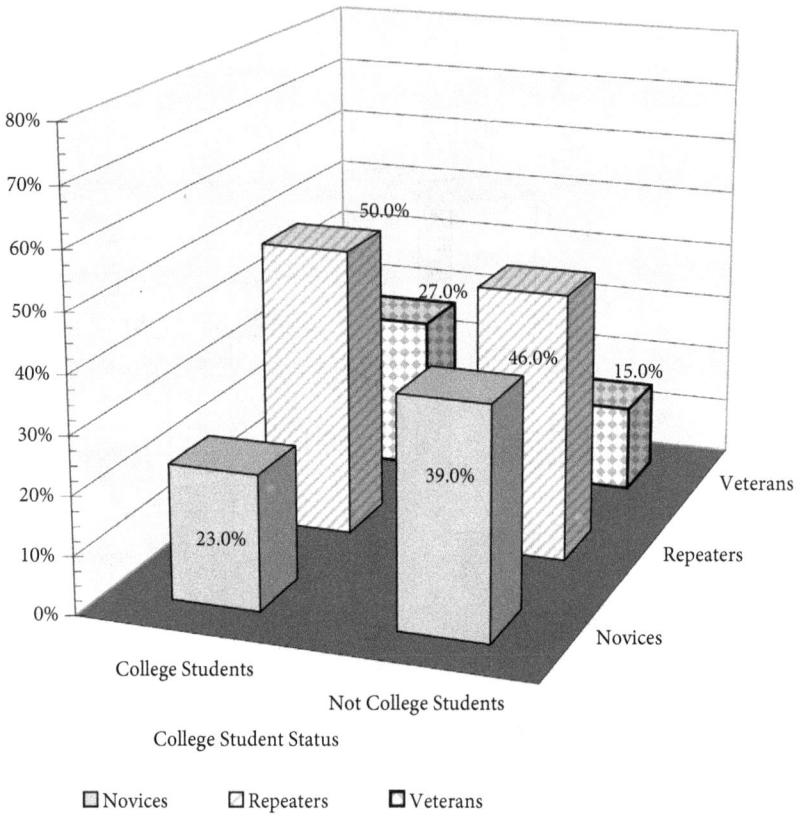

Figure 17.3: Level of Political Experience by College Student Status.

Although interesting, the descriptive statistics do not provide much information about the net relationship between these factors and amount of experience in the immigrant rights movement. In order to address this issue more rigorously, Table 17.2 summarizes results from logistic regression. This table summarizes the results from three logistic regression models. The analysis showed that Latino youth were more likely than those from other racial and ethnic groups to be political novices and repeaters but less likely to be political veterans. Similarly, those who were immigrants were more likely to be repeaters but less likely to be political veterans. Those who were college students were less likely than others to be political novices and more likely to be political veterans. In the multivariate analysis, coming from mixed immigrant-citizen families was not systematically related to levels of political experience.

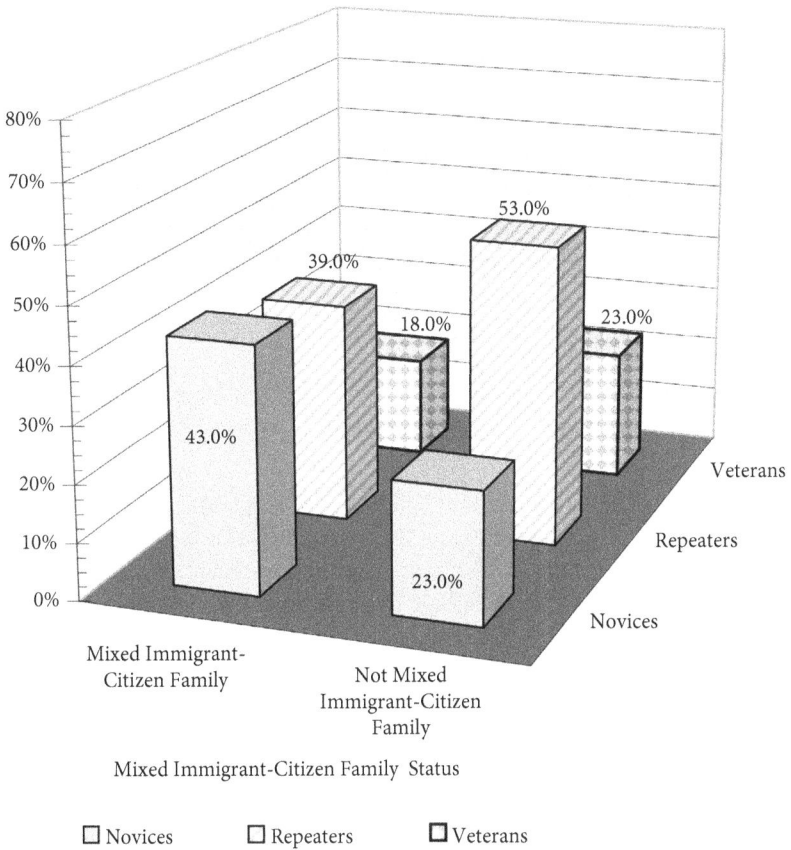

Figure 17.4: Level of Political Experience by Mixed Immigrant-Citizen Family Status.

Table 17.2: Summary of Results from 3 Logistic Regression Models.

Correlates of Political Experience	Novice	Repeater	Veteran
Latino	+	+	—
Immigrant	0	+	—
College Student	—	0	+
Mixed Immigrant-Citizen Family	0	0	0

In short, these results suggest that being Latino, being an immigrant, being a college student matter in ways that are consistent with Hypotheses #1, #2, and #3. Coming from a mixed citizen-immigrant family, while not necessarily inconsistent with predictions, was not statistically significant in this analysis. In particular, the role of having immigrant relatives or coming from mixed immigrant-citizen families were not borne out. Other factors that were not central to theorizing about political experience—e.g., how people found out about the march, marital status, and gender—also appear to be important determinants of levels of experience in unconventional political behavior among young people.

CONCLUSIONS

This chapter began by noting that, in an era of declining political participation, especially among young people, more than one hundred thousand young people participated in the immigrant rights marches that began in 2006. After drawing some parallels between student mobilization in the 1960s, the chapter examined four hypotheses about the determinants of various levels of experience in unconventional political behavior. Based on a literature review, it predicted that Latino youth would be more likely than other youth to be political novices and less likely than others to be political veterans. Similarly, it predicted that immigrant youth would be more likely than other native-born youth to be political novices and less likely to be political veterans. An additional prediction was that college students would be less likely than others to be political novices and more likely to be political veterans. A final prediction was that youth from mixed immigrant-citizen families would be more likely than others to be political novices and less likely to be political veterans.

The analysis showed that Latino youth were more likely than those from other racial and ethnic groups to be political novices and repeaters but less likely to be political veterans. Similarly, those who were immigrants were more likely to be repeaters but less likely to be political veterans. In the multivariate analysis, coming from mixed immigrant-citizen families was not systematically related to levels of political experience. Those who were college students were less likely than others to be political novices and more likely to be political veterans.

There was support for the idea that structural location matters: despite risks to their families and themselves, college students participated because they valued the goals of the movement events. So, despite threats to their well-being, they came forward and participated because they believed in the movement's cause.

Structural locations such as being Latino, being an immigrant, and coming from a mixed immigrant-citizen family matter because they carry varying levels of social, political, and economic power that allow protestors to bear the risks and costs of unconventional activism. Because these factors influence how activists think about the goals of social movements, they should be considered when attempting to understand activism.

References

Almond, Gabriel, and Sidney Verba. 1963. *The Civic Culture*. Boston: Little, Brown.

Andolina, Molly, Krista Jenkins, Cliff Zukin, and Scott Keeter. 2003. "Habits from Home, Lessons from School: Influences on Youth Civic Engagement." *PSOnline* April: 275–280.

Camino, Linda and Shepherd Zeldin. 2002. "From Periphery to Center: Pathways for Youth Civic Engagement in the Day-To-Day Life of Communities." *Applied Developmental Science* 6: 213–220.

Chavez, Leo. 2001. *Covering Immigration*. Berkeley, University of California Press.

Flores-Gonzales, Nilda. 2007. "Marching for My People: Youth Activism and the Immigrant Marches." Paper presented at the American Educational Research Association Meetings, Chicago, Illinois.

Flores-Gonzalez, Nilda, Amalia Pallares, Cedric Herring and Maria Krysan. 2006. *UIC Immigrant Mobilization Project: General Survey Findings*.

Ginwright, Shawn, Pedro Noguera and Julio Cammarota. 2006. *Beyond Resistance: Youth Activism and Community Change*. New York: Routledge.

Hart, Daniel and Robert Atkins. 2003. "Neighborhoods, Adults, and the Development of Civic Identity in Urban Youth."*Applied Developmental Science* 7: 156–164.

Hart, Daniel and Robert Atkins. 2002. "Civic Competence in Urban Youth."*Applied Developmental Science* 6: 227–236.

Herring, Cedric. 1989. *Splitting the Middle: Political Alienation, Acquiescence, and Activism among America's Middle Layers*. New York: Praeger.

Koffler, Daniel. 2005. "On the New Student Politics." *Dissent* 52: 76–79.

Lipset, Seymour Martin. 1960. *Political Man*. Baltimore: Johns Hopkins University Press.

Lopez, Marc Hugo. 2003. *Electoral Engagement Among Latino Youth*. The Center for Information and Research on Civic Learning & Engagement.

Marcelo, Karlo Barrios, Marc Hugo Lopez and Emily Hoban Kirby. 2007. *Civic Engagement among Minority Youth*. The Center for Information and Research on Civic Learning and Engagement.

Martinez, Lisa M. 2005. "Yes We Can: Latino Participation in Unconventional Politics." *Social Forces* 84: 135–155.

McAdam, Doug. 1986. "Recruitment to High-Risk Activism: The Case of Freedom Summer." *American Journal of Sociology* 92: 64–90.

McAdam, Doug, and Ronnelle Paulsen. 1993. "Specifying the Relationship Between Social Ties and Activism." *American Journal of Sociology* 3: 640–67.

Mora, Carlos. 2007. *Latinos in the West: The Student Movement and Academic Labor in Los Angeles*. Lanham, MD: Rowman and Littlefield.

Morris, Aldon D. 1984. *Origins of the Civil Rights Movement*. New York: Free Press.

Morris, Aldon and Cedric Herring. 1987. "Theory and Research in Social Movements: A Critical Review." *Annual Review of Political Science* 2: 137–193.

Oropeza, Lorena. 2005. *¡Raza Sí! ¡Guerra No! Chicano Protest and Patriotism During the Viet Nam War Era*. Berkeley: University of California Press.

Paral, Ron, Timothy Ready, Sung Chun, Wei Sun. 2004. *Latino Demographic Growth in Metropolitan Chicago*. University of Notre Dame: Institute for Latino Studies.

Paulsen, Ronnelle. 1991. "Education, Social Class, and Participation in Collective Action." *Sociology of Education* 64: 96–110.

Pichardo, Nelson A. and Cedric Herring 2004. "Sacrificing for the Cause: Another Look at High-Risk/Cost Activism." *Race and Society* 7: 113–129.

Piven, Frances F. and Richard Cloward. 1979. *Poor Peoples' Movements*. New York: Pantheon. Sanchez-Jankowski 2002

Schlozman, Kay Lehman, Nancy Burns and Sidney Verba. 1994. "Gender and the Pathways to Participation: The Role of Resources." *Journal of Politics* 56: 963–90.

Sherrod, Lonnie R. 2003. *Promoting the Development of Citizenship in Diverse Youth*. New York: Cambridge University Press.

Verba, Sidney, and Norman Nie. 1972. *Participation in America*. Harper and Row.

Verba, Sidney, Norman Nie and Jae-On Kim. 1978. *Participation and Political Equality: A Seven Nation Comparison*. Cambridge University Press.

Verba, Sidney, Kay L. Schlozman and Henry E. Brady. 1995. *Voice and Equality: Civic Voluntarism in American Politics*. Cambridge, MA: Harvard University Press.

Wiltfang, Gregory, and Doug McAdam. 1991. "The Costs and Risks of Social Activism: A Study of Sanctuary Movement Activism." *Social Forces* 69: 987–1010.

Youniss, James, Susan Bales, Verona Christmas-Best, Marcelo Diversi, Milbrey McLaughlin, and Rainer Sulbereisen. 2002. "Youth Civic Engagement in the Twenty-First Century." *Journal of Research on Adolescence* 12: 121–48.

Zukin, Cliff, Scott Keeter, Krista Jenkins, and Michael X. Delli Caprini. 2006. A New Engagement? Political Participation, Civic Life, and the Changing American Citizen. New York: Oxford University Press.

CHAPTER EIGHTEEN

RACE, POVERTY, AND DISABILITY: A SOCIAL JUSTICE DILEMMA

Yolanda Suarez-Balcazar, Fabricio Balcazar, Tina Taylor-Ritzler,
Asma Ali, and Rooshey Hasnain

INTRODUCTION

Living with a disability means more than managing limitations. It also means dealing with a complex mix of social and environmental forces that place people with disabilities in a socially disadvantaged position. This challenge becomes even greater for people from diverse ethnic, racial, and linguistic backgrounds. According to the American Community Survey (ACS) the prevalence of disability by race is 12.4 percent for Whites, 13.7 percent for Black/African Americans, 16.8 percent for Native American or Alaska natives, 6.7 percent for Asians, and 8.4 percent for Hispanics. In addition, the ACS indicated that in 2007 only 39.3 percent of all people with disabilities ages 18 to 64 from all education levels were employed, 25.3 percent lived below the poverty line, and 23.9 percent had less than a high school education (U.S. Census Bureau 2007). Given the current economic crisis it is expected that these statistics have increased.

Compounding challenges of limited education and poverty, individuals with disabilities from ethnically and racially diverse backgrounds are less likely to achieve positive health, employment, rehabilitation, and independent living outcomes (Balcazar, Suarez-Balcazar, Taylor-Ritzler and Keys 2010; Capella 2002; Erickson, Lee, Von Schrader 2010; Sen 2002; Taylor-Ritzler, Balcazar, Suarez-Balcazar and Garcia-Iriarte 2008; Wilson 2002). Although the connection between poverty and disability has been widely documented, the impact of race in this combination of factors has not been fully explored.

In this chapter, we discuss the relationship between race, poverty, and disability from a social justice perspective. We argue that people from diverse ethnic and cultural backgrounds confront multi-layered marginalization due to the interaction of racial and socio-economic status adding to their experiences of oppression and discrimination. We first examine the relationship between poverty, disability, and race. We then examine the association between these factors and social justice, and the influence of social justice on the debate about race, poverty, and disability. We also discuss the implications of multiple marginalizations–including poorer health and economic outcomes– in light of the Kerner Commission's findings and whether or not progress has been made in the 40 years since the Kerner report was issued. Finally, we propose a social justice agenda to address the marginalization of low-income, multiethnic people with disabilities.

RACE, POVERTY AND DISABILITY

People from diverse ethnic and racial backgrounds who have a disability, including Latinos, African Americans and Native Americans, are more likely to live in poverty than White people with disabilities. Block, Balcazar, and Keys (2001) and Balcazar, et al. (2010) call this "triple jeopardy," referring to the additive effects of factors like race, poverty and disability that exacerbate social inequalities. As a group, people from diverse ethnic and racial background with disabilities are at higher risk of being discriminated against when looking for jobs than Whites with disabilities (Balcazar, et al. 2010). They are also less likely to have completed a secondary or post-secondary education and are more often marginalized from the social and economic life of the broader community (Wilson and Senices 2010).

Block, Balcazar and Keys (2002) conducted an analysis of theoretical models that explain the interaction between disability and race. They reported that throughout the twentieth century, theories of biology and culture presented images of race, class, and disability in terms of deficiency and dependency. While biological models represent some ethnically diverse groups as genetically inferior, cultural models present low-income ethnic groups as being trapped in an inescapable cycle of poverty. Both models position people from diverse ethnic and racial backgrounds with disabilities as social victims and/or social outcasts (Block et al. 2002). Policies and practices based on these theories project pejorative images of low-income individuals, ethnic and racial minorities *and* of people with disabilities. Individuals belonging to more than one of these categories or to all three are especially vulnerable to social stigma (Cook, Razzano, and Jonikas 2010).

To illustrate this point consider the following example: A Black woman with a disability has specific experiences that are influenced by her race and disability. These experiences are particular to her combination of identity categories, contributing to her experience of race and disability. This individual experiences her disability differently than an individual who is White and male. The Black woman is likely to experience more barriers than Whites in seeking employment, housing, and overall community integration (Smith and Alston 2010).

Crenshaw (1995) writes that experiences of the world and strategies for living it are not equal for members of minority groups and those of the mainstream population. From a social justice perspective, the basic rights of all individuals, regardless of their race, ethnicity, economic condition or disability should be protected (Braveman and Suarez-Balcazar 2009). Thus, a confluence of minority identities and other factors, such as socio-economic status, can alter an individual's experience of disability.

POVERTY, DISABILITY AND RACE

Poverty is both a cause and consequence of disability. The intersection of poverty and disability has been explored (Yeo 2001) but real solutions are elusive. People living in poverty are more likely to be unemployed, have limited education and often lack access to health care and/or insurance. Fears of increased costs, inflexibility in considering necessary accommodations, and outright prejudice all contribute to a reduction in job market opportunities for people with disabilities. Even when included, people with disabilities often work fewer hours and in lower-paying or lower-skilled positions (Atkins and Guisti 2004).

Several studies and reports have found a strong correlation between disability and poverty and have described them as being cyclical in nature (see Block, Balcazar, and Keys 2001; Moore and Yeo 2003). In fact, living in poverty has been found to put people at increased risk for developing a disability. For example, people living in poverty are more likely to eat either insufficient or unhealthy food, and to live in conditions that put them at higher risk for exposure to malnutrition, hazardous working conditions, and unhygienic living conditions, thereby increasing their likelihood of developing impairments and/or secondary disabilities. Thus, their overall life experience is one of marginalization and oppression (Elwan 1999; Kielhofner, De Las Heras and Suarez-Balcazar 2011).

On the other hand, having a disability can lead to poverty. It is estimated that people with disabilities are three times more likely to live in poverty than the population as a whole (Saunders 2006). Individuals with disabilities experience additional stressors and expenses related to daily living, including the need to purchase assistive devices and adaptive equipment to increase functioning, to have access to home modifications expenses, attendant health care costs, and special services such as interpreters for the Deaf and assisted transportation expenses (Suarez-Balcazar and Cooper 2005). Moreover, individuals with disabilities are more likely to receive welfare benefits and are less likely to have health insurance (Mont 2007).

Even among individuals with disabilities who work, many face significant barriers in receiving needed healthcare benefits. It is estimated that 18.2 percent of non-institutionalized people aged 21 to 64 with a disability in the United States were uninsured in 2008 (Erickson, et al. 2010). In addition, many individuals with disabilities rely on Medicaid for their health care. However, the paperwork required to maintain these services is complex, many people are denied benefits, and many doctors do not accept these patients because of low reimbursement rates or delays in payments by the government.

Furthermore, family members of people with disabilities may also experience work force marginalization and other work-related challenges. For example, caregivers may have to quit their jobs or accept only part-time work so that they can care for the family member with a severe disability (Batavia and Beaulaurier 2001; Brantlinger 2001). This situation places the whole family at greater risk of poverty.

Table 18.1 shows the sequence of events that often lead people with disabilities to chronic poverty. Starting with the impairment, which can take place at birth or at any time during the lifespan, the individual develops a disability which in turns leads to multiple types of exclusion from society's resources and opportunities, and in turn, to chronic poverty.

Table 18.1: Disability/Poverty Cycle.

Impairment ➡ Disability ➡ Exclusion[1] ➡ Consequences of Exclusion[2] ➡ Poverty [3]

[1] Includes exclusion from formal/informal education and employment; limited social contacts; low expectations from community and of self; exclusion from political/legal processes; lowest priority for access to many limited resources; lack of support for high costs directly associated with impairment (e.g., accessible housing, transportation, communication devices, etc).

[2] Includes low self esteem; lack of ability to assert rights; fewer skills; poor health/ physically weak; and further reduced income generating opportunities.

[3] Includes further exclusion and chronic poverty.

Of significance is the disproportionate and increasing rate of disability among ethnically and racially diverse individuals. Braithwaite and Mont (2008) offer several reasons for the steady increase in disability rates: a) Emergence of new diseases and other causes of impairment, such as HIV/AIDS, stress and alcohol and drug abuse; b) increase in the life span and increasing numbers of elderly persons, many of whom have impairments; c) projected increases in the number of disabled children over the next 30 years, particularly due to malnutrition, diseases, child labor and other causes; and d) armed conflict and violence. Understanding the relationship between race, poverty and disability is therefore a current priority.

The Kerner Commission Report

The Kerner Report (1968) was released after seven months of investigation by the National Advisory Commission on Civil Disorders and took its name from the commission's chairman, Illinois Governor Otto Kerner. President Lyndon B. Johnson appointed the commission on July 28, 1967, while rioting was still underway in Detroit, Michigan. The long, hot summers since 1965 had brought riots in the Black sections of many major cities, including Los Angeles (1965), Chicago (1966), and Newark (1967). Johnson charged the Kerner Commission with analyzing the specific triggers for the riots, the deeper causes of the worsening racial climate of the time, and with identifying potential remedies (Harris and Curtis 1998).

The commission presented its findings in 1968, concluding that urban violence reflected the profound frustration of inner-city Blacks and that racism was deeply embedded in American society. The report concluded that growing racial inequality in urban areas caused increased tension among Blacks and Whites, escalating to violence. The report's most famous passage warned that the United States was "moving toward two societies, one Black, one White—separate and unequal." The commission marshaled evidence on an array of problems that fell with particular severity on African Americans, including not only overt discrimination but also chronic poverty, high unemployment, poor schools, inadequate housing, lack of access to health care, and systematic police bias and brutality.

The report recommended sweeping federal initiatives directed at improving educational and employment opportunities, public services, and housing in Black urban neighborhoods and called for a "national system of income supplementation." The call for national action at the end of the Kerner Report echoes several basic tenants of social justice:

(a) opening up opportunities to those who are restricted by racial segregation and discrimination, and eliminating all barriers to their choice of jobs, education and housing; (b) removing the frustration of powerlessness among the disadvantaged by providing the means for them to deal with the problems that affect their own lives and by increasing the capacity of our public and private institutions to respond to these problems; and (c) increasing communication across racial lines to destroy stereotypes, to halt polarization, end distrust and hostility, and create common ground for efforts toward public order and social justice. By the end of 1968, however, Richard M. Nixon had gained the presidency through a conservative White backlash, and the Kerner Report's recommendations were largely ignored in national policy.

To conclude, although the Kerner Commission called attention to an escalating racial divide in American Society, more than 40 years later we continue to see evidence of the same racial divide, magnified when considering the additive effects of race, poverty and disability to social and economic marginalization. The growing racial divide in disability and poverty is one illustration of the findings of the Kerner Report. Clearly, racial status affects disability outcomes. Compounding the issue, these outcomes are further affected by an individual's poverty status.

A social justice approach to understanding and addressing issues of race, poverty and disability encourages self-advocacy and self-determination among marginalized individuals in society and for overall structural changes in society to support the empowerment process. In this way, the individual can impact his/her own life, and perhaps the lives of others, but societies also have the responsibility of promoting structural changes that support equality and fairness and affect public policy.

The Role of Social Justice

The Disabilities Rights Movement of the 1970s, based on social justice and advocacy principles, promoted more local, individualized solutions to the challenges of the racial divide among those with disabilities. A social justice approach adds benefits to the individuals affected by these large-scale problems. First, a social justice approach promotes critical awareness of the issue among the individuals affected. Second, it places the responsibility for finding solutions to the challenges equally in the hands of policy-makers and the individuals affected by the issues. Third, a social justice approach emphasizes local solutions to the issue, leading to solutions that are targeted to the specific manifestations of the problems in each community. Fourth, a social justice approach emphasizes the role of societies in promoting and protecting the rights of individuals. In short, social justice approaches allow individuals to affect their own lives and the lives of future generations as an alternative to frustration and violent responses to social inequality and place responsibility on social structures to promote change.

The social justice approach adds an individually-based response to the social polarization identified in the Kerner Commission Report. Social justice is a broad term that encompasses several interrelated concepts, such as equality, empowerment, fairness in the relationship between people and the government, equal opportunity, equal access to resources and goods, and human rights (Abberley 1995; Fondacaro and Weinberg 2002; Longres and Scanlon 2001; Young 1990; Braveman and Suarez-Balcazar 2009). The concept of social justice has focused on the moral and philosophical meaning of individual rights, free society and free will. Social justice also encompasses the relationships between society and government and the accountability of the masses (Lowery 1998).

The concept of social justice has been used to understand the predicament of marginalized groups, including people with disabilities. As noted above, people with disabilities are marginalized in various spheres of society including employment, access to public buildings and spaces, and access to affordable and accessible housing and transportation (Charlton 1998, Garate, Charlton, Luna, and Townsend 2010). From a social justice perspective, we argue that people with disabilities should have the same rights and be treated with the same level of dignity and respect as nondisabled individuals.

Scholars often discuss justice using one of two terms: social justice or economic justice. From a social justice point of view, scholars have studied human rights, women's rights, violence, poverty, access to social services, and group and individual empowerment, among other concepts. The study of economic justice focuses on economic distribution, occupation (including employment), economic inequalities and access to goods. Examining these two inter-related aspects of justice helps understand the plight of people with disabilities who are from multiple racial and ethnic backgrounds and experience disadvantaged socio-economic status (Braveman and Suarez-Balcazar 2009).

Social Justice Theories

The best-known theories of social justice are the *Distributive Justice Theory* and the *Procedural Justice Theory* (Longres and Scanlon 2001). *Distributive Justice Theory* "refers to the way economic and social goods and services are distributed in a society" (Rawls 1971: 448). It also discusses provision of resources, access to resources, and economic opportunities. The *Procedural Justice Theory* considers the decision-making process as it describes the relationships between dominant and subordinate groups and the participation level of individuals within larger societal structures. *Procedural Justice Theory* articulates that the principles and laws that govern the relationships between dominant and subordinate groups lead to decisions about the distribution of resources (Young 1990). Distributive and procedural justice can complement each other. For example, an individual might be able to increase distributive justice by participating in the decision-making process about the use of available resources, which is an aspect of procedural justice.

From the perspective of distributive social justice, people with disabilities, in particular low-income minorities have been excluded when it comes to the acquisition of wealth. Charlton (1998) and Garate et al. (2010) argue that poverty among ethnic minorities with disabilities is the result of prejudice, racism and social and economic discrimination. They also argue that these conditions can only be eliminated by changing unequal power relations and by the re-distribution of wealth, which would mean providing accessible employment opportunities for people with disabilities. From a procedural social justice perspective, research suggests that racially diverse individuals with disabilities are less likely than Whites with disabilities and the nondisabled to be integrated into their communities, to have choices and control over decisions that matter to them, and to achieve independent living outcomes (Charlton 1998). Having choices and control over decisions that matter to people is often associated with power, wealth and status. As such, those in situations of power and/or higher income are more likely to enjoy these freedoms.

At the core of social justice are the concepts of human rights (Bowring 2002; Lowery 1998) and empowerment (Kielhofner, et al. 2011; Prilleltensky and Nelson 2002). Moreover, the concept of human rights has been considered a global value that lies at the core of social justice (Austin 2001; Fondacaro and Weinberg 2002). Smith (1998), a proponent of the protection of human rights, asserts that governments have legal and moral responsibility to provide for the basic needs of their citizens, including the preservation of liberties and protection from harm. According to Austin (2001), "the central assumption of the rights paradigm is that every person can make certain claims based solely on their humanness" (p. 184). Individuals with disabilities are more likely than nondisabled individuals to report that their rights have been violated, including their access to voting polls, to educational facilities, to employment settings, businesses, and transportation among others (Braveman and Suarez-Balcazar 2009).

SOCIAL JUSTICE AND THE AMERICANS WITH DISABILITIES ACT (ADA)

In an effort to protect the rights of people with disabilities in the United Sates, the U.S. government passed the American with Disabilities Act (ADA) in 1990. The ADA act protects people with disabilities' rights to accommodations in the workplace, access to government services (State and Federal), access to businesses and places of public accommodations, and the right to access assistive communication devices. Despite passage of the ADA, which heralded a new era for the independent living movement, minorities with disabilities are still behind in benefiting from this legislation, particularly in the areas of employment, housing, and community integration (Fujiura, Yamaki, and Czechowicz 1998; Fujiura and Drazen 2010). Although many have benefited from the ADA, more than 20 years after its passage evidence suggests that racially and ethnically diverse populations are still experiencing violations of their rights, discrimination, and other barriers to become productive members of society (National Council on Disability 2009; Taylor, et al. 2010). Even racially diverse individuals with disabilities who are employed and are receiving adequate wages may experience violations of their rights; they may lack accommodations and accessibility in the workplace and therefore be barred from participating in work-related or community activities.

Several approaches to addressing the marginalization of multicultural individuals with disabilities have been suggested. Based on the empowerment literature, we propose an empowerment approach to promoting social justice for individuals with disabilities.

AN EMPOWERMENT APPROACH TO PROMOTING SOCIAL JUSTICE

Rappaport (1977) introduced a theoretical and psychological view of empowerment. He defined empowerment as the process of giving voice to individuals and enabling them to participate in making decisions that impact their lives. Although the empowerment tradition emphasizes the individual's aspiration to control his or her life and resources, those in positions of power, such as government agencies and organizations that control resources, can either facilitate or hinder such aspirations (Fawcett, White, Balcazar et al. 1994; Balcazar, Suarez-Balcazar, et al. 2011). According to Fawcett et al.'s contextual model of empowerment, the interaction between environmental and personal factors determines the empowerment outcome. Capacity building at the individual level–in terms of developing awareness, skills and knowledge in order to increase personal effectiveness–becomes critical in attempts to change power imbalances. The context can either support or obstruct such efforts (Suarez-Balcazar 2005). For instance, most agency policies are designed to protect and maintain the status quo, therefore blocking demands for change. Fondacaro and Weinberg (2002) argue that empowerment is mostly rooted in the principles of procedural justice. An empowerment outcome might refer to distributive justice (e.g., access to resources) that is attained through procedural justice (e.g., making decisions). For example, a Black male in a wheelchair who has the skills and motivation to search for employment might discover that the type of jobs that require the skills he has are not accessible, or lack accommodations, and/or are given to White people and those without disabilities. Furthermore, individuals who experience marginalization and lack of community integration are more likely to lack information about jobs and the support network that can facilitate job seeking.

Empowerment theory is rooted in the assumption that people value the opportunity to be involved in making decisions that affect their lives, and that such participation has a positive impact on their psychological well-being (Zimmerman 2000), increases the number of choices at their disposal, and motivates them to improve their condition and fulfill their goals (Balcazar, Keys and Suarez-Balcazar 2001; Balcazar, Keys, Kaplan, and Suarez-Balcazar 1998; Fawcett et al. 1994; Garate et al. 2010). According to Fondacaro and Weinberg (2002), although early empowerment efforts were concentrated mostly on individualistic notions of autonomy, self-control, personal responsibility, and psychological issues, later studies and conceptualizations of empowerment concentrated on systemic factors, issues of distributive justice, and social responsibility at the group and systemic level (Riger 1993). The emphasis on systemic factors came from the realization that individuals in disadvantaged situations (e.g., multicultural populations with disabilities) are often disempowered (Suarez-Balcazar and Balcazar, 2007), in part due to their experiences of oppression and marginalization (i.e. the lack of distributive and procedural justice).

Fawcett and his colleagues (1994) propose a contextual-behavioral model of empowerment that is characterized as a process of gaining control over relevant aspects of one's life. This model highlights the ongoing contextual interaction between individual and environmental factors. Based on this model, Table 18.2 summarizes the action strategies that our research team compiled as part of an advocacy training program for individuals with disabilities. The action steps can be used to pursue power redistribution in any context. The strategies are numbered according to their degree of complexity and difficulty. Easier tactics are listed first, while more complex tasks and those with greater consequences are listed last. The advocacy process requires the development of critical awareness about the oppressive situations that impact the person or group, particularly of the person or group's capacity to transform their social reality. The utilization of these tactics implies the gradual acquisition of knowledge and skills, including learning about disability rights, and self-advocacy skills, among others.

Freire (1970) highlighted the importance of critical reflection and developing critical awareness in combating oppression. This includes reflecting on one's personal experiences, understanding the historical asymmetric context of power distribution, and realizing one's capacity to engage the controlling agent and seek redistribution of resources or opportunities. People have to discover and realize their capacity to transform their social reality. The unfortunate dilemma, as Freire (1970) pointed out, is that most people who experience social oppression do not take the necessary steps for such transformation. Freire also argued that most people do not have the critical awareness that allows them to see the injustice or the oppression in their lives. Poor individuals with disabilities who are from ethnically, racially and/or linguistically diverse backgrounds often perceive their oppressive context as the result of destiny, bad luck, the "normal" way of life for people like themselves or simply god's will–in other words, forces beyond their control. This is one reason why they tend to be passive and are often unable to recognize their capacity to transform their oppressive reality.

The process of taking action to change power imbalances also requires a way of sorting out and understanding complex problems. Seekins, Balcazar and Fawcett (1993) propose a simple way to identify issues in terms of four basic categories that can then be associated with the action steps presented in Table 18.2. Table 18.3 summarizes the types of issues and the general goals that people could pursue to address them. Table 18.3 also includes the list of actions that could be utilized to pursue each of the four proposed goals. We have found that this simplified view of the main issues

Table 18.2: Empowerment Strategies: The Action Index[1]

1. Postpone action	20. Conduct a study
2. Personally compliment favorable action	21. Develop a proposal
3. Organize an award/celebration ceremony	22. Conduct a fund raising activity
4. Provide public support	23. Sponsor a community conference or public hearing
5. Volunteer to help others	24. Offer public education
6. Document evidence of a complaint	25. Develop a consensus between groups
7. Criticize unfavorable action	26. Build a coalition
8. Establish a formal communication mechanism	27. Initiate legal action
9. Request formal justification	28. Seek enforcement of existing laws, policies or ordinances
10. Express opposition publicly	29. Seek enactment of new laws, policies, regulations, or ordinances
11. Gather more information	30. Organize consumer service audits
12. Prepare a fact sheet to distribute information about your group or the issue	31. Conduct a petition drive
13. Request participation	32. Conduct a letter-writing campaign
14. Watchdog decision process	33. Flood the system
15. Provide corrective feedback	34. Media expose
16. Remind those responsible	35. Organize passive resistance
17. Make an informal complaint	36. Organize public demonstrations
18. Seek a mediator or negotiator	37. Organize a boycott
19. File a formal complaint	38. Establish an alternative system or program

[1] Adapted from Seekins, Balcazar, and Fawcett. (1993).

Table 18.3: Issue/Goal Chart

SITUATION/ISSUE TYPES	GOALS
GOOD NEWS ➤	REINFORCE/PROTECT
(e.g., new services, positive changes in policy or budget allocations; potentially beneficial proposals, etc.)	(From Table 3, Actions # 2, 3, 4, 5, 8, 12, 13, 22, 23, 24, 25, 26, 32)
CONTRADICTORY INFORMATION ➤	INVESTIGATE
(e.g., rumors, complex issues, incomplete, conflicting information, etc.)	(From Table 3, Actions # 1, 5, 6, 8, 9, 11, 12, 13, 14, 20, 23, 25, 26, 30)
UNMET NEEDS ➤	DEVELOP A SOLUTION
(e.g., what is lacking in terms of services, resources, opportunities, etc.)	(From Table 3, Actions # 2, 4, 5, 8, 11, 12, 13, 14, 15, 16, 17, 18, 19, 20, 21, 22, 23, 25, 26, 28, 29, 30, 31, 32, 37, 38)
BAD NEWS ➤	OPPOSE
(e.g., negative changes in services, policies, or budget allocations; potentially harmful proposals, unresponsiveness, offensive actions or language, discrimination, etc.)	(From Table 3, Actions # 1, 6, 7, 9, 10, 12, 15, 16, 17, 18, 19, 20, 23, 24, 25, 26, 27, 28, 29, 30, 31, 32, 33, 34, 35, 36, 37)

in people's lives can be very helpful in guiding individual and group action and facilitating the generation of solutions. Complex issues often require the deployment of multiple tactics at different times. In other words, escalation may sometimes be necessary in order to achieve the intended outcome. We should be reminded however, that the objective is often reached through compromise, which means that there are no winners or losers, but the most satisfactory accommodation that could be attained at that particular time and under specific circumstances.

STEPS FOR ACTION

Researchers can play a critical role in helping oppressed populations develop advocacy skills and action plans. The majority of individuals with disabilities from diverse racial and ethnic communities need support in developing a critical view of the world and in seeing themselves as agents of change. Participatory action research, also known as PAR, is one approach that allows researchers to build partnerships with community organizations or groups in order to promote critical awareness and social change (see Selener 1997; Balcazar, et al. 1998; Balcazar and Hernandez 2002; Jason, Keys, Suarez-Balcazar, Taylor, Davis, Durlak, and Isenberg 2004; Suarez-Balcazar, Hammel, and Helfrich 2005). PAR has been conceptualized as "a process by which the members of a group or oppressed community collect and analyze information about the factors that maintain or precipitate their oppression, and take actions to address their own problems and transform their social reality" (Selener 1997: 17).

Strategies to address environmental factors include reducing and removing barriers, developing networks and educating others in the community, creating opportunities for capacity-building, advocating for changes in policies, programs, and services, among others. To promote social justice at the environmental and societal levels, it is also important to examine national, state, and local policies, and programs and services that inadvertently create barriers and stressors for people with disabilities instead of creating facilitators of the empowerment process and promoters of social justice.

Mitra (2006) offers an integrated perspective for defining disability and understanding its economic causes and consequences. The capability approach was developed by Sen (1985) as a framework for analyzing different concepts of economic welfare, including standard of living, personal well-being, quality of life, and poverty. Sen advocates for focusing on a person's ability (i.e., capability) to function, that is, on what the person can do or be rather than on the person's real income or utility indicated by traditional welfare economics. Using Sen's approach, capability does not constitute physical or mental ability; it is instead understood as a practical opportunity. In general, Sen argues that public policy should deal with capabilities rather than functional limitations, however in practice a person's capabilities are difficult to observe and data are usually available only on functioning.

Mitra (2006) provides a useful example. Consider the following two people with disabilities referred to as Case A and Case B. They have similar personal characteristics: both are 35-year-old women who suffered a similar physical injury and now use a wheelchair. Both have a bachelor's degree and both worked as administrative assistants prior to their injury. Finally, they have similar financial assets, mainly savings. A and B live in different environments: A lives in Washington DC and B lives in rural Vermont. A found a job in the city, and uses public transportation; she used her savings to buy an adapted car. B cannot find a job in her area; she could move to another location but prefers to stay where her social network is located. She is unsure whether she can find a job and she cannot afford personal assistance, so she applied for SSDI. A and B clearly have different capabilities, despite similar personal characteristics and resources. The local socioeconomic environment is a facilitator for A and a barrier for B. In cases like these, the woman's capability sets are typically evaluated within a standardized environment, the US economy, rather than within the local environments in which they live; it also does not consider the constrained resources a person may have. This illustrates the complexity of determining who is disabled due to a limited capacity to work and who is not.

Sen's framework also takes into account the "capability deprivation" of factors such as race, ethnicity, immigration or gender discrimination, all of which match well with the World Health Organizations' (1980) International Classification of Functioning, Disability, and Health framework (ICF) and its focus on two important contextual dimensions often overlooked by the U.S. system: the capability level and the functioning level as discussed here. Rather than seeing disability only as a medical dysfunction, the ICF takes into account the social aspects of disability. In other words it 'mainstreams' the experience of disability and recognizes it as a universal human experience rather than a unique issue. Imagine how the dynamics would change if A were a new Muslim immigrant from Somalia who was fluent in five languages but had few English skills and B was Caucasian. How would the dimensions change or vary in their contexts in light of such differences? Our point is that new and more integrative conceptual models and frameworks need to be explored in order to address the experiences and worldviews of diverse ethnic and cultural populations in the larger U.S. society.

CONCLUSION

A social justice approach that is based on empowerment concepts accounts for the systemic inequalities faced by low-income people with disabilities from different racial and cultural backgrounds who are attempting to overcome their multiple sources of oppression and marginalization. For people with disabilities, disability may be only one of the many stigmas they face. Scholars and practitioners need to recognize the multiple barriers resulting from the "triple jeopardy" of race, poverty, and disability in their work to promote the well-being of individuals with disabilities who are from diverse racial and cultural backgrounds. A social justice framework of analysis, which incorporates an understanding of multifaceted issues can serve as a catalyst for helping people to overcome multiple barriers that thwart their efforts to seek positive social and economic change. This framework encourages people from diverse backgrounds to develop a common agenda based on their shared experiences, regardless of their background. It also promotes self-reliance and an increased awareness of contextual factors, as well as an understanding of the social forces that perpetuate oppression and discrimination, and strategies for increasing opportunities for greater choice and control.

Empowered individuals or groups are more likely to challenge the status quo and pursue remedies to the historical inequality that characterizes the existence of minorities with disabilities. An empowerment framework specifies actions through which individuals from marginalized groups can gain the social, political, and economic support needed to overcome barriers to their full participation in society. Minority individuals with disabilities who live in poverty can find the strength, understanding, and motivation to learn about their own conditions and pursue change. They can develop a critical consciousness about their oppressed status and then plan and take action to address the impact of negative societal attitudes and policies.

The barriers faced by culturally diverse individuals with disabilities who are living in poverty should not be underestimated. Racism, ableism, and poverty severely limit opportunities for individuals with disabilities. Established community-based organizations, as well as large-scale government programs, are usually ill-equipped to serve minority populations with present multiple barriers to social equality. What is needed is greater implementation of empowerment approaches that address the nexus of race, poverty, and disability. In addition, leaders, policies, and organizations with experiences working at different community levels and in different social arenas to meet the multi-faceted needs of minorities with disabilities are essential to this important mission. Professionals—researchers, policymaker, and other community leaders – are often part of the problem, as we tend to reproduce oppressive practices and enforce misguided policies in our work with minority populations. But we can become part of the solution as we seek to develop our critical awareness and assume our social responsibility to benefit those who we serve.

We should be concerned with developing our critical consciousness so we can become part of a greater effort to build a more just world for all.

REFERENCES

Abberley, P. (1995). Disabling ideology in health and welfare. The case of occupational therapy. *Disability and Society, 10*, 221–232.

American with Disabilities Act of 1990, 42 U.S. C.A.@ 12101 et seq. Retrieved from http://www.ada.gov/pubs/ada.htm

Atkins, D. and Guisti, C. (2004). *The Confluence of Poverty and Disability, in The Realities of Poverty in Delaware, 2003–2004*. Dover: Delaware Housing Coalition. http://www.housingforall.org/

Austin, W. (2001). Using the human rights paradigm in health ethics: The problems and the possibilities. *Nursing Ethics, 8*, 183–195.

Balcazar, F.E., and Hernandez, B. (2002). Violencia y discapacidad: Un modelo de intervención basado en la investigación-acción participativa. *Intervención Psicosocial, 11*(2), p. 183–199.

Balcazar, F.E., Keys, C.B., Kaplan, D., and Suarez-Balcazar, Y. (1998). Participatory action research and people with disabilities: Principles and challenges. *Canadian Journal of Rehabilitation, 12*, 105–112.

Balcazar, F.E., Keys, C.B., and Suarez-Balcazar, Y. (2001). Empowering Latinos with disabilities to address issues of independent living and disability rights: A capacity-building approach. *Journal of Prevention and Intervention in the Community, 21*(2), 53–70.

Balcazar, F.E., Suarez-Balcazar, Y., Adames, S.B., Keys, C.B., Garcia-Ramirez, M., Paloma, V. (2011). A Case Study of Liberation among Latino Immigrant Families with Children with Disabilities, *American Journal of Community Psychology*.

Balcazar, F.E., Suarez-Balcazar, Y., Taylor-Ritzler, T., and Keys, C.B. (Eds.). (2010). *Race, culture and disability: Rehabilitation science and practice*. Sudbury, MA: Jones and Barlett Publishers.

Batavia, A.I., and Beaulaurier, R.L. (2001). The financial vulnerability of people with disabilities: Assessing poverty risks. *Journal of Sociology and Social Welfare, 28*(1),139–162.

Block, P., Balcazar, F.E. and Keys, C.B. (2001). From pathology to power: Rethinking race, poverty, and disability. *Journal of Disability Policy Studies, 12*(1), 18–27. Block, P., Balcazar, F.E., and Keys, C.B. (2002). Race poverty and disability: three strikes and you're out! Or are you? *Social Policy, 33*, (1), 34–38.

Bowring, W. (2002). Forbidden relations? The UK's discourse of human rights and the struggle for social justice. *Law, Social Justice, and Global Development Journal, 1*, 1–17.

Braithwaite, J., and Mont, D. (2008). Disability and poverty: A survey of World Bank poverty assessments and implications. Social Protection Discussion Papers, Geneva: World Bank. Retrieved from http://siteresources.worldbank.org/DISABILITY/Resources/280658-1172608138489/WBPovertyAssessments.pdf

Brantlinger, E. 2001. Poverty, class, and disability: A historical, social, and political perspective. *Focus on Exceptional Children, 33*(7): 1–19.

Braveman, B., and Suarez-Balcazar, Y. (2009). Social justice and resource utilization in a community-based organization: A case illustration of the role of occupational therapist. *American Journal of Occupational Therapy, 63*, 13–23.

Capella, M.E. (2002). Inequities in the VR system: Do they still exist? *Rehabilitation Counseling Bulletin, 45*(3), 143–153.

Charlton, J.I. (1998). *Nothing about us without us: Disability oppression and empowerment*. Berkeley: University of California Press.

Cook, J.A., Razzano, L.A. and Jonikas, J.A. (2010) Cultural diversity and how it may differ for programs and providers serving people with psychiatric disabilities. In F.E. Balcazar, Y. Suarez-Balcazar, , T. Taylor-Ritzler, and C.B. Keys. (Eds.) *Race, Culture, and Disability: Rehabilitation Science and Practice* (pp. 115–135).

Crenshaw, K. (1995). *Critical raze theory: the key writings that formed the movement.* New York: New Press.

Elwan, A. (1999). "Poverty and Disability: A Survey of the Literature," Social Protection Discussion Paper Series 9932. The World Bank, December 1999. Retrieved from http://siteresources.worldbank.org/DISABILITY/Resources/280658-1172608138489/PovertyDisabElwan.pdf

Erickson, W., Lee, C., Von Schrader, S. (2010, March 17). Disability Statistics from the 2008 American Community Survey (ACS). Ithaca, NY: Cornell University Rehabilitation Research and Training Center on Disability Demographics and Statistics (StatsRRTC). Retrieved Aug 25, 2010 from www.disabilitystatistics.org

Fawcett, S.B., White, G.W., Balcazar, F.E., Suarez-Balcazar, Y., Mathews, R.M., Paine, A. L, Smith, J.F. (1994). A contextual-behavioral model of empowerment: Case studies with people with physical disabilities. *American Journal of Community Psychology, 22* (4), 475–496.

Fondacaro, M.R., and Weinberg, D. (2002). Concepts of social justice in community psychology: Toward a social ecological epistemology. *American Journal of Community Psychology, 30,* 473–492.

Freire, P. (1970). *Pedagogy of the oppressed.* New York: Continuum Publishing Corporation.

Fujiura, G.T., Yamaki, K. and Czechowicz, S. (1998). Disability among ethnic and racial minorities in the United States: A summary of economic status and family structure. *Journal of Disability Policy Studies* 9(2), 111–130.

Fujiura, G.T. and Drazen, C. (2010). "Ways of Seeing" in race and disability research. In F.E. Balcazar, Y. Suarez-Balcazar, , T. Taylor-Ritzler,, and C.B. Keys (Eds.), *Race, Culture, and Disability: Rehabilitation Science and Practice* (pp. 15–32).

Garate, T., Charlton, J., Luna, R. and Townsend, O. (2010). Implications for Practice in Rehabilitation. In F.E. Balcazar, Y. Suarez-Balcazar, T. Taylor-Ritzler, and C.B. Keys (Eds.) *Race, culture and disability: Rehabilitation science and practice* (pp. 357–367). Boston, MA: Jones and Barlett.

Harris, F.R., and Curtis, L.A. (Eds.). (1998). *Locked in the Poorhouse: Crisis, Race, and Poverty in the United States.* Lanham, MD: Rowman and Littlefield Publishers Inc.

Jason, L.A., Keys, C.B., Suarez-Balcazar, Y., Taylor, R.R., Davis, M., Durlak, J., Isenberg, D. (Eds.) (2004). *Participatory Community Research: Theories and Methods in Action.* Washington, DC: American Psychological Association.

Kerner Report. (2010). *History Matters.* Accessed August 7, 2010 from http://historymatters.gmu.edu/d/6545/.

Kielhofner, G., De Las Heras, C.G., and Suarez-Balcazar, Y. (2011). Human occupation as a tool for promoting social justice. In Fr. Kolberg, S., Algado, N., Pollard Occupational Therapy without Borders. London: Elsevier Publishers.

Longres, J.F., and Scanlon, E. (2001). Social justice and the research curriculum. *Journal of Social Work Education, 37,* 447–463.

Lowery, C.T. (1998). Social justice and international human rights. In M. Mattaini, C. Lowery, and C. Meyer (Eds.). *The foundation of social work practice: A graduate text* (pp. 20–24). Washington, DC: NASW Press.

Mitra, S, (2006). The Capability Approach and Disability. *Journal of Disability Policy Studies, 16,* 4, 236–247.

Mont, D. (2007). Measuring disability prevalence. *Social Protection the World Bank*, March. Retrieved from http://siteresources.worldbank.org/DISABILITY/Resources/Data/MontPrevalence.pdf

Moore, K., and Yeo, R. (2003). Poverty and disability: breaking the vicious cycle through inclusion. *Insights* (46) [2 p]. Retrieved from http://www.eldis.org/id21ext/insights46art5.html

National Council on Disability. (2009) National Disability Policy: A Progress Report. Retrieved from http://www.ncd.gov/newsroom/publications/2009/Progress_Report _HTML/NCD_Progress_Report.html

Prilleltensky, I., and Nelson, G. (2002). *Doing psychology critically: Making a difference in diverse settings*. London: Palgrave Macmillan.

Rappaport, J. (1977). *Community psychology: Values, research, and action*. New York: Holt, Rinehart, and Winston.

Rawls, J. (1971). *A theory of justice*. Cambridge, MA: Harvard University Press.

Riger, S. (1993). What's wrong with empowerment? *American Journal of Community Psychology*, 21 (3), 279–292.

Saunders, P. (2006). The Costs of Disability and the Incidence of Poverty, SPRC Discussion Paper No. 147, *The Social Policy Research Centre*, University of New South Wales. Retrieved from http://www.sprc.unsw.edu.au/media/File/DP147.pdf

Seekins, T., Balcazar, F.E., and Fawcett, S.B. (1993). Consumer involvement in advocacy organizations: Project planning guide (Vol. III). RRTC on Independent Living, University of Kansas. Retrieved at http://disabilityempowerment.org/Advocacy _Products.html

Selener, D. (1997). Participatory action research and social change. Cornell University: *The Cornell Participatory Action Research network*, Ithaca, NY.

Sen A.K. (1985). *Commodities and Capabilities*, Amsterdam: North Holland.

Sen, A.K. (2002) Why health inequality? *Health Economics, 11*, 659–666

Smith, D.L. and Alston, R. (2010). Employment and rehabilitation issues for racially and ethnically diverse women with disabilities. In Balcazar, F.E., Suarez-Balcazar, Y., Renee, T.T., Keys, C.B (Eds.). Race, culture and disability: Rehabilitation science and practice (159–183). Sudbury, MA: Jones and Bartlett Publishers.

Smith, M.K. (1998). Empowerment evaluation: Theoretical and methodological consider-ations. *Evaluation and Programming Planning, 21*, 255–261.

Suarez-Balcazar, Y. (2005). Empowerment and participatory evaluation of a community health intervention: Implications for occupational therapy. *Occupational Therapy Journal of Research, 25*, 133–142.

Suarez-Balcazar, Y. and Balcazar, F. (2007). Empowerment approaches to identifying and addressing health issues in minorities with disabilities. In C. Dumont and G. Kielhofner (Eds.). *In Positive Approaches to Health* (pp. 153–168). Nova Science Publishers, Inc.

Suarez-Balcazar, Y., and Cooper M.B. (2005). Poverty and Disability (pp. 1281–1284). In G. Albrecht, Encyclopedia of Disability, Volume 2, Thousand Oaks, CA: Sage Publications.

Suarez-Balcazar, Y., Hammel, J., and Helfrich, C. (2005). A model of university-community partnerships for Occupational Therapy scholarship and practice. *Occupational Therapy in Health Care, 19*, 47–70. Reprinted with permission in Crist, P. and Kielhofner, G. (2005). The Scholarship of Practice: Academic-Practice Collaborations for Promoting Occupational Therapy. The Haworth Press. New York.

Taylor-Ritzler, T., Balcazar, F.E., Suarez-Balcazar, Y., and Garcia-Iriarte, E. (2008). Conducting disability research with people from diverse ethnic groups: Challenges and Opportunities. *Journal of Rehabilitation, 74*(1), 4–11.

Taylor-Ritzler, T., Balcazar, F., and Suarez-Balcazar, Y., Kilbury, R., Alvarado, F., James, M. (2010). Engaging ethnically diverse individuals with disabilities in the VR System: The Paradox of empowerment and oppression. *Journal of Vocational Rehabilitation, 33*, 3–14.

U.S. Census Bureau (2006). American Community Survey table B1802: Selected Economic Characteristics for the Civilian Non-institutionalized Population By Disability Status. Washington, DC: U.S. Census Bureau. Retrieved from http://factfinder.census.gov/ home/saff/main.html?_lang=en

U.S. Census Bureau (2007). Statistical Abstract of the United States: Resident Population by Race, Hispanic or Latino Origin.

Wilson, K.B. (2002). Exploration of VR acceptance and ethnicity: A national investigation. *Rehabilitation Counseling Bulletin, 45*(3), 168–176.

Wilson, K. B and Senices, J. (2010) Access to Vocational Rehabilitation Services for Black Latinos with Disabilities: Colorism in the 21st Century. In F.E. Balcazar, Y. Suarez-Balcazar, T. Taylor-Ritzler, and C.B. Keys (Eds.). *Race, culture and disability: Rehabilitation science and practice.* Boston, MA: Jones and Barlett.

World Bank (2010) Data and statistics on disability. *Disability and Development,* Retrieved on August 29, 2010 from http://web.worldbank.org/WBSITE/EXTERNAL/TOPICS/EXTSOCIALPROTECTION/EXTDISABILITY/0,,contentMDK:21249181~menuPK:282717~pagePK:148956~piPK:216618~theSitePK:282699,00.html

World Health Organization (1980). *International Classification of Impairments, Disabilities and Handicaps.* Geneva: WHO.

Yeo, R. (2001, August). Chronic Poverty and Disability. Chronic Poverty Research Centre: Background Paper Number 4, ISBN Number: 1-904049-03-6. Retrieved on August 29, 2010 from: http://www.chronicpoverty.org/uploads/publication_files/WP04_Yeo.pdf

Young, I.M. (1990). *Justice and the politics of difference.* Princeton, NJ: Princeton University Press.

Zimmerman, M.A. (2000). Empowerment theory: Psychological, organizational, and community level of analysis. In J. Rappaport and E. Seidman (Eds.), *Handbook of community psychology* (pp. 43–63). New York: Plenum.

CHAPTER NINETEEN

CONCLUSION:
RACISM AND NEORACISM CONTRIBUTIONS OF THIS BOOK

John J. Betancur

We started this project with an open invitation to scholars to celebrate the 40th Anniversary of the Kerner Commission by examining post-1960s developments in race, especially new versions and expressions of racism that we tentatively named "neoracism" along with advances in the struggle against it. As is fully known, in contrast with the Moynihan Report of 1965, *The Negro Family: The Case For National Action*, explaining the black condition by flaws in the black family, The National Advisory Commission on Civil Disorders, known as the Kerner Commission, attributed that condition to racism and called for an all out national effort to end it. Contributors to this volume chose their own topics and perspectives to examine racism forty years after the issuing of the Kerner report. Now, having completed this journey, we close this collection by examining the contributors' views, their contributions and the possible directions emerging from their work. I examine the issues and materials critically paying special attention to the various questions the authors raised and pointing to the openings and challenges they spelled out. To do this, we start with an overview of themes and approaches in the book to then examine the more general question of neoracism and associated implications both for theory and practice.

The first issue to address relates to the ancestral ties of race and racism to European colonization of territories and peoples it turned into today's Third World. Identifying colonization as the foundational matrix of race and racism, Tomás Almaguer argues in this volume that today's racializing practices are rooted/fused upon colonial constructions of race. This, we believe, is a critical connection that, when neglected, leads to naturalizations and misunderstandings for instance on the relationship of race to class and other sources of minoritization. It is crucial to continuously distinguish race and racism from forms of oppression with different roots and dynamics as race is to colonization what gender is to patriarchy or sexuality to religious beliefs. Along these lines, Martinot (2003) for instance explains how the modern construction of race started in the United States with the differentiation between colonizers and colonized. Along these lines, many historians conclude that the root of racism in the United States is the enslavement of blacks, the elimination and reclusion of American Indians, and the exploitation of Mexicans, Puerto Ricans and other Latinos, all part and parcel of or legacies of colonization and the ensuing construction of empire on the backs of non-white races (Acuña 1981; Carmichael and Hamilton 1967; Martinot 2003; Cox 1948; Foner 1983; Janes 2000; Stein and Stein 1970; Steinberg 2007). We could not possibly situate race properly unless we realize this political-economic, European (and hence white)-centered form of minoritization that continues producing many of the same effects generation after generation.

Closely related to the constitution of race is the relationship between race and ethnicity. Manipulated effectively in the United States in the reproduction of unequal social relations, along or in combination with other factors, race and ethnicity have followed somewhat separate trajectories, at times converging, others diverging and for our case, merging into large racial groupings (e.g., whites and blacks – named by skin color, or Latinos and Asians – named by region of origin and defined as ethnic but also assigned color identifiers). Initially, ethnicity was used principally for European nationals (the collective "Us") establishing hierarchies in the pecking order and level of whiteness among them. Race was originally assigned to the bipolar white-black divide with other conquered groups either placed in this divide as surrogates, differently classified as tribes (e.g., Indian Americans) or nationals (e.g., Chinese and Japanese) or viewed as ethnics with a racial ascription (e.g., Latinos). In this structure, Blacks emerged as the absolute other of colonizers and their heirs while for some time non-whites-non-blacks assumed apparently non-racial roles as peons/servants, indentured laborers, or exotic savages. Finally, by the 1960s, peoples with Third World ancestries were racialized (Omi and Winant 1994) by continent of origin (e.g., Asians, and Latinos), as subcategories of the general 'Other.' All these differences helped perpetuate the racial order through separate identities/ascriptions largely pre-empting the unity of disadvantaged groups and eventually forcing them into a 'competition' for higher standing in the racial hierarchy – as I argued earlier in this book.

In the late 1960s and 1970s, building on the realities of colonialism and neocolonialism, authors such as Carmichael and Hamilton (1967) and Blauner (1972) coined the term internal colonialism to explain the relationship between whites and non-whites in the United States. Elaborating on these ideas, Barrera (1979: 212) classified Chicanos (and blacks for that matter) into "subordinate ascriptive class segments:" even those among them ascending in the class order operated as segments within classes and often owed their class position to relationships of class with their own. Such subordinate and differential social relationships were formalized into laws and practices dictating the rights and obligations of each group but, most importantly, the entitlements of the colonizer. Correspondingly, they were elaborated into and maintained through ideologies and representations justifying the status quo.

Rather than wiping out the colonial order, after independence, primal race relationships were maintained and, over time, 'naturalized' and reshaped. Although the formal elimination of slavery, enactment of labor laws and, ultimately, the prohibition of racism in the 1960s changed this primal order, racialized structures, institutions, practices and discourses maintained the divisions and entitlements in newer versions. Along the way, as Almaguer argues in this book, ties to colonialism have been blurred making way for claims that racism has become something else; against this, we insist that today's races continue to be rooted in yesterday's colonial and in post-colonial structures maintaining quasi-colonial relations of subordination under new clothes permeating all corners and aspects of US society. Thus, although recognizing new forms in the trajectory of racism, research needs to trace, through re-enactment of such relations, a continued relationship of race-based domination, hegemony, and advantage.

This is in part what researchers, pragmatically tracing the continued presence of race-based inequalities, do when they examine the racial effects of policies such as welfare and public housing reform –with some of them explicitly tying these interventions to racism and others presenting them simply as racial effects. This collection is rich in them. Professor Edward Goetz points to higher levels of displacement of blacks than of other groups in the implementation of HOPE VI. Following on the footsteps of urban renewal, this federal program has carried out the most massive recent removal of blacks from strategic locations in cities like Chicago. Whether by intent or default (they have been veiled under languages of renovation for everyone's benefit), such policies have disproportionately negative effects on racial minorities (Manning Thomas and Ritzdorf 1997; Nelson 2008; Drake and Cayton 1993). Echoing this, Robert Mier, (1993: 236) argued, "The fundamental lesson I learned from my years as director of development in Chicago under Mayor Harold Washington is that race should be the first way to frame a local planning or development problem...race is a ubiquitous reality that must be acknowledged."

Indeed, race and racism are so ingrained in US society that they operate as a default setting. Indeed, racial power is tattooed in the minds and bodies of all sides of the racial divide, the profiteers and the oppressed on the basis of their race. Paraphrasing Van Dijk (1989a: 27), we can argue that "The consensus-shaping power of these [dominant] ideologies provides the conditions that make a 'conspiracy' of these groups unnecessary."

This is not to say that racism 'just happens' and nobody can be blamed for it because it is produced by 'the system' regardless of the intentions of individuals. It certainly is structurally ingrained and perhaps inadvertently regurgitated by many who find no reason to engage in critical self-reflection fearing having to recognize racially-based advantages. But structures reproduce through the daily practices of individuals and institutions. Confusion, obfuscation and perhaps convenience have led many to blame factors other than race for racial effects. Professor William Julius Wilson (1980) made a name for himself by suggesting a shift from race to class in the United States today. Such a statement certainly was music to the ears of a mainstream that only had to read the title of his book, *The Declining Significance of Race*, to embrace this claim because it provided yet another 'escape' from racism. But the reality of race is there to see: widely available statistics on the distribution of wealth and assets, incarceration, deportations, or criminalization (to mention a few), ghettoes and barrios, accounts and visuals are living testimonies to a race gap that tends to decrease when the country decides to address it frontally to then go back up once these actions stop. Although people may put on blinders or seek alternative explanations, the facts are overwhelming and nobody with an open mind can avoid them.

Indeed, HOPE VI and the other policies examined in this book worked on the widespread belief that policies were race-neutral, racism was over, the playing field had been leveled and actually race-based solutions were forms of reverse racism. Against this, authors in his book show the racial bias of many policies and government interventions. Karen Gibson, for one, explains how, closely assisted by government, the real estate industry continues reproducing the racial divide 'locking' poor blacks in neighborhood reservations or selling their neighborhoods to gentrification. Moreover, rather than benefiting from investment in the inner-city, black residents get displaced or become the 'other' in their own neighborhoods. Operating subtly but not blindly from the guts of the system, structural racism combines with institutional practices to conceal racial exclusion under apparently neutral discourses of development and revitalization. Focusing on the effects of recent welfare legislation (passed largely on claims that welfare was a white man's burden), Professors Kecia R. Johnson and Jacqueline Johnson conclude that, although depressing the earnings of all racial groups across the board, incarceration has the most deleterious effects on blacks followed by Latinos and whites last. Cedric Herring points out even more insidious effects of elevated rates of incarceration, especially among people of color and their communities. He shows that America's disastrous "War on Drugs"—and prison-born infections such as HIV/AIDs and Hepatitis C—has negatively affected the health and well being of the families and communities to which ex-offenders return – most particularly racial minorities. He further shows the link between incarceration and increased need for access to health care and other social support programs for ex-offenders (most of them racial minorities) as they return to their communities upon release.

Further reinforcing this, Melvin Thomas, Hayward Horton, and Cedric Herring show the different perceptions of whites and African Americans regarding government responses to and the effects of Hurricane Katrina by class and race. Exempted from the negative effects of racism and dwelling in privilege, mainstream whites do not seem to perceive these racial effects or to see them as race-related or as forms of racism. In contrast, suffering from the constraints and deleterious effects of race, even when everything is held constant, blacks and Latinos feel such differences deeply inside. Again, although differently perceived by different groups, we cannot simply discard these patterns as non-racial. Today, possibly no white person would feel comfortable admitting to unearned privileges of race and less to racism, preferring to think that their condition is a result of effort and to deny their part in the script of racism—structural, institutional, or else. Differently, for obvious reasons, the disadvantaged are more likely to perceive racism and race-based disadvantages in their daily lives. Studying the differential effects of skin tone and looks on black women at work, Michelle Hughes and Cedric Herring identify different levels of harassment and exclusion –in this case related to the perceived threat or levels of proximity that their looks and lighter or darker complexions represent. Their research suggests that when interacting with whites, African American women with lighter complexions generally receive better treatment. This pattern shows that the notion that America is colorblind is a fabrication. Hughes and Herring's results also show that when interacting with blacks, the lighter an African American woman's complexion, the better is the treatment she receives. These patterns point to the emergence of a neoracism that may have also infected African Americans and Latinos themselves.

With examples from program after program and policy after policy, researchers in this collection and many others elsewhere demonstrate continuing unequal outcomes by race. Notice, however, that these outcomes are not equal across the board but change in intensity and frequency by a number of factors. Actually, most of the above authors explore racial effects on the most vulnerable sectors of minority communities: Gibson focuses on inner-city blacks, Johnson and Johnson on incarcerated (predominantly low-income) males, and Goetz on public housing. Although differentiating by class, Thomas, Herring and Horton also found more intense effects on the poor. Putting them together, we can notice the most deleterious effects at the intersections of race, class and gender, especially among the poor. In this way, these pieces prove the need to disaggregate the effects of race and differentiate between those that are more universal and those that are more particular as well as the differential effects of racism and other sources of minoritization associated with intersections. Rather than assuming monolithic races and across the board equal racial effects, as some of the traditional literature does, these analyses incorporate internal differentiations within races pointing to the need for nuanced analyses to determine which racial effects occur across the board and which are mitigated by factors such as middle and upper class, or are made worse at particular clusterings of race, class, gender and other factors.

Most of the chapters in this book focus on how public policies and practices disadvantage racial minorities and increase social polarization by race –again especially within the most vulnerable. They demonstrate the resilience of race-based inequalities intensified by convergences of the various sources of inequality and the structural workings of racism in ever more nuanced ways over time. In particular, they show how the mediation of other sources of alienation makes racial effects more difficult to tackle. Whereas the ascension to middle and upper class positions has accommodated some minorities mitigating the effects of race, these seem most entrenched and perverse among low-income, female and other vulnerable subgroups such as the incarcerated or those trapped in formations such as the inner-city.

Researchers Yolanda Suarez-Balcázar, Fabrizio Balcázar, Tina Ritsler-Taylor and Asma Ali add the dimension of disability. Although also sources of minoritization, not all disabilities are equal. According to these authors, low-income racial minorities with disabilities fare the worst suggesting that when all things are equal, by default, middle and upper classes and whites with disabilities are still privileged vis-à-vis their low-income and racial minority counterparts. This is a critical consideration as single issue analyses and interventions such as the feminist, disability, and queer movements often operate on 'universalizations' that do not necessarily reflect differences within them – and subsequently do not lift all boats or distribute gains or losses equally by race, gender and other sources of difference and disadvantage. Non white, non-middle class and other voices within them have raised such concerns pushing movements in more nuanced, less generic directions and diversified agendas. Apparently, the more sources of minoritization converge, the deeper the marginalization, the lesser the gain for some from apparently universal solutions, the more attention has to be paid to the added resilience coming from the presence of various sources of alienation. Led often by white middle and upper class members, the priorities and courses of action pursued in these movements may prioritize white perspectives and, thus, get tailored to them –perhaps by default, yet with differential effects by race. Ultimately, this type of evidence suggests that whiteness dominates across the board, even when combined with other sources of inequality.

Elizabeth Sweet extended this analysis to the intersection of race, gender and immigrant status for 'brown" women. Racism, she argues has been re-enacted around immigration. It is important to realize that not only have Latinos become the preferred targets of the US office of Citizenship and Immigration Services and of legislatures at all levels but also the undocumented mantra has been extended to all, stereotyping Latinos into 'illegal aliens' (a highly racist code) or 'illegal alien suspects.' Such ascriptions not only have attracted the animosity of growing numbers of Nativist Americans and others but have justified the sternest measures against them. Defining children of Latino unauthorized immigrants as "anchor babies" (and all Latino children by extension), Nativists have gone as far as calling for repeal of the 14th amendment –to deny citizenship to their offspring born in the United States. Hostility against Latinos has led to practices of profiling and witch hunting that remind those of Jewish people under Nazism—all in the name of patriotism. In her story, Sweet depicts Latino women as one of the major casualties of racism in the 'anti-immigrant city.'

But this level of race and racism is not sustainable unless supported by discourse and perceptions justifying race-based practices of exclusion in the eyes of the majority and actually socializing new generations to accept it or view it as inevitable. A significant amount of research has been actually produced on the ways in which conversations, language, discourses of all sorts, politicians, movies or the media naturalize and perpetuate racism (e.g., Anderson, 1989; Slayden and Slyden 1995;

Solomon and Wrench 1993; Smitherman-Donaldson and van Dijk 1987; Wilson and Gutierrez 1985; Wolak 1989). Of particular interest here is the relationship between the structures of discourse and those of power reflected in media depictions of race and its role in shaping public opinion on behalf of elites and the status quo. Examining the media's discourse on immigration of people from the Third World in Europe and the United States, Teun A. van Dijk (1989: 219) concluded that immigration "is construed as a permanent threat, as a conflict between 'us' and 'them,' between those who want to get in and do not belong here, and those of 'us' who belong here." In this collection, Professor Isabel Molina-Guzmán's research on the *New York Time*'s coverage of the 2006 mobilizations against HR 4437 establishes a relationship between the negative ways in which the media frames issues such as immigration and ethnic and racial relations –in this case applied principally to Latinos. Along these lines but on the topic of crime, Lisa Marie Cacho shows that racialized representations exclude young people of color of the democratic principles of development and equality—a double jeopardy as race also deprives them from economic and other opportunities. In both cases, using Cacho's quotation of Denise Ferreira da Silva, *"whiteness* and only *whiteness* signifies *universality"* and, hence, gets naturalized as the norm –or the universal 'us.' Differently, Latinoness and blackness stand for particularity and, thus, abnormality, suspicion and otherness.

But people of color are not passive recipients of this notion of abnormality. Indeed, from time to time they rise up against efforts to exclude them. Angela Mascarenas and Cedric Herring write about the 2006 mass demonstration of more than one hundred thousand participants protesting in Chicago in favor of immigrant rights. They show that early participants differed from others who subsequently participated in the immigrant rights mobilizations. Similarly, expanding on this, Loren Henderson showed how youth of various races differ in their levels of experience in unconventional political participation and how factors such as race/ethnicity, immigrant status, having immigrant family members, income, and work status affect their levels of experience in participation. Her analysis shows three distinct groups of youth: political novices, political repeaters, and political activists. These patterns of participation, however, were racialized.

Authors also recognize conflicts and openings in the media that actually can advance the struggle against racism and for equal opportunity. Devorah Heitner illustrates in this book how black power generated advances in the production of positive media shows of black affairs while opening doors for black producers, journalists and technicians for generations to come – although still bare-bones compared to whites. Discourse and other critical analyses combating racist rhetoric are part and parcel of recent struggles against racism facilitated by research pieces as those featured in this book. In particular, commenting on the need for new approaches and instruments to counter the new forms and expressions of racism, Junaid Rana illustrates the importance of multi-racial organizing. As racism sets minorities against each other, and as internalized and increasingly coded racism confuses the struggle, a multiplicity of organizing strategies and new tactics focused on common causes are needed. As Rana warns, racial minority, group-specific struggles against racism have come to compete with those of other groups further fragmenting and confusing the field. Good examples of this are drives against Latino and Arab immigrants often with the support of blacks enticed to believe that these groups have preference in the pecking order vis-à-vis them and that their worsening conditions are caused by Latinos' snatching of redress and job opportunities that correspond to them. Similarly, racialized depictions of terrorism and insecurity push other minorities to support racism against Muslims. Lastly, through enthronement of Asians as 'model minorities' this group is enticed to join stereotypes and actions putting blacks and Latinos down and making Asians feel superior. Although many authors argue that minority racism amounts more to prejudice than actual oppression, racial minorities in higher class positions may also identify with and partner with others against lower income minorities.

Similarly, internalization of racism causes minorities to join others in highly racialized causes (e.g. against Muslims –racialized war on terrorism), Latinos (e.g., racialized war on immigrants on claims that they threaten American culture, snatch public resources or are 'illegal aliens'), the poor (e.g., presented as the white man's burden), the undocumented (e.g. racialized efforts to deny them access to human rights such as education), and many others. Along these lines, in chapter two I suggest that inter-minority animosities are largely the product of power manipulations generating a hierarchical racial order that makes groups compete against each other –rather than against racism. At the end, as the production of race self-entitled whites to the monopoly of wealth, power and opportunity, a competitive struggle for opportunities legitimates racism and race-based inequalities by focusing on the distribution of a fixed pie dictated by the race in power –instead of on the end of race-based domination. The reproduction of race depends largely on such distractions and on the acceptance (even if partial) of a racial order. To a large extent, people have accepted the division into races as a natural order focusing on race-based disputes for power, wealth and opportunity and competing for position in the opportunity queue –ratifying along the way the game and the legitimacy of race-based (unequal) competition.

These trappings have helped reproduce racism by turning race-based struggles into circles with apparently no exit. Dividing the world of minority communities/neighborhoods between the two forces of insiders (power holders) and outsiders (minorities) that at the same time complement and contest each other, Doug Gills posits racism and classism as both causes and effects of community development/underdevelopment. As much as the field of community development was established by outsiders to resist the adverse interventions of insiders, insiders manipulated them to advance their interests and shape communities to their advantage – or according to their logics. In this process, the mutual dependency of insiders and outsiders results in adaptations and co-optations in which the forces of resistance and social change become irrelevant vehicles of social change—in fact middlemen giving up to the pressures of insiders in order to maintain their standing by obtaining something for their outsider constituents. At the end, they get tangled in a dialectics of multidirectional causality, opposition and complementarity and, ultimately co-optation, somewhat confirming Hegelian dialectics in which contradictions end up moving in circles and cycles of repetition. The possibility then exists of a perverse mutuality assuring the reproduction of the system. Along these lines, structural racism and classism can be viewed as engaged in a logic in which the other never seems to win and its gains get turned upside down accommodating/swallowing their resistance/opposition. In this framework, racism assumes the form of endless dialectics of opposition turned into dialectics of accommodation reproductive of the status quo.

At this point, we can ask, who is listening? As some of the authors suggest, beneficiaries of racism neither like it nor want to give up their advantages. Most of them prefer to think that it does not exist and that what they have has been duly earned in an open competition in which no one has advantages. This apparent impasse illustrates the ways in which institutional racism reincarnates to reproduce the advantages and disadvantages of race. Can we assume that it occurs more as a by-product of a society of inequality than of racism or that it does not have a clear perpetrator but an abstract system of which we all are to some extent victims? Unfortunately, one of the effects of structural analyses is the sense that inequalities are produced by some 'hidden hand' and that ultimately nobody but the abstract collective can be held accountable. This is certainly how it feels when those benefiting from racial inequality explain that they did not create race or racism and that they worked hard for what they have which, hence, is not the product of their (white) race. Can we bring a white person to court on claims of discrimination for being ahead of the game? Certainly not. Can we bring institutions to court for 'acting rationally' when they invest in those that pose the least risk because they received the most opportunity? No. Still, inherited advantages are being reproduced on a daily basis by the same practices that constitute people's lives; moreover, risk is socially (and racially) determined as the practice of assigning value to race in the determination of real estate's worth illustrates. Are those doing the valuation exempt from fault? Probably, they just 'follow the rules.' Thinking of racism as structural places the perpetrator apparently out of reach, in an abstract and hard to reach "it."

Overall, this book examines the timely issues of racialization of new groups and causes; the differential effects of public policies and actions by race; the effects of racial perceptions; sources of contention and collaboration among racial minorities; the differential effects of racism at the overlapping of race, gender, class, sexuality and disability; processes of production and reproduction of race and racism today; the relationship between structures of racial power and ideology; the ubiquity of racism and the ways in which racial minority struggles are neutralized; developments and structures of racial minority relations with each other; effects at the intersection of race and other sources of minoritization; and differences between and within the races. In part continuation of ancestral forms, in part new forms and strategies, expressions of race and racism today, generally included under the neoracism umbrella, point to practices of inequality in which deep structural inertias combine with institutional practices and individual cooperation, aided by discourses that advance racism by denying it –as discussed below. In the same way as neocolonialism maintained the structure of inequality and value extraction established by colonialism without the much hated direct dictatorship of colonial powers, neoracism maintains a race-based system of subordination and advantages without the formal and blatant practices and laws that put it in place (governmentality). In the latter version, racism often hides behind cultural and other masks producing the appearance that differences result from group and individual characteristics, behaviors and traits – rather than race-based structures and practices. This is not new as white race was a proxy for European ethnocentrism and colonialism and non-white a proxy for conquered nations and peoples from Africa and from the colonized world generally. As in a self-fulfilling prophesy construction of the non-European-origin 'Other' turns this 'Other' into the antithesis of "Us-whites;" along the way, all ascriptions and the actual being of this otherness are turned into uncivilized or less civilized traits and behaviors, thereby delegitimized and even criminalized and used to 'explain' their inferior condition –making a relationship of domination appear as one of deficits and self-infliction. I explore this further below.

RACISM AND NEORACISM

A stream of European authors differentiate between overt and individual 'classic,' biological racism and covert and institutional cultural neoracism (Fréjuté-Rakauskiené 2006: 13). The literature specifically on neoracism is largely inspired by 'European racism' against the recent wave of immigrants flooding Europe; it claims that classical racism associated with colonialism has now assumed the form of ethnic strife reacting to South-North migration. Rather than focusing primarily on "the essential black subject" (Balibar and Wallerstein 2004), Neo-racism would work on the "exclusion and generalization of others according to cultural inheritance" (Fréjuté-Rakauskiené 2006: 14).

Balibar (1991) actually argues about the existence of a racism that does not have as a root the pseudo-biological concept of race and whose prototype is anti-Semitism ("racism without race") referring to it as neoracism. He equates today's racism with this form, differentiating it from classical racism along these lines. I find this formulation troublesome as it tends to dissociate racism from European colonization and the subsequent imposition of Manifest Destiny on the non-European world, and the associated outcome and justification of white rule. I certainly prefer to avoid this route for, if it is the case that there is a different racism (without race) it may belong rather with other sources of minoritization and oppression such as competition between religions than with European colonization and imposition of rule over the rest of the world.

Far less used in the United States where the dominant characterization today is structural racism, the term and the European definition of neoracism can be reconciled with the realities of racism on both sides of the Atlantic Ocean today if we take into consideration that race and racism as we know them today emerged from European colonization. Perhaps the major difference between the United States and Europe comes from the fact that Europe did not bring slavery to its shores as the US did. Yet, today, when the composition of Third World immigrants in European countries increased to the point of being considered a threat to the integrity of European white societies (or 'ethnicities'), colonizing practices and perceptions get re-enacted vis-à-vis immigrants from former colonies. In reality, the Othering and subordination of non-Europeans that were part of colonization, never subsided and, indeed continued in international relations to be fully applied to peoples from the Third World providing today cheap workers to an increasingly Neoliberal Europe. We argue that the European characterization of racism as predominately cultural today is not a departure but a continuation of so-called classical racism. Ultimately, the primal relationship is and continues to be colonial, whether it is exercised in the name of biological, cultural or other rationalizations.

Indeed, in the United States, racism has been also coded in terms of culture. Following on the predicament that Western culture is universal and civilized in contrast to the particularity and primitivism of other cultures, racism is coded in both Europe and America today under claims that US racial minorities and people from the Third World in general are threats to "*our* way of life" and coded under racist bites such as "brownization, Muslimization or ThirdWorldization of America," "creation of Mexamerica" (Pat Buchanan), Mexican colonization of the US Southwest (Border Patrol), "the welfare queen," the black face of crime, the (black and Latino) culture of poverty, the (black) underclass, 'brownization of America,' and so forth. Carnegie Foundation scholar John Judis (2008) presents the anti-immigration movement in the US today as primarily cultural as articulated by mayor of Myrtle Beach, South Carolina, "It's absolutely a cultural problem. If you want to come here, I believe you want to come here to be an American," that he quotes.

The dressing of racism in cultural terms is actually a way of softening/coding the realities of race and racism at the same time as it brings Manifest Destiny and the alleged superiority of 'white civilization' through the back door. Although, confronting the discredit/fall of the old justifications of racism, white power over racialized others is now reinstated in the name of culture and civilization, the primal action and the effects are the same.

Unless we agree that the root of racism is the colonial submission of Third World people initially consecrated in legislation and biological, religious or other explanations and reinstated on an ongoing basis through the combination of white monopoly of wealth, power and opportunities, structural and institutional racism, accumulated advantages, race management, symbolic power and others, we may reduce racism to a simple prejudice, to a generic, 'natural' condition and ultimately, justify it by 'blaming the victim.' If it is the case as Balibar (1991) argues that there is no racism without theory, we argue that culture is the new theoretical dress for the old reality of race and racism – that certainly have evolved but whose historical reality continues the primal colonial project of submission and civilization of peoples from the Third World.

Thus, we propose neoracism as an encompassing term for the continuation/re-enactment of racism following its legal prohibition and, indeed, the corresponding discredit of prior justifications of it. As many authors agree, this version of racism is veiled, subtle, implicit and coded. If the abolition of blatant racism and the development of 'politically correct' forms of racial management, indeed the anti-racist pronouncements and mea culpas of Western white society ended the most explicit forms of racism, they did not end racism –only its formal legality, while making room for accommodation of enough minorities to formulate (manage) new versions –apparently a racism without perpetrators. In other words, legal abolition formally removed the faces of racism that now hides under structures and veiled practices. Still tangled in the logic of 'classical' racism, courts look today for intention to determine whether a practice or outcome is racist or not. Racism, the argument goes, requires intentional harm and a perfectly identifiable perpetrator. Under the circumstances, racism today shines through effects so subtly produced or veiled as to make it apparently invisible – and thus requiring equally sophisticated tools to unveil the forms it hides under.

Absent the visible face (cause) of blatant and legislated racism, apparently free standing effects are orphan, thus facilitating, by default, the attribution of effects to its bearers –hence the urgent necessity for activists and researchers to bring out the new faces of racism and for society at large to address the continued production and reproduction of race-based effects; more than before, we need to address excuses and exceptions (e.g., if there is no visible cause, there is no victim and, thus, there is no racism but deficits); or we all regret racial differences but cannot attribute them to anybody's racism; lastly, "I did not create racism and do not practice it, what happens is not my fault," –in short, denial.

Studies of discourse, conversations, media, movies, the courts, political rhetoric, parliamentarian debate, legislation, nationalism, textbooks, socialization, hiring, and immigration debate and practices show the subtle ways in which racism is practiced today. Van Dijk (1992 and 1995) summarizes today's racist discursive practices into positive self-presentation and negative presentation of the other on the part of dominant white society and white dominated institutions –along with nationalist self-glorification and denial. According to him, while reinforcing the claim of superiority of the white race, such practices encourage people to engage in racism even more blatantly than "politically correct" elites. Depictions of minorities in these outlets and practices as deviant, violent, disruptive, welfare cheaters, law-breaking, inassimilable, or threats to US culture and safety encourage and justify all forms of racism and racial inequality on the name of American (read white) cultural integrity and traditions. No matter how veiled, racism is alive and well; regardless of its denial, it is perpetrated and reproduced on a daily basis by a system that empowers its agents to exercise it legally. At the end of the day, the unwillingness to recognize it is a form of complicity and the denial of racial advantage a form of (implicit or explicit) acceptance of Manifest Destiny.

Authors such as John Judis (2008) explain that the anti-immigrant movement as caused by fear of terrorism and social and economic uncertainties/anxieties associated with a shaky economy particularly among the most threatened and affected classes. According to him, "These workers have seen themselves as "producers" victimized by "parasites"—by Wall Street and big business from above and by an underclass of African Americans and immigrants from below." Although such arguments make sense, their effect is to justify rather than address the roots of the problem, namely a racism that causes them to react in this way and to support opportunistic white politicians resorting to equally racist scapegoating of minorities, to be elected. Actually, racial minorities are more deeply affected by the current crisis than whites due to the mediation of race. No matter how well intended, these types of explanations, indeed, are among the forms of denial and complacence that legitimize racism. They correspond closely with explanations and efforts to conceal the race relationship or blame the victims for higher unemployment among minorities, absence of new anti-racist initiatives and legislation, inferior education and health services for minorities, minority criminalization, police harassment and profiling, or inner-city decay and disinvestment – all of them racial effects.

Denial may be the most formidable mechanism of perpetuation of neoracism today because it naturalizes the status quo while undermining and de-legitimizing efforts to address it. In the words of Van Dijk (1993: 181),

> ... denials of racism have a *sociopolitical function*. Denials challenge the very legitimacy of anti-racist analysis, and thus are part of the politics of ethnic management: as long as a problem is being denied in the first place, the critics are ridiculed, marginalized or delegitimated: denials debilitate resistance. As long as racism is denied, there is no need for official measures against it, for stricter laws, regulations or institutions to combat discrimination, or moral campaigns to change the biased attitudes of whites."

Similarly, "If tolerance is promoted as a national myth [part and parcel of the claims of universalism of Western culture]... it is much more difficult for minority groups to challenge remaining [race-based] inequalities, to take unified action and to gain credibility and support among the (white) dominant group." (Van Dijk 1992: 96)

As people take exception to racism at the same time that they practice it through claims such as "I am not racist but..." racism subtly slips into individuation, exceptionalism or separation from the perpetrator (it is not me or that race but individual members and particular practices). In other words, fault is displaced to behaviors and individuals and racism brought through the back door: the blaming itself re-instills the right of a culture to judge another and the norms as universalistic and superior.

Another possible veil of racism today is diversity. In principle, diversity stands for acceptance of or celebration of 'people as they are,' of their differences, calling for practices of tolerance and *convivencia*. Advertently or inadvertently, this figure assumes that a person's race, gender, sexual orientation, age, or else determines that person's *natural* identity and that the person's characteristics/traits are racially or otherwise inherited. In other words, this construct departs from or actually essentializes a socially constructed, imposed source of identification (the minority condition of the "other") and then calls for relations of tolerance with people having such conditions. Along the way, diversity tends to glorify and culturize race and call on people to feel proud of it. Such a practice and call turns a socially constructed source of inequality into a natural condition (of being a minority). Differently, researchers and activists need to see through such apparently positive versions of race and racism, deconstruct them into what they do, the racial effect they produce, and act strategically. It may be the case that such versions open doors of conversation and action that can be used against racist representations and practices; yet, clarity is necessary as to how far to go with them. Racism cannot be eradicated by re-enacting it on the basis of philosophies that actually make the division by race legitimate and racism far more resilient. Racism will be eradicated when the construct of race is delegitimized along with race-based practices, judgments or representations feeding into or reproducing racial inequality, when people recognize it and act to end it. So long as we continue to see the world through colored lenses, classify people's worth by race and construct race into a culture or other comparable essence, we are reproducing it. The day when race is not a source of unequal differentiation or distribution we may want to have a diversity based on who everybody makes of her/himself different from the other, rather than on ascribed deficiencies of any kind.

Ultimately, to eradicate racism, we need to engage in all-out efforts in discourse and practice such as those that Western society has staged against terrorism or communism.

References

Acuña, Rodolfo. Occupied America: a history of Chicanos. New York: Harper & Row, 1981.

Anderson, J.A. (Eds) 1989. Communication Yearbook 12. Newbury Park, CA: Sage.

Balibar, Etienne. 1991. "Is There a New Racism?" In Race, Nation, Class: Ambiguous Identities by E. Balibar and I. Wallerstein. London: Verso:

Balibar, Etienne and Immanuel Wallerstein. 1991. Race, Nation, Class: Ambiguous Identities. London: Verso:

Barrera, Mario. Race and Class in the Southwest: A Theory of Racial Inequality." Notre Dame, IN and London, UK: University of Notre Dame Press.

Carmichael, Stokely and Charles V. Hamilton. Black power; the politics of liberation in America New York, Random House, 1967.

Cox, Oliver. Caste, class & race; a study in social dynamics. Garden City, N.Y., Doubleday, 1948.

Drake, St. Claire and Horace R. Cayton. 1993. Black Metropolis, A Study of Negro Life in a Northern City. Chicago, the University of Chicago Press.

Foner, Eric. Nothing but freedom: emancipation and its legacy. Baton Rouge: Louisiana State University Press, 1983.

Jaynes, Gerald D., (Ed.) 2000. Race and Immigration: New Challenges for American Democracy. New York and London: Yale University Press.

Judis, John. "Phantom Menace: the Psychology Behind America's Immigration Hysteria." The New Republic, February 13, 2008. Online version <http://www.tnr.com/article/phantom-menace> July 24, 2011.

Manning Thomas, June and Marsha Ritzdorf. 1997. Urban Planning and the African-American Community: In the Shadows. Thousand Oaks, CA, London, UK and New Delhi, India: Sage Publications.

Nelson, Jennifer J. 2008. Razing Africville, A geography of Racism. Toronto, Buffalo and London: University of Toronto Press.

Omi, Michael, and Howard Winant. Racial Formation in the United States: From the 1960s to the 1990s. New York: Routledge, 1994.

Slayden, R.K. and D. Slayden (Eds). 1995. Hate Speech. Newbury Park, CA: Sage.

Solomon, J.J. and J. Wrench (Eds). 1993. Racism and Migration in Western Europe. Oxford: Pergamon Press.

Smitherman-Donaldson, G. and T.A. van Dijk (Eds). 1987. Discourse and Discrimination. Detroit, MI: Wayne State University Press.

Stein Stanley J. and Barbara H. Stein. 1970. The colonial heritage of Latin America; essays on economic dependence in perspective. New York, Oxford University Press.

Steinberg, Stephen. Race Relations, A Critique. Stanford, CA: Stanford University Press, 2007.

Van Dijk, Teun A. 1993. "Denying Racism: Elite Discourse and Racism." Pp. 179–193 in Racism and Migration in Western Europe edited by J.J. Solomon and J. Wrench. Oxford: Pergamon Press.

Van Dijk, Teun A. 1992. "Discourse and the Denial of Racism." Pp. 87–118 in Discourse and Society. London, Newbury Park and New Delhi: Sage.

Van Dijk, Teun A. 1989a. "Structures of Discourse and Structures of Power." Pp. 18–59 in Communication Yearbook 12 edited by J.A. Anderson. Newbury Park, CA: Sage Publications.

Van Dijk, Teun A. 1989b. "Mediating Racism: The Role of the Media in the Reproduction of Racism." Pp, 199–226 in Language, Power and Ideology, edited by R. Wolak. Amsterdam and Philadelphia: John Benjamins Publishing Company

Wilson. C.C. and Felix Gutierrez. 1985. Minorities and Media. Beverly Hills, CA: Sage Publications.

Wilson, William Julius. 1980. The Declining Significance of Race: Blacks and American Changing Institutions. Chicago: The University of Chicago Press.

Wodak, R. (Ed). 1989. Language, Power and Ideology.

INDEX OF NAMES

SUBJECT INDEX

www.ingramcontent.com/pod-product-compliance
Lightning Source LLC
Chambersburg PA
CBHW060019030426
42334CB00019B/2105